Introducing
INTERCULTURAL COMMUNICATION

$\circledS$SAGE | 50 YEARS

SAGE was founded in 1965 by Sara Miller McCune to support the dissemination of usable knowledge by publishing innovative and high-quality research and teaching content. Today, we publish more than 750 journals, including those of more than 300 learned societies, more than 800 new books per year, and a growing range of library products including archives, data, case studies, reports, conference highlights, and video. SAGE remains majority-owned by our founder, and on her passing will become owned by a charitable trust that secures our continued independence.

Los Angeles | London | Washington DC | New Delhi | Singapore

Introducing INTERCULTURAL COMMUNICATION

Global Cultures and Contexts

SHUANG LIU, ZALA VOLČIČ & CINDY GALLOIS

Los Angeles | London | New Delhi
Singapore | Washington DC

Los Angeles | London | New Delhi
Singapore | Washington DC

SAGE Publications Ltd
1 Oliver's Yard
55 City Road
London EC1Y 1SP

SAGE Publications Inc.
2455 Teller Road
Thousand Oaks, California 91320

SAGE Publications India Pvt Ltd
B 1/I 1 Mohan Cooperative Industrial Area
Mathura Road
New Delhi 110 044

SAGE Publications Asia-Pacific Pte Ltd
3 Church Street
#10-04 Samsung Hub
Singapore 049483

Editor: Mila Steele
Assistant editor: James Piper
Production editor: Imogen Roome
Indexer: Cathryn Pritchard
Marketing manager: Michael Ainsley
Cover design: Jen Crisp
Typeset by: C&M Digitals (P) Ltd, Chennai, India
Printed and bound in Great Britain by Ashford
Colour Press Ltd

Library of Congress Control Number: 2014939151

British Library Cataloguing in Publication data

A catalogue record for this book is available from the British Library

ISBN 978-1-4462-8590-9
ISBN 978-1-4462-8591-6 (pbk)

At SAGE we take sustainability seriously. Most of our products are printed in the UK using FSC papers and boards. When we print overseas we ensure sustainable papers are used as measured by the Egmont grading system. We undertake an annual audit to monitor our sustainability.

CONTENTS

PREFACE

> We may have different religions, different languages, different-coloured skin,
> but we all belong to one human race.
>
> Kofi Annan, 7th UN Secretary-General, 2001 Nobel Peace Prize Winner

This new edition of *Introducing Intercultural Communication: Global Cultures and Contexts* reflects theories and practices in the current field of intercultural communication and related disciplines. The global perspectives that the first edition adopts made the book stand out among other competitors in the market. The realization that the first edition was so well received by scholars, colleagues, and, more importantly, students across the world in the past three years left us with a sense of achievement and appreciation. We interpreted this success to mean that a book with global perspectives has resonated with an international audience. We embrace the opportunity to refine and improve on the content and features that have proven successful in the first edition, while concomitantly advancing contemporary theories and research in the field. This second edition has added new features in relation to theories, models, concepts, questions, exercises, and case studies, which take students into some new territory, empower them in active learning, and foster critical thinking. Further, we have broadened the applications to suit a greater range of users from diverse disciplinary areas, including communication, linguistics, business, management, social psychology, political science, public relations, and journalism.

This new edition continues our commitment to presenting intercultural communication theories and applications through a global prism and in a lively, interesting, relevant, and easy-to-follow writing style. At the same time, it maintains the high standard of intellectual depth and rigour in scholarly discussions. We have updated the content of each chapter to reflect state-of-the-art knowledge and current research in the field. Moreover, every chapter has been enriched with more examples from a diverse set of cultures, including Scandinavia, Italy, the Netherlands, Sweden, Russia, Saudi Arabia, Finland, and the USA. This edition has a stronger emphasis on blending theory with practice. More challenging questions are included throughout the text to give students opportunities to exercise their potential, and possibly to target postgraduate students. In response to the reviews, we have also re-ordered the chapters to better streamline the presentation of various topics. At every point in the writing of this new edition, we have endeavoured to put ourselves in the student's place, drawing upon the learning experiences of hundreds of culturally diverse students whom we have been privileged to teach.

NEW TO THIS EDITION

- *Streamlining of the chapters*. Immigration and Acculturation (Chapter 9) is placed before Developing Intercultural Relations with Culturally Different Others (Chapter 10); Categorization, Subgroups and

Identities (Chapter 6) is placed immediately after Cultural and Value Orientations (Chapter 5) and before Verbal Communication and Culture (Chapter 7). This re-ordering presents a more logical flow of the topics.

- *Updated content.* New sections are added to fill in the gaps identified in the reviews and to reflect current development in the field. They include emic–etic approaches to studying culture (Chapter 3, Understanding Culture); Schwartz's value orientations (Chapter 5); religious identity and subgroups based on sexual orientation – gay, lesbian, bisexual and transsexual individuals (Chapter 6); discourse and politeness across cultures (Chapter 7); refugees, Indigenous people and additional acculturation models (Chapter 9); and management of diversity in organizations (Chapter 11, Managing Intercultural Conflicts).

- *Theory in Practice.* This feature accompanies each 'Theory Corner' to highlight the application of theories in different disciplinary areas, including linguistics, business, organizations, advertising, political science, social psychology, and the mass media. In each 'Theory in Practice' box, we also include challenging questions to take students further in their application of knowledge.

- *More in-depth discussion on theories and concepts.* Chapter 2 (Understanding Communication) is substantially revised to raise the level of the discussion on communication models. As well, more theoretical depth is added to Chapter 13 (Becoming an Effective Intercultural Communicator), with concrete examples from multiple cultures.

- *Join the Debate.* 'Key Terms' at the end of each chapter has been replaced by 'Join the Debate', which poses challenging questions and debates in the field. This feature enables students to develop interest and talent.

- *Emphasis on critical thinking.* Critical-thinking questions are incorporated throughout each chapter to engage students in deep learning.

- *More examples from European countries.* More examples from Germany, France, the Netherlands, Switzerland, Sweden, and Scandinavia are added in the text and in case studies. Where appropriate, questions pertaining to case studies are revised to encourage application in a wider context.

- *Communication in cyberspace.* The role of social media and the issues of cyber-bullying in intercultural relations are elaborated in Chapter 10 as well as mass media in the digital age (Chapter 12, Mass Media, Technology, and Cultural Change).

RETAINED FROM THE PREVIOUS EDITION

- *Case studies.* All reviewers and our own students embraced and endorsed them. To build on the success of this feature, we have updated a number of case studies and expanded the domains to humanities, linguistics, business, organizations, and public relations.

- *Theory Corners.* Positive feedback has been received on the 'Theory Corners'. We have updated the theories and added application ('Theory in Practice') to illustrate theories in action.

- *Further readings.* Further readings at the end of each chapter consolidate and complement students' learning. In this new edition, the number of further readings is reduced to five per chapter but they are annotated. In addition, a list of further readings is provided in the Instructor's Manual.

- *Chapter summaries*. The summary of each chapter highlights the key points covered. In response to the reviews, the chapter summaries in this new edition are in the form of bullet points to make them more concise and easier to follow.

- *Pictures*. The illustrative pictures were praised by reviewers and students as original and interesting. We have retained this feature and updated pictures to further align with the revised text and enhance their illustrative power.

- *Glossary*. The glossary, containing definitions of all key terms used in the text, is retained to give users a quick index of the key concepts covered and their definitions. A list of key terms by chapter is provided in the Instructor's Manual.

- *Instructor materials on the companion website*. This new edition has updated all the exercises and activities, as well as multiple choice questions, to align with the new content in this edition. The original sections have been retained: lecture notes, key terms, PowerPoints, further readings, exercises and activities, and multiple choice questions. The companion website can be found at https://study.sagepub.com/liu2e

ACKNOWLEDGEMENTS

We would like to thank all those who have helped us as we progressed through the journey to complete this second edition. We thank the reviewers for their insightful comments on the first edition and valuable suggestions for improvement. A special note of thanks goes to the many instructors who have adopted the first edition over the past two years, as well as to the scholars who have provided their feedback through various channels, including the website of SAGE Publications. Their positive comments on the first edition are especially gratifying, and their suggestions for improvement have helped us rethink and reshape this second edition. We have all had the privilege of teaching and doing research in intercultural communication, and these experiences have formed our outlook on this fascinating field.

We are indebted to our colleagues, friends, and students, both at the University of Queensland and at other institutions around the world where we have studied, worked, or spent periods of research leave; all of them have contributed to this book in various ways, including providing feedback on our intercultural communication classes, sharing their ideas with us, and lending us references and photos from their collections. In particular, we are grateful to Professor Carley Dodd from Abilene Christian University, who granted us permission to include his model of culture; to Alison Rae for granting us permission to use the photos she took while travelling around the world collecting stories as a reporter; and to UNESCO for granting us permission to include some photos from their photobank. We express our sincere gratitude to the Centre of Communication for Social Change in the School of Journalism and Communication at the University of Queensland for offering financial support to employ a research assistant, Laura Simpson Reeves, who assisted with the development of the Instructor's Manuals for the companion website. Special thanks go to everyone who has given us support, time, and encouragement.

We express sincere appreciation to the Senior Commissioning Editor at SAGE Publications, Mila Steele. Without her encouragement and support, this second edition would not have come to fruition. Special thanks also go to the assistant editor, James Piper, others on the editorial staff, and the anonymous reviewers, who reviewed early and final drafts of the manuscript. Their insightful suggestions have greatly contributed to an improved book. We would like to thank everyone from SAGE whose work has transformed the manuscript into its present form.

Finally, we are deeply indebted to our families for their support, love, encouragement and patience throughout the writing of this book. Special thanks, therefore, go to Annie Liu, Mark Andrejevic, and Jeff Pittam.

COMPANION WEBSITE

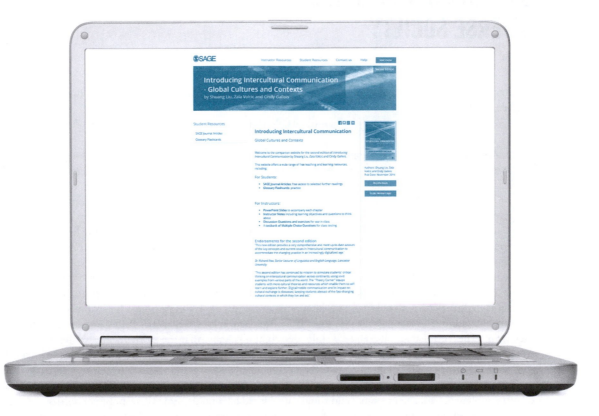

This book is supported by a brand new companion website (**https://study.sagepub.com/liu2e**). The website offers a wide range of free teaching and learning resources, including:

For Students:

- **SAGE Journal Articles**: free access to selected further readings
- **Glossary Flashcards**: practice

For Instructors:

- **PowerPoint Slides** to accompany each chapter
- **Instructor Notes** including learning objectives and questions to think about
- **Discussion Questions and exercises** for use in class
- A **testbank of Multiple Choice Questions** for class testing

INTRODUCTION

COMMUNICATING IN A CULTURALLY DIVERSE SOCIETY

> Human beings are drawn close to one another by their common nature, but habits and customs keep them apart.
>
> Confucius, Chinese thinker and social philosopher, 551–479BC

Since ancient times, clear geographic or political borders have always been marked between countries, states, cities, and villages. Natural boundaries such as rivers, oceans, and mountain ridges, or artificial borders such as walls, fences and signs, all function as landmarks to separate country from country, region from region and people from people. However, the spread of culture has never been confined to these geographic or political territories. For example, as early as the fifteenth century, *Aesop's Fables* were translated from Greek, the language in which they were originally written, into English, thus making them accessible to entirely new cultural, national and geographical audiences. Today, the fables, available in many languages across the world, including Chinese, Japanese, French, Russian, and German, have permeated our culture as myths and legends, providing entertainment and moral truisms for children and adults alike. Regardless of where we live, the colour of our skin or what language we speak, it is likely we have at some time encountered many of the morals or adages of *Aesop's Fables*: for instance, 'A liar will not be believed, even when telling the truth' from The Boy Who Cried Wolf; 'Slow and steady wins the race' from The Tortoise and the Hare. While we might not know that the stories were written by Aesop, exactly when they were written or how many languages they have been translated into, the tales still teach us universal virtues such as honesty, perseverance, modesty, and mutual respect. In addition to the spread of folk literature like *Aesop's Fables*, cultural products like tools, technology, clothing, food, furniture, electric appliances, music, customs, and rituals are spread beyond geographic or political borders.

Culture is defined as the total way of life of a people (Rogers and Steinfatt, 1999). The word 'culture' is derived from the Latin root *colere*, meaning 'to cultivate'. Our language, customs, expectations, behaviours, habits – our way of thinking, doing and being – have and continue to be formed over a long period of cultivation within the specific physical environment and social context in which we were born, with which we grew up, and in which we presently live. During the process of learning and adapting to the environment, different groups of people have learned distinctive ways to organize their world (Dodd, 1998). A group's unique ways of doing and thinking become their beliefs, values, worldviews, norms, rituals, customs, and their communication styles – ultimately, their cultural traditions.

Cultural traditions vary across different groups. For example, the concept of a wedding has a universal meaning, but specific wedding customs and rituals vary from culture to culture. In southern regions of China, the gifts that the groom's parents give to the bride's family often include two coconuts. In the Chinese language, the word 'coconut' is similar in sound to the words 'grandfather and son'. Thus, the gift of coconuts symbolizes a wish for both the longevity of the family's older generations and the ongoing presence of the younger generations, as an extended family of three or four generations is treasured in Chinese culture. In India, the cultural tradition is for the bride to enter her in-laws' home for the first time on her right foot and to knock over a container of uncooked rice, so as to bring good luck to the house. At a Sudanese wedding, seven broomsticks are burned and thrown away, to symbolize the couple discarding any bad habits that could pose a threat to their marriage. Japanese couples only become husband and wife after they take the first sip of *sake*, a rice wine drink, at the wedding. In Sweden, before leaving for the church to be married, the bride-to-be receives a gold coin from her mother to put in her right shoe, and a silver coin from her father to put in her left shoe. This is to ensure that she will always have sufficient financial resources. In the Netherlands, it is a custom to create a wedding 'wish tree'. At the reception a tree branch is placed next to the bride and groom's table, and paper leaves attached to pieces of ribbon are placed at each guest's place setting. Guests write their wishes for the couple on their leaves, which the bride and groom read and hang on the tree. And in France, the groom customarily walks his mother down the aisle before arriving at the altar to be married. Such are the rich variants of cultural traditions.

Culture defines a group of people, binds them to one another and gives them a sense of shared identity. It is the means by which a society expresses its structure and function, its views of the physical universe, and what it regards as the proper ways to live and to treat each other. Cultural traditions go through a process of development and sedimentation, and are passed on from generation to generation. Central to this entire process of development and maintenance is human communication. The word 'communication' is derived from the Latin word 'to make common', as in sharing thoughts, hopes and knowledge. Every cultural pattern and every act of social behaviour involves communication. Culture and communication are inseparable.

Human communication is a product of continual and ongoing development. In the villages of our early ancestors, information sharing was largely done on a face-to-face basis. The successive historical breakthroughs of print, telephone, broadcasting, television, and internet have progressively expanded the domain of communication beyond the immediate cultural and geographic borders. Correspondingly, our identities today have expanded from social groups, ethnic communities, and nations to incorporate factors that are no longer bound by politics, geography, or culture. The ease of global interaction in business, politics, education, and travel has brought strangers from different parts of the globe into face-to-face contact. This increased interconnectedness requires us to communicate competently with people whose cultures are different from our own; that is, to engage in intercultural communication. This ability does not come naturally, but must be learned. We must be able to communicate effectively and efficiently in our increasingly diverse society.

THE STUDY OF INTERCULTURAL COMMUNICATION

The roots of intercultural communication can be traced to the Chicago School, known for pioneering empirical investigations based on the theories of German sociologist Georg Simmel (1858–1918) (Rogers and Steinfatt, 1999). Simmel studied at the University of Berlin, and taught there and at the University of Strassburg in the late nineteenth and early twentieth centuries. Simmel analysed concepts related to his own life. As the son of Jewish parents, the anti-Semitism he experienced in Germany undoubtedly influenced his development of the concept of *der Fremde* or 'stranger', the intellectual descendants of which are key concepts in the fields of both sociology and intercultural communication today. The stranger (Simmel, 1950) is a member of a system, but not strongly attached to it or accepted by the other members of the system. Simmel's insights on the role of the stranger are part of his general concern with the relationships between individuals. His examination of reciprocal interactions at the individual level within a larger social context inspired much of the research at the Chicago School (Rogers, 1999) and subsequent research in the field of intercultural communication. The notion of communicating with someone who is different from us – an intercultural 'stranger' – lies at the heart of intercultural communication.

The key scholar in translating and applying Simmel's concept of the stranger was Robert E. Park, a former newspaper reporter who also earned his PhD degree in Germany. In 1900 Park took Simmel's course in sociology at the University of Berlin, and in 1915 began teaching sociology at the University of Chicago. Inspired by Simmel's notion of the stranger, Park developed the concept of social distance, which he defined as the degree to which an individual perceives a lack of intimacy with individuals different in ethnicity, race, religion, occupation or other variables (Park, 1924). Park's student Emory S. Bogardus later developed a scale that measured the social distance people perceive between themselves and members of another group. For example, in the scale respondents are asked such questions as, 'Would you marry someone who is Chinese?' and 'Would you have Chinese people as regular friends or as speaking acquaintances?' (Bogardus, 1933). The Bogardus Social Distance scale quantified the perceived intimacy or distance of an individual's relationships with various others.

As social distance is largely culturally prescribed, intercultural communication is invariably affected. For instance, Australians often use first names with someone they have just met, and in a university setting it is common for students to address the lecturers by their first name. This can be very puzzling to Korean students, who are more formal in their social relationships, only using first names with very close friends who are usually of the same age or social status as themselves. For example, an American Korean who has taught in the United States for over 30 years still feels some discomfort when students address her by her first name. When asked why she did not explain her preference to her students, she answered that she would only do it indirectly, a preferred Asian communication style. If a student addressed her by first name, instead of calling her 'Professor', she would respond in an unenthusiastic, subdued manner, in the hope that her student would gradually learn the 'appropriate' way to address her as a professor.

Simmel's concept of the stranger and subsequent derivative concepts all deal with individual relationships, both with others and the larger society. The concept of the stranger implies that the individual does not have a high degree of cohesion with the larger system of which he or she is a part. Park also conceptualized the 'marginal man'. A marginal person is an individual who lives in two different worlds, and is a stranger in both. Park studied the children of European immigrant parents in the United States, who typically rejected the European culture and language of their parents, but did not consider themselves to be true North Americans either. Their freedom from the norms of both systems led to a relatively high crime rate. To Park, the marginal person is a cultural hybrid, an individual on the margin of two cultures which never completely fuse. Park's concept was later extended to 'the sojourner', an individual who visits another culture for a period of time but who retains his or her original culture. The experience of sojourning or visiting often gives individuals a unique perspective for viewing both the host and home cultures. The sojourner later became a favourite topic of study for intercultural communication scholars, leading to concepts such as the U-curve of adjustment model, culture shock, and reverse culture shock (see Chapter 9).

Although the concepts of stranger, social distance and marginality are among those at the heart of intercultural communication, the field did not really emerge until after the Second World War. At that time, the United States had emerged as a leading world power and, with the advent of the United Nations, a number of new programmes, such as the World Health Organization, the United Nations' assistance programmes and the World Bank, were initiated to provide assistance to developing nations. However well-intended, not all development programmes were successful, largely because of a failure to comprehend the multifaceted and interrelated nature of culture. In Thailand, for example, where obtaining pure water was identified as the highest-priority problem, most of the hand-pump wells drilled in hundreds of villages by American development workers were broken within six months (Niehoff, 1964). An investigation into the problem showed that no local person was responsible for the maintenance of the pumps. When a well was dug on Buddhist temple grounds, the monks would look after the pump; other wells were neglected. The well-drilling project, conceived and implemented as separate and independent from the church, had not considered the important role that Buddhist monasteries played in Thai culture and the vital contribution they could make to the success of the project. It was clear that cultural issues had to be taken into account along with economic, political, and technical dimensions (Rogers, 1995).

US diplomats also experienced cultural frustrations. They were often poorly trained, lacking in cultural awareness and intercultural communication insight. They usually lived and worked in a small circle of English-speaking individuals, seldom venturing outside the capital city of their posting. In 1946, the US Congress passed an act to provide training to American diplomats and technical assistance workers in the Foreign Service Institute (FSI). Edward T. Hall, a leading anthropologist and teacher at FSI, and his anthropological and linguistics colleagues initially taught the participants the language and anthropological concepts of the nation to which they were assigned. The language programme was successful, but participants reported to Hall that they needed to communicate *across* cultures and thus wanted to understand intercultural differences, rather than simply gaining an understanding of the single culture in which they were to work. In response to these requests, Hall and his colleagues created a new approach that he called 'intercultural communication'. The publication of his famous book, *The Silent Language* (1959), signals the birth of intercultural communication study.

At the FSI, intercultural communication meant only communication between individuals of different national cultures. However, as teaching and research in intercultural communication developed over the decades, the meaning of 'culture' in intercultural communication broadened from national culture to any type of culture or subculture. Intercultural communication came to mean communication between individuals who might differ, for example, in ethnicity, socioeconomic status, age, gender, or lifestyle. This broader definition of the field is reflected in most intercultural communication textbooks today. A key figure in broadening this field was William B. Gudykunst, a professor of communication at California State University. In 1983, Gudykunst published an article in which he applied Simmel's concept of the stranger, arguing that the stranger is perceived as unfamiliar by other members of the system, so that a high degree of uncertainty is involved. This perspective was later carried through in a textbook, co-authored with Young Yun Kim from the University of Oklahoma, *Communicating with Strangers: An Approach to Intercultural Communication* (Gudykunst and Kim, 1984), in which communication with a stranger was made the key intellectual device to broaden the meaning of intercultural communication. Cultural differences, according to Gudykunst and Kim, could involve national or other culture, for example organizational culture or the culture of the deaf. The focus on the uncertainty involved in intercultural communication has led scholars to investigate how individuals reduce uncertainty by means of communication, a key area of intercultural communication study.

ORGANIZATION OF THIS NEW EDITION

This new edition of *Introducing Intercultural Communication* reflects our commitment to present intercultural communication concepts, theories, and applications through global perspectives, and emphasizes the application of knowledge to resolve practical problems. Striking a balance between theory and practice, this book enables you:

1. To learn fundamental concepts and principles of communication between people from different social and cultural backgrounds.

2. To generate insights into social, cultural, and historical dimensions of cultural and subcultural groups around the world.

3.   To reflect critically upon the influence of your own culture on how you view yourself and others.

4.   To compare communication behaviour, verbal and nonverbal, of different cultural groups, and interpret the behaviour through culture.

5.   To apply knowledge and skills to demonstrate autonomy, expert judgement, adaptability, and responsibility as an effective and ethical communicator across multiple cultural contexts.

This book begins by identifying different contributors to diversity in our society and the various challenges that we face in an increasingly globalized society (Chapter 1). When Canadian media culture analyst Marshall McLuhan coined the expression 'global village' five decades ago, many thought emerging communication technologies would restore social relations and bring back village-like intimate interactions. Of course, the technology McLuhan wrote about was not nearly as developed as it is today; recent developments like satellite communications and the rise of the internet make his vision seem almost prophetic. We watch and read about the same things at the same time, and exchange ideas with people on the other side of the world with the same speed and ease that our ancestors did with members of their own village. Yet the rules and guidelines for this interaction are not the same as those of our ancestors, and we have many issues still to explore: Do we really have a unified world because the media bring us closer? Who are the inhabitants and the players in this global village? What roles can intercultural communication play in meeting these challenges?

Chapters 2–5 introduce a range of theories to address historical questions at the intersection of identity, communication, and culture, as well as a number of key issues about the influence of culture on communication. Culture is a construction of reality that is created, shared, and transmitted by members of a group (Bonvillain, 2014). To explore and express our internal states of being, we must engage in communication. Our cultural value orientations influence how we see the world and how we communicate with others who we see around us. In what ways does culture shape our thinking, doing, and being? How does culture influence our perception of ourselves and that of others who are culturally different from us?

Understanding how our culture influences our communication reminds us of the boundaries of the different groups we belong to. Chapters 6 examines groups, subgroups, and various types of identities, including religious identity and identity based on sexual orientation. We belong to many different groups, on the basis of a range of characteristics shared with other members (culture, religion, social activities, gender, occupation, interest, etc.). These shared characteristics serve to categorize us into groups and subgroups, and the identities we derive from our group memberships develop, transform, and reshape our attitudes and behaviours. How do our group memberships give us a sense of location in the world? How are our identities formed and transformed as we move from group to group?

Chapters 7 and 8 focus on verbal and nonverbal codes of communication. Language is our most visible medium of exchange. Language is a set of symbols shared by a community to communicate meaning and experience, that abstract experience. Growing up, we learn to receive, store, manipulate, and generate symbols, through a process shared with others. Cultural values and norms are part of this process, so that problems may arise when people from different cultures interact with one another. If verbal communication can cause intercultural misunderstandings, the chance of misunderstanding is even greater for nonverbal behaviour, which is less explicitly coded. How is culture reflected in what we say and the way we say it?

Chapter 9 addresses issues surrounding immigration. The migration of people is linked to movements of capital and commodities, as well as to global cultural interchange, which is facilitated by improved transport infrastructure and the proliferation of electronic and print media. We pay special attention to migration as part of a transnational revolution that is reshaping the world's societies. The 'globalization of migration' will play a major role in the next decade, and we explore the acculturation of both migrants and people from host cultures. What attitudes should ethnic majorities have towards ethnic minorities, and vice versa? How should we interpret multiculturalism – as a threat or as a benefit?

Chapter 10 discusses cultural influences on relationships with others, including refugees, immigrants, and Indigenous people. Initiating and maintaining relationships with people in different groups is an important way to develop our own personal identity. From our relationships with others we receive feedback that we use to assess ourselves. But this emphasis on shared group experiences and rewards leads to the questions: How do people from different cultures establish relationships with others? How does culture influence ongoing human relationships? What are the potential barriers to developing intercultural friendships or interracial romantic relations?

Chapter 11 focuses on conflict management in intercultural communication and intercultural relations. Conflicts are inevitable in all interactions, and they occur at multiple levels: interpersonal, social, ethnic, national, and international. As conflicts everywhere increase in number and severity, this chapter explores the role of intercultural communication in understanding and transforming these conflicts. We also offer some advice on managing intercultural conflicts, including the management of diversity in organizations. Special attention is paid to the historical reasons for conflicts, such as historical antagonism between ethnic groups (for example, Arabs and Jews, Serbs and Albanian Kosovars). We present the approaches of different cultures to address legacies of widespread or systematic human rights abuses as they move from a period of violent conflict or oppression towards peace, democracy, the rule of law, and respect for individual and collective rights. How is conflict conceptualized and dealt with by members in different cultures? What are the communication styles preferred by people from different cultures to resolve conflicts?

Chapter 12 addresses the impact of the mass media on identity and cultural change. We present ways of thinking about media and identity in different geographical, political, and cultural contexts by offering examples of how the mass media influence us and shape our identities and belongings. We show how the mass media have historically played an essential part in the imagination of national communities. The creation of a national culture would have been impossible, for example, without the contribution of print and broadcast media. This chapter also addresses the mutual influence of mass media and technology, and their joint impact on cultural change; we take up issues related to online media and social networking sites. For example, how do different cultures use Facebook, based on their existing communication practices? What is the role of mass media in this increasingly connected and digitized world?

Finally, Chapter 13 brings us back to the issues raised in Chapter 1 regarding the challenges of living in a culturally diverse society. It explores the dialectic of homogenization and fragmentation of cultures. We present arguments about understanding the global context through the local context, and how local cultures challenge, negotiate, and adjust to globalization. This chapter raises issues for the study of communication and culture, preparing you for further investigation in the field of intercultural communication. Is globalization a form of Westernization? How do we develop intercultural competence to enable us to function effectively in intercultural communication?

This textbook does not simply raise questions and provide answers. We aim to enable you to ask further critical questions, so that you not only learn intercultural knowledge and skills, but also become a critical consumer of information. In learning, debating, and applying knowledge and skills, your journey to become a skilled intercultural communicator starts now!

‘I do not want my house to be walled in on all sides and my windows to be stuffed. I want all the cultures of all the lands to be blown about my house as freely as possible. But I refuse to be blown off my feet by any.’

Mohandas K. Gandhi, political and spiritual leader of India, 1869–1948

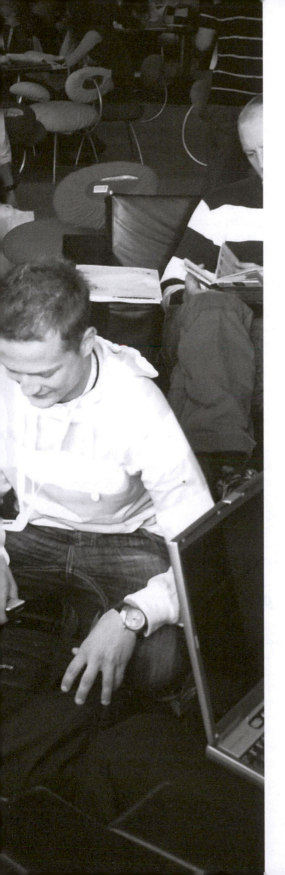

1

CHALLENGES OF LIVING IN A GLOBAL SOCIETY

LEARNING OBJECTIVES

At the end of this chapter, you should be able to:

- Identify different contributors to cultural diversity in our society.

- Analyse the challenges we face living in a global village.

- Appreciate unity and harmony amid diversity.

- Recognize the importance of developing the solid knowledge and skills of intercultural communication.

INTRODUCTION

Our early ancestors lived in small villages; most of them rarely ventured far from their own communities. They lived and died close to where they were born, and much of their information sharing was done through face-to-face communication with people who were much like themselves. Over the years, advances in transportation, improvements in telecommunication technologies, increases in international business, and political exchanges have brought strangers from different parts of the world into face-to-face contact. In 1964, Canadian media culture analyst Marshall McLuhan coined the term 'global village' to describe a world in which communication technology, such as television, radio, and news services, brings news and information to the most remote parts of the world. Today, McLuhan's vision of a global village is no longer considered an abstract idea, but a virtual certainty. We can exchange ideas as easily and quickly with people across the world as our ancestors did within the confines of their villages. We form communities and societies, and we encounter people from different cultures in business, at school, in public places, in our neighbourhood, and in cyberspace. We may wear clothes made in China, purchase seafood from Thailand, dine out with friends in an Italian restaurant, work at a computer made in the United States, drive a car manufactured in Japan – the list goes on. Each encounter with new food, clothing, lifestyle, art, language, or practice teaches us new things outside our 'village' culture.

'Globalization lies at the heart of modern culture; cultural practices lie at the heart of globalization' (Tomlinson, 1999: 1). This quote raises questions about the challenges that we face living in a global village. This chapter first identifies different contributors to cultural diversity in our society. Advances in technology, modern transport systems, global economy, international business transactions, and mass migration make our 'village' more culturally diverse. In this global village, people are constantly moving across borders and engaging in international exchange. This chapter explores theories of globalization and the context in which they are applied, describes various challenges we face living in such a global village, and explains the roles intercultural communication can play in meeting those challenges. By recognizing the importance of developing the sound knowledge and skills of intercultural communication, we can appreciate unity and harmony amid diversity in our global village.

CONTRIBUTORS TO CULTURAL DIVERSITY

Advanced technology and transport system

Globalization is the process of increasing interconnectedness between societies, so that events in one place of the world have more and deeper effects on people and societies far away (Baylis and Smith, 2001). Today, we can watch and read about the same events at the same time, regardless of time and space distance. With emails, social media, bulletin boards, satellites, fax and mobile phones, we can contact people anywhere and anytime. If we want a more personal exchange, Skype or video desktop technology can bring a person at the other end of the globe onto the computer screen right in front of us. Words like 'blogs' (an abridgment of the term 'web log') and 'podcasting' (an amalgam of 'iPod' and 'broadcasting') have appeared in our dictionaries since the beginning of the twenty-first century. Facebook is now a global phenomenon, allowing people from all walks of life to post their profiles online and communicate with other users across the world. Voice-over-Internet Protocol (VOIP), one of the fastest-growing internet technologies, allows people to talk online as if they were on a landline telephone. Instant messaging and texting messages and images by mobile phone can carry visual messages, if an audio channel is inconvenient. The choices of media to connect with other people anywhere and anytime are multiplying.

Critical thinking...

Do we actually partake of a more unified or diversified world because communication technologies bring us closer? What are the biggest differences? What remains the same?

THEORY CORNER

GLOBAL VILLAGE

The notion of global village and the process of globalization pose more questions than answers. Anura Goonasekera (2001) defines globalization as the widening, deepening, and speeding up of worldwide interconnectedness in all aspects of contemporary social life. This interconnectivity breaks down the boundary between East and West. The metaphor of a global village has caught the imagination of many people, including political leaders and intellectuals. Goonasekera further argues that 'paradoxically, we find that while technology has given the world the means of getting closer together into a global village, this very same technology has also given rise to unprecedented fears of domination by the technologically powerful nations' (2001: 278). Some Asian leaders feel that globalization creates fears of cultural liquidation, particularly among smaller nations. Consequently, the global village is viewed more as a threat to cultural identities than as an opportunity to create a more consensual culture among people.

Reference

Goonasekera, Anura (2001) 'Transnational communication: establishing effective linkages between North and South', in N. Chitty (ed.), *Mapping Globalization: International Media and a Crisis of Identity*. Penang: Southbank. pp. 270–281.

Further reading on globalization and cultural hegemony

Castells, Manuel (2007) 'Communication, power and counter-power in the network society', *International Journal of Communication*, 1: 238–266.

Theory in Practice

LOCALIZED GLOBALISM AT TOURIST SITES IN CHINA

The increasing mobility of goods and people on a global scale has challenged the traditional, static, and universal definition of place. In tourist destinations, for example, the construction of places for tourists' consumption involves the strategic mobilization of resources on a global–local continuum. Gao (2012) studied a tourist site, West Street, in Yangshuo County, China, to illustrate how a former residential neighbourhood was gradually transformed into a 'global village' for local tourists, in part through appropriating English as a semiotic resource. Situated in the picturesque Yangshuo County, West Street is full of craft shops, calligraphy and painting shops, cafés, bars, and Chinese Kung Fu houses. It is also the gathering place for the largest number of foreigners, with more than 20 businesses being owned by foreigners. The place is called the 'global village', since all the locals can speak foreign languages. Gao analysed County Chronicles, media reports, promotional materials on local government websites, and held interviews with foreign and local business owners in West Street to uncover how linguistic devices are used to localize globalism at tourism sites. Findings from this study show that the 'global village' in Yangshuo is not simply Westernization, but a social construct whose significance corresponds to ideologies of language and culture at societal level.

Questions to take you further

Tourist sites provide an opportunity for minority languages and cultures to enhance their value through the commodification of local languages and identities. Can you identify another arena for exploring the social construction of place?

Reference

Gao, Shuang (2012) 'Commodification of place, consumption of identity: the sociolinguistic construction of a "global village" in rural China', *Journal of Sociolinguistics*, 16(3): 336–357.

Further reading on globalization

Blommaert, Jan (2010) *The Sociolinguistics of Globalization*. Cambridge and New York: Cambridge University Press.

Advanced communication technologies also affect how we form relationships with others. In past centuries, social relationships typically were circumscribed by how far one could walk (Martin and Nakayama, 2001). With each technological advance – the train, motor vehicle, telephone, or the internet – social relationships have been transformed and expanded manyfold. There are millions of global users of the internet every day. The average user spends over 70 per cent of his or her time online, building personal relationships, including online friendships, sexual partnerships, and romances (Nua Internet Survey, 2007). Evidence of the legitimacy and social acceptance of these types of relationship is found, for example, in Warner Brothers' popular 1998 movie *You've Got Mail*, which played on the increasing mainstream acceptance of romantic relationships formed over the internet.

The internet has led to new ways of socializing that seem especially to attract young people. The research shows that, for example, in Western European countries most people know someone who has met a romantic partner on the internet. As Sveningsson (2007) writes, one of Sweden's most popular online meeting places is a web community called Lunarstorm (www.lunarstorm.se), which is visited weekly by 85 per cent and daily by 29 per cent of all Swedes aged 15–20. Most young Swedes seem to have become members of Lunarstorm – the media have even called it 'Sweden's largest online youth recreation centre'. Whitty, Baker and Inman (2007) show that there are still the usual steps leading to the establishment and development of a love relationship, when initiated on the web: meeting in specific online places, communicating online, and meeting in real life are factors in successful and unsuccessful online-initiated relationships. They assess the role of Facebook in the escalation of romantic relationships and argue that new media technologies are supplementing or replacing face-to-face interaction in relationship development for a growing number of individuals.

Photo 1.1   We continue to be 'connected' during our work or leisure time. Copyright © Jaka Polutnik. Used with permission.

The idea of internet-based romantic relationships is gaining popularity as the mobility of society increases. Unlike the telephone, postage, and physical travel, the cost of email, instant messaging and chat rooms does not depend on either message length or the distance the message travels. The internet, therefore, provides many opportunities to maintain and receive support from long-distance romantic partners, as it is inexpensive, convenient, quick, and similar to a conversation. The people we exchange emails with on the internet are now more than ever likely to come from different countries, be of different ethnic or cultural backgrounds, and have different life experiences. Advanced communication technologies make our community more culturally diverse than ever before.

Critical thinking...

In what ways can online communication shape the structure and development of interpersonal relationships, such as friendships? Do you think our continued reliance on technology-mediated communication will lead to a weakening of interpersonal communication skills?

Not only do we come in contact with more people in cyberspace, but modern transport systems also bring us into contact with more people physically. Our society is more mobile than in the past. For example, in the 1930s, travel from China to Singapore took several months; travellers started the journey in winter and arrived at their destination in summer. Nowadays, the same distance by airplane would take only a few hours! Such ease of mobility changes the nature of society. On the one hand, families and individuals easily and often move for economic, career or lifestyle opportunities. A New Zealander can work in Australia; an Australian can work in the USA; an American can work in England; a Briton can work in

France; a French person can work in Belgium – or in Tahiti. Increasing mobility and technology make our global village smaller but more diverse.

On the other hand, as Brown (2011) argues, ever since the fall of the Berlin Wall, there has been a strange increase in wall-building, in order to separate people. It is not simply that there is a resurgence in the construction of physical walls, such as the Israeli West Bank barrier, the US–Mexico border fence, or similar barriers on the edges of the European Union or the borders of India, Saudi Arabia, and a host of other countries (or the non-physical boundaries in maritime countries like Australia). There is also a rise of attempts at enclosure, as if nations could wrap themselves safely behind walls. Think of the town of Michalovce in Slovakia, where residents built a cement barrier to separate themselves from the town's majority Roma population. This wall has nothing to do with sovereignty or security, but with aversion and xenophobia. Thus, while changes in technology have facilitated the exchange of ideas, they also have magnified the possibility for misunderstandings. If we consider that people with the same cultural background may experience problems communicating with each other, we can appreciate more fully the difficulties that people from different cultures may encounter when trying to communicate. Understanding other cultures is a challenge we face today, living in a global society.

Further online reading   The following article can be accessed for free on the book's companion website https://study.sagepub.com/liu2e: Cunningham, William A., Nezlek, John B. and Banaji, Mahzarin R. (2004) 'Implicit and explicit ethnocentrism: revisiting the ideologies of prejudice', *Personality and Social Psychology Bulletin*, 30(10): 1332–1346.

THEORY CORNER

PERSPECTIVES ON GLOBALIZATION

In the academic literature (Held and McGrew, 2007), there are three different perspectives on globalization: a globalist perspective, a traditionalist perspective, and a transformationalist perspective.

Globalists view globalization as an inevitable development which cannot be resisted or significantly influenced by human intervention, particularly through traditional political institutions, such as nation-states. Traditionalists argue that the significance of globalization as a new phase has been exaggerated. They believe that most economic and social activity is regional, rather than global, and they still see a significant role for nation-states. Transformationalists contend that globalization represents a significant shift, but they question the inevitability of its impacts. They argue that there is still significant scope for national, local, and other agencies.

Reference
Held, David and Anthony, McGrew (eds) (2007) *Globalization Theory: Approaches and Controversies*. Cambridge: Polity Press.

Further reading on globalization
Baylis, John, Steve, Smith and Patricia, Owens (2011) *The Globalization of World Politics: An Introduction to International Relations* (5th edn). Oxford: Oxford University Press.

Theory in Practice

ONGOING CONFLICTS BETWEEN GLOBALISTS AND SCEPTICS

Research on media globalization has grown rapidly in recent years. Within the field of global media studies, there is an ongoing conflict between two basic positions: globalists and sceptics. Globalists emphasize the possibility of transnational media systems and communication technology to create a global public sphere, whereas sceptics stress the persistent national features of the news media, and the continuing stability of the nation-state paradigm. In her study on the emergence of a transnational (European) identity in national news reporting on global climate change, Olausson (2013) analysed climate reporting in Indian, Swedish, and US newspapers. Findings showed that some domestic discourses created explicit interconnections between the national or local and the global, for example, by situating Earth Hour in a small city in Sweden within the global framework of the event. Other discourses worked in a counter-domestic manner; that is, they lacked nationalizing elements around the issue of climate change. The author argues that the national and global are not mutually exclusive, but reinforce and reconstruct one another; they constitute two sides of the same coin.

Questions to take you further

Think about media audiences. Can you give examples to show what types of event covered in the media are more likely to activate our national identity positions? Under what circumstances do we accept global outlooks provided by the media?

Reference

Olausson, Ulrika (2013) 'Theorizing global media as global discourse', *International Journal of Communication*, 7: 1281–1297.

Further reading on global media

Sparks, Colin (2007) 'What's wrong with globalization?', *Global Media and Communication*, 3(2): 133–155.

Global economy and business transactions

Information and communication technologies (ICTs) transform the potential reach and influence of our economy and business transactions from a local to a global level. *Global transformation* refers to the worldwide economic and technological changes that influence how people relate to one another (Cooper, Calloway-Thomas and Simonds, 2007). For example, people in nearly every part of the world can buy Reebok shoes, Levi jeans or an iPhone! Cross-cultural business transactions today are as common as trade between two persons in the same village was centuries ago. The clothes we wear, the food we purchase from the local supermarket, the cars we drive, the electric appliances we use at home, the movies we watch may all be from different countries. Indeed, we are being multiculturalized every day. Our local market is as culturally diverse as the global market. Cultural diversity brings many opportunities, particularly in the economic realm, and helps to make our society the cosmopolitan, dynamic and exciting place it is today. However, one of the biggest economic and social challenges facing us today is to unlock the barriers to the

Photo 1.2   Ethnic shops in Chinatown in Brisbane, Australia. Copyright © Shuang Liu. Used with permission.

acceptance of cultural diversity in the economy and society as a whole (Beamer and Varner, 2008).

In response to the economic transformations, businesses are continually expanding into world markets as a part of the wider process of globalization. Cultural diversity shapes market demand and economic behaviours. For example, in 1991, India began to open its economy to wider trade, and the United States quickly became its primary trading and investment partner – investing some US$687 million in 1997, almost three times as much as in the previous year (Cooper et al., 2007). Billions of dollars in goods and services are exchanged each year in international businesses. Similarly, multinational corporations are increasingly moving their operations overseas to take advantage of lower labour costs, a trend that has far-reaching implications.

Ethnic diversity within workplaces is continually changing the organizational composition of most parts of the world. For example, the number of emigrants joining the European workforce from Africa, Asia, and the Middle East increases each year. In the United States, the proportion of non-white (Asian, black, and Hispanic American) men is growing, and this trend is expected to continue (Oetzel, 2002). In the Middle East, many workers come from India, the Philippines, and Southeast Asia. For example, Saudi Arabia's population of foreign workers has increased significantly over the last few decades, with a particularly significant increase of 38 per cent between 1975 and 2000. This population grew dramatically again in 2004, when there were approximately 12.5 million foreign workers in the country, making up 37 per cent of the overall population and 65 per cent of the entire labour force (Looney, 2004). The Kingdom of Saudi Arabia emerged in 1932 upon the ascendance of King Abdulaziz to the throne. During the middle of the twentieth century, the discovery of oil reserves in the country led to rapid industrialization, and subsequent economic development. Early on, the oil wealth led to a great demand for skilled labour that was not present in Saudi Arabia.

Similarly, in Asian countries like Malaysia, the workforce is also becoming more diverse. Even though Malays make up a large proportion of the workforce (65 per cent), the term 'Malaysian', more often than not, is used to refer to the people of different ethnicities, including Indians and Chinese in Malaysia. Working in cross-cultural teams allows organizations to make use of scarce resources and thus increase their competitive advantage. As a result of such economic and cultural shifts, people with diverse cultural backgrounds are working side by side in many countries, creating a workplace that is intercultural (Beamer and Varner, 2008).

The flow of migrant workers as a result of economic transformation also leads to an increase in ethnic competition. Migrant workers tend to flow from regions with lower economic opportunities towards those with greater opportunities. In Western European countries, for example, with the opening up of national borders within the European Union, European nation-states have been granting social rights, although no real political rights, to migrants (Soysal, 1994). This change has increased the perception of competition on the part of the native population. For example, there is a large North African presence in Europe. Reaching 3.5 million today, North Africans began arriving in Europe as early as the 1940s to help rebuild fledgling European economies severely weakened by the war. This migration accelerated in the 1950s and 1960s to meet the high demand for low-skilled workers in factories and mines and to compensate for slow demographic growth in Western Europe. For many years, North African immigrants were considered temporary residents (guest workers) and had no share in the social, political, and cultural life of the host societies. Now, these groups form communities with a generation born in the new country.

Further online reading The following article can be accessed for free on the book's companion website https://study.sagepub.com/liu2e: Castells, Manuel (2008) 'The new public sphere: global civil society, communication networks, and global governance', *Annals of the American Academy of Political and Social Science*, 616(1): 78–93.

It was only after the 1974 policies of family reunion that immigrants, their families, traditions, and religions became visible in everyday life. France, for example, is home to the largest number of North African immigrants, due to its long colonial involvement in Algeria, Morocco, and Tunisia, followed by Holland, Belgium, Spain, Italy, and Germany. Different citizenship and immigration laws, as well as the socio-political climate of each host country, determine to a large extent how North Africans have engaged with the host culture. While acknowledging the benefits that can be obtained from an ethnically and culturally diverse workforce, studies consistently indicate problems often experienced by multi-ethnic workers, such as conflicts in expectations, lack of communication competence, and attitude problems such as mistrust. Thus, understanding the cultural tensions created by economic transformations is a challenge we face in the business context of intercultural communication.

THEORY CORNER

CONCEPTUALIZING ETHNICITY

As is widely known, 'ethnicity' and 'ethnic' are derived from the Greek. At the time of Homer (between 750 and 650 BC) the term *ethnos* was applied to various large, undifferentiated groups (warriors as well as bees and birds) and meant something like 'throng' or 'swarm'. According to Hutchinson and Smith (1996: 6), ethnicity is named after a 'human population with myths of common ancestry, shared historical memories, one or more elements of a common culture, a link with a homeland and a sense of solidarity among at least some of its members'. Special attention is paid to the extremes of human experience, which are always a fertile ground for cultural myths and memories that sustain a large group culture. Similarly, Anthony D. Smith (2007) views myths and memories as part of a culture, remembered as a part of a golden past and the commemoration and celebration of heroic events. Every ethnic group, according to Smith, has a mythologized version of its past, in which heroic events (victories/glories and sacrifices/traumas) and heroes (actual historical figures and/or mythologized characters) occupy a prominent position. These events and characters are often evoked during different occasions and ceremonies to inspire the members of the group, to build social cohesion among them, and to particularize their common identity. For example, the French celebrate their Independence Day to honour the storming of the Bastille, the beginning of the revolution, and the birth of the modern French nation. These celebratory activities have the purpose of enhancing the cultural group's sense of belonging and togetherness.

References
Hutchinson, John and Anthony D. Smith (1996) *Ethnicity*. Oxford: Oxford University Press.
Smith, Anthony D. (2007) *Myths and Memories of the Nation*. Oxford: Oxford University Press.

Further reading on ethnicity
Hecht, Michael, Ronald L. Jackson II, Sheryl Lindsley, Susan Strauss and Karen E. Johnson (2001) 'A layered approach to ethnicity: language and communication', in P. Robinson and H. Giles (eds), *The New Handbook of Language and Social Psychology*. Chichester, UK: Wiley. pp. 429–449.

Theory in Practice

ETHNICITY AS A MANAGEMENT ISSUE AND RESOURCE

There has been recognition for some time that the management policies in international operations of multinational companies are complex and complicated. This is not only due to diverse business or product market strategies, but also because the political, economic, social, legislative, and cultural environment varies between locations. In particular, a neglected aspect of the context is ethnicity, especially in multi-ethnic locations. Such environments provide not only 'constraints', but also 'opportunities' in terms of management, write Bhopal and Rowley (2005). Ethnicity is not only an issue which calls for 'management', but is itself a potential managerial resource. Ethnicity is important for organizations at both external (contextual) and internal (operational) levels.

Bhopal and Rowley specifically write about the Malaysian context. They argue that for political management, the creation of ethnic boundaries assists in creating ethnic bonds. In this sense, ethnicity is a resource in the developmental process, because it undermines the potential of employer–employee conflicts of interest, and can act as a solvent for the basis of political organization and support. In this study, the idea of ethnic identification – either with the values of rural Malays or with Chinese-educated Chinese – acts to ensure that there is a desire to reduce cultural distance and seek commonalities rather than highlight differences.

Questions to take you further
To what extent are issues of ethnicity functional and dysfunctional for organizational management? What are the key factors that improve the situation? What aspects of ethnicity make things worse?

Reference
Bhopal, Mhinder and Chris Rowley (2005) 'Ethnicity as a management issue and resource: examples from Malaysia', *Asia Pacific Business Review*, 11(4): 553–574.

Further reading on global business citizenship
Logsdon, Jeanne M. and Donna J. Wood (2005) 'Global business citizenship and voluntary codes of ethical conduct', *Journal of Business Ethics*, 59(1): 55–67.

Critical thinking...

Skilled migrants form an important migration element; they are accepted into the receiving country to fill in skill shortages. However, international research has found that many of them are under-employed or unemployed in the country of settlement. Why do you think this is so? What training programmes could we offer to enhance their employability in the job market? What does this have to do with intercultural communication?

Mass migration and international exchange

One of the most significant contributors to our multicultural environment is the ever-increasing flow of people through migration and international exchange (see Chapter 9). According to the Population Division of the Department of Economic and Social Affairs of the United Nations (DESA, 2013), 232 million people, or 3.2 per cent of the world's population, were international migrants in 2012, compared with 175 million in 2000 and 154 million in 1990. In 2013 a growing concentration of international migrants was found in ten countries, with the USA hosting the largest number (45.8 million). The Russian Federation hosted 11 million, followed by Germany (9.8 million), Saudi Arabia (9.1 million), the United Arab Emirates (7.8 million), the United Kingdom (7.8 million), France (7.4 million), Canada (7.3 million), Australia (6.5 million), and Spain (6.5 million). Asians and Latin Americans living outside their home regions form the largest global diaspora group. Statistics from the Population Division of the United Nations reveals that in 2013 Asians accounted for 19 million migrants living in Europe, some 16 million in Northern America, and about 3 million in Oceania. International migrants originating from Central America, including Mexico, represented another large group of migrants living outside their home region. The majority of Central American migrants (about 16.3 million out of 17.4 million) live in the USA. Migration increases cultural diversity in the composition of populations for receiving countries, and contributes to social and economic development both in the countries of origin and in the countries of destination. Therefore, it is crucial to enhance the benefits of international migration, while reducing its negative implications.

A steadily increasing proportion of migrant populations are made up of international students, particularly in developed English-speaking countries such as the USA, Australia, and the UK. To date, the United States has been the world's largest receiving country for international students. In 2005–06, the number of international students enrolled in higher education institutions remained steady at 567,766, according to the *Annual Report on International Academic Mobility* published by the Institute of International Education (IIE, 2006). This marks the seventh year in a row that the USA has hosted more than half a million foreign students. Asia remains the largest region of origin, accounting for 58 per cent of the total of US international enrolments. India is the leading country of origin for international students, followed by China, Korea, Japan, Canada, Taiwan, Mexico, Turkey, Germany, and Thailand. International students contribute approximately US$13.5 billion to the US economy through their expenditure on tuition and living expenses. The Department of Commerce describes US higher education as the country's fifth largest service sector export.

A similar trend was found in Oceanic countries such as Australia, where education has recently replaced tourism as the country's largest service export, according to IDP Education, a global company that informs and advises international students on Australian education and assists in enrolment in Australian institutions across all sectors (IDP Education, 2008). Higher education is the largest sector for international students, with an average annual growth rate of 7.7 per cent since 2002. Students from China accounted for 40.2 per cent of all international student higher education enrolments in 2011 (International Education Advisory Council [IEAC], 2012). Australia's top five source countries for international students are China, India,

Photo 1.3 Signs in market squares are in different languages to cater to multicultural customers.
Copyright © Shuang Liu. Used with permission.

South Korea, Vietnam, and Malaysia (Australian Education International, 2013). Figures released by the Australian Bureau of Statistics (ABS) show that international education contributed A$16 billion (approximately US$15 billion) to the Australian economy in the 2010–11 financial year, and created over 100,000 jobs. According to commentators, education is now a bigger drawcard for visitors to Australia than the Great Barrier Reef and all other tourist attractions combined. The flow of international students, particularly those from non-English- to English-speaking countries, inevitably creates both opportunities and challenges for intercultural communication.

Of more permanent residential status than international students are those people who migrate to the host country to make a living. They are a significant contributor to the multicultural environment of society today. In Australia, for example, immigration has always been a central part of nation building. Since the end of the Second World War, around over 7 million migrants have moved to Australia. In the immediate post-war period, only 10 per cent of Australia's population was born overseas (Marden and Mercer, 1998). Today, nearly 25 per cent of the Australian population was born overseas (including all three authors of this book), and approximately 200 languages are spoken in the country. The proportion of people from Asian countries is on the increase. Between 2000 and 2005, the number of East Asians in Australia rose by 17 per cent (from approximately 850,000 to 1 million). In comparison, the total Australian population grew only by approximately 5 per cent (from 19.4 million to 20.3 million) during the same period (Australian Bureau of Statistics, 2005).

Migrants move to their host countries for a variety of reasons, including access to a better living environment or to give their children a good education in an English-speaking country. Other people intend to explore business opportunities unavailable in their home country, while some migrate to seek refuge or political protection. Regardless of the reasons for migration, migrants worldwide dream of the freedom to be their own boss, to have autonomy in their choice of work, and to achieve prosperity in the host country. Small businesses, such as take-away shops, convenience stores, trading companies or video shops, are considered by many migrants as ways to realize their dreams of freedom and financial security. As a result, walking along a street in Sydney, Auckland, San Francisco or London, one would not have difficulty finding an Indian restaurant, a Chinese take-away shop, a Vietnamese greengrocery store, an Italian deli, a Japanese sushi bar – the list goes on. For example, in Brisbane market squares, signs are in different languages to cater to the linguistic diversity of customers.

NECESSITY AND BENEFITS OF INTERCULTURAL COMMUNICATION

Multiculturalism

All over the world, nations are trying to come to terms with the growing diversity of their populations (Beamer and Varner, 2008). Behind the overt, visible symbols of cultural diversity is a complex and often implicit concept of *multiculturalism*. At a descriptive level, multiculturalism can be used to characterize a society with diverse cultures. As an attitude, it can refer to a society's tolerance towards diversity and acceptance of equal societal participation. In attempting to maximize the benefits of cultural diversity, there has been an accompanying awareness of some potential threats to our cultural uniqueness. Globally, host nationals have expressed concerns over the threat that new ethnic cultures may pose to mainstream cultural values, the political and economic power structure, and the distribution of employment opportunities. Some countries are addressing these concerns by trying to control diversity through tighter entry requirements. Other countries are developing governmental policies concerning the rights of immigrants to preserve their home culture within the host country.

Australia, during the nineteenth century, had no restrictions on anyone entering what was then a set of colonies, provided that they were not convicts serving out their time. Consequently, free settlers moved in from Great Britain, Germany, America, Scandinavia, and Asia. Similarly, the slogan of the post-Second World War immigration programme was 'Populate or Perish'! However, since 2007, a citizenship test has been in place to check migrants' knowledge of the English language and comprehension of Australian moral principles and history, as well as national and Aboriginal symbols. The test is available in English only, and a migrant applicant for citizenship must pass the test before an application for citizenship can be lodged. This restriction of citizenship opportunities is also evident elsewhere. In some countries, such as the People's Republic of China and the USA, dual citizenship is not recognized. In Germany, immigrants are considered 'Ausländer' (foreigners) and their naturalization is only possible if they agree to renounce their original citizenship and demonstrate loyalty to their 'adoptive' country (these laws were slightly relaxed when the Social Democrats gained power in the 1990s). Even so, there is a raging controversy regarding the amendment of the citizenship laws and the implications for German national identity (Blank, Schmidt and Westle, 2001). France has built its nation-state, since the nineteenth century, on the premise that all regional and cultural differences should be eliminated. French citizens have to show loyalty to a powerful, centralized, secular nation-state, and to adhere to universal political values. Linguistic as well as cultural diversity within France has always been seen as a sign of regression and a hindrance to achieving national unity. Even in the United States, a country that historically afforded a home to people of diverse cultures, the advantages and disadvantages of acknowledging diversity are hotly debated (Cooper et al., 2007). Maintenance of nationalism and continuity of the mainstream culture have been key issues of concern in all countries that receive migrants.

Migrants, on the other hand, have long been forming associations to maintain their ethnic and cultural heritage and promote the survival of their languages within a host country's mainstream institutions. In Australia, for example, the Asian-values debate has attracted considerable media attention, particularly in response to increased Asian immigration and the continuing emphasis placed on Australia's role in the Asian region as being closely tied to the policy of multiculturalism (Marden and Mercer, 1998).

Central to this debate is the question of whether the preservation of ethnic cultures creates a threat to mainstream society. An interesting example, from Australia, involves the game of football (soccer), the 'world game' (or the 'beautiful game'). This code of football had not been popular in Australia, but began to gain followers with the European migrations in the 1950s and 1960s (see the Case Study). These people formed teams with names similar to those in their countries of origin ('Juventus', 'Olympic'). During the 1990s, the national football association pushed for a change to these names and the composition of the teams, so that the game would be seen as 'less ethnic'. Clubs like the Sydney Football Club and the Brisbane Roar gained followers from their home cities (a long Australian tradition in many football codes). Today, with Australia's improved performance in world football, the clubs feel sufficiently integrated into mainstream society to celebrate their multi-ethnic and multicultural character; they advertise that they reflect the 'real', multicultural Australia. Even so, multiculturalism is on fragile ground. The challenge we face is how to promote intercultural understanding so as to reap the benefits of cultural diversity and reduce intercultural tensions. The key to building the necessary understanding between cultural groups is effective intercultural communication.

Critical thinking...

To what extent should migrants maintain their ethnic cultural traditions and practices without posing a threat to the unity of the mainstream host culture? To what extent should they adapt to their new society? Do you agree with the admonition 'Leave your old conflicts at home – there is no place for them here'? Why or why not?

Further online reading The following article can be accessed for free on the book's companion website https://study.sagepub.com/liu2e: Ho, Robert (1990) 'Multiculturalism in Australia: a survey of attitudes', *Human Relations*, 43(3): 259–272.

Building intercultural understanding

Understanding is the first step towards acceptance. The biggest benefit of accepting cultural differences is that cultural diversity enriches each of us. Throughout history, people around the world have accumulated a rich stock of cultural traditions and customs, but we are often not aware of the cultural rules governing our own behaviour until we encounter behaviours different from our own. Local laws and customs vary from country to country; if you are unaware of them and act according to your own learned customs when in the new country, you may very well end up in prison! For example, it is illegal in Egypt to take photographs of bridges and canals (including the Suez Canal), as well as military personnel, buildings and equipment. In India, trespassing on and photography of airports, military establishments and dams is illegal, with penalties ranging from 3 to 14 years' imprisonment. Similarly, maiming or killing a cow in India is an offence which can result in a punishment of up to five years' imprisonment. In Thailand, lengthy prison terms of up to 15 years can be imposed for insulting the monarchy; this includes destroying bank notes bearing the king's image.

If some of these local laws do not make much sense to you, you may find some local customs even stranger. Behaviours which are considered perfectly appropriate and acceptable in one culture may appear harsh or offensive in another. For example, in Saudi Arabia, women are legally required to wear the abaya, a long black coat that conceals their body shape, in all public places, while men are to avoid wearing shorts, short-sleeved or unbuttoned shirts. Public displays of affection, including kissing and holding hands, are considered offensive. Hotels may refuse accommodation to couples unable to provide proof of marriage, because it is illegal for unmarried couples to live together. In Thailand, simple actions such as showing the soles of your feet or touching the top of a person's head are likely to cause grave offence. Even unknowingly breaching local customs may either get you into trouble or make you unwelcome!

We acquire many of our cultural beliefs, values, and communication norms at an unconscious level. Cultural socialization, in addition, can encourage the development of ethnocentrism. *Ethnocentrism* means seeing our own culture as the central and best one, and seeing other cultures as insignificant or even inferior. Ethnocentrism may lead to prejudice, stereotypes, or discrimination (see Chapter 4). It is a barrier to effective intercultural communication because it prevents us from understanding those who are culturally different from ourselves. In contrast to ethnocentrism is *cultural relativism*, which is the degree to which an individual judges another culture by its context (Rogers and Steinfatt, 1999). Cultural relativists try to evaluate the behaviours of a culture using that culture's assumptions about reality. Although one element of a culture, by itself, may seem strange to a non-member, it generally makes sense when being considered in light of other elements of that culture (see Chapter 3). To understand another culture, therefore, we need to communicate with its people and broaden our understanding of its practices and beliefs, thus enhancing our sense of cultural relativism – hence the need and benefit of intercultural communication.

As members of the global village, we can celebrate the richness of the human imagination along with its diverse products. The key to appreciating cultural differences is to acquire intercultural knowledge and develop intercultural skills. Intercultural knowledge opens doors to the treasure house of human experience. It reveals to us myriad ways of experiencing, sensing, feeling, and knowing. It helps us to start questioning our own stance on issues that we may have once taken for granted. It widens our vision to include an alternative perspective of valuing and relating. By understanding the beliefs, values, and worldviews that influence alternative communication approaches, we can understand the logic that motivates the actions or behaviours of others who are culturally different from ourselves. Cultural differences do not prevent us from communicating with each other; rather, they enrich us through communication. Culturally sensitive communication can increase relational closeness and deepen cultural self-awareness (Ting-Toomey and Chung, 2005). The more that culturally diverse people get to know each other, the more they can appreciate the differences and perceive the deep commonalities among them. The key to building a stock of intercultural knowledge, therefore, is to engage in intercultural communication. Intercultural communication can help us to build our knowledge of other peoples and their cultures, as well as enhancing and consolidating our knowledge about our own culture. The result is invariably greater intercultural understanding.

Further online reading The following article can be accessed for free on the book's companion website https://study.sagepub.com/liu2e: Jairrels, Veda (1999) 'Cultural diversity: implications for collaboration', *Intervention in School and Clinic*, 34(4): 236–239.

Promoting international business exchange

The 'International Business Trend Report' produced in 1999 (*Training and Development*, 1999) identified three competencies that are essential in the global workplace of the twenty-first century: intercultural communication skills, problem-solving ability, and global leadership. When money and jobs cross borders, there are challenges and opportunities facing individuals of different backgrounds who live and work together. People of different ethnic backgrounds bring their cultural baggage to the workplace. In a multinational organization, for instance, Malay employees may heavily emphasize the values of family togetherness, harmony in relationships, and respect for seniority, whereas North American employees may value individuality and personal achievement more highly. A workgroup consisting of members from different cultural backgrounds is more likely to experience difficulty in communication or to experience miscommunication, dysfunctional conflict, and turnover if group members are not interculturally competent. This is clearly reflected in research conducted by Cox, Lobel and McLeod (1991), who studied the effects of ethnic differences in groups, and the cooperative and competitive behaviours of group members. Their findings indicate that Asian, black and Hispanic employees have a more cooperative task orientation than Anglos. Ethnic diversity in the workplace creates challenges for management in today's businesses, but attention to diversity issues has the potential to bolster employee morale, create an inclusive climate in organizations, and spark creative innovation.

Communicating in unfamiliar cultures does not simply mean finding a translator to facilitate discussions in a foreign language (Beamer and Varner, 2008). Communication is about unarticulated meanings and the thinking behind the words, not just the words *per se* (see Chapter 2). To understand the significance of a message from someone, you need to understand that person's perception and the most important values in that person's view of the world. You need to know what to expect when someone engages in a particular behaviour. *Guanxi*, for example, is a special type of Chinese relationship which contains trust, favour, dependence, and adaptation. It constitutes a highly differentiated and intricate system of formal and informal social subsets, which are governed by the unwritten law of reciprocity (Zhou and Hui, 2003). The Chinese people view human relationships as long-term, and consequently place great emphasis on cultivating a good relationship with their business partners prior to any business transaction. While economic factors are important to the Chinese, those factors alone cannot sustain the motivation to maintain long-term business relations. In fact, non-economic factors such as acceptance, face-giving, complementary social reciprocity, and trust may play a bigger role in influencing decision making. The emphasis on developing *guanxi* is reflected in business negotiations with Chinese partners, which tend to be much lengthier than those with a Westerner. As culture profoundly influences how people think, communicate, and behave, it also affects the kinds of deals they make and the way they make them. A good understanding of cultural differences is a key factor in promoting mutually productive and successful international business exchanges.

Facilitating cross-cultural adaptation

Cross-cultural adaptation has to be understood as a manifestation of broader social trends that are not confined to the experience of immigrants, but rather as extending to many other kinds of associations and networks as well as into cultural life at large.

Globalization is a process by which geographic borders as boundaries between nations and states are eroding. There are new contours of transnational spaces and societies, and new systems of identity. Advances in technology and transport systems now provide people with greater freedom to travel beyond national borders as well as more choices for belonging. Ultimately, interconnectedness between people and the erosion of geographic borders make our 'village' more global, but our world smaller. The arrival of immigrants brings various changes to the host cultural environment. Intercultural encounters provide opportunities for understanding between people as well as the potential for misunderstanding.

Cross-cultural adaptation is not a process that is unique to immigrants; host nationals also have to experience cultural adjustments when their society is joined by culturally different others (see Chapter 9). The tension between immigrants and host nationals often centres on the extent to which immigrants can maintain their heritage culture in the host country. Research conducted on immigrants' cultural adaptation strategies indicates that they identify integrating into the host culture and, at the same time, maintaining their ethnic cultural heritage as their preferred acculturation strategy (Liu, 2007). A key question is whether or not the host society provides immigrants with an environment in which they feel welcome to integrate. In countries receiving many immigrants, ethnically different populations can become perceived threats to collective identity and to the standard of living of the natives. For host nationals, multiculturalism can be interpreted as a threat to their cultural dominance. For migrant groups, however, multiculturalism offers the possibility of maintaining their own culture and still integrating into the host society. Thus, policies of multiculturalism that highlight the importance of recognizing cultural diversity within a common framework, as well as equal opportunities, can lead to inter-ethnic distinctions and threaten social cohesion.

The extent to which host nationals allow members of immigrant groups to maintain their own culture and partake in relationships with the dominant cultural group plays an important role in the construction of a truly multicultural society. Promoting inter-ethnic understanding facilitates cultural adaptation by both migrants and host nationals; the key to inter-ethnic understanding is intercultural communication.

Interacting with immigrants is often difficult for host nationals because of differences in language and cultural values, and this adds anxiety to intercultural interactions. To reduce anxiety of this nature, we must equip ourselves with knowledge about other cultures. Intercultural knowledge reduces anxiety and uncertainty, making the communication process smoother and more successful. Intercultural knowledge and intercultural communication skills, however, do not come naturally; they have to be acquired through conscious learning.

SUMMARY

- Advancement in communication technologies, modern transport systems, global economy, international business, mass migration, and international exchange are major contributors to cultural diversity in our society.
- While geographic borders that used to separate people from people and country from country are receding, there are various issues associated with globalization and challenges we face by living in a global village, which highlight the necessity of acquiring skills in intercultural communication.
- Our culture governs our behaviour; however, our way of doing may be neither the only nor the only right way. Different cultural customs and practices need to be interpreted in their own contexts.
- In order to harness the benefits of cultural diversity in our society, we need to develop sound knowledge and skills in communicating with people from different cultures.
- The study of intercultural communication equips us with the necessary knowledge and dynamic skills to manage differences efficiently and effectively.

JOIN THE DEBATE

Will globalization result in the disappearance of local cultures?

There have been ongoing debates about the interaction of global trends and influences with local cultures and realities. Pervasive rhetoric on globalization within and outside academia has revealed a tendency to provide a polarized vision of the world in which we live: it is either celebrated for its global unity and interconnectivity which communication technologies facilitate, or it is deplored for the erosion of differences. While the interconnectivity can hardly be contested, it has not erased the differences. The reconfiguration of the sociocultural, political, and economic landscape of the world keeps reminding us that while the 'global village' continues to draw more tightly together into a single system of consumption, it increasingly multiples its circulation of differences. Local cultures and traditions as a site of resistance or liberation are finding ways of asserting themselves or reclaiming spaces in the global society. The global and the local are becoming increasingly interlocked and interdependent, albeit in an asymmetrical way. What are the multiple ways in which local cultures and practices interact with, respond to, adjust, or reject global cultures?

CASE STUDY

Migration and diversity in Australia

Australia has become one of the most culturally diverse countries in the world. One can hardly walk along a major city street without passing a Chinese restaurant, a Vietnamese grocery store, an Italian deli or a Japanese sushi bar. The most significant contributor to this multicultural environment is the ever-increasing levels of immigration. As Castles (1992: 549) pointed out, nowhere is this more apparent than in a country like Australia, where 'immigration has always been a central part of nation building'. Since 1945, over 7 million people have come to Australia as new settlers. Their contribution to Australian society, culture and prosperity is an important factor in shaping the nation.

In the eighteenth century, transported criminals were the basis of the first migration from Europe. Starting in 1788, some 160,000 convicts were shipped to the Australian colonies. From that time, free immigrants also began coming to Australia. The rapid growth of the wool industry in the 1820s created an enormous demand for labour and sparked an increase in the migration of free people from the United Kingdom. The social upheavals of industrialization in Britain also resulted in many people emigrating to escape widespread poverty and unemployment. The myth of 'terra nullius', or empty land, encouraged immigration, and many people in the indigenous population were pushed from their traditional territory to cede the land, willing or not, with the newcomers. This pressure, along with conflict and serious discrimination against them, began to tell on the Indigenous population, whose numbers, influence, and visibility steadily decreased.

A major impetus for Australian immigration following its initial post-convict settlement was the discovery of vast alluvial goldfields that attracted a mass influx of immigrants in the 1850s, coupled with the extension of parliamentary democracy and the establishment of inland towns. During the Gold Rush era of 1851 to 1860, early migration peaked at arrivals of around 50,000 people a year; Chinese immigrants were the largest non-British group. More restricted immigration began by the 1880s, at the start of the movement known as 'White Australia', when the colony of Victoria introduced legislation to discourage immigration by taxing Chinese migrants. The 'White Australia Policy' reflected Australians' fear of the 'yellow hordes', as they perceived Asian immigrants – indeed, as they perceived any migrants who were not from Britain or northern Europe. This policy was strongly assimilationist, and also reflected the belief current at that time that a population must be culturally homogeneous to be truly egalitarian and democratic. Pressure to assimilate was applied both to immigrants and to the indigenous population, so that the dominant Anglo-Celtic group came to be seen as 'native' Australians.

In the mid-twentieth century, Australia's outlook on the world was significantly changed because of the Second World War. Australia then had a population of only 7 million people, and the devastating effects of the Depression and the war led to a policy of 'Populate or Perish'. Australia opened the floodgates for mainly British and European migrants, many of whom had been displaced by the war and the Nazi Holocaust. Immigration policies aimed to attract migrants to the industrial workforce. A more ambitious part of Australia's migration programme followed the end of the Second World War. The resettling of ex-servicemen, refugees, and young people were significant chapters in Australian immigration history. Australia negotiated agreements with other governments and international organizations to help achieve high migration targets. For example, a system of free passage for United Kingdom residents (the 'ten-pound migrants'), and an assisted passage scheme for British Empire and United States ex-servicemen vastly increased immigration. Australian immigration drew heavily on its traditional connections with the British who, until the 1960s, continued to get virtually free passage for themselves and their families. At various times in the 1950s and 1960s, the Netherlands, Germany, Italy, Greece, Turkey, and Yugoslavia were also important sources of immigrants.

The 'White Australia Policy' was removed in 1973, by the then Whitlam Labor Government. Furthermore, in 1967, Indigenous people had been recognized as full Australian citizens through a national referendum.

When legislation removed race as a factor in Australia's immigration policies, the assimilation policy was still in force, reflecting both the perceived national need for homogeneity and an opportunistic political aim of nation building through imported population growth. In the 1980s, the nation implemented this policy of multiculturalism, adopting an institutionalized diversity. The evolution of Australia's immigration policies at several phases over time was reflected in Fact Sheet 4 of the Australian Government's Department of Immigration and Border Protection (2013).

The policy of multiculturalism enhanced the situation of immigrants in Australia for 20 years. Unfortunately, prejudice and discrimination against the non-immigrant indigenous population was affected little by this policy. In addition, a change of government in 1996 allowed the policy to be eroded to some extent, as immigration was increasingly restricted. The situation for immigrants today is thus more fragile than in the recent past, as recent conflicts illustrate (see the Cronulla riots in the Chapter 9 Case Study). Today, nearly one in four of Australia's more than 22 million people were born overseas, and approximately 200 languages, including indigenous languages, are spoken in the country. New Zealand and the United Kingdom are still the largest source countries for migrants, but other regions, notably Asia, have also become more significant contributors.

References

Castles, Stephen (1992) 'The Australian model of immigration and multiculturalism: is it applicable to Europe?', *International Immigration Review*, 26(2): 549–567.

Department of Immigration and Border Protection (2013) 'Fact sheet 4: More than 65 years of post-war migration' [online]. Accessed 30 September 2013 at: www.immi.gov.au/media/fact-sheets/04fifty.htm.

Questions for discussion

1. What factors can influence immigration flow and what effects can immigration have on receiving countries?

2. What factors can influence immigration policy change in immigrants-receiving countries?

3. When immigrants enter a new country, they often feel 'out of place'. What roles does the host cultural environment play in influencing their sense of place?

4. Does multiculturalism pose a threat to our cultural uniqueness? Why or why not?

5. Do you think host nationals and immigrants view multiculturalism as equally beneficial? Why or why not?

FURTHER READINGS

All articles listed next to the mouse icon below can be accessed for free on the book's companion website: https://study.sagepub.com/liu2e

Cultural diversity

Cunningham, William A., John B. Nezlek and Mahzarin R. Banaji (2004) 'Implicit and explicit ethnocentrism: revisiting the ideologies of prejudice', *Personality and Social Psychology Bulletin*, 30(10): 1332–1346.

This article reports two studies that investigated relationships among individual differences in implicit and explicit prejudice, right-wing ideology, and rigidity in thinking. The first study examined these relationships

focusing on white Americans' prejudice towards black Americans. The second study examined implicit ethnocentrism and its relationship to explicit ethnocentrism by studying the relationship between attitudes towards five social groups. The results lead to the conclusion that implicit ethnocentrism exists and it is related to and distinct from explicit ethnocentrism.

Martin-Barbero, Jesús (1993) *Communication, Culture and Hegemony: From the Media to Mediations*. Newbury Park, CA: Sage.

This book is the first English translation of this major contribution to cultural studies in media research. Building on British, French, and other European traditions of cultural studies, as well as a brilliant synthesis of the rich and extensive research of Latin American scholars, Martin-Barbero offers a substantial reassessment of critical media theory.

Globalization and global citizenship

Baylis, John, Steve Smith and Patricia Owens (2011) *The Globalization of World Politics: An Introduction to International Relations* (5th edn). Oxford: Oxford University Press.

This text provides a coherent, accessible, and engaging introduction to the globalization of world politics from a unique non-US perspective. Its fifth edition has been fully revised and updated in light of recent developments in world politics. New chapters on post-colonialism and post-structuralism give the most comprehensive introduction to international relations available. This text is ideal for students who are approaching the subject for the first time. Features include figures, tables, maps, questions, lively examples, and case studies.

 Castells, Manuel (2008) 'The new public sphere: global civil society, communication networks, and global governance', *Annals of the American Academy of Political and Social Science*, 616(1): 78–93.

This paper discusses the relationships between government and civil society and their interaction via the public sphere, which defines the polity of society. The process of globalization has shifted the debate from the national domain to the global debate, prompting the emergence of a global civil society and of *ad hoc* forms of global governance. Accordingly, the public sphere as the space of debate on public affairs has also shifted from the national to the global and is increasingly constructed around global communication networks. The paper illustrates how public diplomacy intervenes in this global public sphere, laying the ground for traditional forms of diplomacy to act beyond the strict negotiation of power relationships by building on shared cultural meaning, the essence of communication.

Oxley, Laura and Paul Morris (2013) 'Global citizenship: a typology for distinguishing its multiple conceptions', *British Journal of Educational Studies*, 61(3): 301–325.

The promotion of global citizenship has emerged as a goal of education in many countries, symbolizing a shift away from national towards more global concepts of citizenship. This paper constructs a typology to identify and distinguish the diverse conceptions of global citizenship. The typology incorporates the political, moral, economic, cultural, social, critical, environmental, and spiritual conceptions. The paper illustrates how the typology can be used to evaluate the critical features of a curriculum plan to promote global citizenship in England.

> 'There are four ways, and only four ways, in which we have contact with the world. We are evaluated and classified by those four contacts: what we do, how we look, what we say, and how we say it. '

Dale Carnegie, American author and trainer, 1888–1955

2

UNDERSTANDING COMMUNICATION

LEARNING OBJECTIVES

At the end of this chapter, you should be able to:

- Recognize the multifaceted nature of communication.
- Identify components and characteristics of communication.
- Critically examine widely known models of communication.
- Evaluate the influence of culture on communication.

INTRODUCTION

As the opening quote by Carnegie indicates, we make our contact with the world through 'what we do, how we look, what we say, and how we say it'; each of these actions communicates a message to the people around us. Babies arrive in this world crying. Before they learn to use language, crying and smiling are their tools of communication. 'Communication – our ability to share our ideas and feelings – is the basis of all human contact' (Samovar, Porter, McDaniel and Roy, 2013: 27). The English word 'communication' is derived from the Latin root *communicare*, meaning 'to make common', as in sharing thoughts, hopes, and knowledge. For example, greeting one another is a basic communication act practised in every culture. We may do this by saying 'hello', or by using touch, eye contact, or gesture to exchange greetings. These methods of interaction reflect the functions and characteristics of communication; that is, we use a shared code to exchange messages. Communication requires that all parties understand a common 'language' or code. There are auditory means of exchanging this code, such as speaking, singing, and tone of voice; there are physical means, such as body language, sign language, touch, eye contact, or writing. People communicate to accomplish tasks, achieve goals, share understanding, exchange information, to be heard and even be appreciated. Whether we live in a large city like New York, a small Peruvian village like Los Molinos, a remote region like Christmas Island, or a metropolitan city like Cape Town, we all participate in communication.

Communication is sharing who we are and what we know. We all share our ideas and feelings with others; however, *how* we share them with others varies from culture to culture. As our contact with people from other cultures expands, the need for competent intercultural communicators increases. This chapter first explores the multifaceted nature of the concept of communication and then examines its components and characteristics. Following this, we will critically examine widely used models of communication – linear and interactive – and their theoretical underpinnings. The chapter concludes by challenging the conventional notions of communication in the digital era and highlighting the influence of culture on communication. The analysis provided in this chapter enables you to understand and appreciate the complexities of communication.

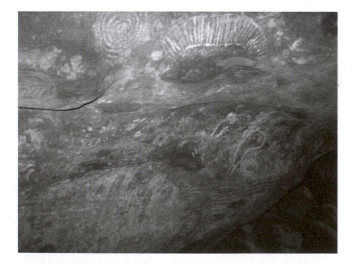

Photo 2.1   Aboriginal rock art paintings in Australia illustrate stories in the everyday lives of the Anangu Aboriginal people who live at Uluru – a red sandstone monolith, the world's largest one – 9.4 km around. Copyright © Zala Volčič. Used with permission.

THE MULTIFACETED NATURE OF COMMUNICATION

Human communication is as old as human history. Cave paintings in prehistoric Europe – for example, the famous rock paintings at Lascaux in France – chart the beginning of human communication. In Australia, paintings by Indigenous people can be found on rocks and caves, illustrating an ancient means of communication. The paintings on the caves and rock of Uluru – a red sandstone monolith in central Australia – reveal that it has been the focus for religious, cultural, territorial, and economic relations among the Aboriginal people of the Western Desert for thousands of years. Many other means of conveying messages have been used throughout history, via members of our own species and other animals. For example, pigeons were used by European armies to carry military intelligence during the First World War (Greelis, 2007), while warriors in ancient China used burning fire and smoke to send messages to fellow soldiers in different military camps. Human beings have long been used as couriers of communication. For example, in ancient times, human messengers were probably the most reliable and efficient means of sending official information and communiqués, even though it meant weeks or months of long, often dangerous travelling time.

Advances in information technology have brought tremendous changes to communication media and to the role of communicators. From print, telephone, radio, telegraph, television, satellites, email, the internet, Facebook, Twitter, and blogs, human communication has expanded beyond the confines of time, space, geographic region, culture, and nation. Every communicator, whether a source or a receiver (or more likely both), is a node on the 'wired' communication network. As Cooper and her associates (2007) point out, when we consider our world from such a compressed perspective, the need for mutual acceptance and understanding becomes apparent.

Critical thinking...

Do communication technologies bring us closer together, or do they separate us from those closest to us? In what ways?

Defining communication

Finding a single definition of communication is a difficult task, as current definitions vary widely. Dance (1970) reviewed some 95 definitions of communication published in the 1950s and 1960s. Since then countless other definitions of communication have been added to the list. He concluded that the definitions differed in so many ways that communication might better be theorized as a 'family' of related concepts, rather than as a unitary concept. This reflects the multifaceted nature of communication. Consider the simple act of greeting a friend. From the secretion of chemicals in the brain to the moving of one's lips to produce sound, thousands of components are in operation. When we add on cultural dimensions, it becomes even more complex – people from different cultures express the same concept or idea differently. For example, in New Zealand a casual hello is acceptable as a form of greeting; in Japan, a bow is expected when greeting one's boss; in Arab culture, friends are commonly greeted with a full embrace and a kiss on the cheek; in Serbia and in Belgium, friends kiss three times on the cheek as a form of greeting; in Malaysia, friends may greet each other by folding two hands in front of the chest.

To overcome problems created by the complexity of the concept of communication, scholars concentrate on the aspects of communication that are most germane to their interests (Samovar et al., 2013). For example, neurologists look at what the brain and nervous system do during communication; psychologists examine issues related to perception; linguists inspect people's use of language; philosophers are more interested in whether communication is essential to thought; anthropologists focus on the question of whether communication is universal; in the electronic world, scientists tend to focus on the transfer of data and information from one location to another; communication researchers are more interested in how people share understanding and meaning through the use of verbal or nonverbal symbols. Each of these disciplines carves out but one piece within the territory of human communication. As each field of study explores its own area of communication, it is very important to be aware that there is no right or wrong definition, and no single definition can include *all* aspects of communication. Given that our interest lies in communication between culturally different people, our focus is on those elements that influence sharing understanding and meaning between cultures. Thus, in this chapter, we define *communication* as *the process by which people use shared verbal or nonverbal codes, systems, and media to exchange information in a particular cultural context.*

The study of communication, therefore, is influenced by a variety of fields as diverse as literature, mathematics, engineering, political science, health science, sociology, and psychology. According to Littlejohn (1996a: 117), the primary source of ideas about communication 'prior to this century, dating back to ancient times, was rhetoric'. In rhetorical theory, which originated with the ancient Greek sophists and traces a long and varied history to the present, communication has typically been theorized as the practical art of discourse. Problems of communication in the rhetorical tradition are regarded as social exigencies that can be resolved through the artful use of discourse to persuade an audience (Bitzer, 1968).

This way of theorizing communication is useful for explaining why our participation in discourse, especially public discourse, is important and how it occurs. A discourse approach to communication holds the possibility that the practice of communication can be cultivated and improved through education and research. We know that some people are better communicators than others, and that the best examples of rhetoric can rise to the level of great art. Skills can be learned and improved through practice. Thus, it is reasonable to think that people can become better communicators by learning and practising communication. Equally important, however, is to recognize that every culture has its own communication rules, and criteria for judging 'good' communicators vary from culture to culture. For example, in Sweden, being a very direct communicator is respected, and as such, 'Say what you mean and mean what you say' is practised.

Further online reading The following article can be accessed for free on the book's companion website https://study.sagepub.com/liu2e: Baraldi, Claudio (2006) 'New forms of intercultural communication in a globalized world', *International Communication Gazette*, 68(1): 53–69.

THEORY CORNER

RHETORICAL THEORY

The rhetorical tradition views communication as a practical art of discourse (Rybacki and Rybacki, 1991). Rhetorical theory dates back centuries to ancient Greece, when Plato, Aristotle, and the sophists were speech teachers. Classical rhetorical theory is based on the philosophical idea that we are rational beings who can be persuaded by compelling arguments. Rhetorical communication deliberately attempts to influence the audience by using carefully constructed messages of verbal and often visual symbols. Those who create rhetorical communication are called rhetors, and the messages they create are rhetorical acts. Aristotle's *Rhetoric* was the most influential rhetorical text for thousands of years and had a significant influence on theories of communication. The model of rhetoric he proposed focuses on three elements in public speaking: (1) *ethos*, based on the personal character or credibility of the speaker; (2) *pathos*, based on inducing specific emotions or putting the audience into certain frames of mind; and (3) *logos*, based on the arguments made in the speech. Rhetorical analysis used to be confined to public speech, but is now also used to interpret mass media products such as those on radio, television, and film.

Reference
Rybacki, Karyn and Donald Rybacki (1991) *Communication Criticism: Approaches and Genres*. Belmont, CA: Wadsworth.

Further reading on rhetorical theory
Hartelius, Johanna and Larry Browning (2008) 'The application of rhetorical theory in managerial research: a literature review', *Management Communication Quarterly*, 22: 13–39.

Theory in Practice

MANAGERS AS RHETORS

Managers are rhetors in that they strategically communicate with organizational members at different levels. Classifying a person in a management position as a rhetor draws attention to the ways in which he or she faces many of the same challenges as does the classical orator, but the notion of rhetor in the management context extends beyond an orator to denote a complex set of meanings, involving audience analysis, contextual sensitivity, and message structure. The manager-as-rhetor notion is a way of understanding how persuasion is part of an organizational leader's role. Just as an effective public speaker uses rhetorical tactics, a manager must construct a persuasive message that reflects the organization's need and goals.

Green (2004) illustrates this rhetorical approach to studying managers in the context of innovation, suggesting that managers play an active role in the diffusion process because 'what managers say and how they say it matter a great deal' (p. 654). For example, using evocative words (e.g., 'I have a dream' versus 'I have an idea') or describing a new production operation as a 'greenfield site' can make a speech more real and more appealing to organizational members. Given the rhetorical skills, a manager can make organizational members feel the power of action, visualize the new production project, and imagine the promise of bringing the innovation to fruition. Managers address organizational challenges, such as innovation and change, in much the same way as does the classical orator. However, managers as rhetors can argue and persuade in a strategic manner to achieve goals. Analysing managers as rhetors enables researchers to discover new dimensions of organizational leadership communication.

Questions to take you further
What kind of rhetoric makes employees describe an organization as toxic? What makes people describe a CEO as a transformational leader?

Reference

Green, Sandy E., Jr (2004) 'A rhetorical theory of diffusion', *Academy of Management Review*, 29: 653–669.

Further reading on rhetorical theory in practice

Sillince, John and Frank Mueller (2007) 'Switching strategic perspective: the reframing of accounts of responsibility', *Organization Studies*, 28(2): 155–176.

Components of communication

Although definitions of communication vary from discipline to discipline, scholars tend to agree that embedded in all definitions of communication are the factors of people, message, channel, and context. Based on this consensus, we can identify eight components of human communication, which usually operate simultaneously. In their most basic form, these components are found in every culture. They are source, message, channel, receiver, encoding, decoding, noise, and feedback. All these components exist in the specific context in which the communication act occurs. Context permeates all communication processes (Jandt, 2007).

Source. A source is the origin of information. A source is someone who needs and wants to exchange information with others. The need may be conscious, such as asking someone directions (seeking information), expressing feelings about a wedding attended (sharing experience), or assigning tasks to an employee (accomplishing tasks). The need to communicate may also be non-conscious – for example, frowning when hearing music one does not like or in disagreeing with another's opinion. Conscious or non-conscious, communication is the sharing of thoughts and feelings, with varying degrees of intention by the source, and it affects the feelings and behaviour of another person or a group of people.

Message. The message is the verbal and/or nonverbal form of ideas, thought or feelings that one person wishes to communicate to another person or group in some place at some time within a specific context. A message is the composition of verbal codes such as language (see Chapter 7) and/or nonverbal codes, including facial expressions, body movements, tone of voice, use of space, time orientation, and so forth (see Chapter 8). Each culture has its own way of forming and expressing messages. In India and Bulgaria, 'wiggling' the head from side to side indicates 'Yes' whereas a Dutch person would shake her head to express the same idea.

Channel. Messages must have a means by which they move from one person to another. This route is known as the channel (or channels, as much communication involves several channels at once). The channel can be sound, sight, words, telephone, the internet, fax, and so on. We receive messages when we listen to and watch each other. The degree to which an individual prefers one channel over another is often determined by his or her culture. In the United States, words are highly valued, while in some Mediterranean cultures, touch is a major communication channel. In Finland and Japan, silence is as significant a carrier of messages as words and sound.

Receiver. The receiver is the intended target of the message. He or she normally shares the same code as the source. Of course, in most interpersonal communication, participants are both sources and receivers, whereas mass communication may be (but is not always) one way. Unlike programmed computers or machines, human beings do not respond uniformly to all messages, nor do they always compose the same message in exactly the same way (Pearson and Nelson, 1997). Individual characteristics, including those related to race, sex, age, education, culture, values, and attitudes, all affect how people both send and receive messages.

Encoding. The code refers to a shared language used by individuals to categorize their experience and communicate it to others (Rogers and Steinfatt, 1999). Feelings and ideas cannot be shared directly; they must be converted into words and actions in order to be communicated to others. Encoding is the process by which the source uses shared codes to convert concepts, thoughts, and feelings into a message. This is distinguishable from the encoding process, in that the message can be thought of as separate to the source, while encoding is the source's internal process (Samovar et al., 2013). Although symbolic representation is universal, the particular words and actions selected, and how these are strung together, are culturally based. In encoding, we select and arrange verbal and nonverbal symbols according to rules that are known and shared by the group. For example, a member of one culture might see a close friend and decide to smile, encoding her message of greeting according to the 'rules' of her language community. A member of another culture might instead place her hands in front of the chest and bow to her friend, encoding the message of greeting according to a different set of cultural rules.

Photo 2.2   People in Jordan using nonverbal code to communicate. Copyright © UNESCO; photographer: Jane Taylor. Used with permission.

Decoding. Decoding is the process by which the receiver, as the target of the message, converts the coded message back into meaning. It is a process of assigning meaning to codes. Decoding permits the person in the receiver's position to attach meaning to the source's behaviour. Like encoding, interpretation of the message is influenced by culture. The same coded message, therefore, may be decoded differently by different people. For example, Italians may regard animated conversation and loud laughing in public as a sign of happiness, whereas a Thai woman might believe that such an outward display of emotions should be reserved for the privacy of one's home. Swedes tend to speak softly and calmly. It is rare that you witness a Swede demonstrating anger or strong emotion in public. This is because Swedes prefer to listen to others as opposed to ensuring that their own voice is heard.

Noise. Noise interferes with the receipt of the message. All factors that interfere with information transfer can be referred to as noise. Noise can be physical, such as distracting sounds or sights, but noise can be psychological too, such as having a headache or worrying about bills. Noise can also be semantic, such as different interpretations of a concept. For example, participants of an interpersonal communication act may have different interpretations of a concept like individualism. In Germany, individualism is a positive concept, referring to people as independent, assertive, and goal-oriented. In South Korea, however, individualism is more likely to be associated with selfishness and a lack of concern for the group – a negative feature in a culture that traditionally values collectivism and a group orientation. Therefore, a message sent about this concept from a German person to a Korean may not be well received because of the culturally influenced semantic noise that affects the encoding and decoding of the message. When source and receiver have (even subtly) different interpretations of the same concept, the effect of communication will inevitably be affected. The more heterophilous (culturally dissimilar) the source and receiver are, the more difficult clear understanding of each other's communication will be (Rogers and Steinfatt, 1999).

Critical thinking...

What is some potential 'noise' that will affect effective communication online?

Feedback. Feedback refers to the response of the receiver after receiving the message. Feedback is information generated by the receiver and made available to the source, allowing the source to judge the communication while it is taking place. Feedback can function to adjust the attitudes and behaviours of both source and receiver and is yet another component that is modified by culture. For example, while members of US culture would feel comfortable saying, 'I don't agree with what you said' as a means of feedback in a conversation, members of Chinese culture would communicate the same thought by taking a deep breath.

Characteristics of communication

Just as scholars agree upon some basic components of communication, so too is there consensus on some of the key characteristics of communication.

Communication is a dynamic process. A process is anything that is ongoing and continuous. Communication is a process; you cannot talk about the exact beginning or the end point of a communication exchange. David Berlo (1960) provided a particularly clear statement about communication as a process:

> If we accept the concept of process, we view events and relationships as dynamic, ongoing, ever-changing, continuous. When we label something as a process, we also mean that it does not have a beginning, an end, a fixed sequence of events. It is not static, at rest. It is moving. The ingredients within a process interact; each affects all of the others. (Berlo, 1960: 24)

Although individual verbal messages have definite beginning and ending points, the *overall* process of communication does not. Meanings are dynamic, continually changing as a function of earlier usages and of changes in perceptions and meta-perceptions. For example, imagine you came across a classmate in a shopping centre and started exchanging ideas about an assignment due in a week's time. Your conversation would presume an earlier exchange of information (perhaps during class on the previous day) and the communication process would not necessarily end after you have said 'good bye' to each other. You might go home and modify your previous assignment framework as a result of your talking with your classmate – a continuation of your communication in the shopping centre.

As a dynamic process, communication is more like a motion picture than a single snapshot. A word or action does not stay 'frozen' when we communicate; it is immediately replaced with another one. Communication is also dynamic, because once a word or action is employed, it cannot be retracted. We probably all know the saying 'You cannot step into the same river twice', by the ancient Greek philosopher Heraclitus, who was known for his doctrine of change being central to the universe. People cannot experience exactly the same thing twice with exactly the same feeling. As an example, you may see the same film twice, but you may have some different feelings each time. You cannot recapture or repeat exactly the same experience of seeing the film for the first time. Similarly, we cannot take back what we have communicated. Once you have said and done something, it is irretrievable – many people have found this out the hard way when using emails, Facebook, and Twitter, but it applies to all modes of communication. If you have hurt a friend's feelings, you can apologize, but you cannot unsay what you said or undo what you did. A process is irreversible and unrepeatable (Cooper et al., 2007).

Communication is interactive. Communication is interactive because it requires the active participation of at least two people. To communicate, one has to address another person or persons. Of course, you can communicate with yourself (intrapersonal communication), but you are still interacting with an imagined self. You must act as if you were two people. Human communication not only calls for a response, but also is shaped in its very form and content by the anticipated response. The encoding and decoding of messages are influenced by prior interactions between communicators, and feedback influences the subsequent exchange of messages. During this interactive process, communicators may modify the content or form of their conversation. Their thoughts and feelings may also be adjusted during the interaction process. For example, a late arrival to a meeting might be interpreted by the other attendees as bad manners and they might react with frowns or silence. However, if they learned that the person's reason for being late was stopping to help someone injured in a car accident, their reactions would most likely change from negative to positive.

Communication is symbolic. A symbol is an arbitrarily selected and learned stimulus that represents something else. Symbols can be verbal or nonverbal, such as a sound, a mark on paper, a statue, Braille, a movement, or a painting. They are the vehicles by which the thoughts and ideas of one person can be communicated to another. Human beings are able to generate, receive, store, and manipulate symbols (Samovar et al., 2013). Words are not actual objects or ideas, but we use these symbols to create meaning. Meaning resides in people. Imagine how difficult communication could become if two people from different cultures come together with different symbolic understandings. Not only are their languages different, but the same gesture can have different meanings. Patting a child on the head in Australian culture usually indicates affection; however, in Thai culture, it may be considered offensive as it is thought to damage the spirit of the child, which resides in the head.

Communication is contextual. Communication is dependent on the context in which it occurs. A context is the cultural, physical, relational, and perceptual environment in which communication occurs (Neuliep, 2012). A context is also historical, and cultures that are past-oriented may emphasize this facet of context. We interact with others not in isolation but in a specific setting. Communication always occurs in a context, and the nature of communication depends largely on this context (Littlejohn, 1996b). Dress, language, topic selection and the like are all adapted to contexts. For example, attending a graduation ceremony without wearing a shirt or using profanity in the classroom are likely to be frowned upon, whereas in other contexts these behaviours might be more acceptable. Similarly, how do you feel when someone keeps you waiting for 15 minutes? What do you say when you have to leave a conversation while the other person is still keen on talking? This probably depends

Photo 2.3   The motorbike is an import means of transportation in Vietnam. A man (and passengers) weaving in and out of traffic on his scooter in Hanoi. Copyright © Alison Rae. Used with permission.

on the context. Context influences what we communicate and how we communicate – once again, these rules are culture bound. In Mexico, for example, children are encouraged to move around the classroom and to interact verbally and physically with their classmates; in Hong Kong, it is expected that students remain in their seats during class, and they are expected not to talk to one another unless the teacher gives permission. Context influences how we communicate with others.

Critical thinking...

Is all behaviour communication behaviour? If so, how does this assumption align with several generally accepted postulates of communication, such as that it is interactive, encoded, and symbolic? Does communication depend more upon the receiver's interpretation of behaviours or on the sender's intentions and orientation to those behaviours? Who is the best judge of what a communication means: senders, receivers, or outside observers?

THEORY CORNER

COMMUNICATION ACCOMMODATION THEORY

Communication accommodation theory was developed in the context of intercultural communication in the 1970s (e.g., Gallois, Ogay and Giles, 2005). The theory is based on three general assumptions: (1) interactions are embedded in a socio-historical context; (2) communication is both about exchanges of referential meaning and negotiation of personal and social identities; and (3) interactants achieve these functions of communication by accommodating their communicative behaviour, through language, paralanguage, discourse, and non-linguistic moves, to their perception of the others' individual and group characteristics. Accommodation is the process through which interactants regulate their communication. Key concepts of this theory are:

- Ingroups and outgroups: Individuals are attracted to groups to which they belong and tend to create group boundaries to exclude people from outgroups.

- Accommodation (or attuning): Communicators adjust their behaviour to take account of their interactants' communication needs and style because of a conscious or unconscious desire for social integration, approval, identification, or communication effectiveness.

- Non-accommodation (or non-attuning): Speakers maintain social distance from others by accentuating differences and treating interactants as group members rather than as individuals.

Since its development four decades ago, the theory has stood the test of time and is still generating research up to the present day.

Reference

Gallois, Cindy, Tania Ogay and Howard Giles (2005) 'Communication accommodation theory: a look back and a look ahead', in W. B. Gudykunst (ed.), *Theorizing about Intercultural Communication*. Thousand Oaks, CA: Sage. pp. 121–148.

Further reading on communication and culture

Halualani, Rona T. (2008) 'How do multicultural university students define and make sense of intercultural contact? A qualitative study', *International Journal of Intercultural Relations*, 32: 1–16.

Theory in Practice

COMMUNICATION ACCOMMODATION IN INSTANT MESSAGING

Communication accommodation has been applied to study the mass media, doctor–patient communication, family relations, job interviews, police–citizen encounters, and even messages left on telephone answering machines and online communication. Lexical convergence has been documented as a primary means of accommodation, represented, for example, by the use of politeness terms to influence perceptions of rapport and to build trust. An interesting area is the application of this theory to investigate temporal convergence, such as in instant messaging conversations. Not only temporal cues, but also the extent to which communicators adapt to each other's use of these cues, influence the outcomes of communication. For example, Riordan, Markman and Stewart (2012) conducted a study to examine temporal convergence in instant messaging conversations between friends on social and task-related interactions. Findings from their study revealed a general tendency towards convergence on both length and duration. However, the level of convergence was also influenced by the conversational context (task versus social) as the conversation continues.

Questions to take you further

What are the key ways to show liking and to create an ingroup in instant messaging, on Facebook, or on Twitter? What about showing dislike or excluding people? How is 'flaming' on the internet related to non-accommodation? What cultural norms do you think are emerging around these practices?

Reference

Riordan, Monica A., Kris M. Markman and Craig O. Stewart (2012) 'Communication accommodation in instant messaging: an examination of temporal convergence', *Journal of Language and social Psychology*, 32(1): 84–95.

> **Further reading on communication accommodation**
> Bunz, Ulla and Scott W., Campbell (2004) 'Politeness accommodation in electronic mail', *Communication Research Reports*, 21: 11–25.

MODELS OF COMMUNICATION

In the broadest sense, a model is a systematic representation of an object or event in idealized and abstract form. Models are somewhat arbitrary by nature. The act of abstracting eliminates certain details in order to focus on other factors. Communication models are representations of communication processes and characteristics; they illustrate the main components of communication and their relationships to each other. The key to the usefulness of a communication model is the degree to which it conforms to the underlying determinants of communicative behaviour (Mortensen, 1972). Communication models help us to recognize and explain complexities and regularities in the communication process. Just as models are a simplified expression of theory, they are the basis of communication theory. If theories need modification, so too do models.

> **Further online reading** The following article can be accessed for free on the book's companion website https://study.sagepub.com/liu2e: Bowman, Joel and Andrew Targowski (1987) 'Modelling the communication process: the map is not the territory', *Journal of Business Communication*, 24(4): 21–34.

The linear model

Early scholars conceptualized communication as transmitting information, concepts, understanding, and thought, as if along a pipeline. According to this model, the communication process is *linear*. The most influential linear model is Claude Shannon and Warren Weaver's mathematical model of communication, presented in their book *The Mathematical Theory of Communication* (1949). Shannon developed the basic model of communication while conducting cryptographic research at Bell Laboratories during the Second World War. When the field of communication study first emerged in the 1950s and 1960s, Shannon and Weaver's basic communication model was adapted to the process of human communication. As an engineer for the Bell Telephone Company, Shannon's goal was to formulate a theory to guide the efforts of engineers in finding the most efficient way of transmitting electrical signals from one location to another (Shannon and Weaver, 1949).

The model conceives of a linear and literal transmission of information from one location to another. The message is like an object in a parcel. The receiver opens a parcel to get the message (Fiske, 1982). Later the concept of feedback was added to the model – the information that a communicator gains from others in response to his or her own verbal or nonverbal behaviour. Shannon and Weaver were mainly concerned with the technical problems associated with the selection and arrangement of discrete units of information (Mortensen, 1972), so their model does not apply to semantic dimensions of language; that is, it does not address issues of meaning in communication. Nevertheless, Shannon and Weaver's (1949) linear model is, perhaps, the most widely cited communication model in existence. The mathematical theory of information principles upon which it is based are sometimes given by communication scholars as evidence of their field's scientific status (Craig, 1999).

Today, this model is known as the *transmission model* of communication, viewing communication as a process of transferring information from one mind to another. The transmission model is useful, as it allows us to distinguish between communication sources and receivers and map the flow of information through systems. It also allows for messages to be conceptualized as 'containers' of meaning, and for communication to be understood as an act performed in order to achieve anticipated outcomes. Although viewing communication as a linear process, this model makes us alert to the ever-present danger of distortion and misunderstanding in communication. The linear model was elaborated by non-mathematical scholars to study media effects. A typical example of this endeavour was reflected in Harold Lasswell's (1948) 5W model: 'Who?', 'Says What?', 'In Which channel?', 'To Whom?', and 'With What effect?'. Lasswell's primary interest was in the mass media and propaganda, and the 5W model embraced the 'administrative research' dominant among the pioneers of communication at the time (Gitlin, 1978). Although the 5W model was intended to direct people to media effects research, it has also been found to be useful when applied to other forms of communication, such as persuasion.

Linear models of communication, particularly the transmission model, have encountered criticism since the 1980s and 1990s because they do not account for the complexity of communication. The critics have argued that the transmission model is philosophically flawed, full of paradoxes, and is ideologically backward. By limiting content to transmission, the model reduces communication to a merely technical process (Shepherd, 1993). It assumes that senders, receivers, and meaningful content all exist independently prior to the event of transmission, ignoring that all of these components are actually constituted symbolically during communication (Deetz, 1994). The critics suggest that the linear model should at least be supplemented, if not entirely replaced, by a model that conceptualizes communication as a constitutive process that produces and reproduces shared meaning (Pearce, 2005). Deetz (1994: 568) further points out that new disciplines will arise 'when existing modes of explanation fail to provide compelling guidance for responses to a central set of new social issues'. Those central social issues are concerned with who participates in what ways in the social processes to construct personal identities, the social order, and codes of communication. Corresponding with this perspective, therefore, is the need for a model that reflects this element of communication.

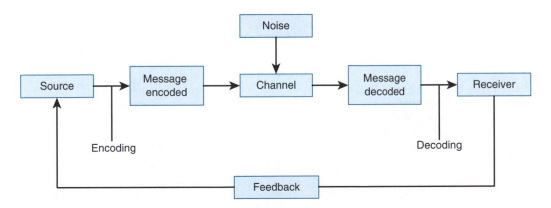

Figure 2.1   The linear model of communication

Source: Adapted from Shannon, Claude and Warren Weaver (1949) *The Mathematical Theory of Communication*. Urbana, IL: University of Illinois Press. p. 5.

The interactive model

Wilbur Schramm (1971) was one of the first to challenge the mathematical model of Shannon and Weaver. He conceived of decoding and encoding as activities maintained simultaneously by sender and receiver; he also made provision for a two-way interchange of messages. In the actual communication process, speaking and listening are not separate activities, nor do they occur one at a time. The view of communication as interactive recognizes that communicators simultaneously send and receive messages rather than act exclusively as either senders or receivers (Lanigan, 2013). Even mass communication is a two-way process. For example, media organizations examine audience ratings to gauge the impact of their programmes. In this sense, both the audience and the media organization are senders and receivers. The strength of Schramm's model is that it provides the additional notion of a field of experience of the interactants. The model includes context and postulates that a message may be different in meaning, depending on the specific context. Nevertheless, Schramm's model, while it is less linear, still accounts only for bilateral communication between two parties. Complex, multiple levels of communication across several sources are beyond the scope of both this model and the Shannon and Weaver model.

Following Schramm, communication scholars such as Everett Rogers and Thomas Steinfatt (1999) put forward a more elaborate interactive model, based on their understanding of communication as a process through which participants create and share meaning in order to reach mutual understanding. One of the major changes human communication scholars made to Shannon's model was to emphasize the subjectivity of communication. When the source and receiver are individuals instead of machines, their perceptions, paradigms, and past experiences inevitably filter the encoding and decoding process. This subjectivity is one reason why the receiver seldom decodes a message into exactly the same meaning that the source has in mind. Furthermore, the participants exert mutual control over the process, rather than serving as either active sources or passive receivers. This principle of communication applies as much to intercultural communication as it does to other types of human communication. Advocates of the interactive model of communication propose that communication systems operate within the confines of

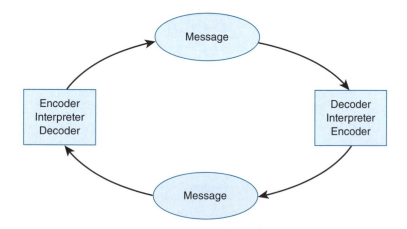

Figure 2.2   Schramm's interactive model of communication

Source: Adapted from Wilbur Schramm (1971) 'The nature of communication between humans', in W. Schramm and D. F. Roberts (eds), *The Process and Effects of Mass Communication*. Urbana, IL: University of Illinois Press. p. 24.

cultural rules and expectations: a message may have different meanings associated with it, depending on the culture in which it is sent or received.

In this chapter, we adopt the interactive model proposed by Rogers and Steinfatt (1999) to explain intercultural communication phenomena. This model replaces the terms 'sender' and 'receiver' with 'communicator'; in addition, it incorporates communicator perceptions into the model. This model represents communication as a process of creating and sharing meaning in order to reach mutual understanding. The process itself is influenced by communicators' perceptions of the context and of each other. The model also theorizes each communication action as building upon the previous experience of the communicators and as having consequences for future communication. A number of theories in intercultural communication (e.g., communication accommodation theory; see Theory Corner) share the assumptions of the interactive model. Rogers and Steinfatt's model reflects the dynamic nature of the communication process as much as the potential influence of perceived cultural differences on the communication process. Indeed, James Carey (1977) called the interactive model a 'ritual' model. He claimed that a ritual model of communication is about sharing, participating, drawing people together, and building a community through communication processes.

Critical thinking...

What are the indicators of successful communication? Who is at fault when communication goes wrong? Does it make sense to say that two parties in conflict are communicating successfully if they decode each other's messages correctly, even though they continue to disagree?

CURRENT ISSUES SURROUNDING THEORIZING COMMUNICATION

Communication study has a long tradition, with its roots in ancient philosophy and rhetoric, yet as an independent discipline, it can still be considered a young field. Borrowing from psychology, sociology, anthropology, political science, information technology, and other social sciences, the field of communication is highly interdisciplinary (Cooren, 2012). There is no single object of communication study, nor is there a universal definition of the concept. A model is a simplified picture of part of the real world; as such, it represents and explains characteristics of reality, but only some of them. In the same vein, a communication theory which consists of concepts and relationships among them can only represent or explain certain aspects of communication phenomena. Any communication act takes place in a context, and it is through context that the different levels of communication study – intrapersonal, interpersonal, group, organization, and mass – come together.

Nevertheless, the multidisciplinary nature of the communication field and the proliferation of the objects of communication study do not necessarily mean that communication is a fragmented field. The development of communication theories has been informed by two general approaches: a linguistic approach associated with the humanities, and a quantitative approach associated with the life and social sciences (Cobley and Shulz, 2013). These two broad approaches have informed investigation into communication, both at the level of forming theories and at the level of the collection of data. In his seminal article, 'Communication as a field', Robert T. Craig (1999) advanced a constitutive meta-model of communication theory. He

Table 2.1 Levels of Communication

Level of communication	Characteristics	Examples
Intrapersonal communication	The process of understanding and sharing meaning within the self.	Imagine you find a pair of shoes and a dress that you would like to purchase – unfortunately, your budget will only allow you to purchase one item, not both. In this case, you may engage in intrapersonal communication; that is, communicating within yourself before making a decision.
Interpersonal communication	The process of understanding and sharing meaning between at least two people when relatively mutual opportunities for speaking and listening exist.	It can be used to resolve conflicts, solve a problem, share information, improve our perception of ourselves, or fulfil such social needs as belonging or love. Most intercultural communication is interpersonally oriented.
Group communication	Purposeful communication in limited-sized groups in which decision making or problem solving occurs.	Small-group communication occurs in social organizations such as clubs, civic groups, and church groups, and in business settings such as workgroups.
Organizational communication	Communication in large cooperative networks including virtually all aspects of both interpersonal and group communication.	It encompasses concepts such as the structure and function of organizations, human relations, the process of organizing, and organizational culture. The purpose of this type of communication may range from completing a task to creating and maintaining satisfying human relationships.
Mass communication	The process of understanding and sharing meaning with a broad audience through mediated channels. Mass media like radio, television and newspapers are specifically conceived and designed to reach a large audience.	The internet continually creates new configurations of sources, messages, and receivers. Sources of messages on the internet can range from one person in email communication to a social group or a group of professional journalists. The messages themselves can be traditional journalistic news stories created by a reporter, or stories by non-professional reporters such as bloggers. The receivers or audience of these messages can also number from one to potentially millions; they may move fluidly from audience to producers.

summarized communication study into seven traditions: rhetorical, semiotic, phenomenological, cybernetic, socio-psychological, sociocultural, and critical. For theories in the rhetorical tradition, communication is considered a practical art of discourse that can be learned and practised. Theories in the semiotic tradition consider communication a process of signification that mediates subjectivity via signs. The phenomenological tradition takes communication to be an experiential encounter of self and other through authentic dialogue. In the cybernetic tradition, communication is synonymous with information processing. The socio-psychological tradition considers communication to be expression, interaction, and influence. In the sociocultural tradition, communication exists in social and cultural patterns that allow interaction among members. Theories in the

Photo 2.4   The internet has become an inseparable part of people's life; men from Koutiala, Mali, take computer courses.
Copyright © UNESCO; photographer: Serge Daniel. Used with permission.

critical tradition consider communication to be discursive reflection, particularly on ideology and power. These traditions of communication theories, according to Craig's constitutive meta-model, encompass social sciences, humanities, and arts.

There may be many communication theories, each proceeding from a different understanding of communication phenomena and each contributing to scholarship proceeding from that understanding. Over the past decades, scholars have applied communication theories to study the ways in which communication is used to shape public opinion, to transmit information, to develop relationships, and to define, interpret, and critique culture (Eadie and Goret, 2013). Each domain of study explores one slice of the communication discipline. An understanding of the traditions that have shaped the theorizing of communication study can help us to appreciate the diversity of this field.

THEORY CORNER

CONCEPTUALIZING 'WHOM' IN DIGITAL MEDIA

In Lasswell's (1948) model of communication, the 'whom' (the objects of communication messages) receive the output of communication, and as a result may change their opinions or behaviour. The advent of digital media, however, allowed 'whom' to enter the sphere of media content producers, and they therefore become 'influencers' themselves. Receivers have now become hyperactive audiences: people who read, view, listen, watch, post, tweet, and comment on media products. New digital media technologies have not just changed the information world, but have also blurred the boundaries between interpersonal and mass communication. Social media have allowed the simultaneous existence of a mass audience and a collective of individuals (Shoemaker, Riccio and Johnson, 2013).

The interactive model of communication highlights the importance of context. This context becomes increasingly important in the world of digital media, where technological advances reconfigure traditional boundaries between interpersonal and mass communication. For digital and social media, 'whom' may differ greatly from communication offline. The norms governing communication in a digital setting are different from those in face-to-face interactions, and also different from the traditional mass communication spectrum of print, television, and radio. The intersection between interpersonal and mass communication necessitates a reconceptualization of audience in digital media. This is the beginning of an ongoing theoretical journey to enhance our knowledge about how audiences create media and media create audiences.

Reference

Shoemaker, Pamela J., Jaime Riccio and Philip R. Johnson (2013) 'Whom', in P. Cobley and P. J. Schulz (eds), *Theories and Models of Communication*. Berlin/Boston, MA: Walter de Gruyter. pp. 383–395.

Further reading on digital media

Noor Al-Deen, Hana S. and John A. Jendricks (2012) *Social Media: Usage and Impact*. Lanham, MD: Lexington Books.

Theory in Practice

NAVIGATING THROUGH VIRTUAL SOCIAL WORLDS

Digital technology has not only challenged traditional definitions of interpersonal and mass communication, it has also changed the way through which we develop relationships with others. This can be illustrated in virtual social worlds, where inhabitants live a virtual life similar to their life in the real world. In virtual social worlds, 'residents' appear in the form of avatars and interact in an apparent three-dimensional virtual environment that more and more closely resembles real-life settings (Kaplan and Haenlein, 2009). Arguably, the most prominent example of virtual social worlds is the Second Life application, founded and managed by the San Francisco-based company Linden Research, Inc. Residents of Second Life can do simple things that are possible in real life, such as speaking to other avatars, taking a walk, and enjoying the virtual sunshine. Second Life also allows users to create content (e.g., to design virtual clothing or furniture items) and sell this content to others in exchange for Linden Dollars, a virtual currency traded against the US dollar on the Second Life Exchange. Many companies today are taking advantage of a multitude of opportunities offered by virtual social worlds for advertising, marketing, virtual product sales, and even human resource management.

Questions to take you further

Who is the 'whom' in virtual communication? Is virtual communication taking over from face-to-face communication? If so, what might be the costs and benefits?

Reference

Kaplan, Andreas and Michael Haenlein (2009) 'The fairyland of Second Life: about social words and how to use them', *Business Horizons*, 52(6): 563–572.

Further reading on internet-mediated communication

Yus, Francisco (2011) *Cyberpragmatics: Internet-Mediated Communication in Context*. Philadelphia, PA: John Benjamins.

COMMUNICATION AND CULTURE

Culture is a code we learn and share, and learning and sharing require communication (Jandt, 2007). Culture and communication, therefore, mutually influence one another, producing different behavioural patterns in different contexts. Culture influences how we adapt and learn, our perception of reality, our language patterns, habits, customs, expectations, norms, and roles – in other words, it shapes what we do, how we look, what we say, and how we say it. Communication and culture are inseparable. One implication of this insight, as Dodd (1998) noted, is that culture generates symbols, rituals, customs, and formats. In Western cultures, the symbols for success include an individual's acquisition of degrees, promotions, certificates, material objects, and technology. In other cultures, the achievements of the primary group are more important than those of individuals. Cultural misunderstandings occur when we fail to match the symbols and communication system to a culture.

Here is an example. As a cultural practice of modesty, a Chinese technician in a joint venture factory expressed some doubt over how to fix a machine breakdown when interacting with his American manager. The technician's hesitation was intentional and was meant to 'give face' to the American manager by showing that he does not know much more than the American manager who is supposed to be more knowledgeable. However, this hesitation might be misinterpreted by his American manager as lack of confidence or ability. Many cultural imprints are subtle and elusive, if not beyond conscious recognition, but we tend to become more aware of the cultural rules governing our behaviour when we interact with culturally different others. Communication involves sharing, such as sharing a meal or experience – what is shared and understood in the communication process is meaning. Difficulties may arise when we try to share meaning with people whose communication behaviours are governed by cultural rules different from our own.

The intricate link between culture and communication can be illustrated in a number of ways. In the first place, *culture teaches us significant rules, rituals, and procedures*, such as our orientation towards time, perceived power relations, how to dress, when and what to eat, and how to work. The overall process of learning these things is called *socialization*, which refers to the process by which we develop a sense of proper and improper behaviour and communication within the confines of those cultural rules (Dodd, 1998). Think of one of many thousands of rules your culture or your family may have taught you. As a young child, when you went to dinner at a friend's house, your mother probably told you that before you leave, you should thank the hostess and say the food is very nice and you enjoyed it very much. In this way, you consciously learned the rule of politeness. Politeness may involve very different rules. In the more traditional homes of Slovenia (part of the former Yugoslavia), guests are greeted with bread and salt to show that they are part of the family (in the past, this was also a practice in Great Britain and Ireland, but it no longer is). When meeting people in Denmark, introductions are often made on a first-name basis with a handshake. It is important not to speak in a loud voice – Danish culture views this as being disrespectful. In Russia, when you are invited to a meal, you need to expect the hosts to offer you a lot of food, and also they will expect you to finish it all – it is through food that their generosity and respect for you as a guest is expressed. What is polite, rude, or expected falls under the rubric of rules, rituals, and procedures taught by our culture. These rules are very important: they are the means by which we determine inclusion and self-worth, and they help to define boundaries between 'us' and 'them'.

Further online reading The following article can be accessed for free on the book's companion website https://study.sagepub.com/liu2e: Midooka, Kiyoshi (1990) 'Characteristics of Japanese-style communication', *Media, Culture & Society*, 12: 477–489.

More than simply determining and teaching the 'rules', *culture cultivates and reinforces beliefs and values*. Our core understanding of the world is taught in a cultural context. Consequently, we develop culturally reinforced approaches to thoughts and beliefs about the world. These beliefs and values are reflected in our communication behaviour. For example, Australian culture teaches people the values of a 'fair go': independence, privacy, competition, mateship, and directness. 'Fair enough' – a common Australian expression – reveals the value placed on equality in this cultural context. In reflecting these values, Australian communication styles tend to be more direct. It is common for two people to confront each other to 'sort things out' when there is interpersonal conflict. In an Asian context, however, a third party might be brought in to act as an intermediary to resolve the conflict. This communication style avoids direct confrontation and loss of face, and reflects the values of harmony, non-competitiveness, and loyalty to superiors in Asian culture. Both the Asian and Australian approaches are valid within their cultural context, and they serve to highlight the impact of cultural beliefs and values on communication behaviour.

Furthermore, *culture teaches us how to develop relationships with others*. Every communication event establishes a certain relationship. Initiating and maintaining relationships with others is one of the most necessary and challenging functions of human survival. From our relationships with others we receive feedback that we use to evaluate ourselves. The relationships formed in a cultural context generate a dynamic of roles and expectations. Where to stand, how far to stand from each other, when to talk to others, when to visit, when to call/not to call people at home, and the level of formality in language are highly influenced by the nature of the relationship between the communicators. According to Yum (1988), East Asian cultures tend to foster a long-term interpersonal relationship characterized by complementary social reciprocity (see Chapter 10). In this type of relationship, people always feel indebted to others. For example, the Chinese saying 'to return a drop of kindness with a fountain of kindness' indicates how important it is for one to return the favour in a social interaction. On the other hand, North American culture does not treat commitments or obligations as such important elements in interpersonal relationship development as do East Asian cultures. Instead, they might consider extra generosity in a relationship as a potential threat to freedom or autonomy, and tend to prefer reciprocity – returning another's generosity at the same level. Hence, for example, it is common for Westerners to split the bill when having dinner together with friends.

THEORY CORNER

CAN ONE NOT COMMUNICATE?

In 1990, the *Western Journal of Speech Communication* published Michael Motley's article calling for a re-examination of Watzlawick, Beavin and Jackson's axiom that 'one cannot not communicate'. The main theme of Motley's article was that, on the one hand, the axiom 'one cannot not communicate' may be taken to suggest that all behaviour is communicative behaviour. On the other hand, several generally accepted postulates of communication, such as that it is interactive, encoded, and symbolic, clearly suggest that not all behaviour is communication behaviour. Following Motley's article, the journal published a forum on 'Can one not communicate?' featuring a response to Motley. The debate centres on whether communication depends more upon the receiver's interpretation of behaviours or on the sender's orientation to those behaviours.

This is an important debate. Certainly much communication is intentional – we use verbal or nonverbal codes often as an attempt to modify the behaviour of other people. Thus, communication is not random or unconscious activity, but rather a consciously planned action. People may thus be very surprised that their messages are misunderstood by members of another culture. However, other scholars propose that the concept of intentionality does not account for all the circumstances where unintentionally conveyed messages are assigned meaning, such as yawning at a meeting.

Reference
Motley, Michael T. (1990) 'On whether one can(not) not communicate: an examination via traditional communication postulates', *Western Journal of Speech Communication*, 54: 1–20.

Further reading on communication
Craig, Robert T. (1999) 'Communication theory as a field', *Communication Theory*, 9(2): 119–161.

Theory in Practice

INFERRED MOTIVES OF COMMUNICATION

In virtually any communicative encounter, interactants make inferences about fellow interactants' intentions or motives, and individuals' evaluations of interactions and of each other can inform their desire to engage in future interaction. Making adjustment of others is an integral part of successful communication, and the appropriateness of the adjustment depends on the communicators' ability to interpret each other's communication behaviours. Gasiorek and Giles (2012) conducted two studies to investigate the role of inferred intentionality and motive in people's evaluations of non-accommodation. Non-accommodation refers to communicative behaviour that is inappropriately adjusted for participants in an interaction. Data were collected from a sample of over 200 university students. The findings show that when participants inferred that a non-accommodative communication was intentional and negatively motivated, they evaluated both the communication behaviour and the speaker more negatively than if the non-accommodative communication was inferred to be either unintentional or intentional but positively motivated. This research suggests that people infer meanings and assign intentionality to each other's behaviour during interaction. Sometimes the inferred intentionality might not be consistent with the intended one. If this happens, it can lead to misunderstanding or further miscommunication. Thus, there is a need for a better understanding of what leads individuals to attribute positive, negative, or non-existent intentions to others' behaviour in interaction.

Questions to take you further

To what extent does interactants' present and past relationship to each other play a role in inferring speaker intentions? Are there individual differences that make some see the 'best' or the 'worst' in others?

Reference

Gasiorek, Jessica and Howard Giles (2012) 'Effects of interred motive on evaluations of nonaccommodative communication', *Human Communication Research*, 38: 309–331.

Further reading on intentionality

Trope, Yaacov and Ruth Gaunt (2003) 'Attribution and person perception', in M. A. Hogg and J. Cooper (eds), *The Sage Handbook of Social Psychology*. London: Sage. pp. 190–208.

Our verbal and nonverbal behaviours reflect our cultural imprints. Each culture expects a particular communication style. Features such as loudness, pitch, tempo, turn-taking, and gestures characterize communication behaviours and they vary considerably across cultures. If you buy clothes from a marketplace stall in Hong Kong, you have to be prepared to engage in intensive bargaining, loud and hard. Hence, the stereotypical perception is that Asians are good at haggling over price. In another example, in America it would seem unusual to see two male friends kissing in public, while in Peruvian culture, this behaviour would be perceived as commonplace. In Norway, the traditional, national costume is called *Bunad*, dating back to the early 1800s. The costume is adorned with lots of embroidery and jewellery. It is part of Norway's culture to wear the *Bunad* as folk dress for folk dancing, at official celebrations, weddings, and especially on 17 May, which is Constitution Day in Norway. Wearing it also means communicating your cultural identity to the world. But it is also important to understand the diversity of *Bunad* dress: it comes in different shapes for different regions of Norway. Communication shows us that we are alike and we are different. We are similar in that each of us experiences the same feelings, such as anger, joy, sadness, anxiety. However, our unique cultural experiences and habits keep us apart. Misunderstanding occurs because we do not understand each other's cultural rules governing communication behaviour.

Critical thinking...

What could be the communication outcomes if one party over-accommodated the other during a communication act? We know that men sound more masculine and women sound more feminine in romantic relationships: how does this non-accommodation still show liking and attraction?

SUMMARY

- Human communication is multifaceted in nature, and finding a single definition of communication is difficult, if not impossible; the same is true for finding a single theory of communication study.

- Scholars tend to agree on some basic components of communication and its characteristics, and there is a consensus that communication occurs in a particular context which potentially affects every element of the communication process.

- The widely known communication models are linear and interactive. The interactive model is more applicable in the context of intercultural communication.

- Intercultural communication can occur at different levels, from interpersonal, to group, organizational and mass communication.

- Our past experience becomes an inventory consisting of values, sets of expectations, and preconceptions about the consequences of acting one way or another. The receiver's background of experience and learning may differ enough from that of the source to cause significantly different perceptions and evaluations of the topic under discussion.

- The key to successful intercultural communication is to recognize differences and adjust our communication behaviour according to context and communicators.

JOIN THE DEBATE

Universal or culture-specific theories of communication?

The traditions of communication theory identified by Craig (1999) all originated in European thought, and most current theories of communication and media have been developed within those traditions. The key question is whether theories of communication can express universal principles that apply to all cultures, or whether the phenomenon of communication is so culturally variable that culture-specific theories are needed. If theories are universally valid, then the problem of cultural bias is largely irrelevant. On the other hand, if theories must be culture-specific, then the current reliance on Western theories and methods around the world arguably represents a form of cultural domination that can only be overcome by replacing them with theories grounded in local cultures; indeed, many researchers believe this to be the case. What is your view on this debate? Are there intermediate positions between these two extremes?

CASE STUDY

Hanging out in the public square

In order to communicate with fellow citizens, we need to have access to different public spaces. The term 'public' comes from the Latin root *publicus*, usually denoting something which belongs to the community. Each culture creates its own public spaces, and public squares, markets, coffee shops and so on have historically provided the opportunity to share information, convey news, and engage in communication. Hannah Arendt (1958) argues that there is a need for the existence of a common ground where people can relate to each other and physically gather together. What she emphasizes as an explicitly formed space is first of all the *space of communication* – a space in which one can be seen and heard.

An example of a space of communication is that of the Turkish public bath, known as 'Hamam'. This is the Middle-Eastern version of a steam bath, much like what many Westerners know as a sauna. The Hamam has an important role in the cultures of the Middle East, serving as a place for gathering, communicating, ritual cleansing, and even as educational and architectural institutions. Hamams usually have three rooms: the grand steamy hot room (*caldarium*) for steam-soaking and massage, the warm room (*tepidarium*) for washing with soap and water, and the cool room for resting or napping after the bath with a cup of Turkish coffee or a cup of tea. Men and women use separate sections of a Hamam, and they enjoy spending time in these public spaces in order to get to know each other, debate, and relax. In Turkish culture, Hamams are used for social contact, and sometimes for financial and cultural transactions. However, many Western women, upon experiencing Hamams for the first time, express their shock when they have to walk in their underwear in front of other naked women, as well as bathe for several hours.

Different medieval marketplaces also provide a setting for contact among people, a space devoted equally to commerce and culture, a venue for festivals and fairs, and the exchange of books and pamphlets. Over the past 200 years, market squares have been replaced by commercial streets (Judd, 1995). Today, major cities incorporate spaces of consumption with an emphasis also on spaces of exchange and commerce (Lefebvre, 1991). Shopping malls are the public spaces that we occupy most frequently today – these are the spaces where we meet and encounter each other. As critics point out, not only are we shopping – we are also communicating in these spaces (Sennett, 1992).

Another example of an ideal public space for communication is the public square of ancient Greece. Arendt (1958) writes that public spaces depend on public habits, manners, and talents: the ability to welcome strangers and to communicate with others. She writes that this was precisely the case in ancient Greece, that a clear line between public and private realms could be observed in the difference between the *polis* (the sphere where citizens would debate the public affairs, a kind of a city-state) and *oikos* (private sphere of household).

The agora, for example, was a big public square and the marketplace where the Athenians gathered to walk and chat. It was here that they would discuss and communicate about important public issues; thus, openness, accountability, and accessibility were the conditions for the Athenian urban architecture. Later, the ability to see and hear other people on equal basis became a new ordering principle: the merchant's quarter was located around the agora. It was the place where theatres emerged and where the works of Euripides, Sophocles, and Aeschylus were written and performed. The agoras contributed to the development of philosophy – Socrates, Plato, and Aristotle were among the philosophers who would frequently give public lectures – and from this, other disciplines emerged, such as rhetoric and history. In public life at this time, there was a great concern with honour and reputation, which were expressed in a vital, vibrant public communication, and in which all citizens were expected to participate. This was the assembly that established the laws of the land.

References

Arendt, Hannah (1958) *The Human Condition*. Chicago, IL: University of Chicago Press.

Judd, Dennis R. (1995) 'The rise of the new walled cities', in H. Liggett and D. C. Perry (eds), *Spatial Practices*. London: Sage. pp. 144–167.

Lefebvre, Henri (1991) *The Production of Space*. London: Blackwell.

Sennett, Richard (1978/1992) *The Fall of Public Man*. New York: W.W. Norton & Co.

Questions for discussion

1. What are some of the public spaces that exist in different cultures, where people can meet and communicate?
2. How is 'Hamam' being used in this case study? Do you have similar facilities in your culture?
3. How would you describe a Greek *polis*?
4. Do you think shopping malls are public spaces? Why?
5. What are the characteristics of the ancient Greek public square? Do we still have such public squares today? How could the ancient Greek public square be compared to an internet forum today?

FURTHER READINGS

All articles listed next to the mouse icon below can be accessed for free on the book's companion website: https://study.sagepub.com/liu2e

Communication and culture

Baraldi, Claudio (2006) 'New forms of intercultural communication in a globalized world', *International Communication Gazette*, 68(1): 53–69.

This article takes the view that globalization involves the worldwide expansion of a functionally differentiated European society through intercultural communication. It reviews the changing functions of intercultural communication from the seventeenth century to the twentieth century, and to the last decade of that century, in which a transcultural form of communication based on dialogue was proposed as a basis for cross-cultural adaptation, multicultural identities, and a construction of a hybrid multicultural society. This article discusses the paradoxes and difficulties in intercultural communication, mixing the preservation of cultural difference with the search for synthesis, and argues for the need of a new form of intercultural dialogue, dealing with incommensurable differences and conflicts.

Communication models

Craig, Robert T. (1999) 'Communication theory as a field', *Communication Theory*, 9(2): 119–161.

This essay reconstructs communication theory as a dialogical-dialectical field according to two principles: the constitutive model of communication as a meta-model, and theory as meta-discursive practice. The essay argues that all communication theories are mutually relevant when addressed to a practical life world in which 'communication' is already a richly meaningful term. Each tradition of communication theory derives from and appeals rhetorically to certain commonplace beliefs about communication while challenging other beliefs. The complementarities and tensions among traditions generate a theoretical meta-discourse that intersects with and potentially informs the ongoing practical meta-discourse in society.

Eadie, William F. and Robin Goret (2013) 'Theories and models of communication: foundations and heritage', in P. Cobley and P. J. Schulz (eds), *Theories and Models of Communication*. Berlin/Boston, MA: Walter de Gruyter. pp. 17–36.

This chapter provides a comprehensive chart of the historical influences on the theories and models that shaped the communication discipline. It illustrates the importance of US and European scholars from not only the beginnings of the communication discipline, but also including those who were pre-eminent in other academic disciplines, such as sociology, psychology, political science, and journalism. The chapter also examines emerging scholarship from Asia that focuses on understanding cultural differences through communication theories.

Communication technologies

Kaplan, Andreas M. and Michael Haenlein (2010) 'Users of the world, unite! The challenges and opportunities of social media', *Business Horizons*, 53: 59–68.

Business executives and consultants today endeavour to identify ways in which companies can make profitable use of social media applications such as YouTube, Facebook, and Twitter. Despite the widespread interest, there seems to be limited understanding of what 'social media' exactly means. This article provides a classification of social media applications by characteristics: collective projects, blogs, content communities, social networking sites, virtual game worlds, and virtual social worlds. It offers ten pieces of practical advice for companies which decide to utilize social media for their business.

Rhetoric and discourse

Bonvillain, Nancy (2014) *Language, Culture and Communication: The Meaning of Messages* (7th edn). Upper Saddle River, NJ: Pearson Prentice-Hall.

This book presents a discussion of the multifaceted meanings and uses of language. It emphasizes the ways that language encapsulates speakers' meanings and intentions, using data from cultures and languages throughout the world in order to document both similarities and differences in human language. It explores the many interconnections among language, culture, and communicative meaning. This book is a useful source of reference particularly for students who are entering the field of intercultural communication from the field of language or linguistics.

'*Culture is the name for what people are interested in, their thoughts, their models, the books they read and the speeches they hear, their table-talk, gossip, controversies, historical sense and scientific training, the value they appreciate, the quality of life they admire. All communities have a culture. It is the climate of their civilization.* '

Walter Lippmann, American journalist and sociologist, 1889–1974

3

UNDERSTANDING CULTURE

LEARNING OBJECTIVES

At the end of this chapter, you should be able to:

- Recognize the multifaceted nature of culture.

- Identify different components and characteristics of culture.

- Define different types of subcultures.

- Evaluate different approaches to studying culture.

INTRODUCTION

The word 'culture' originated from the Latin word *cultura*, which is from the verb *colere*, denoting 'to till' (as in to till the soil or land). In its original meaning, therefore, culture is a process related to the tending of something, such as crops or animals. The word shares its etymology with modern English words such as agriculture, cultivate, and colony. Eventually, the term was extended to incorporate ideas related to the human mind and a state of being 'cultivated'. Generally, the study of culture ranges from aspects that are associated with the arts to the study of the entire system of meanings and the way of life of a society. As Edward T. Hall (1966: x) states, culture is 'those deep, common, unstated experiences which members of a given culture share, communicate without knowing, and which form the backdrop against which all other events are judged'. Culture fosters a sense of shared identity and solidarity among its group members. Being a member of a cultural group implies that you have been nurtured by its core values and understand what constitutes 'desirable' and 'undesirable' behaviours in that particular system (Ting-Toomey and Chung, 2005). While different people might have different norms for judging behaviours in a particular cultural environment, common to all people is that they see their world through cultural glasses – we all view the world through culturally tinted lenses, and we rarely take them off.

Basically, any process or product of human activity can be named as 'culture'. In this general sense, culture consists of a group or community's traditions, customs, norms, beliefs, values and thought patterns passed down from generation to generation. This includes food, music, language, dress codes, artefacts, family, organization, politics, stories, the production and distribution of goods, and so on. Culture is not instinctive or innate; culture is learned. Communication and culture are intertwined. To study intercultural communication without exploring culture is like studying physics without exploring matter. This chapter discusses the pervasive nature of culture and explores the relationship between culture and communication. Components and characteristics of culture are identified, and various subcultures are examined. The chapter concludes by highlighting the importance of valuing cultural diversity.

DEFINITIONS AND COMPONENTS OF CULTURE

For decades, scholars across the academic spectrum have attempted to define culture. Almost 200 definitions can be located, each attempting to delineate the boundaries and inclusions of the concept by drawing upon such synonymous ideas as community, minorities, social groups, social class, nationalities, geographic units, societies and so forth. This highlights the multifaceted nature of the term.

Defining culture

Scholars in philosophy, anthropology, cultural studies, and communication, among many others, have grappled with and attempted to define culture. For example, the Italian philosopher Antonio Gramsci (2000) conceptualized culture as the creative meaning-making process, constantly being produced and reproduced by multiple groups. He conceives of culture as the means by which people make sense of their social world and represent their active relation to the wider social and material world. Alternatively, American anthropologist Clifford Geertz (1973) defines culture as a web that people themselves have spun. He proposes that 'culture is the fabric of meanings in terms of which human beings interpret their experience and guide their action' (p. 145). There are three aspects to Geertz's 'web' metaphor: firstly, as a web, culture both confines members to their social reality and facilitates their functioning in this reality; secondly, culture is both a product and a process; and thirdly, culture provides contexts for behaviour. Raymond Williams (1989), a British cultural studies scholar, argues that culture is the product of individuals' whole committed personal and social experience; it is the product of a whole people and offers individual meanings. Rogers and

Steinfatt (1999: 79) define culture as 'the total way of life of a people, composed of their learned and shared behavior patterns, values, norms, and material objects'. While Gramsci, Geertz, Williams, and Rogers and Steinfatt represent only a small number of the scholars who have attempted to define culture, they serve to illustrate the many ways in which culture is conceptualized across disciplines.

Although definitions of culture vary across different fields, scholars agree that culture is pervasive in human life and governs people's behaviours. Building on this consensus about culture, this chapter defines *culture* as the particular way of life of a group of people, comprising the deposit of knowledge, experience, beliefs, values, traditions, religion, notions of time, roles, spatial relations, worldviews, material objects, and geographic territory. This definition emphasizes the pervasive nature of culture; it also confirms that culture is a process as well as a product of communication. Our attitudes towards work and age, ethical standards, clothing, artistic expressions, rituals and customs, beliefs about health, concepts of time, social and political institutions, religious practices, even our superstitions – these, are all reflections of culture. As Dodd (1998: 37) argues, 'Culture is like the luggage we carry', and when we open each pocket of our cultural suitcase, we explore an interrelated set of group identities, beliefs, values, activities, rules and customs, institutions, and communication patterns arising from our daily needs.

Critical thinking...

Do you agree that culture is the production and exchange of meanings between members of a society or group? If so, how do you think that ordinary daily activities form a part of a culture? For example, is wearing a T-shirt an example of reproducing a culture? Or having a morning coffee?

Components of culture

Dodd (1998) groups cultural components into three levels, as shown in the model in Figure 3.1. The inner core of culture is made up of history, identity, beliefs, values, and worldviews; the intermediate layer consists of activities as cultural manifestations, such as roles, rules, rituals, customs, communication patterns, and artistic expressions; the outer layer involves the larger cultural system and includes economic, health, educational, religious, family, and political systems.

The inner core of culture

The inner core of culture consists of the history, identity, beliefs and values, and worldviews of a cultural group (Dodd, 1998). Every culture has a history that is the deposit and carrier of cultural heritage and development. Totems, archives, architecture, ancient languages, and paintings are just some of the ways in which a culture records and expresses its heritage and tradition. The power of origin and heritage demonstrates the continuity of a culture. Culture is passed on from generation to generation, binding its members together and providing a sense of *identity*. The multifaceted nature of our identity (or, more appropriately, identities) is experienced and negotiated by many of us in everyday life. Hardly a day passes when we do not come across an identity issue being (re)addressed in a newspaper article, a radio show, a TV programme, or in a conversation with a friend. For example, you know the popular saying, 'We are what we eat'. Nowadays, food from many different cultures is available to us, and we can ask how the consumption of 'foreign' food might affect our sense of cultural identity. Daily life and events unfold within an entire spectrum of identities, including our ethnic, national, gender, racial, social, corporate, professional, and sexual identities. Identity gives us a location in the world and reflects the link between us and the society

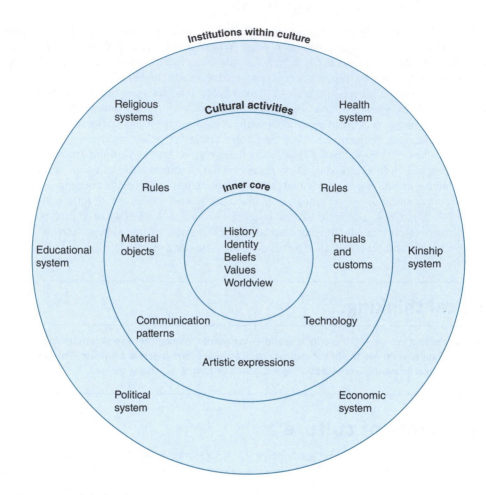

Figure 3.1   A model of culture

Source: Adapted from Dodd, Carley H. (1998) *Dynamics of Intercultural Communication* (5th edn). Boston, MA: McGraw-Hill. p. 38. Used with permission.

in which we live. For example, pre-colonial Maori society in what today is New Zealand was communal and tribally based. Maori tribes occupied and cultivated ancestral (tribal) lands. Work, tools, and living areas were also shared. Within Maori society, identity was determined by satisfactory fulfilment of social obligations towards biological kin through *whanau* (extended family based on shared genealogy), *hapu* (sub-tribes comprising several *whanau*) and *iwi* (tribes comprising *hapu*) (Houkamaua, 2010). In this regard, *whanau* obligations were central to self-identity. Further, conducting the self in a way that honoured the collective mode of operation enabled individuals to achieve social acceptance, a sense of purpose and meaning, and indeed a cultural identity.

Further online reading   The following article can be accessed for free on the book's companion website https://study.sagepub.com/liu2e: Nederveen Pieterse, Jan (1994) 'Globalisation as hybridisation', *International Sociology*, 9(2): 161–184.

THEORY CORNER

CONCEPTUALIZING IDENTITY

The concept of identity has been examined extensively from both psychological and sociological perspectives. Erik Erikson (1968), a post-Freudian psychologist working in the USA, states that identity has two forms: identity and difference. The first is identity as a self-differentiation, or self-awareness and a sense of personal continuity. The second is the identity that derives from a primary relationship, where identity is connected with differentiation of the self from the Other – this leads to an awareness of one's personal distinctiveness.

Manuel Castells (1997), a well-known sociologist, writes that as communication networks become central to economies and societies, identity becomes an organizing principle of social action in the emerging information society. Castells argues that identities are plural, and such a plurality is a source of stress and contradiction in both self-representation and social action. Importantly, identity should be distinguished from what sociologists have traditionally called roles. Today, questions of culture, identity, and difference have become central to contemporary global issues of politics, equality, and justice. Issues of culture and identity have moved to the centre of analysis across the humanities and social sciences. This has been linked to the decline of traditional forms of social affiliation and action and the emergence of new forms of solidarity and collective identities, captured in the notion of identity politics from the 1960s.

Reference
Castells, Manuel (1997) *The Power of Identity*. Oxford: Blackwell.
Erikson, Erik (1968) 'Identity, Psychological', in *International Encyclopaedia of the Social Sciences* (Vol. 7). New York: Macmillan. pp. 46–48.

Further reading on identity
Shore, Chris and Annabel Black (1994) 'Citizens' Europe and the construction of European identity', in V. A. Goddard, J. R. Llobera and C. Shore (eds), *The Anthropology of Europe: Identity and Boundaries in Conflict*. Oxford and Providence, RI: Berg Publishers. pp. 275–298.

Theory in Practice

IDENTITY AMONG INDIGENOUS PEOPLES

Rosengren (2003) explores the indigenous constructions of how competing identity models affect the articulation of the local sense of community. Today, the situation in the Amazon is characterized by political tensions between Indigenous and non-Indigenous peoples. As a consequence, Indigenous peoples are organizing themselves in order to defend themselves and their land against the encroachment of representatives from the national Peruvian society. To the Matsigenka, who live in the mountains of south-eastern Peru, the processes of creating an identity and mobilizing around it is relatively recent, and so is the conceptualization of understanding conflicts in ethnic terms. Although ethnic criteria for constructing social identity is largely alien to most Matsigenka, it has, to the indigenous organizations, come to serve as the model for defining political issues, mainly because it is imposed by the dominant national society. As Rosengren writes, categories of beings that are defined in notions of the cosmogony remain a significant factor in the Matsigenka conceptualization of the social world.

Questions to take you further

Do you think exposure to positive stereotypes about identities in the media and through education is important? Why or why not? Why might we describe identity as a personalized social construction, formed by social contexts and shaped by socio-historical conditions? Can you give some examples?

References

Rosengren, Dan (2003) 'The collective self and the ethnopolitical movement', *Identities Journal*, 10(2): 221–240.

Further reading on identity construction

Eakin, Paul J. (1999) *How Our Lives Become Stories: Making Selves*. New York: Cornell University Press.

It is generally agreed that the term 'identity' refers primarily to a person's subjective experience of herself/himself in relation to the world, and it should, therefore, be differentiated from concepts like 'character' or 'personality'. While one can share character traits with many people, the sharing of such traits does not require any active engagement of our being. On the other hand, sharing an identity implies that we actively engage part of our being in order to identify with a certain group. This notion of active engagement indicates that one's identity is formed through *cultural* processes, which are in turn determined by a culture's structures.

Culture is captured for individual human beings as beliefs and values. Each culture has a window through which its members perceive reality and other people. *Beliefs* are an individual's representations of reality viewed through that cultural window. Some beliefs are seen as very likely to be true; others are seen as less probable. When a belief is held by most members of a culture, it is known as a cultural belief. For example, Aboriginal cultural beliefs are based on spiritual beliefs, where there are direct links between land, language, dreaming, and people. Aboriginal and Torres Strait Islander people in Australia traditionally have a strong physical and spiritual bond with the Australian landscape through 'the Dreaming', which is believed to be reality. Another example is that most Chinese people believe that having the number eight in their phone number symbolizes prosperity, and having the number six symbolizes smoothness; thus, having both the numbers eight and six suggests a smooth path to prosperity. A further example of a belief from Slovenian culture is that people hang horseshoes over their doors to bring positive spirits and good luck.

Cultures also have concepts of ultimate significance and of long-term importance, known as *values*, which go beyond statements of truth. Values are what people who share a culture regard as good or bad; they tell the cultural group members how to judge good or bad, right or wrong. Values enshrine within a culture what is worth fighting for, what is worth sacrificing, what should be protected, and what should be given up. Cultural values involve judgements, and so values differ across cultures. For example, US American culture teaches people the values of independence, privacy, and competition. Asian culture teaches people the values of harmony, reciprocity, non-competitiveness, loyalty to superiors, and thrift. Hierarchy is valued in Korean culture, while equality is treasured in Switzerland. Our core understanding of good and evil, right and wrong, true and false, is taught in a cultural context.

Consequently, members of a cultural group share thoughts and beliefs about the world. A culture's belief about nature and the working of the universe is called a *worldview*. Understanding the worldview of a culture can help predict its members' thoughts and behavioural patterns. For example, according to the Judaeo-Christian understanding of human nature, the first humans were created in the image of God. *Genesis* declares that God said, 'Let us make [humans] in our image, in our likeness and let them rule over the fish of the sea and the birds of the air, over the livestock, over all earth, and over all the creatures that move along the ground.' In Shinto (an ancient Japanese religion), the Gods, called Kami (deities), take the form of wind, rain, mountains, trees, rivers, and fertility. Nature is sacred; to be in contact with nature is to be close to the Gods, hence, natural objects are worshipped as sacred spirits. Believers of Shinto also respect animals as messengers of the Gods. From the above examples we can see that a worldview is a belief system about the nature of the universe, its perceived effect on human behaviour, and humans' place in the universe (Dodd, 1998).

Critical thinking...

Are culture and behaviour interchangeable? Are they the same thing? Remove culture, and there will be no behaviour; remove behaviour, and there will not be culture. What do you think?

The intermediate layer of culture

The intermediate layer of culture is connected to the inner core, but has more capacity to change. This layer consists of activities as manifestations of culture. According to Dodd (1998), cultural activities can be expressed in many ways: technology, material objects, roles, rules, rituals, customs, communication patterns, and artistic expressions. The rituals and customs people observe and the festivals people celebrate reflect culture. The celebration of Queen's Day in the Netherlands on 30 April every year reinforces the belief that the Dutch Queen is an embodiment of hope and unity in times of war, adversity, and natural disaster. In a different arena, the power of football (soccer) in many countries, starting in Europe and South America, to symbolize a core value of pride in the nation is astonishing – one only needs to look at the TV viewing parties and celebrations around the football World Cup to understand that.

Artworks are cultural products. In many paintings by Western artists people tend to be portrayed

Photo 3.1 A colourful array of spices in the Deira Spice Souq in Dubai. Copyright © Alison Rae. Used with permission.

as the focal point, whereas in paintings produced by Eastern artists (such as those of the Chinese), natural scenes or animals are more likely to be at the centre of the painting. This reflects the importance and power of nature in the Chinese culture, versus the power of human agency and action in Western European and American culture. In addition to artwork, technology is a very salient feature of a culture, reflected in its transportation, communication, food, clothing, shelter, and tools. What people wear, how they eat and prepare food, the kinds of tools they use for work – all these reflect the culture of a particular group. As Everett Rogers (1995) states, technology has form (what it is or how it looks), function (what it does and how it works), and meaning (what it represents).

THEORY CORNER

POPULAR CULTURE AND FOLK CULTURE

Popular culture refers to artefacts and styles of human expression developed from ordinary people (Lull, 2000). It stands in contrast to what early European scholars referred to as 'high' or elite culture. Popular culture can include such cultural products as music, talk shows, soap operas, cooking, clothing, consumption, and the many facets of entertainment such as sports and literature. The recognition that a 'pop' culture icon such as Madonna might in fact provide a rich repository of American society's attitudes, values, practices, and beliefs has led to the emergence of popular cultural studies as a discipline.

Folk culture is the localized lifestyle of culture. It is usually handed down through oral tradition. Geertz (1973) writes that a local or a folk culture is composed of the taken-for-granted and repetitive nature of the everyday culture of which individuals have mastery. Elements of folk culture are often imbued with a sense of place. They carry strong connotations of their original site of creation, even when they are moved to a foreign locale. Handmade patchwork quilts are an example of American folk culture. Folk culture often informs popular culture and even filters into high culture. The minuet dance of European court society, for example, is based on a peasant dance. The consciously self-centred culture of the Amish has been portrayed for comic value in Hollywood films and media reality shows. Similarly, the archetypal costume of the cowboy has been reinvented in gleaming silver by disco dancers.

References

Geertz, Clifford (1973) *The Interpretation of Cultures*. New York: Basic Books.
Lull, James (2000) *Media, Communication, Culture: A Global Perspective* (2nd edn). New York: Columbia University Press.

Further reading on popular and folk culture

Beer, David (2013) *Popular Culture and New Media: The Politics of Circulation*. New York: Palgrave Macmillan.

Theory in Practice

WATCHING POPULAR TELENOVELAS AROUND THE WORLD

Latin American telenovelas are considered to be a part of popular culture and are extremely popular worldwide. Huge audiences that go beyond national, class, generational, and gender differences sit daily in front of their television to watch episodes of one of the most globally watched television genres. By 1988, Brazil had exported telenovelas to more than 128 countries, and, in 1992, more than 200 million people regularly watched the Mexican production *Los Ricos También Lloran* (*The Rich Also Cry*) in Russia (Alcosta-Azuru, 2003). Globo (Brazil), Televisa (Mexico), and Venevisión (Venezuela) are the leading telenovela producers, selling their products to diverse markets in North America, Europe, Asia, and the Middle East. Telenovelas are a part of popular, television culture: they are serial melodramatic genres that are characterized by a central story of heterosexual love. The main couple is faced by many different obstacles and have to overcome problems to achieve happiness together. In addition, the 'ignorance of an identity' is always central to the story. Becoming blind, crippled, or pregnant are staples of the genre, whose heroines experience these dilemmas, only to overcome them before the happy ending (Alcosta-Azuru, 2003).

Questions to take you further

Do you think the inclusion of political topics into telenovelas, such as domestic abuse, homosexuality, or abortion, will be accepted by viewers? Why or why not? How could popular culture shows like telenovelas make international audiences understand the genre's melodramatic codes as a part of their own, local cultures?

Reference

Alcosta-Azuru, Carolina (2003) 'Tackling the issues: meaning making in a Telenovela', *Popular Communication*, 1(4): 193–215.

Further reading on telenovelas

Rios, Diana I. (2003) 'US Latino audiences of "telenovelas"', *Journal of Latinos and Education*, 2(1): 59–65.

What we do in a cultural context forms relationships with others; these relationships generate a dynamic of roles and expectations. The behavioural norms associated with these roles and expectations are defined by culture. As well as influencing roles, rules, norms, customs, and rituals, each culture expects particular communication patterns. Communication behaviours such as turn-taking, gestures, loudness, directness, and rate are all expected to conform to a culture's expectations. In this, the contrasts between cultures are striking. For example, Ghanaian culture dictates that people address elderly men as 'grandfather'. In Australia and many other Western countries, children often address adults by their first name to show equality. In Hong Kong, indirectness in conversation is valued as it functions to preserve harmony between the speakers; in Germany, 'speaking your mind' is preferred in an interpersonal communication act. Intercultural misunderstandings often occur because we do not share the cultural rules governing the communication behaviour of others.

Not only verbal but also nonverbal communication behaviour is influenced by culture. Our posture, gestures, and concepts of time and space also influence communication. In Western countries, people view time with great precision, and punctuality is a cultural expectation. People make an appointment or reservation to see a doctor, go to a hairdresser, or dine in a restaurant. Being late is regarded as bad manners. For example, the Dutch and Germans are very punctual, and being even five minutes late for an appointment is considered inappropriate – if anything, people arrive a minute or two early as a sign of respect. In Africa, Malaysia, or Latin America, however, people are deliberately a little late, in order not to disturb their hosts' other activities. Meetings may not start until everyone arrives. A doctor may schedule all patients for the 8:00am appointment, and it is the patients' responsibility to negotiate among themselves whose turn it is to see the doctor. There are core cultural values in both these time orientations – and people with one orientation tend to think those with the other are lazy or over-punctual. Both culture and communication, therefore, are a way of living and a whole social process. The intermediate level of culture reflects our definitions of social and cultural rules, and our communication patterns.

Further online reading The following article can be accessed for free on the book's companion website https://study.sagepub.com/liu2e: Merolla, Andy J., Shuangyue Zhang and Shaojing Sun (2013) 'Forgiveness in the United States and China: antecedents, consequences, and communication style comparisons', *Communication Research*, 40(5): 595–622.

Critical thinking...

If a global culture can be said to be emerging, on whose/which cultures will it be (primarily) based? Is it possible, or desirable, for all cultures to get equal play in a global culture? Why, or why not? How might local cultural values and beliefs be affected?

THEORY CORNER

CULTURAL THEORISTS

Biological theories, inspired by the work of Charles Darwin, in most cases construe any human behaviour as physical processes that have developed as an inherent part of human evolution. Biological theories posit humans as merely 'biological species', underplaying the significance of culture. Cultural theorists, on the other hand, understand culture as a powerful force that affects our behaviour and the ways we experience the world. Culture always stands as the opposite of nature. It is not unified or one-dimensional, but fragmented and multidimensional. According to Bourdieu (1977), we shape a culture in accordance with its dominant economic and political system. For example, the collapse of systems such as communism at the end of the 1980s brought incredible transformations to Eastern European cultures, and with that, their way of life. If 'communist culture' propagated solidarity, a one-party political system, state property, and working hard, the new system, called liberal-democratic, fosters a completely different culture – one that mobilizes mostly around private property, individualism, consumption, and entertainment.

Reference

Bourdieu, Pierre (1977) *Outline of a Theory and Practice*. Cambridge: Cambridge University Press.

Further reading on global culture

Ladegaard, Hans J. (2007) 'A global corporation', *Journal of Intercultural Communication Research*, 36(2): 139–163.

Theory in Practice

DIGITAL YOUTH CULTURES

The rapid spread of digital media in most parts of the world has been attributed to many global social, political, cultural, and economic changes. The scholarly tendency has been to treat young people born in and after 1990 as the digital generation, with an orientation towards digital culture. Digital culture refers to the multiple ways in which young people engage with digital media and technologies in their daily lives.

Pathak-Shelat and DeShano (2013) discuss the case of youth digital cultures in rural/small-town Gujarat, in India. India has the largest youth population in the world, with approximately 600 million people under the age of 25. This group of Indian citizens alone accounts for almost 10 per cent of the world's population. There is immense diversity in the Indian youth population. India is a country with strong cultural divides. These divides heavily influence the life experiences of young people. Class, caste, gender, geographical location, beliefs, values, schools, and infrastructure are only some of the elements that influence digital culture of the youth. Pathak-Shelat and DeShano (2013) applied the cultural theory approach to examine how the location and dominant discourses intersect with digital technologies and reconfigure aspects of daily lives, such as study, leisure, and friendship; how youth negotiate their interactions with digital media as one aspect of their real life; and how these negotiations influence cultural practices within structural environments. Youth in this study treat new media and technologies as one component of their lives and social experiences.

Questions to take you further

Which cultural values and beliefs do you think influence youth digital cultures in your cultural context? How would you describe this influence? How is the culture changing as a consequence?

Reference

Pathak-Shelat, Manisha and Cathy DeShano (2013) 'Digital youth cultures in small town and rural Gujarat', *New Media and Society*, 1(2): 1–19.

Further reading on digital youth cultures

Livingstone, Sonia (2009) *Children and the Internet: Great Expectations, Challenging Realities*. Cambridge: Polity Press.

The outer layer of culture

The outer layer involves the *institutions of a culture* (Dodd, 1998). Like the intermediate layer, elements of this layer of culture are also tied to the inner core and remain an area for flexibility and change. According to Dodd, institutions constitute the formalized systems, including religion, economy, politics, family, healthcare, and education. These systems are products of culture.

Religion refers to any system of thought that provides answers to the big question of life, death, and of life beyond death. According to Dodd (1998), religious systems involve beliefs, ceremonies, worship, norms of respect, and spiritual issues. Religion supplies maps for individuals in their journeys towards belief and faith. For example, the 'Abrahamic' faiths (Judaism, Islam, and Christianity) are called monotheistic religions – meaning that each believes in only one God. Hindus tend to be both monotheistic and polytheistic. Buddhism offers the possibility for personal self-realization, and the Buddha is considered a teacher, not a God. Aboriginal people in Australia value integrated communities, based on beliefs about connections between people and the environment, including land and animals. In modern societies, religion is sometimes used to explain events in life, including death, accidents, illness, and even natural disasters. In this sense, religion and culture are intertwined. According to the Pew Research Report (2008), in Indonesia, Tanzania, Pakistan, and Nigeria, nine-in-ten people acknowledge that religion is very important, and religion is central to their lives. Knowledge of religious practice, such as the fasting month of Ramadan in Islam, the annual pilgrimage to the holy places of Mecca, and the Friday prayers, can help one to understand a particular culture, and avoid cultural mistakes and prejudice. Like culture, however, no religion is superior or inferior to any other.

In addition to religious systems, the economic system of a society reflects its culture. In some remote villages, people still use barter trade for business transactions, whereas in more developed regions, people are more likely to use cash or credit cards to make a purchase. Cultural influences are also reflected in family size. In Western countries, the nuclear family (a unit referring to father, mother, and children) is the major family structure. In other cultures, the extended family, which includes the nuclear family along with grandparents, uncles and aunts, cousins and so on, is valued and more likely to be the norm. Although it may vary in expression, the relationship between the economic system, culture, and family system is intrinsic to all cultures.

Political, health, and educational systems are also element of culture, and they vary across cultures. For example, some countries have a one-party system (e.g., communist regimes), whereas others have two or more parties (e.g., democratic regimes) governing the country. In some cultures, religion and politics are separate, whereas in other cultures they are interrelated – the religious leader may also be a political figure. For example, the Roman Catholic Pope, as the leader of his church, has full legal, executive, and judicial power in its seat, the Vatican City. On the one hand, religion offers the possibility of peace and unites people. On the other hand, religion can play a divisive role when different ethnic groups or nations struggle over resources.

In addition, people's beliefs about health and medical care are also shaped by culture. Some societies rely on Western medicine to cure illness; others have more faith in traditional herbal medicine; and still others believe praying is a way to relieve pain and illness. Similarly, a society's educational system also reflects its culture. In some Asian cultures, such as Malaysia, Singapore, or Hong Kong, memorization or rote learning is the preferred pedagogy, whereas in Anglo-Saxon cultures, the skills of creative thinking and problem solving are more valued in the classroom. The religion a society practises, the festivals a country observes, the events a people celebrate, the healthcare practices, and the educational system all reveal something about the culture of a group or nation. The outer layer of cultural systems includes numerous aspects of a culture's ultimate survival in ways that are accepted and often sanctioned by law. They are fundamental to the economic, legal, social, and spiritual nature of a culture (Dodd, 1998).

THEORY CORNER

EMIC AND ETIC APPROACHES

Generally, there are two main approaches that investigate culture: emic and etic, developed by Kenneth Pike (1967). The emic approach views each culture as a unique entity that can only be examined by constructs developed from inside the culture. In other words, this approach focuses on identifying culture-specific aspects of concepts and behaviour which cannot be compared across all cultures. Emic knowledge and interpretations are those existing within a culture, which are shaped by local customs, values, meanings, and beliefs and are best described by a 'native' or an 'insider' of a culture. The cultural anthropologist's endeavour to understand a culture from 'the native's point of view' is the main foundation of the emic approach.

In contrast, the etic approach assumes that culture can be examined with predetermined categories that can be applied to all cultures in the search for cultural universals. Etic researchers attempt to identify universal aspects of human behaviour and seek to find universal processes that can be utilized across cultures. In other words, this approach assumes that all cultures can be compared in terms of generalizable phenomena, and researchers should seek to segregate common components of culture and test hypotheses.

Reference
Pike, Kenneth L. (1967) *Language in Relation to Unified Theory of the Structure of Human Behavior*. The Hague, the Netherlands: Mouton.

Further reading on emic and etic approaches
Fukuyama, Mary A. (1990) 'Taking a universal approach to multicultural counseling', *Counselor Education and Supervision*, 30(1): 6–17.

Theory in Practice

MEASURING CULTURE IN INTERNATIONAL BUSINESS

How to measure culture has been a challenge for intercultural scholars. Lu's (2012) paper provided a critical analysis of how the emic and etic approaches can be applied to measure culture in international business research. For managers in multinational corporations, one of the most difficult aspects of doing business in a foreign country is to understand the similarities and differences in cultural insights and values. Cross-cultural studies using an etic approach with quantitative methods have led researchers to compare the similar elements (etic) of national culture around the world. However, critiques argue that the etic approach may be too generalized because they presume a group of people living in a society or country to be relatively homogeneous. Moreover, etic researchers pay little attention to cultural diversity in a country or to interactions between mainstream and ethnic cultures. Therefore, it is time to explore the relationship between different parts of culture (emic) and international business activities. While the etic categories may be useful for comparative analysis, they need corroboration from fieldwork and must be open to new elements collected by an emic approach. The paper argues that the etic and emic approaches are complementary and researchers should combine both approaches in cross-cultural study.

Questions to take you further
What is the relationship between culture and national culture? How can etic and emic approaches be used to study cultural identity?

Reference
Lu, Lung-Tan (2012) 'Etic or emic? Measuring culture in international business research', *International Business Research*, 5(5): 109–115.

Further reading on etic and emic approaches
Harris, Marvin (1976) 'History and significance of the emic/etic distinction', *Annual Review of Anthropology*, 5(1): 329–350.

Critical thinking...

Do you agree that we live in a consumer culture today, premised upon the expansion of global capitalist commodity production? How would you define consumer culture and its main features?

CHARACTERISTICS OF CULTURE

As we have seen, culture manifests itself at three levels: inner core, cultural activities, and institutions. We now turn to discuss some important characteristics of culture.

Culture is holistic

To this point, we have isolated components of culture, for ease of description and explanation. In reality, culture functions as an integrated and complex whole. While the various parts of culture are interrelated (Samovar et al., 2013), the whole is more than simply the sum of these interconnected parts. As Hall (1977: 13–14) said, 'You touch a culture in one place and everything else is affected.' You might, for example, explore a specific cultural formation, such as Hindu Annaprasanam, a festive event to celebrate the first birthday of a child. During the Annaprasanam the baby is given a mixture of rice, sugar and milk, which is generally his/her first solid food after a year of a liquid diet. All aspects of the event are interrelated and must be interpreted as a whole – none makes sense on its own.

Photo 3.2 The Vatican City in Rome is one of the most sacred places and attests to a great history.
Copyright © Shuang Liu. Used with permission.

Another example of culture as a whole is the ritual of drinking tea. People in more than 100 countries and regions all over the world drink tea every day. But, in different local contexts, the ritual of tea drinking is not the same. In some places, it is considered to be an art; in other places, it is viewed as a way of character cultivation. The custom of tea drinking can symbolize culture, from which different values and cultural orientations can be learned. One very specific example is the Japanese tea ritual. *Chadō*, or the 'Way of Tea', is a key part of Japanese culture. The tea ritual is a detailed procedure, which takes years to learn and which can take up to four hours to perform. In 2002, officials at Japan's National Space Development Agency declared a plan to include a tea room in their section of the International Space Station. Even when confronted with restrictions on time and space, they preferred to include the tea ritual, in order to make a symbolic statement about what was most important to them as a culture. The aim of the tea ceremony is to achieve inner peace and harmony, which are valued in Japanese culture. It also aims to open the mind in preparation for meditation (Anderson, 1987). Thus, the tea ritual must be interpreted as an integral part of the whole cultural system.

Culture is learned

The Dutch psychologist and sociologist Geert Hofstede (1991: 32) writes that every person 'carries within him or herself patterns of thinking, feeling, and potential acting which were learned throughout his or her lifetime. Much of these patterns are acquired in early childhood, because at that time a person is most susceptible to learning and assimilating.' We continue to learn culture throughout our lives. For example, we constantly have to learn specific rules and norms governing our behaviours within the communities in which we live. A group of people may have potatoes as a staple food, or they may depend on hunting for animals as their main source of food. They may grow wheat or breed cattle, they may use science to explain natural phenomena, or they may attribute wind and storms to the Gods fighting in the heavens – these are all products of cultural learning.

We learn our cultural rules and norms through communication, both at the conscious and unconscious level. A Chinese mother might tell her daughter that once married, she should follow her mother-in-law's ways of doing things around the house, and in doing so, the daughter learns about the expected roles of a married woman. This is cultural learning at a conscious level. Identifying cultural learning at the unconscious level is more difficult, but just as significant nevertheless. While we may be unable to specify a particular experience that taught us about our view of ageing, for example, the attitudes we have developed are still the product of our cultural environment. As an example, the French convention of addressing older relatives with the formal pronoun for 'you' – 'vous' – whereas younger relatives are called by the more informal and intimate 'tu', reinforces the value of respect for older people that is central to this culture, even with the changes of modern life. Culture is pervasive; it is like the water fish swim in and the air we breathe (Beamer and Varner, 2008). We consciously and unconsciously learn cultural rules as we grow up, from sources such as family, friends, teachers, proverbs, adages, and folk-tales. Often we are not able to see their effects on our lives until we encounter different cultural rules or practices.

Culture is dynamic

Culture is subject to change over time; it is not fixed or static. When different cultures are in contact, cultural change may occur. For example, think of how Russian culture has been changing over the past few years – many aspects of its culture have noticeably changed since the collapse of communism in 1991. A new cultural and political order, economic recovery, growth, and increasing openness to Western ideas have led many to see present-day Russia as more 'individualistic' and 'Western'. Credited with facilitating these changes are people like Kseniya Sobchak, who is the daughter of St Petersburg's first democratically elected mayor. She co-hosts a popular reality TV show, designs fashionable clothes, promotes expensive perfumes, and adorns the covers of glossy magazines, bringing Western cultural products into Russia.

As our cultural environment changes, so does our view of cultural practices. The waltz was considered savage during the 1700s. During the 1800s, the tango was viewed as a primitive dance, too sexual to be socially acceptable – in fact, it was banned in Argentina. Today the tango is very popular all over the world, even in places far from its origins, like Finland. Similarly, in the USA, rock 'n' roll was decried as too sexual in the 1950s and the 1960s. Nowadays, the waltz, the tango, and the music and dance associated with rock 'n' roll are accepted as part of our social life.

In recognizing the dynamic nature of culture, we also need to be aware that different elements of culture or different layers of culture may not change at the same speed or at the same time. While technology, transport systems, material objects, and architecture are becoming increasingly similar across different cultures, our beliefs, values, and worldviews – the inner core of culture – can prove more resistant to change. An American may wear the traditional costume of an Indian woman, but her beliefs, values, and worldviews may still differ considerably. We could build a city in Africa similar in appearance to New York, but it would still not be New York.

Culture is ethnocentric

The term 'ethnocentrism' refers to the belief that one's own culture is superior to other cultures (see Chapter 4). Anthropologists generally agree that ethnocentrism is found in every culture (Samovar et al., 2013). Ethnocentrism builds fences between cultures and thus creates barriers for intercultural communication. How we view a culture invariably affects how we interact with people from that culture. When Captain James Cook arrived in Hawaii in 1778, he described their culture as being savage, animal-like, or heathen, comparing (unfavourably) the practices of the Hawaiian people to the European culture of which he was a part.

Today, we know that no culture is superior to any other, but simply that some cultural practices might appear strange or inappropriate to members of other cultures. Australians think it is cruel that Koreans eat dog meat; Koreans feel it is heartless that Australians and other Anglo-Saxons send their elderly parents to nursing homes. Similarly, people in Sweden think Anglo-Saxons are cruel for spanking their children, but many Anglo-Saxons think that corporal punishment is central to bringing up a child properly. Even when cultures are closely related, as the ones in some of these examples are, they can clash about core values – and when they do, members of each culture feel that they are 'right' and the other culture is 'wrong'. Of course, we do not have to accept or practise what is acceptable in other cultures; in intercultural relations it is recognizing and respecting the differences that is more important. Culture is what is distinctive about the way of life of a people, community, nation, or social group. This implies that no culture is inherently superior to any other.

Critical thinking...

How do new technologies influence the preservation of traditional cultural practices? Is it true that as the world becomes more global, our attitudes will become more provincial? What's your view on this?

THEORY CORNER

ETHNOGRAPHY

Classical ethnography refers to a specific research methodology that has been employed to study different cultures and subcultures. According to Gribich (2007: 40), this approach has 'strong links with the anthropological tradition of observation of culture *in situ*'. The purpose of classical ethnography is to describe the whole culture, be it a tribal group or a professional group. Key informants are sought and their voices highlighted. The role of the researcher is that of a 'neutral' reflective observer who documents observational and visual images, and asks questions in both informal conversation and formal interviews. This is done in order to identify, confirm, and cross-check an understanding of the societal structures, social linkages, and behaviour patterns, beliefs, and values of people within the culture. This will usually involve participation for several years in the setting, learning the language, and collecting data. One important characteristic of ethnography is the notion of immersion: the attempt to understand another culture while immersing oneself in it. Many ethnographers today spend a shorter time in the field but use a number of data collection techniques to speed up the process of data collection, including focus groups, face-to-face interviewing, participant observation, and document analysis. Data gathered from ethnographic studies often cast light on our understanding of the life and culture of particular communities.

Reference

Gribich, Carol (2007) *Qualitative Data Analysis: An Introduction*. London: Sage.

Further reading on ethnography

Singer, Jane B. (2009) 'Ethnography', *Journalism & Mass Communication Quaterly*, 86(1): 191–198.

Theory in Practice

RESTAURANT ETHNOGRAPHY

In her book on restaurants, Gatta (2002) combines interviews and several months of participant observation in a variety of restaurant spaces, from fast-food to expensive restaurants. Her goal is to look at the strategies used by servers to negotiate their emotions when confronted with rude and demanding customers, as well as managers and co-workers: 'Customers can be rude to servers, managers can place unachievable demands on workers, cooks can make mistakes when preparing food, and bartenders can spill drinks on customers. Servers can feel a multitude of emotions, such as frustration, anger, hurt, annoyance and joy, all during the same workshift' (p. 5). Thus, Gatta believes that restaurants provide a stage to explore how workers attempted to maintain, lose, and regain emotional balance amid these potentially disturbing situations. She carefully observed and listened to mostly waitresses and their stories. She claims there are different strategies used by servers that can be inward-directed or outward-directed, active or passive. They range from spitting in a customer's food (relatively rare) to withdrawing friendly service, 'blowing off steam' at other employees, stealing food or alcohol from their restaurants, re-engaging in routines that allow one to forget a particular incident, or engaging in various stress-management techniques outside work, such as excessive drinking and yoga. From her ethnography research in restaurants, she provides a sense of the daily culture of servers, their coping strategies, and the ways that they create a sense of community in response to the challenges posed by the job.

Questions to take you further

How likely is it that researchers bring their own cultural values, beliefs, and biases to their research in new cultures? How should ethnographic researchers address such researcher bias when interpreting data they have collected by 'living with' the people with whom they do their research?

References

Gatta, Mary L. (2002) *Juggling Food and Feelings*. Lanham, MD: Lexington Books.

Further reading on ethnography

Richardson, Laurel (2000) 'Evaluating ethnography', *Qualitative Inquiry*, 6(2): 253–255.

SUBCULTURES

Within any dominant culture, there are microcultures, often referred to as *subcultures*. Some scholars call subcultures co-cultures. Subcultures can be categorized by a number of indicators, including gender, ethnicity, religion, profession, social class, organization, and geographic region. In this section, we introduce four types of subculture defined by ethnicity, social class, organization, and geographic region. Subculture gives its members identity. Members of a subculture group can mark their identity through dress code, hairstyle, rituals, and language.

Ethnic culture

Ethnicity is frequently the basis of a subculture within a larger national culture. *Ethnic groups* are identifiable bodies of people who have a common heritage and cultural tradition passed on through generations. Examples include Chinese Australians, Mexican Americans, Vietnamese Italians, and Greek New Zealanders. Ethnic identity refers to identification with a group with shared heritage and culture. Some people use this term and the term 'racial ethnic groups' interchangeably; others differentiate the two terms by specifying that racial groups emphasize genetically transmitted traits of physical appearance (Dodd, 1998). Examples of racial groups are Asian, European, Anglo-Celtic, and Aboriginal Australians. It is important to note that racial group boundaries are very fluid and blurred, and very few people today (if any) belong to only one racial group. Therefore, many people resist the use of the term 'race' altogether, preferring a term like 'ethnic [or cultural] group'.

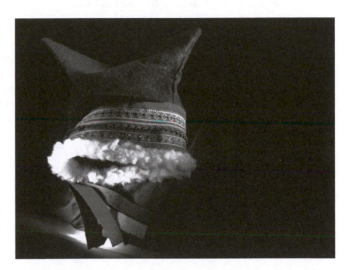

Photo 3.3   The traditional hat of the Sami people – an indigenous group of the Fennoscandian area, more or less disconnected from the European civilization.
Copyright © Jaka Polutnik. Used with permission.

Ethnic groups in the host country are often referred to as minority groups, even though they may be the numerical majority. Vietnam, for example, is a multi-ethnic country with over 50 distinct ethnic groups (54 are recognized by the Vietnamese government), each with its own language, lifestyle, and cultural heritage. They are all considered as ethnic minority groups, in contrast to the mainstream cultural group. They observe their ethnic cultural traditions and celebrate their own ethnic cultural festivals. An example of the complexity of belonging to ethnic groups comes from Latin America. There is a notion 'Latina/o', which is a grassroots, pan-ethnic identity label used by scholars and some grassroots activists to describe people from a variety of ethnic and linguistic backgrounds but who are of Mexican, Latin American, and Spanish Caribbean descent and living in the United States. 'Chicana/o' is a political grassroots identity label used to describe people of Mexican descent, and is most widely used in California. People of Mexican descent living in the south-west USA often prefer the label 'Hispanic'. However, as studies by the Pew Hispanic Foundation demonstrate, most people of Mexican, Latin American, and Spanish Caribbean descent prefer to identify by specific nationality rather than by pan-ethnic labels (Mayer, 2003).

More than just describing a group's population status in relation to the mainstream group, the term 'minority' is sometimes associated with disadvantage and lower social status. The Sami people in

Scandinavia, for example, have long been an economically and socially disadvantaged indigenous minority in the relatively (but not completely) homogeneous cultures of Sweden, Norway, and Finland. Communication between people from an ethnic minority and those from the ethnic majority can be problematic, due to language and cultural barriers as well as negative stereotypes (see Chapter 4). For example, it is reported that recently arrived immigrants in Portugal, mostly from former colonies in Africa and Asia, are residentially segregated in neighbourhoods with poor housing, and they experience cultural barriers and other difficulties.

Social – class culture

Socioeconomic status (SES) can be the basis for a subculture (Brislin, 1988). SES can be derived from a person's income, education, occupation, residential area, and family background. For example, your income can determine where you are most likely to reside, the type of occupation you have and the position you hold, the brand of clothes you wear, the kind of people you tend to associate with, whom you marry, or which school your children attend. The Indian caste system is an example of a hierarchically ordered social class ranking. Class ranking predicts attitudes and communication between different castes within the larger Indian culture. Similarly, previous research in Western countries has found differences between middle-class and working-class parents in regard to the values placed on raising their children (e.g., Gilbert, 2003). Jandt (2007) argues that working-class parents' emphasis on obedience can transfer to their children as obedience to authority, acceptance of what other people think, and hesitancy in expressing desires to authority figures outside the home. Research also reveals differences between people of different SES with regard to friendship, prestige, and trust. For instance, prestige and achievement may be more valuable to middle-class members, whereas working-class people may be less trusting of authority used by more powerful people (Daniel, 1976).

Organizational culture

Subcultures also include *organizational cultures*. Each organization has its ways of doing things and its ways of communicating, which together constitute its organizational culture (Pacanowsky and O'Donnell-Trujillo, 1983). Employees hold beliefs, values, and assumptions to organize their behaviour and interpret their experience. Through communication, these beliefs and values develop into organizationally-based understanding and shared interpretations of organizational reality. These expectations and meanings form the framework of organizational culture. The IBM Corporation, for example, has a distinctive organizational culture, in which male employees are expected to wear dark blue suits, white shirts, and conservative neckties. The dress code reflects unity and conformity to IBM's management style. On the other hand, innovativeness is an espoused value of the 3M Corporation. Employees who put forward suggestions become heroes for demonstrating the spirit of innovation. In Japanese companies, employee loyalty is highly valued, whereas opportunities for career advancement may be seen as more important in Western organizations. In some organizations, subordinates can address people in management by their first name; in other organizations, employees of lower rank must address senior-level managers by their last name and their title. Even subsidiaries of the same company (e.g., IBM) operating in different countries may report value differences (Hofstede, 1980). Members of each organization share knowledge of appropriate behaviours and use this knowledge to guide their activities at work. Organizational cultures give members a sense of identity.

Regional culture

Geographic region is also a basis for categorizing people into different cultural groups. Regional differences often imply differences in social attitudes, lifestyle, food preferences, and communication. People from rural areas are different from people in urban areas. The Dutch distinguish between two major cultural urban–rural subdivisions in their nation. The most important distinction is between the Randstad (Rim City) and non-Randstad cultures. Randstad culture is distinctively urban, located in the provinces of North Holland, South Holland, and Utrecht. The non-Randstad culture follows the historical divide between the predominantly Protestant north and the Catholic south. Interpersonal relationships may seem tighter in rural communities than in urban regions, partly due to apartment living and busy lifestyles in urban environments.

Language or regional dialects are also markers of regional cultures. For example, the Swedish language has been standardized for more than a century, but regional variations in pronunciation between urban areas and rural ones persist. Similarly, the Japanese language spoken in Okinawa, for example, differs from the Japanese spoken in Tokyo, and Mandarin spoken in Beijing is different from Mandarin spoken in Shanghai. Likewise, the American English spoken in Virginia is different from that spoken in Ohio (much less the English spoken in London, Sydney, or Singapore). In addition, climate contributes to regional differences, separating people into different groups. For example, in southern China, where the climate is warm all year round, farmers plant and harvest rice three times a year; in northern China, however, farmers can only plant and harvest rice once a year, because of the long and cold winter. As a result, southerners tend to view northerners as 'lazy', and northerners consider southerners as too money-minded because they seem to devote all their time to making money. Of course, with the development of technology, these attitudes are changing. There are many other jobs (such as working in village food-processing factories) that now keep farmers in the northern part of China as busy throughout the winter as their southern counterparts.

SUMMARY

- It is difficult to have a concrete definition of culture because the characteristics used to denote cultural differences are not universally applicable.

- There are different definitions of culture, and subcultures can be defined by ethnicity, social class, organization, and geographic region. Identification with a cultural group gives us a sense of identity.

- Culture in this book is defined as a particular way of life of a group of people, comprising the sum of knowledge, experience, beliefs, values, traditions, religion, concepts of time, roles, spatial relations, worldviews, material objects, and geographic territory.

- Cultural identity is a process; it is never complete; it is always in flux, contextual, and subject to transformations. Understanding the term 'culture' helps us to value our own cultural identity as well as appreciate that of culturally different others.

- Although there are many reasons why we identify cultures and cultural groups, one purpose of such identification is to indicate that groups of people are different from each other. In this way, we recognize differences and value diversity.

- We can achieve greater knowledge and awareness of the issues of cultural expression, creativity, and art through interdisciplinary thinking about culture. Both emic and etic approaches help us to study cultures from within and from outside the system.

JOIN THE DEBATE

Are we what we eat?

It is often said 'we are what we eat'. Food, cooking, and eating habits constitute an integral part of every culture. The consumption of food is more than a purely biological activity: is always imbued with meaning. Food choices, eating habits, and cooking are expressions of culture and cultural identity. Food is also an important part of religion, separating one creed from another by means of dietary taboos. The techniques utilized to prepare food and the ways of consuming it have an important influence on social and familial relationships. Fast-food like KFC (Kentucky Fried Chicken), for example, does not encourage people to spend the whole evening with friends or family members over a meal either at home or at a restaurant, which is a favourite social activity for continental Europeans. On the other hand, eating quickly is popular in the USA, which places a high value on saving time and getting things done. Thus, people who eat different foods, or eat the same foods in different ways, are often thought to be different. With the increasing variety of cuisines from different cultures readily available, and with our gradual acquisition of culturally diverse foods, will we gradually assimilate different cultures, cultural values, and cultural identity? What will be the impact on our original cultures? Will we become increasingly similar as we eat more similar foods in similar ways?

CASE STUDY

Mobile banking in rural Papua New Guinea

Papua New Guinea (PNG) is located in the southwestern Pacific Ocean, in a region described since the early nineteenth century as Melanesia. The capital is Port Moresby. The country occupies the eastern half of the island of New Guinea, just north of Australia, and many outlying islands, with a total territory of 463,000 square kilometres. Papua New Guinea has a population of approximately 6.7 million. Most of the people are Melanesian, but some are Micronesian or Polynesian. There are over 800 known languages in the country. English, Tok Pisin (Pidgin), and Hiri Motu (the lingua franca of the Papuan region) are the official languages. Lifestyles there range from traditional village-based life, dependent on subsistence and small cash-crop agriculture, to modern urban life in the main cities of Port Moresby, Lae, Madang, Wewak, Goroka, Mt Hagen, and Rabaul. Some 85 per cent of the population directly derives their livelihood from farming, and only 15 per cent of the population lives in urban areas.

Papua New Guinea has a dual economy comprising a formal, corporate-based sector and a large informal sector where subsistence farming accounts for the majority of economic activities. The formal sector provides a narrow employment base, consisting of workers engaged in mineral production, a relatively small manufacturing sector, public sector employees, and service industries including finance, construction, transportation, and utilities. The majority of the population is engaged in the informal sector, which relies on farming. Today, information and communication technologies (ICTs) are rapidly changing the life of the people working in the informal sector (farmers) and the culture of the rural communities. Smart phones, tablets, and social networking sites such as Twitter and Facebook as well as the convergence of print, online, and broadcast media have all significantly altered how and when the farmers communicate to each other.

The past few years have seen an influx of mobile phone technology spreading across the developing world. This widespread and affordable access to mobile phone technology has enabled rural communities in the area to 'leap-frog' (or jump over) traditional tools like landlines to more modern technologies such as mobile phones. Some scholars argue that this 'leap-frogging' can also stimulate economic growth in poorer regions (Mansell, 2002). Others are concerned that mobile phone ownership might become more important than some essential needs, with significant portions of income being spent on technologies instead of on education or healthcare services (Heeks, 2010). Nevertheless, the benefits of using mobile phones have been widely discussed, and as a cultural manifestation, new technologies are changing the way people relate to one another.

Communication technologies have brought about cultural transformation in rural PNG. Local

Photo 3.4   Mobile banking in a Papua New Guinea rural community, as a result of the introduction of new communication technologies. Copyright © Laura Simpson Reeves. Used with permission.

and regional communities are finding new and innovative ways to utilize this technology. In addition to being able to transfer mobile phone credit and purchase pre-paid electricity credits, the widespread ownership of mobile phones and the abundance of mobile phone towers have led to the introduction of SMS-based mobile banking systems to PNG. First trialled in late 2011, the Bank South Pacific (BSP) has teamed up with mobile provider Digicel to develop new financial services that can be securely and efficiently conducted through a mobile phone. The mobile banking service is particularly targeted towards the rural community, which was traditionally made up of 'unbanked' members of the population. It is estimated that between 85 per cent and 90 per cent of the population of PNG had little or no access to banking services (Komon, 2013).

Many farmers sell their produce, such as cocoa or copra (coconut meat), in bulk to local buyers, who pay the farmers in cash. The farmers then may need to travel several hours with the cash either to home or the nearest bank, often via remote roads, which creates ample opportunities for theft and armed robbery. With this technology, the farmers can be paid via electronic funds transfer, available to anyone with a mobile phone number. New accounts can be set up instantly using applications on portable tablets and other similar devices. Customers can then use their mobile phones to view their current balance or to transfer funds to anyone with a Digicel mobile. Most importantly, the phones do not need to be internet-enabled – customers simply need to dial a special number and follow the prompts. If cash is needed, it can be withdrawn via local bank branches or ATMs, or through a local shop that operates as an agent for the bank. This means that the farmers can not only receive their payments securely and safely, but also save a great deal of time as they no longer need to travel to the major centres to deposit or withdraw cash. For rural farmers, mobile banking creates opportunities for safer transactions.

In addition to creating a safer environment for business transactions, mobile banking is also changing a previously unrealized savings culture. This new savings culture in a previously cash-only environment will promote responsible spending and long-term planning, particularly for children and within family settings. This savings culture can also create opportunities for farmers or other members of the local community to apply for small bank loans. These can be used to expand their produce or help fund new cooperative development projects. While there are some ongoing fees linked to transaction accounts, savings accounts are free to set up, free of monthly charges, and free to deposit into, meaning that the service is accessible to any user with an active mobile phone number. Similar schemes are being introduced across the Pacific region by international banking groups such as Westpac and ANZ. It is hoped that greater wealth creation and poverty reduction can be achieved by expanding access to new technologies.

References

Heeks, Richard (2010) 'Do information and communication technologies (ICTs) contribute to development?', *Journal of International Development*, 22: 625–640.

Komon, Peter (2013) 'BSP's Rural Banking Opens Up Market Access' [online]. Accessed 6 October 2013 at: www.businessadvantagepng.com/banks-take-high-tech-approach-for-remote-customers.

Mansell, Robin (2002) 'From digital divides to digital entitlements in knowledge societies', *Current Sociology*, 50(3): 407–426.

Questions for discussion

1. How has the introduction of mobile banking changed the culture of rural communities in Papua New Guinea? Do you think similar systems can be introduced in other developing regions?

2. Why do you think the financial services are being targeted towards the rural population? What are the 'costs' and 'rewards' of introducing new technologies in rural regions?

3. In what ways do you think fostering a savings culture will affect how farmers in PNG relate to one another and what possible changes might this savings culture bring to the economy of the country?

4. What can you learn about the characteristics of culture from this case study?

5. What might be some of the challenges that the farmers in rural PNG will face when new communication technologies become manifestations of their island culture?

FURTHER READINGS

All articles listed next to the mouse icon below can be accessed for free on the book's companion website: https://study.sagepub.com/liu2e

Cultural customs and practices

Broom, Alex, Phillip Good, Emma Kirby and Zarnie Lwin (2013) 'Negotiating palliative care in the context of culturally and linguistically diverse patients', *Internal Medicine Journal*, 43(9): 1043–1046.

There is an increasing emphasis on meeting the healthcare needs of culturally and linguistically diverse (CALD) communities in Australia. This paper outlines some of the key challenges currently facing many clinicians in the context of CALD patients, with particular reference to the transitioning of patients to specialist palliative care. Negotiating the point of futility and the transition to specialist palliative care requires not only effective communication, but also sensitivity to cultural and linguistic specificities. The paper suggests a focus on further research that can systematically document and model existing CALD-specific clinical processes and pathways, which can then support the development of targeted educational interventions. This includes developing a multi-stakeholder understanding of the CALD experience that moves beyond cultural stereotyping and predicting need.

 Merolla, Andy J., Shuangyue Zhang and Shaojing Sun (2013) 'Forgiveness in the United States and China: antecedents, consequences, and communication style comparisons', *Communication Research*, 40(5): 595–622.

This study examined forgiveness communication in American and Chinese people to better understand how culture influences the interpersonal forgiveness process. Four key forgiveness antecedents – social harmony, empathy, apology, and blame – were examined as predictors of forgiveness communication. Social harmony, counter to predictions, positively predicted direct rather than indirect forgiveness in Chinese relationships. Empathy, expected to be a robust predictor of forgiveness communication across cultures, was not a good predictor in either. The research found that instead, the best predictors of forgiveness communication were offender apology and, to a lesser extent, blame. In both cultures, apology positively predicted direct and conditional forgiveness and negatively predicted non-expression, while blame positively predicted conditional forgiveness. These findings suggest that direct forgiveness is an important component of relationship repair in individualistic and collectivistic contexts.

Culture and globalization

Johnson, Michelle (2013) 'Culture's calling: mobile phones, gender, and the making of an African migrant village in Lisbon', *Anthropological Quarterly*, 86(1): 163–190.

This paper explores how immigrants from the West African nation of Guinea-Bissau living in Portugal use mobile phones in their daily lives in Lisbon. The ethnographic fieldwork conducted in Lisbon from 1999 to 2003 shows that mobile phones, as imagined and used by the Guinean immigrants, revealed less about transnationalism and globalization than they did about constructing community and identity in a new locale. As Guinean immigrants in Portugal reconfigured their relationship to their former colonizers and struggled to make their way in a new, multicultural Europe, they used their mobile phones to engage local networks, shape local identities, and transform Lisbon's sprawl into an African migrant village. The study also shows variations in Guinean men and women in relation to their uses of mobile phones in Lisbon.

Ossman, Susan (2013) *Moving Matters: Paths of Serial Cultural Migration.* Stanford, CA: Stanford University Press.

This book is a rich portrait of a culture of serial migrants: people who have lived in several countries, calling each one at some point 'home'. The stories told here are both extraordinary and increasingly common. Serial migrants rarely travel freely – they must negotiate a world of territorial borders and legal restrictions – yet as they move from one country to another, they can use border-crossings as moments of self-clarification, and they create their own culture. They often become masters of settlement as they turn each country into a life chapter. Ossman follows this diverse and growing population not only to understand how they produce certain cultures, but also to illuminate an ongoing tension between global fluidity and the power of nation-states.

Subcultures

Peck, Janice (2009) *The Age of Oprah: Cultural Icon for the Neoliberal Era*. Boulder, CO: Paradigm.

Over the last two decades Oprah Winfrey's journey has taken her from talk show queen to one of the most important figures in popular culture. Through her talk show, magazine, website, seminars, charity work, and public appearances, her influence in the social, economic, and political arenas is considerable and, until now, largely unexamined. In her book, Janice Peck traces Winfrey's growing cultural impact and illustrates the fascinating parallels between her road to fame and fortune and the political-economic rise of neoliberalism. While seeking to understand Oprah's culture, Peck's book provides a fascinating window into the intersection of global politics and culture over the past quarter-century.

> *However, no two people see the external world in exactly the same way. To every separate person, a thing is what he thinks it is – in other words, not a thing, but a think.*

Penelope Fitzgerald, British author, 1916–2000

4

THE INFLUENCE OF CULTURE ON PERCEPTION

LEARNING OBJECTIVES

At the end of this chapter, you should be able to:

- Define perception and identify three stages of the perception process.

- Analyse the influence of culture on our perception.

- Explain the ways in which ethnocentrism, stereotypes, prejudice, and racism can affect intercultural communication.

INTRODUCTION

We receive information about the world around us through our sense of sight, sound, smell, taste, and touch. These stimuli are selected, organized, and interpreted, and from them we create a meaningful picture of our world. Much like a computer, the human mind processes information in a sequence of stages akin to data entry or storage and retrieval, with each stage involving a specific operation on incoming information. The first stage of information processing is that of *perception*, which refers to how we see or sense things around us. Human perception is an active process, in which we use our sensory organs to selectively identify the existence of stimuli and then subject them to evaluation and interpretation. Since the way we behave is influenced by how we perceive the world around us, perception is the very basis of how we communicate with others. The information we select from the stimuli available in our environment is affected by our personal experiences, our psychological states, our values, and our culture, among many other factors (Cooper et al., 2007). Based on those perceptions, we make judgements of others and adapt our communication accordingly.

According to psychologist Blaine Goss (1995), the information we manage every day has two origins: external and internal. People, events, and objects are sources of *external* information, while knowledge, past experiences, and feelings make up our *internal* world of information. Successful information processing depends on the merging of external and internal information. In other words, how people enter, store, and retrieve information is a combination of what they are experiencing (external) with what they know and feel (internal). We form images of our world based on this assimilation of internal and external information (Boulding, 1956). Once formed, images become filters that we use to guide further interpretation of the external world. We bring with us a perceptual frame of reference through which all of our messages are filtered every time we enter into a communicative exchange. Although information processing is a universal phenomenon, it is nevertheless influenced by culture. It follows, therefore, that if culturally different people vary in their interpretation of reality, communication problems may occur. For example, the French people consider snails as delicacies, whereas a Samoan might baulk at eating this food.

Similarly, while two Americans engaged in face-to-face communication expect direct eye contact as an indication of engagement and interest in the conversation, in South Korea it is considered polite to cast one's eyes downwards during some communication situations (such as when a student is speaking to a teacher). The handshake is considered common business protocol in many countries, but while a firm handshake is acceptable in Australia, a gentle handshake is preferred in the Middle East. Violating expectations of culturally determined behavioural rules potentially impairs further communication. Consequently, it is important for us to understand the nature of perception and how it is influenced by cultural experience. This chapter concentrates on the human perception process. Firstly, we identify the different stages of this process, and then we illustrate how perception is connected to our beliefs, values, worldviews, and attitudes. The formation of stereotypes prejudice, racism, and their relationship to perception is explained and a discussion of how stereotypes and prejudice can affect intercultural communication concludes the chapter.

Photo 4.1   Chinese BBQ shop in Chinatown, Brisbane, Australia.
Copyright © Shuang Liu. Used with permission.

STAGES OF THE PERCEPTION PROCESS

The perception process consists of three stages: selection, categorization, and interpretation.

The selection stage

The first stage in the process is selection, in which information is received via the senses, attended to, and interpreted by the brain (Jandt, 2007). Selection plays a major part in the larger process of converting environmental stimuli into meaningful experience. We are bombarded with an enormous array of stimuli as part of our everyday lives, but we are limited in the number of stimuli we can meaningfully process. This is where the selection process helps us to discern those stimuli which are immediately or potentially useful to us. For example, if you intend to buy a new car, you are more inclined to pay attention to the 'motor vehicles' section of your daily newspaper before you make the decision to purchase a car.

Scholars argue that we do not consciously 'see' an object unless we are paying direct, focused attention to that object, engaging in what is known as selective perception. *Selective perception* involves three steps: selective exposure, selective attention, and selective retention (Klopf, 1995). We *selectively expose* ourselves to certain kinds of information from our environment, *pay attention* to a subset of elements of this information that is immediately relevant to us, and *selectively retain* for later recall that part of the information that is likely to be used in the future and is consistent with our beliefs, attitudes, and values. For example, if the budget for your new car is $6,000, as you read the 'vehicles for sale' section of the newspaper you will disregard vehicles priced above your limit and remember the cheaper ones. Likewise, a dieter is more inclined to attend to and remember ingredients and nutritional values on food labels than someone who is not concerned about their weight. A different example is that a mortgage holder pays more attention to the activity of interest rates as reported on TV than someone who is not paying off a home loan.

Perception, including selective exposure, attention, and retention, is influenced by culture. As a result, differences in perception can lead to misunderstandings during interactions, especially when those involved are from different cultural backgrounds (Chen and Starosta, 2005). Goss (1995) identified three common perceptual tendencies, all influenced by culture: closure, familiarity, and expectations.

Closure refers to humans' tendency to see things as complete wholes instead of incomplete configurations. Based on a tiny amount of data, people often make inferences about an incomplete figure, thought, idea, or sentence. Figure 4.1 illustrates this point – while the triangle and circle are presented as partial forms, most people tend to see a full triangle and a full circle.

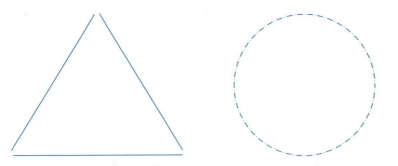

Figure 4.1   Incomplete triangle and circle

Familiarity suggests that people use their existing knowledge to identify what they see. We are more inclined to recognize the familiar than the unfamiliar aspects of things. When presented with Figure 4.2, it is likely that people will see two overlapping squares rather than three irregular shapes, the reason being that we are more familiar with the former, and tend to look for the familiar rather than the unusual.

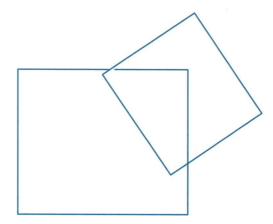

Figure 4.2   Three irregular shapes or two squares?

Expectation can be illustrated in the old adage that we see what we want to see and hear what we want to hear. This saying is particularly relevant to the process of perception. Perception involves expectations; the more frequently we see something, the more inclined we are to form a 'fixed' image of that thing in our mind which informs our future expectations of it. For example, we expect roses to be red, older people to have white hair, and workers in childcare centres to be female. Over time, these 'fixed' images become habits and make different perceptions difficult. This is demonstrated in Figure 4.3. The saying is well known, so you might not immediately detect the duplication of the word 'one', but instead read it according to your expectation of what it should be.

Rome was
not built in
one
one day.

Figure 4.3   Did you notice the grammar error at first sight?

The notions of closure, familiarity, and expectation illustrate that perception is both a product and process. As a process, it is a way of forming recognizable objects, thoughts, ideas, and categories of people. As a product, perception represents what we see and experience and is stored in the memory to be retrieved and utilized when we need it.

Critical thinking...

If an Australian business person met with a person from the Middle East in a business setting and gave a good old-fashioned firm handshake, but the one returned was limp, how might this affect how they view each other?

The categorization stage

Humans are surrounded by such an enormous amount of information or stimuli from our environment that it is impossible to process it all at once. To function within this environment, and select and manage the relevant information from it, we employ mental economy strategies (Neuliep, 2012). *Categorization* is one such strategy, defined as the process of ordering the environment by grouping persons, objects, and events on the basis of their being perceived as sharing similar features or characteristics (Tajfel, 1978). Categories are useful because they help the information processor to reduce uncertainty and increase the accuracy of predictions. Most cognitive psychologists argue that all people, regardless of culture, engage in categorization. Categories assist us in making attributions about the behaviour of others and help us to recall and recognize information. For example, we categorize people based on skin or hair colour, dress, race, sex, language, occupation, interests, geographic location, or desirable/undesirable qualities. Once people are categorized, other associated collective traits and intentions are also attributed to them. The fact that membership categories are associated with specific features and activities provides people with a powerful resource for making sense of their social world, allowing them to make discursive connections to the category membership of the actors (Tajfel and Forgas, 1981). Once assigned, therefore, membership in a category comes to imply much more than the original traits on which categorization was based in the first place.

THEORY CORNER

ATTRIBUTION THEORY

Attribution theory was initially developed by Fritz Heider in 1958 and has been modified since that time by Edward Jones, Keith Davis, and Harold Kelley, all of whom are social psychologists. The theory assumes that a person seeking to understand why another person acted in a certain way may attribute one or more causes to the behaviour in question. According to Heider (1958), a person can make two attributions: internal or external. Internal attribution refers to the inference that a person is behaving in a certain way because of something about that person, such as attitude, beliefs, or personality. External attribution instead ascribes situational causes to a person's behaviour. Attributions, whether internal or external, are significantly driven by emotional and motivational factors. While we commonly attribute our own success and others' failures to internal factors, we tend to attribute our own failures and other people's success to external ones. For example, a student who failed a test may blame the instructor for not providing a clear explanation of the material. This externalization of cause diminishes the responsibility of the student. Attribution theory is relevant to the study of human perception. It has been applied in a wide range of areas, including psychology, management, criminal law, marketing, education, decision making, and ethics.

Reference

Heider, Fritz (1958) *The Psychology of Interpersonal Relations*. New York: Wiley.

Further reading on attribution theory

Jaspars, Jos and Miles Hewstone (1982) 'Cross-culture interaction, social attribution, and intergroup relations', in S. Bochner (ed.), *Cultures in Contact*. Elmsford, NY: Pergamon. pp. 127–156.

Theory in Practice

ATTRIBUTION, EMOTION, AND IDENTITY

Identity can be an important factor shaping the types of attribution judgements and emotions of individuals. The deadly shooting incident on the Virginia Tech University campus in April 2007 killed 32 people and injured 17. The perpetrator was identified as a Korean who migrated to the USA at a very young age. Park and colleagues (2013) compared non-Korean Americans, Korean Americans, Koreans in the USA, and Koreans in Korea in terms of their attributions and emotions concerning the shooting incident. Participants were asked to rate the extent to which they attributed the cause of the incident to American society or the perpetrator, their emotions (e.g., sad, upset), and how they categorized the perpetrator (e.g., American or Korean). Findings showed that people residing in the USA had more negative emotions than Koreans in Korea, regardless of their ethnic heritage. However, how they categorized the perpetrator affected their attributions of the causes of the incident. Americans who viewed the perpetrator as a Korean were more likely to hold the perpetrator responsible, while Koreans who viewed him as an American were more likely to attribute the cause of the incident to American society. Results also showed that categorizing the perpetrator as being a Korean American was the relevant dimension for feeling unhappy, sad, and bad. This study concluded that not only attribution of the cause, but also emotions regarding the incident, can differ depending on individuals' self-categorization and categorization of the perpetrator.

Questions to take you further

As individuals have the tendency to see themselves in more positive terms, they generally make external attributions for negative behaviours of members of their own groups. What strategies may the Korean Americans, in the case above, adopt to distance themselves from the perpetrator?

Reference

Park, Hee S., Doshik Yun, Hye Choi et al. (2013) 'Social identity, attribution, and emotion: comparisons of Americans, Korean Americans, and Koreans', *International Journal of Psychology*, 48(5): 922–934.

Further reading on attribution

Eberly, Marion B. and Christina T. Fong (2013) 'Leading via the heart and mind: the roles of leader and follower emotions, attributions and interdependence', *Leadership Quarterly*, 24(5): 696–711.

People categorize for a variety of reasons – to reduce uncertainty, maintain self-esteem, and draw distinctions between ingroups (the groups to which we belong) and outgroups (the groups to which we do not belong). Research on intergroup relations indicates that, once established, categories have a biasing and filtering effect on perceptions, so that the mere categorization of persons into groups is sufficient to foster bias (Tajfel, 1978). According to social psychologist Henri Tajfel, this leads us to the perception that *we* (the ingroup) are who we are because *they* (the outgroup) are *not* what we are. Most people tend to think in terms of ingroup and outgroup membership when it comes to categorizing people (Neuliep, 2012). In doing so, people also have a tendency to create categories that maximize the advantages of the ingroup. Richard Brislin (1981) claims that we are socialized to believe in the superiority of our ingroups. People also tend to label members of competing outgroups with undesirable attributes, while labelling ingroups with desirable qualities. On the positive side, categorization helps to give incoming information structure and reduces uncertainty in our environment. However, in categorizing people, we can end up overlooking individual elements and overgeneralizing from group membership.

Critical thinking...

Make a list of the groups you belong to. Select one group that you think is most important to you. How does membership in this group affect how you view yourself and those who are not in your group?

The interpretation stage

Interpretation is the attachment of meaning to data obtained through the sensory organs. It is synonymous with decoding. According to Goss (1995), people filter information physiologically (e.g., hearing, eyesight, touch), sociologically (e.g., demographics, group membership), and psychologically (e.g., attitudes, beliefs, and dispositions). We have already examined how perception combines the internal states of the person with external stimuli from the environment. When interpreting, we tend to rely on familiar contexts and compare new stimuli with them in order to look for clues. The more ambiguous the stimuli, the more room there is for differing interpretations (Pearson and Nelson, 1997). As a result, the same situation can be interpreted differently by different people. For example, eating with one's hands is regarded as normal behaviour in India, but may be interpreted as bad table manners in some Western cultures. Figure 4.4 contains a set of images that a psychologist might ask you to interpret. There are no right or wrong answers, but different people interpret them differently depending on their past experiences and their familiarity with the context in which each image is situated.

Further online reading The following article can be accessed for free on the book's companion website https://study.sagepub.com/liu2e: Peng, Kaiping and Eric Knowles (2003) 'Culture, ethnicity and the attribution of physical causality', *Personality and Social Psychology Bulletin*, 29: 1272–1284.

As we have seen, perception is the process by which an individual converts physical stimuli from the environment into meaning based on internal experiences. From Figure 4.4, we learn that while the physical mechanism of perception is much the same in all people – sensory organs such as the eyes, ears, and nose permit us to sense and interpret our environment – assigning meaning is not the same for all people. This is a learned process and therefore subject to cultural influences (Samovar et al., 2013).

While perception is an internal process, it is the external forces of culture that primarily determine the meanings we apply to the stimuli that reach us. For example, American mothers may interpret assertiveness in their children's speech as positive, whereas Korean mothers who observe the same behaviour in

What can you see in the pictures below?

A.

B.

C.

D.

Figure 4.4   Optical illusions

their children might consider their children disrespectful and lacking in discipline. Similarly, the Dutch regard an outspoken person as credible, while Japanese tend to consider constant talking as a sign of shallowness. In Australia, people tend to respond positively to a direct approach to resolving an interpersonal conflict, yet this same behaviour is frowned upon in most Asian cultures. The issue of interpretation becomes more complex when we factor in further variables, such as age, gender, social status, and the relationship between communicators. Misinterpretation of the information perceived has the potential to impede intercultural interactions. The influence of culture on perception and intercultural communication, therefore, cannot be overstated.

Critical thinking...

When we say 'people see the world differently', does it mean that people differ in how they physiologically experience the world or in how they interpret what they experience?

THE INFLUENCE OF CULTURE ON PERCEPTION

People behave as they do because of the ways in which they perceive the world. One learns these perceptions and behaviours as part of cultural experience. The influence of culture on human perception has long been studied by social scientists (Segall, 1979), who have explored the notion that perception is partial because we can never completely know everything about the world surrounding us. As Marshall Singer (1987: 9) notes: 'We experience everything in the world not as it is – but only as the world comes to us through our sensory receptors.' The way we respond to the external world is primarily the result of how our cultural filters influence what we see, hear, smell, feel, and taste. Consistent findings from studies in this area suggest that people's ability to select incoming information, categorize, and interpret it differs across cultures. In short, the world looks, sounds, tastes, and feels the way it does because our culture has given us the criteria to apply to perceiving it. The basic process of perception is the same for all humans, but the content differs because of variations in beliefs, values, and worldviews as well as individual inference habits.

Cultural beliefs, values, and perception

Belief systems are significant to intercultural communication because they are at the core of our thoughts and actions. Beliefs are learned and consequently subject to cultural bias. In some cultures, people believe the weather is a product of God's will and will pray for a drought or flood to be alleviated. Other cultures believe that humans should conquer nature and make use of cloud-seeding technology to break long-standing droughts. Beliefs are the basis of our values, which are enduring attitudes about a preference for one belief over another. Values possess a normative dimension, specifying what is good or bad, right or wrong, in a particular context. For example, harmony in interpersonal relationships is treasured in most Asian workplaces; on the other hand, interpersonal relationships between Western colleagues are believed to benefit from being upfront and direct. Westerners associate aggressiveness (unless it is very negative) with the value of competition and independence, whereas any aggressiveness is interpreted adversely in an Asian workplace. An understanding of cultural values not only helps us to appreciate the behaviour of other people and know how to treat them with respect, but also helps us to interpret our own behaviour.

Culture and categorization

Studies have found cultural differences in how people categorize objects. Nisbett and Miyamoto (2005) argue that people from Western cultures focus on salient objects and rules when categorizing the environment. By contrast, people in East Asian cultures focus more on relationships and similarities among objects when organizing the environment. For example, a study in which both Chinese and American children were presented with pictures of three objects (e.g., man, woman, and baby) and then asked to pick two objects of the three that went together showed that Chinese children tended to group their two objects on the basis of relational-contextual information (e.g., grouping the woman and the baby together because the mother takes care of the baby). American children, on the other hand, tended to group objects based on shared properties or categories (e.g., grouping a man and woman together because they are both adults).

Most people have a tendency to create categories that maximize the advantages of the ingroup (Neuliep, 2012). Naturally, this has implications for initial intercultural interactions. When meeting someone from another culture for the first time, there may be salient features that can lead us to categorize their entire culture. For example, a British tourist first boarding an MTR (subway) in Hong Kong and hearing a local person chatting loudly on a mobile phone might categorize the entire Hong Kong population as discourteous and inconsiderate of others. While categorization performs a useful function in reducing the amount of incoming information, it also leads us to ignore individual elements, particularly when categorizing people from outgroups. This tendency to see members of outgroups as 'all alike', without recognizing the individual differences that we appreciate in ingroup members, is called the *outgroup homogeneity effect* (Mullen and Hu, 1989); this is one of the important bases of group-based prejudice and discrimination, which are most extreme when groups dehumanize each other during war. On the other hand, categorization can also lead us to minimize differences between members of the ingroup on valued characteristics, but to maximize differences between the ingroup and outgroup on these things. Hence, while allowing the human mind to process information more efficiently, categories are also the basis of pre-judgements, which can lead to stereotyping. However, bias of this nature may be reduced by decreasing distance between ingroups and outgroups. According to Tajfel (1978), when we perceive an outgroup as similar to our group on a valued characteristic, we are more likely to think positively about that group and to engage members in interaction. Perceived similarity reduces uncertainty about intergroup interaction.

THEORY CORNER

IMPLICIT PERSONALITY THEORY

Implicit personality theory describes assumed relationships among personality traits (see Schneider, 1973, for a review of the theory). The theory suggests that we organize our individual perceptions into clusters. Thus, individual personality traits are related to other traits. When we identify an individual trait in someone, we assume the person also possesses other traits in the cluster. There are two traditions associated with implicit personality theory. The first is concerned with the role of general bias in the judgements of others. Various researchers have found that people tend to exaggerate the extent of relationships among personality traits. The tendency to presume that someone who has one good trait is likely to have other good traits is called the halo effect. In attempting to explain these perceived patterns, researchers have examined the biases implicit in language that lead us to think relationships among traits are stronger than the evidence indicates. The second tradition concentrates on individual differences in person perception. For example, people were found to cluster 'intelligent', 'quiet' and 'friendly' together so that, if we view someone as friendly, we also attribute to them the characteristics of quietness and intelligence. Once we have formed a first impression of someone, we tend to look for cues that are consistent and supportive of this impression and ignore those that are inconsistent.

Reference
Schneider, David J. (1973) 'Implicit personality theory: a review', *Psychological Bulletin*, 79(5): 294–309.

Further reading on perception and attribution
Maddux, William W. and Masaki Yuki (2006) 'The "ripple effect": cultural differences in perceptions of the consequences of events', *Personality and Social Psychology Bulletin*, 32: 669–683.

Theory in Practice

EGOCENTRIC PATTERN PROJECTION

People all face the task of forming impressions of others based on incomplete information. In making such inferences, we often rely on implicit personality theories, that is, beliefs about how personality traits tend to be associated within people (e.g., 'submissive' suggests someone who is also 'weak'). Critcher and Dunning (2009) conducted five studies on undergraduate students at Cornell University to examine how people construct their implicit personality theories when forming judgements of other people. Participants were asked to rate themselves and their roommates on a number of personality traits (e.g., aggressive, dominant, passive). They were also asked to estimate the percentage of people in the general population who possessed each trait as well as the conditional probabilities that people would possess a particular trait if they showed evidence of possessing another trait. Their research identified 'egocentric pattern projection'. This term refers to the fact that people use the way traits are configured in the self to form beliefs about how traits are related in other people. Critcher and Dunning's studies revealed that if two traits go together in the self, then they are assumed to go together in other people. Their studies concluded that one important source of a person's implicit personality theories is the self. People's knowledge of themselves can have a profound influence on their beliefs about other people.

Questions to take you further
We can classify people in a number of ways – male, female, southerners, Vietnamese, rugby players. What determines which category will be used? How do we decide how to classify people?

Reference
Critcher, Clayton R. and David Dunning (2009) 'Egocentric pattern projection: how implicit personality theories recapitulate the geography of the self', *Journal of Personality and Social Psychology*, 97(1): 1–16.

Further reading on impression consistency
Ng, Audrey S. and Eddie M. W. Tong (2013) 'The relation between implicit theories of personality and forgiveness', *Personal Relationships*, 20(3): 479–494.

Critical thinking...

Our perceptions can obviously be flawed; even skilled observers can misperceive, misjudge, and reach the wrong conclusions. Once we form wrong impressions, they are likely to persist. How do we form impressions of others? How do we combine the diverse information we receive about someone into a coherent overall impression?

Culture and interpretation

Culture affects the variables that people use to interpret what they perceive. A study in which students from different cultures were asked to write down their perceptions of different colours found surprising and significant differences in the responses, based on culture (Chen and Starosta, 2005). For example, red to Chinese represents splendour and wealth and is a wedding colour. In Western cultures, white is a wedding colour because it is perceived as suggesting purity. A car decorated with white ribbons is likely to be a wedding car in Western cultures, but such decoration in Asian cultures may instead suggest a funeral – white is a colour of mourning.

As well as objects, we also interpret meanings of events, based on our past experience (Cooper et al., 2007). All events occur in a social context which has specific meaning to the group of people involved. For example, the onset of the New Year is celebrated across cultures, but in very different ways. Unlike Western New Year (based on the Roman calendar), Chinese New Year is based on the lunar calendar and usually falls between the end of January and the beginning of February. The celebration lasts 15 days. Celebrations begin on the New Year eve. Specific traditional dishes are served at dinner to signify wishes or blessings for the coming year: fish for prosperity, chicken representing good luck, and *jiaozi* (Chinese dumpling) signifying family reunion. People also put up good-luck papers outside their front door and feed the Kitchen God sweets before he ascends to heaven to report to the Jade Emperor on the family's activities during the previous year (this is a bit similar to the European custom of leaving sweets for St Nicholas at Christmas). It is also common to see parents or grandparents give children 'lucky money' in bright red envelopes, signifying wishes for a smooth and happy new year.

Culture also affects what information people emphasize when interpreting events or behaviour. Listening more and talking less is viewed as showing respect in Japanese culture; in Australia, the same behaviour may be viewed as signifying a lack of confidence. People also try to explain an observed behaviour by attributing it to either personal or situational causes. Whenever we explain someone's behaviour in terms of personality, motivation, or personal preferences, we are using personal attributes. When we explain someone's behaviour in terms of unusual circumstances, social pressure, or physical forces beyond their control, we are using situational attributes. When we make attributions of people's behaviours on the basis of either personality or situational factors, we are prone to biases. In particular, we engage in a self-serving bias – we tend to attribute positive behaviour by ingroup members to internal factors, and their negative behaviour to situational variables. In contrast, we tend to attribute positive behaviour by outgroup members to situational variables, and negative behaviour to personality variables (Jaspars and Hewstone, 1982). For example, a student's failure to pass an exam could be attributed to a lack of intelligence on the part of the student (internal factor) or too much social/family pressure as a cause of under-performance (external factor).

Photo 4.2   Red envelopes with lucky money are customarily given to children by parents or grandparents on Chinese New Year eve to wish them a smooth and happy new year.
Copyright © Shuang Liu. Used with permission.

These differences in interpretations also manifest themselves culturally and can result in misunderstandings. The Chinese are reluctant to say 'no' in business negotiations, especially to foreign business partners, because this may upset harmony. When asked a question to which the answer is 'no', they might instead reply, 'maybe'. Difficulties of this nature have arisen in negotiations between an Australian university and a Chinese government agency over the establishment of an institute to be affiliated with the university. Part of the problem in reaching an agreement is the frustration that the Australian representatives feel with either getting no answer or 'maybe' in response to significant or difficult questions. A Westerner is more likely to assume that a response of 'maybe' suggests possibility, whereas to a Chinese 'maybe' is an indirect way of saying 'no'. To improve the accuracy of our attributions so as to be more effective in intercultural communication, we can use techniques such as perception checking, active listening, and feedback. These techniques can help us to ensure that our interpretation of another's words or actions is what was intended.

PERCEPTION AND INTERCULTURAL COMMUNICATION

Culture plays a key role in influencing what information we select from available external stimuli, how we structure the incoming information, and the meanings we assign to the processed information. As a result, it is possible for our cultural socialization to foster ethnocentrism. Higher levels of ethnocentrism can lead to stereotypes, prejudice, and even racism, all of which are barriers to successful intercultural communication.

Further online reading The following article can be accessed for free on the book's companion website https://study.sagepub.com/liu2e: Maddux, William W. and Masaki Yuki (2006) 'The "ripple effect": cultural differences in perceptions of the consequences of events', *Personality and Social Psychology Bulletin*, 32: 669–683.

Ethnocentrism

Ethnocentrism is the tendency for people to see their own culture (or ingroup) as the point of reference, while seeing other cultures (or outgroups) as insignificant or inferior (Neuliep, 2012). Gudykunst (2004) points out that one's cultural orientation acts as a filter for processing incoming and outgoing verbal and nonverbal messages. To this extent, all intercultural communication events are inescapably charged with some degree of ethnocentrism. At its most benign, ethnocentrism has the capacity to foster ingroup survival, solidarity, conformity, loyalty, and cooperation. Many researchers recognize ethnocentrism as a ubiquitous phenomenon. As Charon (2007: 156) states:

> Groups develop differences from one another, so do formal organizations, communities and societies. Without interaction with outsiders, differences become difficult to understand and difficult not to judge. What is real to us becomes comfortable; what is comfortable becomes right. What we do not understand becomes less than right to us.

Ethnocentrism is a continuum; our position on this continuum determines the distance we create when we communicate with people from other cultures or groups. At the high end of the continuum, there is a larger distance between ingroups and outgroups, along with insensitivity to the other group's feelings and perspective. At the other end of the scale, low ethnocentrism reflects a desire to reduce communicative distance between ourselves and others, and the use of inclusive language (Cooper et al., 2007). A high level of ethnocentrism is dysfunctional in intercultural communication as it creates communicative distance (Gudykunst and Kim, 1984). Highly ethnocentric people tend to engage in self-centred dialogue in which they use their own cultural standards to judge the experience of communicating with others. Ethnocentrism at this level may lead to prejudice, stereotypes, or discrimination, and thus prohibits effective intercultural communication by impairing or preventing understanding. In contrast to ethnocentrism, *cultural relativism* is the degree to which an individual judges another culture by its context (Chen and Starosta, 2005). Taken in isolation, a single element of a culture may seem strange to a non-member, but generally makes sense when considered in light of the other elements of that culture (see Chapter 3). Take the earlier example about eating food with the fingers being more acceptable in India than in Anglo-Saxon culture. When one considers this single cultural element within a broader context (i.e., the Indian belief that God gives people hands so that they may give and eat food), then this Indian behaviour makes sense to Anglo-Saxons. Interpreting a person's behaviour through their own cultural frame of reference enhances the chances of effective communication. It follows, therefore, that to understand another culture we need to communicate with its people and broaden our understanding of its practices and beliefs, thus enhancing our sense of cultural relativism.

Stereotypes

Group-based stereotypes are preconceived beliefs about the characteristics of certain groups based on physical attributes or social status. Stereotypes are overgeneralizations and thus may be wrongly generalized to some members of the group (Hilton and von Hippel, 1996). The term 'stereotype' derives from the Greek word *stereos* meaning 'solid' or 'firm' and *tupos* meaning 'impression' or 'engraved mark'. Thus, in its original sense, 'stereotype' stands for 'solid impression'. In 1798, at the outset of the industrial age, two European printers invented a new way to reproduce images that would fix permanently. This image-setting process was called stereotyping. Walter Lippmann brought the term into modern usage when he applied it in his 1922 book *Public Opinion*, using it to refer to a psychological process of forming intellectual images. The mass media's heavy reliance on stereotypes means that we are probably all familiar with those of the ambitious, outgoing American, the laid-back, beach-loving Australian, or the respectful, technology-loving Japanese, among many others based on such factors as national, ethnic, social, or gender characteristics. The term 'stereotype' is often used with a negative connotation when referring to an oversimplified assumption of the characteristics associated with a group.

Stereotypes can be used to deny individuals respect or legitimacy based on their group membership. A stereotype can be a conventional and preconceived opinion or image based on the belief that there are attitudes, appearances, or behaviours shared by all members of a certain group. They can emerge from an illusory correlation or false association between two variables. For example, since 9/11, Muslim airline passengers, or anyone of Middle Eastern appearance, are more likely to draw the attention of Western airport security than other people. Similarly, since the onset of widespread media coverage of natural and military disasters in some

Photo 4.3 Emirate women, wearing traditional abaya, shop in downtown Dubai.
Copyright © Alison Rae. Used with permission.

African countries, a group of dark-skinned children are more likely to be categorized by Europeans as refugees or children from a poverty-stricken African village. Stereotypes are forms of social consensus rather than individual judgements; while we do not construct them ourselves, in using them, we contribute to the consensus that perpetuates them.

Stereotypes often form the basis of prejudice and are usually employed to explain real or imaginary differences, such as those due to race, gender, religion, ethnicity, social class, occupation, or sexual orientation. Research has shown that stereotypes can have an impact on both the holder and the subject (Steele and Aronson, 1995). For example, non-English-speakers are disadvantaged in English-language social and academic settings because of their accent, and their accent is often believed to signify their incapacity to perform as well as the majority group (Woodrow, 2006). Consequently, ethnic minorities may experience anxiety and performance decrement, and withdraw from communication with people of the host culture (Lesko and Corpus, 2006). Should the person perform poorly in a stereotypical domain (e.g., academic performance), the performance can then be concluded as typical, reinforcing the negative stereotype attached to the particular group (Steele, Spencer and Aronson, 2002). Interestingly, Clark and Kashima (2007) have demonstrated the important role played by narratives in encouraging us to maintain our stereotypes about other groups – we tell and remember stories that emphasize stereotype-consistent traits and behaviour.

Critical thinking...

Write down one stereotype, when and where you learned it, who taught it to you, and how it might have affected your attitude and behaviour. How true is this stereotype? Has it changed over time? If yes, what were the causes of the change? If not, what perpetuated the stereotype?

THEORY CORNER

SELF-FULFILLING PROPHECY

A self-fulfilling prophecy is a statement that causes itself to become true by directly or indirectly altering actions. In Robert Merton's book *Social Theory and Social Structure* (1968), he states that a self-fulfilling prophecy is a false definition of the situation evoking a new behaviour which makes the original false conception 'come true'. In other words, a false prophecy may sufficiently influence people's behaviours so that their reactions ultimately fulfil it. For example, if a professor believes all American students are active participants in the classroom, she might treat them as such by giving them more opportunities to speak in class. Thus, the professor self-fulfils her prophecy by encouraging the students to behave in accordance with it. Self-fulfilling prophecy can also be applied to self-concept. When people are given a label that supposedly describes them, they behave accordingly to the label. Calling someone 'lazy' can increase the chances that the person will act that way. If an Asian student believes that 'Asians are good at maths', she might have less trouble with her statistics course than those who declared deficiency in maths, simply because she is self-confident about the subject.

Reference
Merton, Robert K. (1968) *Social Theory and Social Structure*. New York: The Free Press.

Further reading on self-fulfilling prophecies
Biggs, Michael (2009) 'Self-fulfilling prophecies', in P. Bearman and P. Hedström (eds), *The Oxford Handbook of Analytical Sociology*. Oxford: Oxford University Press. pp. 294–314.

Theory in Practice

MYTHS ABOUT OLDER PEOPLE'S USE OF COMMUNICATION TECHNOLOGY

Information communication technology (ICT) has great potential to improve and enrich the lives of older people. However, there have been widespread myths about older people's use of ICTs. Wandke,

Sengpiel and Sönksen (2012) identified six common myths shared among computer scientists, engineers and programmers, the general public, and even older people themselves. They are:

1. Just wait and see. The problem older people currently have with ICT is only temporary; future generations of older people will possess the knowledge and skills to use ICT without problems.

2. Older people consider computers as useless and unnecessary. They may be aware of ICT but consider it unnecessary for their personal lives.

3. Older people lack the physical capabilities to use ICT. Older people have problems with text fonts, contrast, brightness, and other features.

4. Older people cannot understand interactive computer technology. They lack the knowledge and language required to describe computer functions and objects.

5. You can't teach an old dog new tricks. Older people are unmotivated and not cognitively able to learn new technologies.

While each myth might contain an element of truth, they are overgeneralized, resulting in older people avoiding computer usage; that is, each myth becomes a self-fulfilling prophecy. As myths have a tendency to be self-fulfilling and self-reinforcing, the article argues that we should not wait until myths and barriers disappear by themselves, but take responsibility to design user-friendly programs for all age groups and encourage older people to use ICTs.

Questions to take you further

Computer designers, engineers, programmers, and even older people themselves are convinced that 'You can't teach an old dog new tricks'. However, with humans, new tricks can be learned if the motivation is there. How do we differentiate between ability and motivation? How could we facilitate the learning of ICT use for older people?

Reference

Wandke, Hartmut, Michael Sengpiel and Malte Sönksen (2012) 'Myths about older people's use of information and communication technology', *Gerontology*, 58: 564–570.

Further reading on self-fulfilling prophecy

Olsson, Andreas, Susanna Carmona, Geraldine Downey, Niall Bolger, and Kevin N. Ochsner (2013) 'Learning biases underlying individual differences in sensitivity to social rejection', *Emotion*, 13(4): 616–621.

Prejudice

Prejudice is a negative attitude towards individuals resulting from stereotypes (Cooper et al., 2007). Prejudice constitutes generalized evaluations about a person, object, or action that are the result of individual experience, interpersonal communication, or media influence. Prejudiced people distort evidence to fit their prejudice or simply ignore evidence that is inconsistent with their viewpoint (Allport, 1954). Brislin (1981) suggests that prejudice serves several functions, the first of which is utilitarian: our prejudices may be rewarded economically or socially. For example, prejudice against minority groups might put people from the mainstream culture in a more favourable position when competing in the job market. The second function is ego-defensive: prejudice allows us to avoid admitting certain things about ourselves. For example, if you are unsuccessful in some pursuit, you could blame those who were successful and, in doing so, avoid examining the reasons for your own failure and protect your self-esteem. Prejudice also has a value-expressive function, in that it allows people to highlight the aspects of life they value, such as affiliation with a particular social group. Prejudice performs a knowledge function too. This fourth function allows us to organize and structure our world in ways that make sense to us and are relatively convenient. Thus, it is a learned tendency to respond to a given group of people in a certain way. When we are prejudiced against a group, this can manifest in biased actions such as discrimination.

Brislin (1981) further categorized prejudice according to the intensity of action or response: verbal abuse, physical avoidance, discrimination, physical attack, and massacre. The first of these five forms of prejudice, verbal abuse, is often accompanied by labelling. For example, verbal abuse motivated by racial prejudice includes a host of racist labels such as 'chink', 'pom', 'nigger', or 'kaffir'. The second form of prejudice, physical avoidance, occurs when a group of people are disliked and shunned because of their religious beliefs, language systems, and customs. Prejudice of this nature might lead someone to avoid making friends, going out, or working with certain people on the basis of their perceived differences. Discrimination, the third form of prejudice, refers to the denial of opportunities to outgroup members. Discrimination exists in employment, housing, political rights, educational opportunities, and elsewhere. It is usually based on gender, social class, religion, skin colour, or other physical characteristics. The 'White Australia' policy, an immigration guideline which was not repealed until the 1980s, was an example of this form of prejudice. It legitimized discrimination towards potential immigrants who were not of a 'desirable' ethnic background – initially anyone who was not of Western European origin.

As the degree of discrimination intensifies, physical punishment of the targeted group becomes likely. The widely reported Cronulla riot in Sydney in 2005 (see Chapter 9) is an example of the fourth form of prejudice, physical attack, in which racial discrimination against people of Lebanese or Middle Eastern origin manifested as physical violence. The worst form of prejudice is massacre. The burning of women as witches in the American colonies, Hitler's attempted genocide of the Jewish people in Germany, and, more recently, the conflict and ethnic cleansing in Bosnia and Rwanda are examples of this extreme form of prejudice.

Stereotypes and prejudice are developed through socialization. As we grow, we learn stereotypes from our parents, friends, schools, churches, and our own experience. Moreover, mass media also play an important role in fostering stereotypes of social groups by constructing the 'image in our heads'. Because stereotypes and prejudice are based on our beliefs and attitude systems, they affect the way we communicate in intercultural encounters. They can inhibit communication, create negative feelings, and cause conflict. To avoid this problem, we need to develop intercultural empathy, projecting ourselves into the position of the other person's position in intercultural communication.

Racism

Racism refers to the belief that some racial groups are superior and that other racial groups are necessarily inferior. It is grounded in a belief in the supremacy of some races over others and that this superiority is biologically based. It therefore devalues and renders certain racial or ethnic groups inferior based on biological features. As such, racist people believe that race differences cannot be influenced by culture or education, and that biological superiority translates into cultural, intellectual, moral, and social superiority. Racism is usually the product of ignorance, fear, and hatred. It is a worldwide phenomenon, and often reflects and is perpetuated by deeply rooted historical, social, cultural, and power inequalities in society. The misconceptions it engenders are often founded on the fear of difference, including differences in customs, values, religion, physical appearance, and ways of living and viewing the world. Racism, stereotyping, prejudice, and discrimination are often linked. When a racial group is labelled as inferior, stereotypes about it tend to be negative. Because of this, people become prejudiced against the racial group and discriminate against it.

Racism takes different forms in different contexts, and so has been defined in many different ways. Its ultimate effects, however, are universal: it disempowers people by devaluing their identity, destroys community cohesion and creates divisions in society, and it makes it difficult if not impossible for certain groups of people to have political, economic, and social power. It is, therefore, the opposite of the democratic principles of equality and the right of all people to be treated fairly.

Further online reading The following article can be accessed for free on the book's companion website https://study.sagepub.com/liu2e: Murphy, Shelia (1998) 'The impact of factual versus fictional media portrayals on cultural stereotypes', *The Annals of the American Academy of Political and Social Science*, 560: 165–178.

Racist attitudes may be manifested in a number of ways, including expressions of racial prejudice and stereotypical assumptions about other cultures, as well as more extreme forms of prejudice such as xenophobia. Racist behaviour can include ridicule, abuse, property damage, harassment, and physical assault. Its underlying beliefs are reinforced by prevailing social attitudes towards people who are seen as different. In many countries, racism is inextricably linked to a colonial and/or immigrant history. In Australia, the indigenous inhabitants were dispossessed of their land and were discriminated against by European settlers. Over time, the migration of peoples from all parts of the world led to an increased cultural and linguistic diversity of the Australian population, but there has nevertheless been prejudice and discrimination against people of non-English-speaking backgrounds or non-European appearance over much of Australia's history. South Africa, New Zealand, and some Asian countries have similar histories of colonization and dispossession of indigenous groups; in some countries, this has led to a backlash by indigenous groups and subsequent discrimination against long-established immigrant groups. In the United States, on the other hand, racism grew in large part from the history of importing slaves from Africa. In most cases, racism is associated with a chauvinist view of who the 'real' members of the culture are. Like all forms of prejudice, it leads to conflicts and difficulties in intercultural communication.

Critical thinking...

What is the difference between prejudice and racism? Racism is still present in our multicultural society. If you were to design a campaign against racism, what activities would the campaign plan include?

SUMMARY

- Human perception is the basis of communication. The physical mechanism of perception is much the same in all people: sensory organs (eyes, ears, nose, etc.) permit us to perceive stimuli in our environment. The sensations received are subsequently routed through the nervous system to the brain, where they are interpreted.

- Perception is the process of organizing these sensations into recognizable wholes – the first step in assigning meaning. Previous experience produces expectations that act upon further received stimuli.

- The outcome of interpretation and the process of assigning meaning is not the same for all people. Interpretation is a learned process and is thus subject to psychological, physiological, and cultural influences.

- While the propensity to categorize and stereotype is common to all humans, it is our cultural socialization that influences the way in which this process is fulfilled.

- To overcome the barriers to intercultural communication created by stereotypes, prejudice, and racism, we need to practise cultural relativism and keep an open mind when interacting with people from different cultures.

JOIN THE DEBATE

Is ageism the fear of our future self?

Prejudice and discrimination against the aged has been an ongoing problem worldwide. Typically, ageism involves negative attitudes of young people towards older people or just those who are older than they are. Teenagers, for example, may be prejudiced against people over 30, while a middle-aged person may be prejudiced against people who are retired (older people can also be prejudiced against younger people, that is, be ageist). Ageism is manifested in our language, including slang and jokes, and in the way we communicate with older people, such as the use of 'baby talk'. Unlike other categories, such as ethnicity, race, and religion, into which we were born or to which we have a choice not to belong, all of us will grow old one day regardless of cultural differences. Why is ageism so prevalent across cultures? Is it because of the generation gap, or does it stem from our fear of the future self? What strategies can we use to reduce ageism in our society?

CASE STUDY

How are Eastern Europeans perceived by the West?

Since the collapse of communism in 1989 in Eastern European countries (such as Bosnia, Bulgaria, Romania, Serbia, Russia, Poland, the Czech Republic, Slovenia, etc.), there have been heated debates in the public spheres about issues such as how Eastern Europeans are perceived by the West. After the fall of the Roman Empire, the Western European regions became more economically and politically powerful, whereas much of

Eastern Europe was subordinated to the rule of the imperial powers and relegated to inferior social positions. As is often the case, the dominant population developed explanations in the form of stereotypes to explain and justify the power imbalance and the subjugation of Eastern Europeans. Eastern Europe tends to be associated with being backward, lazy, poor, or inferior. Findings from one survey revealed that respondents from Western Europe associated their Eastern neighbours with attributes like greyness, coldness, alcohol, poverty, unhappiness, melancholy, sadness, crime, corruption, and chaos (Hall, 1991).

On the other hand, Eastern European countries see Western Europeans as heartless, efficiency-driven, and soulless. In Slovenia, a popular saying illustrates their assumptions about the West: 'In heaven, the police are British, the cooks are French, the engineers are German, the administrators are Swiss, and the lovers are Italian'. However, 'in hell, the police are German, the cooks are British, the engineers are Italian, the administrators are French, and the lovers are Swiss.' This popular saying also reveals our commonly held stereotypes: Britons are perceived as logical and systematic; French people are seen as having a delicious cuisine; the Germans are often portrayed as efficient and hardworking; the Swiss are seen as well organized; and the Italians are believed to be warm and emotional.

Maria Todorova (1997), a Bulgarian scholar, argues that Western Europeans have historically created the image of Eastern Europe and the regions of the Balkans, including countries such as Serbia, Bulgaria, Romania, Albania, Montenegro, and so forth, as the land of violence, primitiveness, bloodshed, and lawlessness. She believes that such negative stereotypes of Eastern Europeans, specifically, of people from the Balkans, are influenced by the media, popular culture, and especially literature. Those cultural products contribute to creating an image of the Balkans as mystical but dangerous and traditional. Most mainstream cultural texts tend to rely on stereotypes and clichés in their representations of 'us' (the civilized West) and 'them' (the uncivilized East). For example, the famous novel *Dracula*, written by an English/Irish writer Bram Stoker in 1897, displays British perceptions and stereotypes of eastern Europeans, depicting them as uncivilized and barbaric – a potential threat to the civilized British culture.

Since the fall of the Berlin Wall and the collapse of the Soviet Union, 28 countries have emerged out of the eight former communist countries in Central and Eastern Europe (CEE). Different research projects in the last couple of years indeed show that Eastern Europeans are still predominantly perceived by their Western counterparts through stereotypes, such as laziness, backwardness, and violence. Despite the expansion of the European Union towards eastern regions, including countries like Poland, Slovenia, Bulgaria, and Romania, Western European perceptions of the new member states to the east tend to be monolithic and unchanged (Volčič, 2008).

Nevertheless, the newly emerged countries have been engaging in a range of public campaigns during the past 18 years in order to change the negative perceptions or stereotypes that the West have about them into positive ones. They want the West to perceive them as countries with democracy, political stability, and a strong market economy. Many Eastern European countries now attempt to project themselves as cultural, artistic, affordable, modern, sunny, and welcoming places. For example, public campaigns employ attractive slogans: in Serbia, *Serbia is the Guardian of Time*; in Macedonia, *Come to Macedonia and Your Heart Will Remain Here*; in Slovenia, *On the Sunny Side of the Alps*; in Croatia, *Mediterranean as It Once Was*; in Montenegro, *The Pearl of the Mediterranean*; in Bosnia, *The Old Europe*.

Governments also utilizes mass media channels to change negative stereotypes about Eastern European countries. In 2004, the Romanian government backed what was the country's first long-term campaign to change the image of Romania in the West. A comprehensive project, called *Romania: Simply Surprising*, was developed to present Romania as a modern, multicultural, democratic country. TV channels were utilized to advertise the four major Romanian 'assets': Bucharest, Transylvania, the churches of Bukovina, and Maramures, as well as the Black Sea coast. Similarly, in Bulgaria, the mass media played a role in influencing perceptions of Eastern Europe. For example, in 2007, a 45-second commercial with the slogan *Open Doors to Open Hearts* appeared on CNN as part of the 'changing perception' campaign to promote Bulgaria as an attractive tourism destination. It is hoped that public campaigns and media products can change negative perceptions and reduce negative stereotypes about Eastern Europe.

References

Hall, Derek (ed) (1991) *Tourism and Economic Development in Eastern Europe and the Soviet Union*. London: Belhaven.

Todorova, Maria (1997) *Imagining the Balkans*. New York: Oxford University Press.

Volčič, Zala (2008) 'Former Yugoslavia on the World Wide Web: commercialization and branding of nation-states', *International Communication Gazette*, 70(5): 395–413.

Questions for discussion

1. What are some of the negative stereotypes about Eastern Europeans?

2. What are the major sources of those negative stereotypes? What roles do mass media play in creating and reinforcing stereotypes?

3. What do you think are the potential consequences of negative stereotypes against certain groups of people?

4. Eastern Europeans are often grouped together as all being the same – of one culture. Could you use implicit consistency theory to explain this phenomenon?

5. What kind of strategies would you suggest to overcome prejudice and stereotypes against Eastern European countries?

FURTHER READINGS

All articles listed next to the mouse icon below can be accessed for free on the book's companion website: https://study.sagepub.com/liu2e

Attribution and implicit personality theory

Freeman, Jonathan B., Yina Ma, Shihui Han and Nalini Ambady (2013) 'Influences of culture and visual context on real-time social categorization', *Journal of Experimental Social Psychology*, 49: 206–210.

This paper reported a study on the extent to which Chinese and Americans relied on visual context in social categorization. American and Chinese participants were presented with faces varying along a white–Asian morph continuum either in American, neutral, or Chinese contexts. The results show that context systematically influences social categorization, sometimes altering categorization responses and at other times only temporarily altering the process. Further, the timing of contextual influences differs by culture. The findings highlight the role of contextual and cultural factors in social categorization.

Peng, Kaiping and Eric Knowles (2003) 'Culture, ethnicity and the attribution of physical causality', *Personality and Social Psychology Bulletin*, 29: 1272–1284.

This paper reported two studies that investigated the impact of culturally instilled folk theories on the perception of physical events. In Study 1, Americans and Chinese with no formal physics education were found to emphasize different causes in their explanations for eight physical events, with Americans attributing them more to dispositional factors (e.g., weight) and less to contextual factors (e.g., a medium) than did Chinese. In Study 2, Chinese Americans' identity as Asians or as Americans was primed before having them explain the events used in Study 1. Asian-primed participants endorsed dispositional explanations to a lesser degree and contextual explanations to a greater degree than did American-primed participants. Findings showed cultural differences in the perception of physical causality.

Perception and culture

Jain, Parul and Michael D. Slater (2013) 'Provider portrayals and patient-provider communication in drama and reality medical entertainment television shows', *Journal of Health Communication*, 18(6): 703–722.

This study content-analysed 101 episodes (85 hours) of portrayals of physicians on medical dramas broadcast during the 2006–2007 viewing season. Findings indicate that women are underrepresented as physicians on reality shows, although they are no longer underrepresented as physicians on dramas. However, they are not as actively portrayed in patient–care interactions as are male physicians on medical dramas. Asians and international medical graduates are underrepresented relative to their proportion in the US physician population. Many aspects of patient-centred communication are modelled, more so on reality programmes than on medical dramas.

Nisbett, Richard E. (2003) *The Geography of Thought: How Asians and Westerners Think Differently and Why.* New York: The Free Press.

This book takes on the presumptions of evolutionary psychology in a provocative, powerfully engaging exploration of the divergent ways Eastern and Western societies see and understand the world. Using data from experiments, Nisbett shows that different 'seeings' are a clue to profound underlying cognitive differences between Westerners and East Asians. The book argues that people think about and see the world differently because of differing ecologies, social structures, philosophies, and educational systems.

Stereotyping and racism

Lindemann, Stephanie and Nicolas Subtirelu (2013) 'Reliably biased: the role of listener expectation in the perception of second language speech', *Language Learning*, 63(3): 567–594.

Second-language pronunciation research and teaching relies on human listeners to assess second-language speakers' performance. Most applied linguists working in this area have been satisfied that listener ratings are reasonably reliable when well-controlled research protocols are implemented. However, this paper argues that listeners demonstrate a certain amount of reliability in their ratings of speakers, stemming from shared expectations of a speaker's language and social groups, rather than from the speech itself. Drawing upon evidence from perceptual psychology, sociolinguistics, and phonetics, demonstrating a sizeable listener influence on speech perception, the paper suggests ways for research and teaching to acknowledge and contend with the role of the listener.

> '*If we are to achieve a richer culture, rich in contrasting values, we must recognize the whole gamut of human potentialities, and so weave a less arbitrary social fabric, one in which each diverse human gift will find a fitting place.*'

Margaret Mead, American cultural anthropologist, 1901–1978

5

CULTURAL AND VALUE ORIENTATIONS

LEARNING OBJECTIVES

At the end of this chapter, you should be able to:

- Identify Hofstede's five dimensions of culture.

- Define Hall's high-context and low-context cultures.

- Compare and contrast Kluckhohn and Strodtbeck's value orientations.

- Explain Schwartz's cultural value theory.

- Apply the principles governing ethical intercultural communication.

INTRODUCTION

Culture provides the overall framework for humans to organize their thoughts, emotions, and behaviours in relation to their environment. At the core of culture are values, defined as an explicit or implicit conception, distinctive of an individual or characteristic of a group, which influence the selection of behaviours. Values are guiding principles for human behaviour, and each culture treasures some values more than others. For example, some cultures value assertiveness, while others hold the value of harmony in greater esteem. Our values provide criteria for us to evaluate our own behaviours and those of others. The relationship between values and human communication is summarized by Sitaram and Haapanen (1979). First, values are communicated both explicitly and implicitly through symbolic behaviours. Most of our verbal and nonverbal behaviours reflect the values we have learned through the socialization process and they have become internalized in our mind. For example, the Japanese proverb 'A single arrow is easily broken, but not ten in a bundle' illustrates the value of collectivism. Values influence the way we communicate with others. The Koreans often avoid saying 'no' when someone makes a request that probably will not be fulfilled. Instead, such a request would elicit a response such as 'We need to think it over' or 'It is a bit difficult', in order to preserve harmony. In contrast, 'to speak your mind' is preferred by US Americans, who value direct communication. Finns, on the other hand, hold an attitude of only speaking if one has something to say, and not to simply fill a void. Long periods of silence between people sitting at the same table are not uncommon (Carbaugh, Berry and Nurmikari-Berry, 2006). These examples demonstrate that our cultural values serve as a repertoire of our behaviours, as well as criteria for evaluating the behaviours of others.

This chapter concentrates on the influence of cultural and value orientations on behaviours. First, we describe the five widely known cultural dimensions, identified by Hofstede and his associates. Next, we introduce Hall's high-context and low-context dimensions of culture and compare different cultures on them. The value orientations developed by Kluckhohn and Strodtbeck are introduced, followed by Schwartz's cultural value theory. This chapter concludes with a discussion of the principles governing ethical intercultural communication.

HOFSTEDE'S CULTURAL DIMENSIONS

Hofstede (1980) compared work-related attitudes in IBM across more than 53 different cultures, and identified four consistent cultural dimensions influencing the behaviours of 160,000 managers and employees. He suggested that these cultural dimensions have a significant impact on behaviour in all cultures: individualism–collectivism, masculinity–femininity, power distance, and uncertainty avoidance. Later, a fifth dimension of long-term orientation (also known as Confucian work dynamism) was added to the model by Hofstede and Bond (1988). Since the publication of Hofstede's book, *Culture's Consequences: International Differences in Work-related Values*, in 1980, the concept of dimensions of national cultures has been applied in various disciplines, including intercultural training, cross-cultural psychology, management and leadership, organizational psychology, sociology, and communication. Hofstede's work is not without criticisms, though. For example, McSweeney (2002) commented that nations may not be the best units for studying cultures, that a study of the subsidiaries of one company (IBM) cannot provide information about entire national cultures, and that surveys are not suitable ways of measuring culture. It is important to note that Hofstede's work measured cultural dimensions at a national rather than an individual level, and therefore those value dimensions characterize the dominant culture of a particular society. Within the larger culture of any country, various subcultural groups co-exist, and you can find variations across different groups along each value continuum. Nevertheless, over the past decades, researchers from different disciplines have tested and added more validations to the IBM scores and contributed to the overall picture originally developed by Hofstede (e.g., House et al., 2004; Triandis, 1995). Till this date, Hofstede's model has been included in almost all intercultural communication books.

Further online reading The following article can be accessed for free on the book's companion website https://study.sagepub.com/liu2e: Merritt, Ashleigh (2000) 'Culture in the cockpit: do Hofstede's dimensions replicate?', *Journal of Cross-Cultural Psychology*, 31(2): 283–301.

Individualism–collectivism

The *individualism–collectivism* dimension describes the relationship between the individual and the groups to which he or she belongs. In individualistic cultures, emphasis is placed on individuals' goals over group goals (Triandis, McCusker and Hui, 1990). People in an individualistic culture tend to stress the importance of self and personal achievement (Gudykunst, 2004). Social behaviour is guided by personal goals, perhaps at the expense of other types of goals. Individuals are encouraged to pursue and develop their abilities and aptitudes.

In contrast, collectivistic cultures emphasize values that serve and preserve the ingroup by subordinating personal goals to this end. Group membership is more important than individuality, and people are expected to be interdependent and show conformity to ingroup norms and values. In collectivistic cultures,

Photo 5.1 Chinese dragon dance in Brisbane to celebrate Chinese New Year.
Copyright © The Chinese Consulate in Brisbane. Used with permission.

people do not see themselves as isolated individuals but as interdependent with others (e.g., their ingroup), in which responsibility is shared and accountability is collective. Collectivistic societies are characterized by extended primary groups, such as the family, neighbourhood, or occupational group. For example, collectivist values are evident in many traditional Chinese performances, such as the dragon dance, which requires the close cooperation of the group rather than exceptional skills by one individual. Cultures are never completely individualist or collectivist, but can be conceived of as being positioned somewhere along a continuum between high individualism and high collectivism. According to Hofstede's (1980) study, countries such as Australia, the United States, Great Britain, Canada, the Netherlands, New Zealand, Italy, Belgium, and Denmark are ranked high on individualism, whereas Columbia, Venezuela, Pakistan, Peru, Taiwan, Thailand, Singapore, Chile, and Hong Kong are ranked towards the lower end of the continuum.

Critical thinking...

Can a culture be both individualistic and collectivistic? Can you find an example to illustrate this? Where is the culture more individualist and where is it more collectivist? Why do you think this combination exists (if it does)?

A culture's orientation towards individualism or collectivism has important behavioural consequences for its members. Previous research indicates that in collectivistic cultures, distinctiveness of the self-concept does not play as important a role as it does in individualistic cultures (Hofstede, 1980). As seen in large-scale research programmes like GLOBE (House et al., 2004), Confucian Asia (China, Hong Kong, Japan, Singapore, South Korea, and Taiwan) is characterized by a societal collectivism based on networks, trust, and loyalty to ingroups such as organizations or families. Research has demonstrated that people in collectivistic cultures are more concerned with social acceptance and others' opinions than are people in individualistic cultures (Hui and Triandis, 1986). This is because collectivists are more likely to comply with the wishes of the ingroup than individualists. For example, Lee and Green (1991) showed that reference groups, such as the extended family, neighbours, and friends, have greater influence on purchase decisions for Korean consumers than for American consumers.

It is important to note that individualism or collectivism at the cultural level does not mean that every individual in the culture conforms to the culture's position on this dimension. In a seminal review, Markus and Kitayama (1991) pointed to the vast individual differences within cultures on this dimension. They showed the influence of an individualist (or independent) orientation versus a collectivist (or interdependent) orientation on self-concept, motivation, emotion, and thinking. In intercultural communication, we need to be aware not only of cultural values, but also of an individual's orientation to them, as both will influence any interaction.

Individualism and collectivism have been associated with direct and indirect styles of communication; that is, the extent to which speakers reveal intentions through explicit verbal communication. In the direct style, associated with individualism, the wants and needs of the speaker are embodied in the spoken message. For example, saying 'no' to requests made by a friend is both common and acceptable in the USA, the UK, and Germany. In the indirect style, associated with collectivism, the wants and needs of the speaker are not obvious in the spoken message. In China, for instance, requests for help from friends are often made indirectly, so as to avoid embarrassment should the other person have difficulty in honouring the request. Such an indirect request may be made by describing one's problematic situation, 'inviting' the other person to offer help. The initial offer of help is customarily declined, and then later accepted with gratitude upon the second or third offer. Thus, the sincerity of the offer to help can be ensured.

Masculinity–femininity

The *masculinity–femininity* dimension describes how a culture's dominant values are assertive or nurturing. In masculine cultures, people strive for maximal distinction between how men and women are expected to think and behave. Cultures that place high value on masculine traits stress assertiveness, competition, and material success. Cultures labelled as feminine are those that permit more overlapping social roles for the sexes and place high value on feminine traits, such as quality of life, interpersonal relationships, and concern for the weak. For example, in some cultures it is acceptable for the wife to go out to work while the husband stays home minding the children and taking care of domestic chores. In cultures with more masculine values, however, such a practice would probably be frowned upon. According to Hofstede's (1980) study, Japan is at the top of the list of masculine cultures; Australia, Venezuela, Switzerland, Mexico, Ireland, Great Britain, and Germany also belong to this category. Japanese women are traditionally taught to be obedient and to make household skills and domesticity the centre of their life. The Japanese wife is expected to be an able homemaker and mother. However, these traditions are changing, with women increasingly taking on professions and joining the workforce. Sweden, Norway, the Netherlands, Denmark, Finland, Chile, Portugal, and Thailand represent more feminine cultures. For example, in Norway, the softer aspects of culture are valued and encouraged, such as consensus and sympathy for the underdog. Trying to be better than others is neither socially nor materially rewarded.

Power distance

Power distance refers to the extent to which a culture tolerates inequality in power distribution. In cultures with a larger power distance, inequalities among people are both expected and desired. Less powerful people are expected to depend on more powerful people. Children are expected to be obedient towards parents, instead of being treated more or less as equals, and people are expected to display respect for those with higher status. For example, in Thailand, where a status hierarchy is observed, people are expected to display respect to monks by greeting and taking leave of monks with ritualistic greetings, removing hats in the presence of a monk, seating monks at a higher level, and using a vocabulary that shows respect. Cultures with a smaller power distance emphasize equality among people, stressing that there should be interdependence between people at different power levels. In New Zealand, characterized as a low power distance culture, it is common for subordinates to address managers by their first name; in Hong Kong, high in power distance, people of lower rank in the workplace usually address those of higher rank with titles to preserve hierarchical relationships.

Power distance also refers to the extent to which power, prestige, and wealth are distributed within a culture. Cultures with high power distance have power and influence concentrated in the hands of a few rather than distributed through the population. Those cultures may communicate in a way that reinforces hierarchies in interpersonal relationships. High power-distance cultures tend to orient to authoritarianism, which dictates a hierarchical structure of social relationships. In such cultures, the differences between age and status are maximized. The Philippines, Mexico, Venezuela, India, Singapore, Brazil, Hong Kong, France, and Columbia represent high power-distance cultures (Hofstede, 1980). On the other hand, low power distance cultures are characterized by 'horizontal' social relationships. People in these cultures tend to minimize differences of age, sex, status, and roles. Social interactions are more direct and less formal. Countries such as Australia, Israel, Denmark, New Zealand, Ireland, Sweden, Norway, Finland, and Switzerland score low in power distance.

Critical thinking...

In what ways can the ownership of mass media reinforce power distance between people? How does advertising in the media affect power distance?

THEORY CORNER

MICHEL FOUCAULT'S THEORY OF POWER

Michel Foucault (2006), a French philosopher, argues that communication rarely takes place between pure 'equals', even though most of our models of understanding communication make this assumption. Social hierarchies are always present, however subtle, in communication interactions. In every culture, there is a social hierarchy that privileges some groups over others. These groups hold more power, be it economic, political, or cultural, and they determine to a great extent the communication system.

Foucault's work reveals an interest in questions of where power is 'located' in a culture; who has and who does not have it; how power is distributed; how those in power obtain and keep power; and to what/whose ends power is used. Foucault (2006) believes that power is dynamic, flowing through individuals in various contexts and relationships. Importantly, people who are the subjects of power often find ways to resist this power, but this does not mean such resistance is easy. Power is also institutional in that human institutions embody and sustain power relations. This is true of cultural institutions such as marriage, legal-political institutions, and physical institutions such as prisons, schools, or hospitals. Certain institutional roles (e.g., teacher or police) can offer occupants accompanying institutional power.

Reference
Foucault, Michel (2006) *History of Madness*. New York: Routledge.

Further reading on power
Loden, Marilyn and Judy B. Rosener (1991) *Workforce America: Managing Diversity as a Vital Resource*. Homewood, IL: Business One Irwin.

Theory in Practice

FOUCAULT'S INFLUENCE ON SOCIAL WORK

Michel Foucault's theories around power and knowledge have been very influential in a range of disciplines, including development, philosophy, business, and social work. Over the past few years, new policy frameworks have influenced the structure and terrain of 'caring' professions in England, including social work. The introduction of quasi-markets has led to the division of service departments. Quasi-markets refer to institutional structures designed to gain free-market efficiency without compromising the equity benefits of traditional public administration. The governments set budgets and targets for the otherwise autonomous organizations. Powell and Khan (2012: 136) argue that this has led to 'the role of social workers [being] shaped by increasing managerialist demands for information particularly in response to audit and risk assessment'. This, combined with a recent push for a stricter qualification process, has produced a vast array of roles for social workers operating in different segments of the welfare and care sector. Powell and Khan (2012) argue that this kind of 'routinized practice' becomes oppressive, and it may restrict the worker's organization. It is therefore important to review this process in light of the political factors at play, particularly around power relations and worker identities.

Questions to take you further
In what ways can Foucault's theory of power influence an organizational code of conduct? How can it help to explain interpersonal and mediated communication in an organization? Does this theory help to explain the role of journalism and the impact of media ethics? How?

Reference

Powell, Jason L. and Hafiz T. A. Khan (2012) 'Foucault, social theory and social work', *Sociologie Romaneasca*, 10(1): 131–147.

Further reading on power in practice

Alagiah, Ratnam (2011) 'Theory about theories: income theories after Foucault', *Journal of American Academy of Business*, 16(2): 23–30.

Uncertainty avoidance

The *uncertainty avoidance* dimension reflects a culture's tolerance of ambiguity and acceptance of risk. Some cultures have a high need for information and certainty, whereas other cultures seem to be more comfortable dealing with diversity and ambiguity. In high uncertainty-avoidance cultures, people are active and security seeking; cultures weak in uncertainty avoidance are contemplative, less aggressive, unemotional, relaxed, accepting of personal risks, and relatively tolerant. According to Hofstede's (2001) scale, Greece, Portugal, Belgium, Japan, Peru, France, Chile, Spain, and Argentina are high in uncertainty avoidance, whereas Denmark, Sweden, Norway, Finland, Ireland, Great Britain, the Netherlands, the Philippines, and the United States tend to be at the lower end of the scale. These latter cultures are oriented to cope with the stress and anxiety caused by ambiguous situations. They take more initiative, show greater flexibility, and feel more relaxed in interactions. People from high uncertainty-avoidance cultures tend to avoid risk-taking, whereas those from low uncertainty-avoidance cultures are more comfortable with risk and are able to cope with the stress and anxiety that it causes.

High uncertainty avoidance tends to be found in collectivistic cultures. The combined influence of uncertainty avoidance and collectivism can be found in research on consumer behaviour. The decision to purchase imported products, for instance, involves risk-taking. The level of perceived risk associated with the purchase and the extent of uncertainty tolerance will influence purchasing intentions. For example, risk perception is found to be negatively associated with Asian consumers' willingness to adopt online purchasing (Liang and Huang, 1998). Similarly, Greek consumers have greater concerns for security than British consumers (Jarvenpaa and Tractinsky, 1999). However, the results of other empirical research have been equivocal. Weber and Hsee (1998) contend that people from collectivistic cultures may be more willing to take risks because in a collectivistic society family and other ingroup members are expected to help a person bear the possible adverse consequences of risky choices. This claim is supported by Yamaguchi (1998), who argues that people tend to perceive less risk when others are exposed to the same risk situation. Nevertheless, the consensus is that people from cultures with different levels of uncertainty avoidance respond differently to risk situations.

Critical thinking...

Do you think a culture's orientation to risk-taking is related to the political and economic systems of the country? How might uncertainty avoidance also be related to the level of economic security at a particular time in history?

Long-term and short-term orientation

The *long-term and short-term orientation* dimension was added in response to criticisms of Hofstede's work for its Western bias in data collection. This fifth dimension was identified based on the Chinese Value Survey (CVS), which was developed from values suggested by Chinese scholars (Hofstede, 2001). Hofstede originally called this dimension *Confucian work dynamism* because the survey items seemed to be related to the teachings of Confucius. Minkov and Hofstede (2012) later drew upon the World Values Survey (WVS) data to extend the study from originally 23 countries to 38 countries. Based on their analysis, they found high scores among some Eastern European nations on long-term orientation. Hofstede and his colleagues then considered it no longer appropriate to link this dimension with Confucianism. Thus, they now consider the long-term and short-term orientation dimension to be another universal dimension of national culture.

The long-term versus short-term orientation is concerned with values in social relations. Long-term orientation was identified in an international study with Chinese employees and managers (Hofstede and Bond, 1988). People with long-term orientation tend to be dedicated, motivated, responsible, and educated individuals with a sense of commitment and organizational identity and loyalty. Countries and regions high in long-term orientation are Hong Kong, Singapore, Taiwan, South Korea, and Japan – five economic dragons. Long-term orientation encourages thrift, savings, perseverance towards results, ordering relationships by status, and a willingness to subordinate oneself for a purpose. Other studies found that long-term orientation encouraged Chinese consumers to place a greater emphasis on the quality of products when making purchasing decisions. For example, quality and utilitarian values were found to be strong predictors of Chinese consumers' intention to purchase Canadian pork sausages (Zhou and Hui, 2003). Short-term orientation, which characterizes Western cultures, is consistent with spending to keep up with social pressure, less saving, and a preference for quick results (Hofstede, 2001).

HALL'S HIGH- AND LOW-CONTEXT CULTURAL DIMENSION

Hall (1977) divided cultures into *high-context* and *low-context*. This dimension refers to the extent to which we gather information from the physical, social, and psychological context of an interaction (high context), as opposed to the explicit verbal code (low context). This dimension represents a continuum in which some cultures (e.g., China, England, France, Ghana, Japan, Korea) orient to the high-context end, whereas others (e.g., Germany, Scandinavia, Switzerland, the United States) are at the low-context end. According to Hall and Hall (1990: 183–184), high-context and low-context refers to:

> the fact that when people communicate, they take for granted how much the listener knows about the subject under discussion. In low-context communication, the listener knows very little and must be told practically everything. In high-context communication, the listener is already 'contexted' and does not need to be given much background information.

For people in high-context cultures, much meaning is either implicit in the physical setting or in shared beliefs, values, and norms. The context provides much information about the culture's rules, practices, and expectations. Thus, information about background and procedures is not overtly communicated; instead, listeners are expected to know how to interpret the communication and what to do. Thus, information and cultural rules remain unspoken, as the context is expected to be a cue for behaviour. High-context cultures generally have restricted code systems, in which speakers and listeners rely more on the contextual elements of the communication setting for information than on the actual language – interactants look to the physical, social, relational, and cultural environment for information. By contrast, low-context cultures employ an explicit code to send messages. People rely on an elaborated code system for creating and interpreting meaning, so that little meaning is determined by the context. Information to be shared with others is explicitly coded in the verbal message, procedures are explained, and expectations are discussed.

Critical thinking...

What kind of problems might occur if a person from a low-context culture works for a boss who is from a high-context culture? What could they do to avoid miscommunication?

KLUCKHOHN AND STRODTBECK'S VALUE ORIENTATIONS

Kluckhohn and Strodtbeck (1961) argue that all human cultures are confronted with universal problems emerging from relationships with others, time, activities, and nature. Value orientations are the means a society uses to solve these universal problems. The concept entails four assumptions. Firstly, all human societies face the same problems; secondly, they use different means to solve them; thirdly, the means to address universal problems are limited; and fourthly, value orientations are behaviourally observable through empirical studies (Condon and Yousef, 1975). Value orientation theory suggests that cultures develop unique positions on five value orientations: (1) the relationship of people with nature (people should be subordinate to/in harmony with/dominant over nature), (2) activity (state of being/inner development/industriousness), (3) time (past/present/future), (4) human nature (people are good/mixed/evil), and (5) social relations (individualistic/collective/hierarchical). Each orientation represents a way of addressing a universal problem.

Man–nature orientation

The man–nature orientation address the question: What is the relationship of humans to nature? A society's conception of the relationship of humans to nature is determined by the worldview of its people. *Worldview* refers to the outlook a culture has about the nature of the universe, the nature of humankind, the relationship between humanity and the universe, and other philosophical issues defining humans' place in the cosmos. Since prehistoric times, humans have made creation stories in order to explain their relationship to nature. This relationship can be subjugation to nature, harmony with nature, or mastery over nature. Phrases like 'nature as machine', and its variant 'nature as storehouse', justify the exploitative relationship between Western civilizations and the environment, where nature is regarded as something that needs to be conquered. For example, in the United States, people make a clear distinction between humans and nature, with humans assuming a dominant role over nature, valuing and protecting it. This viewpoint is evident in the changing of river courses to accommodate city planning.

In Arab culture, humans are seen as part of nature and are supposed to live in harmony with it. This orientation is related to the Islamic view that everything in the world, except humans, is administered by God-made laws. The physical world has no choice but to be obedient to God. Humans, however,

Photo 5.2   The statue of Buddha symbolizes peace and harmony, both of which are valued in Asian cultures.
Copyright © Shuang Liu. Used with permission.

can choose to obey the law of God; in so doing, they will be in harmony with all other elements of nature. Japanese culture is also characterized by a love of and respect for nature, believing that humans should live in harmony with nature. They cherish the beauty of nature through *hanami* (cherry blossoms) in spring and *momijigari* (maple leaves changing colour) in autumn, and practise traditional flower arrangements known as *ikebana*. Harmony is a central concept in Japanese culture, influenced by Shintoism along with Buddhist and Confucian traditions. The traditional Japanese garden illustrates this harmonious relationship between humans and nature.

Activity orientation

The activity orientation addresses the question: What is the modality of human activity? This refers to the use of time for self-expression and play, self-improvement and development, and work. The activity orientation can refer to being, being-in-becoming, and doing. Protestant cultures, such as in Britain, perceive paid work as essential: a dominant human activity that occupies a central place in human existence. Human work is understood as a duty that benefits both the individual and society as a whole. Many Americans believe that work should be separated from play, and that a feeling of accomplishment is the most important aspect of work. High value is placed on time and efficiency. In Arab cultures, earning a living through labour is not only a duty but also a virtue, and is thus not separable from other aspects of human existence. In some religious cultures, praying is cherished, and a prayer is considered to be more important for humans than is work.

Time orientation

The time orientation answers the question: What is the temporal focus of human life? Cultures differ widely in their conceptions of time. Time orientation can be past, present, or future. Past-oriented cultures emphasize tradition; present-oriented cultures stress spontaneity and immediacy; future-oriented cultures emphasize the importance of present activities to future outcomes (Cooper et al., 2007). Many Western cultures view time in a linear fashion – past, present, and future move in a line, in one direction. This attitude conceives of time as a commodity that can be spent, saved, borrowed, and wasted. When time is considered as a tangible object, it becomes something to be managed and used responsibly. For example, most Americans say that they often lack time. This may be partly due to the fact that they are striving for the 'American Dream' – the metaphor for upward mobility, success, luxury, and happiness – all of which consume time. The concept is often regarded as an ideology; Americans feel pressured constantly to do more, earn more, and consume more, in order to achieve the ideals of their society. This attitude tends to push people to a constantly hurried state of mind. Time decides when Americans make their appointments, when they do their work, and even how they spend their leisure time. Punctuality is important, and being late without a legitimate reason is considered bad manners. Similarly, the Swiss have a reputation for being as punctual and precise as their famous watches. The saying is: *Avant l'heure, c'est pas l'heure, après l'heure, c'est plus l'heure* (Before the hour is not yet the hour, after the hour is no longer the hour). In Switzerland, you are likely to see a clock almost everywhere you go; this is a culture that runs on time and is organized around time.

In other cultures, the past, present, and future may not be as distinct. Mulder (1996) reports three different conceptions of time in Thai society. The first conception is characterized by continuity. This is the belief in the continuity of life, traditions, and the environment, from ancestors into endless future generations. In this sense, time stands still. Past, present, and future are indistinct. The second conception is the 'modern' conception of time – instead of standing still, time in this conception moves ahead towards the future. For example, when a poor Thai farmer

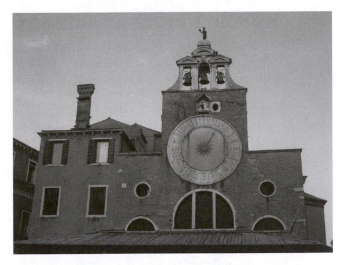

Photo 5.3 A clock in a public place in Venice uses Roman numerals to show the hours of the day.
Copyright © Zala Volčič. Used with permission.

migrated to the city for a better life, she or he had to measure time in terms of working hours in a factory instead of in the field. The third is an animistic conception of time. Communities feel that they are controlled by a strong power beyond their control. Thus, they seek for ways to manage the power through various means, including worship and animal sacrifices. Thai people worship the gods who they believe will help villagers in return by sending rain when it is needed.

There are cultures that do not have a clear sense of time, as revealed in their language. For example, the Hopi language does not have verb tenses, but simply uses two words to express time: one meaning 'sooner' and the other meaning 'later'. The Hopi tribes live for the most part in north-east Arizona, and are well known for being very peaceful. Another example is the Pirahã, a small Amazonian tribe that has a limited language consisting of relatively few sounds and grammatical constructions, and which is whistled for some purposes (like hunting). Their traditional language appears to have no precise numbers, specific past tense, or written form. There is limited art in this culture, and no precise concept of time. Their religion is animistic, and they make little reference to history or ancestors. The Pirahã do not (or did not in the past) have a desire to remember where they come from or to tell cultural stories. In the old days in Venice, similarly, there were clocks on public buildings that showed the position of the sun and moon along with the relative positions of Saturn, Jupiter, Venus, Mercury, and Mars. Today, we can see clocks in public places in Venice that use Roman numerals to show the hours of the day.

Critical thinking...

Do you feel that being punctual at meetings is important? How would you feel if your guest was half an hour late for dinner? What explanation do you feel you need to give if you are late? How does this depend on the situation?

Human nature orientation

The human nature orientation addresses the question: What is the intrinsic character of human nature? Are we born good or evil, or a mixture of good and evil? The Puritan origins in the United States reflects a Christian view that people are born evil but have the potential to become good through self-control and self-discipline. Other contemporary views claim that humans are born with a mixture of good and evil, and thus have a choice to be either. Such a belief in rationality is consistent with the belief in the scientific method of inquiry, whereby truth can be discovered through human reasoning. In other cultures, such as Chinese culture, Confucianism teaches that humans are born free of evil. Buddhism emphasizes the spirituality and goodness of the individual, in what is a more inward-oriented philosophy. The Judaeo-Christian tradition claims that understanding of the person is bound together with the belief that humans are created in the image of God, suggesting a close relationship between the concept of God and the concept of the person. Humans are seen as sinful, but they can be redeemed during the course of life, since God created humans endowed with intelligence and choice. The purpose of human life is to worship God by knowing, loving, and obeying. In Hinduism, a person is defined by his or her membership of a caste, so it is difficult to practise equality for all persons. Differences in human nature orientation are often reflected in a society's criminal laws: some countries believe a suspect is innocent until proved guilty, whereas other countries believe the suspect is guilty until proved innocent.

Relational orientation

The relational orientation addresses the question: What is the modality of a person's relationship to others? It refers to perceptions of the self and the ways in which society is organized. It can be lineal, collateral, and individualistic. In individualistic cultures, people are encouraged to accept responsibility as independent individuals. For example, in such cultures marriage is usually the decision of the individual, and romantic love tends to be the reason for marriage. In collectivistic cultures, such as India, marriage may be considered as too great a decision to be left to the individuals involved, because marriages present opportunities for familial alliances in a culture where families are very important. In such group-oriented cultures, individuals subordinate personal needs to their ingroup, particularly their family. If a Chinese youngster passes the national matriculation test and is offered a place in a good university, both parents and other members of the extended family feel they have been given face because honour is the collective property of the family. In the same way, all family members would feel they had lost face should a single member of the family commit a dishonourable act. Collectivistic cultures tend to be more caring for each other, as there is a strong sense of belonging to some collectivity – family, neighbourhood, village, class, or organization. In Bosnia, for example, elderly people enjoy playing chess in a public square, which creates an atmosphere of collectivity.

Photo 5.4   Elderly people in Sarajevo, Bosnia, enjoy playing collective games like chess in a public square.
Copyright © Zala Volčič. Used with permission.

Further online reading The following article can be accessed for free on the book's companion website https://study.sagepub.com/liu2e: Lee, Hyung-Seok and Jin S. Park (2012) 'Cultural orientation and the persuasive effects of fear appeals: the case of anti-smoking public service announcements', *Journal of Medical Marketing*, 12(2): 73–80.

THEORY CORNER

CONDON AND YOUSEF'S MODEL OF VALUE ORIENTATIONS

Condon and Yousef (1975) extended Kluckhohn and Strodtbeck's five value orientations to include six spheres of universal problems all humans face. They are the self, the family, society, human nature, nature, and the supernatural, all of which are interdependent of each other. Condon and Yousef derived 25 value orientations encompassed by the six spheres. They claim that all value orientations exist in every society, but the preferred response to the problem varies from culture to culture. For example, one value orientation under the sphere of 'supernatural' is 'knowledge of the cosmic order'. In some cultures, people believe this order is comprehensible; in others, they believe it is mysterious and unknowable; in still others, they believe that understanding it is a matter of faith and reason.

Reference

Condon, John C. and Fathi Yousef (1975) *An Introduction to Intercultural Communication*. Indianapolis, IN: Bobbs-Merrill.

Further reading on values

Schwartz, Shalom H. and Lilach Sagiv (1995) 'Identifying culture-specifics in the content and structure of values', *Journal of Cross-Cultural Psychology*, 26(1): 99–116.

Theory in Practice

JAPANESE TIME VERSUS US TIME

Different cultures have different concepts of time and therefore value time in different ways. Masumoto (2004) compared Japanese time orientations with US time orientations. He found that US culture tends to focus on the future, with distinct barriers between work time and personal time (although this is slowly changing). Within the workplace, employees often value change and 'moving forward', with high levels of motivation and ambition. This means that the level of an employee's experience is not necessarily linked to age. Business plans are often focused on 'short-term' goals, such as fiscal quarters or three-year strategic plans. Japanese culture, on the other hand, values tradition and 'longevity'; it is quite common for one employee to stay with the same company for more than 30 years. Seniority is based on years of service, and is highly rewarded. The business world organizes its calendar around seasonal and national holidays, with bonuses being paid at the end of the calendar year and recruitment taking place each April. Extended periods of silence during meetings may be quite common, as Japanese culture values reflection time and often views this process as necessary to process information and extract meaning. Many Japanese people also may not separate work and non-work time, often staying late at the office without expectation of compensation. These different concepts and values of time can negatively affect international business collaborations if not understood.

Questions to take you further
How is time viewed in your culture? Do you think remaining in the same job demonstrates loyalty and perseverance? What does 'efficiency' mean to you?

Reference
Masumoto, Tomoko (2004) 'Learning to "do time" in Japan: a study of US interns in Japanese organizations', *International Journal of Cross-Cultural Management*, 4(1): 19–37.

Further reading on value orientations in practice
Kartal, Ali and Mehmet S. Bozok (2011) 'The effects of socio-cultural variables on the application of ethical standards for Turkish accountants', *South East European Journal of Economics and Business*, 6(1): 7–12.

Critical thinking...

In Western cultures, children's career paths are often their own choice, although they may seek advice from their parents. In many Asian cultures, the parents decide which universities their children will go to, which subject areas their children will be studying, and which career path their children will follow in the future. Can you explain this phenomenon in terms of the value orientation theory?

SCHWARTZ'S CULTURAL VALUE THEORY

Shalom Schwartz developed another cultural values framework to understand the influence of cultural values on attitudes and behaviours. Schwartz (1994: 88) defines values as the 'desirable goals, varying in importance, that serve as guiding principles in people's lives'. Like Hofstede, Schwartz attempted to identify national cultural dimensions that can be used to compare cultures by aggregating the value priorities of individuals. Unlike Hofstede, whose research focused on IBM employees, Schwartz's original research data were collected from teacher and student samples in 38 nations between 1988 and 1992.

Schwartz (1999) argues that there are seven types of value on which cultures can be compared. They are conservatism, intellectual autonomy, affective autonomy, hierarchy, mastery, egalitarian commitment, and harmony (see Table 5.1 for definitions of each value type).

Table 5.1   Schwartz's Seven Cultural Value Types

Value type	Definition
Conservatism	A society that emphasizes close-knit harmonious relations, the maintenance of the status quo and traditional order.
Intellectual autonomy	A society that recognizes individuals as autonomous entities who are entitled to pursue their own intellectual interests and desires.
Affective autonomy	A society that recognizes individuals as autonomous entities who are entitled to pursue their stimulation and hedonism, interests and desires.
Hierarchy	A society that emphasizes the legitimacy of hierarchical roles and resource allocation.
Mastery	A society that emphasizes active mastery of the social environment and an individual's rights to get ahead of other people.
Egalitarian commitment	A society that emphasizes the transcendence of selfless interests.
Harmony	A society that emphasizes harmony with nature.

Source: Adapted from Schwartz, Shalom (1999) 'A theory of cultural values and some implications for work', *Applied Psychology: An International Review*, 48(1): 23–47, p. 29.

Those seven cultural value types were summarized into three dimensions, namely: (1) autonomy versus embeddedness; (2) hierarchy versus egalitarianism; and (3) mastery versus harmony. While each dimension represents a continuum of cultural responses, a culture's preference for one orientation of a given dimension means that the opposite end of the continuum is less important to that culture. Similar to Kluckhohn and Strodtbeck's premise that all cultures face universal problems that they must resolve, Schwartz (1999) argues that there are three issues that all societies face and must resolve. The first issue that confronts all societies is to define the nature of the relation between the individual and the group. Resolutions of this issue give rise to the cultural dimension which Schwartz calls *autonomy versus embeddedness*. In autonomy cultures, people are more independent; they find meaning in their own uniqueness; they are encouraged to express their own preferences, traits, feeling, and motives. Autonomy can occur at intellectual and affective levels. Cultures that value intellectual autonomy, such as France and Japan (Lustig and Koester, 2013), encourage people's independent pursuit of ideas, creativity, intellectual directions, curiosity, and broad-mindedness. Cultures that favour affective autonomy, such as those in Denmark and England (Lustig and Koester, 2013), encourage people to independently pursue pleasure, an exciting life, and a varied life.

In contrast, cultures that are oriented towards embeddedness view the person as an entity embedded in the collectivity and finding meaning in life largely through social relationships. Identifying with the group and participating in its shared way of life are important. This outlook is expressed in values like conservatism, which emphasizes maintenance of the status quo, propriety, and restraint of actions that might disrupt the solidarity of the group or the traditional order. Nigeria, for example, a country that values predictability, obedience to authorities, maintenance of social order, and respect for tradition and elders' wisdom exemplifies embeddedness.

The second issue that Schwartz identifies that confronts all societies is to guarantee responsible behaviour that will preserve the social fabric. Schwartz argues that people must organize and coordinate their activities to preserve and fulfil the goals of the social group and the needs of others. He labels this dimension *hierarchy versus egalitarianism*. Cultures that value hierarchy view the unequal distribution of social, political, and economic power as legitimate and desirable. They prefer the use of power ascribed by hierarchical systems to ensure socially responsible behaviour; compliance with the obligations and rules is emphasized. Countries like Thailand and Turkey, where power distance is relatively high, have a more hierarchical culture. On the other hand, cultures that value egalitarianism believe that responsible social behaviour can be induced by encouraging people to recognize one another as moral equals who share basic interests. People in more egalitarian cultures are socialized to a commitment to voluntary cooperation with others, to transcend selfish interests, and to promote the welfare of others. Countries like Spain and Belgium belong to this category of more egalitarian cultures.

Further online reading The following article can be accessed for free on the book's companion website https://study.sagepub.com/liu2e: Schwartz, Shalom H. and Lilach Sagiv (1995) 'Identifying culture-specifics in the content and structure of values', *Journal of Cross-Cultural Psychology*, 26(1): 99–116.

The third universal issue that Schwartz identifies is the relation of humankind to nature. Resolutions to this issue give rise to the cultural dimension which he calls *mastery versus harmony*. Mastery cultures encourage people to actively control and change the world and to exploit it in order to advance personal or group interests. They emphasize getting ahead through self-assertion; ambition, success, daring, and competence are valued. India and China are ranked high on the mastery end. A culture that values harmony with nature encourages acceptance and fitting harmoniously into the environment, as humans are viewed as an integral part of nature; unity with nature, protecting the environment, and the world of beauty are valued. This cultural orientation is held by the dominant cultures in Italy and Mexico.

Critical thinking...

In what ways are Schwartz's value dimensions, Hofstede's cultural dimensions, and Kluckhohn and Strodtbeck's value orientations similar, and in what ways are they different?

INTERCULTURAL COMMUNICATION ETHICS

Ethics is concerned with what is right or wrong, good or bad, and the standards and rules that guide our behaviour. Ethics is different from morals: morals are our personal beliefs, while ethics is the study of what is good for the individual and society. Communication ethics involves how we engage in communication acts and the consequences of our communication behaviour (Chen and Starosta, 2005). When we engage in intercultural interactions, we evaluate each other's communication based on our own cultural rules. We make decisions about what is right or wrong, albeit sometimes subconsciously, and apply ethical principles. Scholars in intercultural communication debate whether there are overarching ethical frameworks that we can apply to all cultures, or whether each culture determines its own standard for what is right or wrong. Ethical issues are important in intercultural communication, as the variation of cultural norms may mean variation of ethical standards.

Approaches to ethics

Debates on approaches to ethics have largely been about two approaches: universalism versus relativism. Proponents of *ethical universalism* believe that there are universal ethical principles that guide behaviour across all societies. Thus, what is wrong in one place will be wrong elsewhere, regardless of time and circumstance (Lowenstein and Merrill, 1990). Universalist approaches are connected to a unilinear model of cultural development which describes all cultures as progressing along a single line of development and converging on a single universal set of values and norms. The Geneva Convention standards on appropriate warfare, and human rights groups who work across geographic and cultural borders, can be considered as illustrative of this universalistic view. The problem with universalism is that universalist approaches attempt to ground ethics variously in religion, nature, history, and reason, but largely fail because there is no agreement about what is religiously authoritative, natural, historical, or reasonable (Evanoff, 2004).

Contrary to universalism, proponents of *ethical relativism* believe that ethics is closely related to motive, intuition, and emotion. They believe that while people from different cultures share common needs, interests, or feelings, their ways of acting upon these internal states vary because of cultural differences. Relativists deny the existence of a single universal set of values and norms, and instead believe that values and norms are relative to particular individuals or groups (Lowenstein and Merrill, 1990). Relativist approaches are connected with subjectivity in ethics, the preservation of local cultures, and a multilinear model of cultural development which views all cultures as progressing along separate lines of development and diverging with respect to values and norms (Evanoff, 2004). Thus, ethical relativists would not judge another's behaviour by their own ethical standards because they believe that adhering to one's own contextualized truths in intercultural interactions only leads to conflict. Nevertheless relativism, which is widely accepted in the field of intercultural communication, is not without criticisms. While acknowledging that various cultures construct ethical systems, cultural relativists fail to address how conflicts between cultures with different values and norms can be resolved. Moreover, there is often a difference between what is done (descriptive ethics) and what should be done (normative ethics).

Evanoff (2004) states that relativism seems progressive but is in fact conservative because it obligates us simply to accept the values and norms of other cultures instead of encouraging us to critically reflect upon them. He proposes a communicative approach to intercultural ethics as an alternative to both universalism and relativism. The *communicative ethical approach* recognizes that humans are socialized into a particular set of cultural norms, but claims that they are capable of critically reflecting upon and changing them. We are also able to critically review the norms of other cultures and make informed decisions about which of them are worthy of adoption or rejection. Ethical dialogue on intercultural communication can take place between specific cultures in specific contexts in relation to specific problems and specific individuals or groups. Thus, rather than seeing ethics as fixed, a communicative approach views ethics as dynamic and changing. For example, we no longer find slavery acceptable, and we are in the process of creating ethical norms to deal with emerging issues like euthanasia.

Principles of ethical intercultural communication

Bradford Hall (2005) provides a comprehensive overview of intercultural communication ethics. He argues that the controversy between universalism and relativism both enables and constrains creativity and stability in human societies. Therefore, a more appropriate way to examine intercultural ethics is to integrate both universal and relative perspectives (Chen and Starosta, 2005). Just as Hall claims that communication ethics is a combination of constraints and empowerment, one of the golden rules for communication ethics, originally based in religious philosophy, is 'Do unto others as you would have them do unto you'. Similarly, a famous Confucian maxim states, 'Never do to others what you would not like them to do to you.' In this section, we will discuss four ethical principles guiding intercultural communication, based on Chen and Starosta's (2005) work.

Mutuality

Mutuality means we should locate a common space. The key to this principle is human relationships in interacting with others. We need to gain an understanding of the perspective of the other before making any ethical decisions. We also need to build relational empathy with the other party. A spirit of equality, inclusiveness, and supportive climate is conducive to successful communication outcomes. On the other hand, if either party demands that the interaction be conducted according to his or her own cultural norms, intercultural communication is unlikely to be successful.

Non-judgementalism

Non-judgementalism implies a willingness to express ourselves openly and be open-minded about others' behaviours. The key to this principle is to understand the other's point of view, power position, and cultural values. Muslim women cover their head with a scarf in public to observe their religious beliefs; Chinese business people often give gifts to their business partners, not to bribe but to show their desire to establish a good interpersonal relationship, because in China there is an overlap between personal and work relationships. None of these practices may be practised in your culture; the important point is to recognize and appreciate differences.

Honesty

The principle of honesty requires us to see things as they are rather than as we would like them to be. For example, Elliott (1997) examined the cross-cultural tensions created by the 1995 earthquake in Japan. When the Japanese government was slow to accept the assistance offered by the international community, the US media were quick to criticize what it perceived as ingratitude. However, Elliott uncovered the cultural assumptions that underlay the Japanese response, such as collective self-sufficiency, emphasis on local-first action, bottom-up decision making, and lack of emphasis on individual volunteerism. We are socialized into our own cultural rules and norms as we grow up; and hence carry personal biases regarding what is or is not an appropriate way of handling certain situations. In the process of intercultural communication, we must be aware of these biases in order to understand other people's behaviour as it is.

Respect

Respect involves sensitivity to and acknowledgement of other people's needs and wants. Like mutuality, the golden rule with respect is to 'Do unto others as you would have them do unto you'. The platinum rule goes one step further, stating that rather than treating others as you want to be treated, treat them as you think they would want to be treated. For example, religious practices vary widely across cultural and ethnic groups. Muslims fast at a certain time of the year to demonstrate their religious faith; some Buddhists do not eat red meat as an illustration of the religious principle of non-violence; whereas people in Hong Kong offer temple sacrifices of baby pig in return for a deity's protection. To be an ethical intercultural communicator means to be open to and respect all these practices, even though they may seem to contradict each other. We do not necessarily have to practise what other cultures do, but we need to respect the people who observe those customs and rituals.

SUMMARY

- Hofstede's four cultural dimensions include individualism versus collectivism, masculinity versus femininity, power distance, and uncertainty avoidance. A fifth dimension was developed by Hofstede and Bond, long-term versus short-term orientation.

- This five-dimensional model has been widely used in cross-cultural research on organizations, on individuals, and on communities, although it has attracted some criticisms.

- Edward T. Hall's high-context and low-context culture model describes the extent to which individuals rely on verbal codes or contextual codes for information.

- Kluckhohn and Strodtbeck's theory of value orientations include man–nature, activity, time, human nature, and relationships. Condon and Yousef have extended Kluckhohn and Strodtbeck's model, but the variation of cultural values makes it impossible for a single list to be exhaustive.

- Schwartz's value theory identifies seven cultural value types, which are summarized into three dimensions: embeddedness versus autonomy, hierarchy versus egalitarianism, and mastery versus harmony.

- Three approaches to ethics are discussed: universalism, relativism, and a communicative approach. General principles governing all ethical intercultural communication include mutuality, non-judgmentalism, honesty, and respect.

JOIN THE DEBATE

Should same-sex marriage be accepted across the world?

The debate around same-sex marriage, often referred to as marriage equality, is increasingly complex. Despite advocates arguing that there is a growing level of support for marriage equality, the decision or desire to legally redefine 'marriage' is complicated by personal, social, and religious reasons, as well as legal issues. Some cultures, including many religious groups, view the purpose of marriage as the reproduction and balanced upbringing of offspring, which these groups argue is not possible in same-sex relationships. Those religious groups often cite Bible passages that support their view. On the other hand, those in favour of marriage equality maintain that it is a basic human right, and argue that the current legislation is discriminatory based on sexual orientation. By mid-2013, 15 countries had enacted legislation allowing same-sex couples to marry, including Argentina, New Zealand, and South Africa. In many federal countries, such as Australia, Mexico, and the USA, the debate continues nationally despite many states altering their legislation in favour of marriage equality. What's your view on same-sex marriage? Should the definition of marriage be universal or culture-specific?

CASE STUDY

Museums as a site of culture

A museum is an institution that safeguards different collections of material objects of scientific, artistic, cultural, or historical importance and makes them available for the public to visit through exhibits. Most museums are located in urban areas throughout the world, but more local and community-oriented museums exist in smaller towns and the countryside. Most generally, museums are cultural institutions with a major goal of educating the public about different cultures. The city with the largest number of museums is Mexico City, with over 128 museums. According to the World Museum Community (World Museum Community, 2013), there are more than 57,000 museums in 202 countries. In the UK alone, it is estimated that there are about 2,500 museums.

The opening of museums to the public in the seventeenth century and their subsequent use as an educational instrument that shapes middle-class citizenry was crucial in helping to create national cultures (Bennett, 1995). Early museums began as the private collections of wealthy individuals, families, or institutions of art and rare or curious natural objects and other material objects. These were often displayed in so-called wonder rooms or 'cabinets of curiosities'. In France, the first public museum was the Louvre Museum in Paris. It opened in 1793, during the French Revolution, and enabled free access to people from different classes for the first time. The Musée d'Orsay, situated on the left bank of the river Seine, is another world-famous museum in Paris. The museum building was originally a railway station, Gare d'Orsay, and remained in use as a railway station until 1939. The suggestion to turn the station into a museum came from the Directorate of the Museums of France. The idea was to build a museum that would bridge the gap between the Louvre and the National Museum of Modern Art at the Georges Pompidou Centre. The museum officially opened in December 1986 by then-president, François Mitterrand.

Museums, particularly anthropological or ethnographic museums that focus on past representations of cultural worlds, can help to create a version of those worlds that reflects certain cultural attitudes and values. Museums have always been an expression of a particular time and place (MacGregor, 2009). From the constructivist notion of representation, these museum exhibits are not reflecting past cultures; they are actually *creating* a specific version of those cultures (Bennett, 1995). These exhibits of Asian, African, or South American countries, some argue, often reflected Western colonialist discourses and imagination. During the nineteenth and early twentieth century, European and American museums often exhibited 'other' cultures as inferior, primitive, or exotic (MacGregor, 2009). These exhibits reflected a Western political and ideological perspective of colonized parts of the world. For example, an exhibition at the 1904 St Louis World's Fair portrayed the Igorots, a Philippine tribe, as only eating dog meat, a representation that served to represent them as 'primitive', 'uncivilized', or 'savage' (Bennett, 1995).

Types of museum vary, from large institutions (one of the biggest museums in Spain, the Prado Museum in Madrid, features some of the best collections of European art from the twelfth century to the early nineteenth century), to very small institutions focusing on a specific subject, location, or some important person. For example, the Museum of Broken Relationships, a museum in Zagreb, Croatia, is dedicated to failed love relationships. Its exhibits include personal objects left over from former lovers, accompanied by brief descriptions. Museums can involve fine arts, applied arts, archaeology, anthropology and ethnology, biography, history, cultural history, science, technology, children's museums, natural history, and botanical gardens. As culture becomes more globalized, the issues of representation and inclusion become crucial. Ethnic, religious, political, and class minorities, marginalized groups, immigrants, and local communities all claim representation in museums, for they understand the museum as a powerful agent of cultural memory representation and identity construction. Thus, museums have gone from being a national, regional, or local phenomenon to being a worldwide phenomenon.

One of the examples of cultural museums is the national Museum of World Culture that opened in Gothenburg, Sweden, in 2004. Its aim is to interpret the subject of world culture in an interdisciplinary way; that is, in a dynamic and open-ended manner.

> On the one hand, various cultures are incorporating impulses from each other and becoming more alike. On the other hand, local, national, ethnic and gender differences are shaping much of that process. World culture is not only about communication, globalization, reciprocity and interdependence, but also about the specificity, concretion and uniqueness of each and every culture and individual. (Museum of World Culture, 2013)

The question of diversity and the acknowledgement of differences are leitmotifs of cultural confrontation and representation in the Museum of World Culture. Diversity and differences afford the complex issues of confrontation with other histories and cultures. This museum does this without any prejudice, giving way to many voices, ideas, proposals, and disputes. It is a creative meeting place with dynamic exhibitions and programmes about current questions in the world around us. The Museum of World Culture has around 100,000 objects spread across 2,500 collections from around the world that are managed and shown to the public in Sweden and abroad. These different cultural exhibitions highlight contemporary global issues through a combination of their own and borrowed objects and photographs, films and artwork. Vital knowledge about the collections and social issues is kept alive through the collaboration with international researchers. They also have a rich library and archive, including more than 30,000 titles, correspondence by former museum managers, field diaries and old photographs. Children and young people are of particular importance to the Museum of World Culture and their emphasis is on children's and young people's rights to a global history and future.

References

Bennett, Tony (1995) *The Birth of the Museum: History, Theory, Politics*. London: Routledge.

MacGregor, Neil (2009) 'To shape the citizens of that great city, the world', in J. Cuno (ed.), *Whose Culture? The Promise of Museums and the Debate over Antiquities*. Princeton, NJ: Princeton University Press. pp. 35–54.

Museum of World Culture (2013) *Who We Are*. Accessed 20 October 2013 at: www.varldskulturmuseerna.se/varldskulturmuseet/.

World Museum Community (2013) *Cultural Tourism*. Accessed 20 October 2013 at: http://icom.museum/.

Questions for discussion

1. How can museums represent cultures, their values, and identities with an intercultural approach?

2. How can museums face the challenge of representing multiple cultures in contemporary global society?

3. Are museums still laboratories for enhancing experience, education, and cultural dialogue? How can museums play the role of mediators in cultural exchanges?

4. What can happen when the 'peoples' and their cultures implicated in, and at least to some extent constructed in, museum representation shift, change, multiply, fragment, and/or move?

5. The Musée d'Orsay in Paris has an approach somewhat similar to that of the Museum of World Culture. What can you find out about this museum?

FURTHER READINGS

All articles listed next to the mouse icon below can be accessed for free on the book's companion website: https://study.sagepub.com/liu2e

Cultural dimensions

Li, Shu, Harry C. Triandis, and Yao Yu (2006) 'Cultural orientation and corruption', *Ethics and Behavior*, 16(3): 199–215.

Previous studies claim that individuals in collectivist cultures may be more corrupt than those in individualist cultures when they are interacting with outgroup members. This study challenges this claim, and discusses the relationship between deception and cultural orientation. In particular, the authors examined the cultural orientation differences in the propensity to lie in negotiation and family contexts in Singapore. They found a positive correlation between deception and vertical collectivism during an organizational scenario, whereas a positive correlation between deception and individualism occurred during a family setting scenario.

Merritt, Ashleigh (2000) 'Culture in the cockpit: do Hofstede's dimensions replicate?', *Journal of Cross-Cultural Psychology*, 31(2): 283–301.

This paper aims to replicate Hofstede's indexes of national culture by surveying 9,400 male commercial airline pilots from 19 countries. The analysis, which removed the constraint of item equivalence, proved superior, both conceptually and empirically, to the analysis using Hofstede's items and formulae as prescribed, and rendered significant replication correlations for all indexes (individualism–collectivism .96, power distance .87, masculinity–femininity .75, and uncertainty avoidance .68). The successful replication confirms that national culture exerts an influence on cockpit behaviour over and above the professional culture of pilots, and that 'one size fits all' training is inappropriate.

Culture and behaviour

Lee, Hyung-Seok and Jin S. Park (2012) 'Cultural orientation and the persuasive effects of fear appeals: the case of anti-smoking public service announcements', *Journal of Medical Marketing*, 12(2): 73–80.

The purpose of this study is to examine whether the extent to which one is individualistic moderates the persuasive effects of fear appeals in anti-smoking public service announcements. A total of 129 undergraduates in the United States and South Korea participated in an experiment designed to test the hypothesis that individualists respond better to an anti-smoking public service announcement with emphasis on an individualistic fear appeal, whereas a public service announcement stressing a collectivistic fear appeal is more effective among collectivists. The results supported the hypothesis, implying that fear appeals in anti-smoking public service announcements should address the target audience's cultural orientation. The study also showed that an individual's cultural orientation is not necessarily determined by their country of origin. That is, the effects of fear appeals were moderated by the individual's internalized cultural orientation, not their country of origin *per se*.

Value orientations

Ng, Sharon (2010) 'Cultural orientation and brand dilution: impact of motivation level and extension typicality', *Journal of Marketing Research*, 47(1): 186–198.

This research examines cross-cultural differences in brand dilution effects and the moderating role of motivation and extension typicality. Drawing from recent findings that indicate that culture affects the way people treat conflicting information, this research predicts that Easterners and Westerners react differently to failures by a brand extension. In contrast to previous findings that have suggested that failure in a typical extension leads to less brand dilution for Westerners when they are highly motivated (than when they are less motivated), this study argues that Easterners exhibit greater brand dilution when they are less motivated (than when they are highly motivated). The opposite pattern of results should emerge when the extension is atypical. Three studies provide support for these predictions and the underlying processes.

Tsai, Jeanne L. (2000) 'Cultural orientation of Hmong young adults', *Journal of Human Behavior in the Social Environment*, 3(3–4): 99–114.

This study explored whether American-born and overseas-born Hmong young adults differed in levels, models, and meanings of cultural orientation. Fourteen American-born and 32 overseas-born Hmong college students were asked what 'being Hmong' and 'being American' meant to them. Both groups reported being more oriented to American culture than Hmong culture. Despite similarities in mean levels of orientation to Hmong and American cultures and in the meanings of 'being Hmong' and 'being American', American-born Hmong and overseas-born Hmong differed in their underlying models of cultural orientation. For American-born Hmong, 'being Hmong' and 'being American' were unrelated constructs, whereas for overseas-born Hmong, they were negatively correlated constructs.

'You can out-distance that which is running after you, but not what is running inside you. '

Rwandan proverb

6

CATEGORIZATION, SUBGROUPS, AND IDENTITIES

LEARNING OBJECTIVES

At the end of this chapter, you should be able to:

- Define the different types of identity.

- Explain the sources and characteristics of identities.

- Explain theories of identities and identity negotiation.

- Analyse identities within the contexts of history, economics, and politics.

INTRODUCTION

Identity is the cornerstone of our times (Castells, 1997), and it gives us a sense of place. As we grow up, we encounter many situations in which we ask ourselves or are asked the question 'Who am I?', which penetrates to the deepest levels of our being. Identity manifests personal or group characteristics and expresses specific memberships. It is generally agreed that the term 'identity' refers primarily to a person's subjective experience of himself or herself in relation to the world, and as such it should be differentiated from concepts like character or personality. One can share character traits with many people, but the sharing of such traits does not require any active personal engagement. Sharing an identity, however, implies that we actively engage part of our being in order to identify with a certain group. This notion of active engagement indicates that one's identity is formed through cultural processes, which are in turn conditioned by cultural structures. The multifaceted nature of identities is experienced and negotiated constantly in everyday life.

Broadly speaking, identities can be studied at the individual or collective level. *Individual* (or *personal*) *identity* refers to categorizing an individual as distinct from others, along with the specific relationships the individual has with others. *Collective* (or *social*) *identity* refers to categorization based on group membership, to make groups rather than individuals distinctive. Identification with and perceived acceptance into a group involve learning systems of symbols as well as values, norms, and rules, all expressing people's group or cultural affiliation. Racial identity, for example, is a type of collective identity. Generally, racial identity involves a group that characterizes itself and/or is characterized by others as being distinct by immutable biological differences (even in the absence of actual biological evidence). As a defining and controlling characteristic, race has been used for not only social categorization, but also discrimination throughout history. Humans in all cultures desire positive individually-based and group-based identities, which are expressed in their communicative interactions (Ting-Toomey, 2005a).

We categorize people based on their group membership, which gives us social identities and systematically orders the world around us. Throughout our lives, we identify with various social groups, and hence develop multiple identities. As early as the fifth century BC, Greeks used factors such as blood, language, religion, and way of life to identify what they shared in common and what distinguished them from Persians and other non-Greeks (Cooper et al., 2007). In addition to race and culture, identities can be defined by gender, class, ethnicity, religion, political orientation, social group, occupation, and geographic region.

Sometimes we are positioned into categories that we do not want to be a part of. In addition, while some group memberships are voluntary (e.g., political affiliation, occupation), others are involuntary (e.g., sex, age). Because of our multiple group or subgroup memberships, we are always engaged in communicating with people from outgroups (groups we do not belong to). This chapter focuses on categorization, subgroups, and identities. We explain social categorization theories, and describe the formation of different types of identity based on gender, ethnicity, religion, sexual orientation, culture, and nationality. Various historical and contemporary examples are provided, followed by discussions on the role of identity in intercultural communication. This chapter emphasizes that identity is not given and fixed, but rather, it is constantly negotiated and reconstructed.

SOCIAL CATEGORIZATION AND IDENTITIES

As explained in Chapter 4, *categorization* is defined as a process of ordering the environment through the grouping of persons, objects, and events as being similar or equivalent to one another, based on their shared features or characteristics (Tajfel, 1978). When we selectively perceive stimuli from the external world, we organize and arrange them in meaningful and systematic ways. In everyday life, we try to distinguish individuals, groups, or cultures based on their differences. Such categorization has both advantages and disadvantages. On the one hand, it reduces the complexity of the world and helps us to understand our environment by giving it some structure; on the other hand, categorization, particularly of people, can reinforce stereotypes (Tajfel, 1982). Categorizing people into groups gives us identities at both an individual and a group level.

Critical thinking...

Is identity a process or a product, or both? Draw on your personal experience to illustrate your view on this. What are your most important social and personal identities? What are your main outgroups, and how do you feel about these outgroups?

Categorization and the formation of identities

Social identity theory posits that identity formation is a product of social categorization (Hogg and Abrams, 1988). Individuals belong to various social categories (e.g., gender, class, religion, political affiliation), and form identities based on membership of social categories. Through this process, society is internalized by individuals on the basis of social categories. Social identities connect individuals to society through group memberships which influence their beliefs, attitudes, and behaviour in their relationships with members of other social groups.

Broadly speaking, identities can be at individual or group levels. We often use the term *personal identity* to define an individual in terms of his or her difference from others. The individual creates a self-image and responds to the image created. Others also expect the individual to act in accordance with his or her self-image. Aspects of personal identity include physical features, hobbies, interests, family relationships, social circle, as well as personal aspects of age, sex, nationality, religious affiliation, disability, sexual orientation, and so forth. The specific way in which each of us sees ourselves in relation to those around us and those things that make us unique are all a part of personal identity. Personal identity consists of the things that pick us out as individuals and make us distinct from others who are similar in some ways (e.g., the things that make me distinct from my friends, fellow employees, etc.). Part of our personal identity, such as sex and genetic characteristics, is given to us at birth. Other parts are created during our childhood and continue to evolve throughout our lives as we are socialized into society (Denzin and Lincoln, 1998). Personal identity gives individuals a sense of distinctiveness even when they are in a crowd of similar people.

Photo 6.1   Our personal identity picks us out as individuals and makes us distinct from others, even when we are in a crowd.
Copyright © Joan Burnett. Used with permission.

Further online reading   The following article can be accessed for free on the book's companion web-site https://study.sagepub.com/liu2e: Banks, Stephen P., Esther Louie and Martha Einerson (2000) 'Constructing personal identities in holiday letters', *Journal of Social and Personal Relationships*, 17(2): 299–327.

We tend to use the term *social identity* to refer to those parts of an individual's self-concept which derive from his or her membership in a group, together with the value and emotional significance attached to membership (Tajfel, 1978). Social identities pick us out as group members and distinguish our groups (e.g., national groups, sports groups) from other, perhaps competing, groups. Social identity influences how we live within diverse cultural contexts and relate to a range of social groups and institutions (Jenkins, 1996). Social groups can be marked by family connections, ethnic communities, cultural groups, race, nationality, occupation, or friendship circles.

Individuals construct social categories like sports clubs, liberals, and Jews, and use their beliefs, attitudes, feelings, and behaviours as prototypes to differentiate their own groups from other groups. Hogg and Mullin (1999) argue that individuals are more inclined to align themselves with the norms of their group when they experience a sense of uncertainty. Think of racial identities and what it means to be 'white'. Fanon (1990) writes that white individuals in the West are usually unaware of themselves as belonging to a specific racial group, because being white is taken for granted. On the other hand, people from other racial backgrounds are more aware of their minority group membership, as distinct from the majority. An important consequence of categorizing people based on group membership is drawing the boundary between ingroups and outgroups; some types of groups (e.g., those with a strong collective or group-based orientation) and some contexts (e.g., rivalry or competition for scarce resources) lead to sharper boundaries being drawn than others.

THEORY CORNER

STAGES OF IDENTITY DEVELOPMENT

According to Hardiman (2001), there are several stages for social identity development by white people in Western cultures. Firstly, there is an unexamined identity phase, characterized by acceptance of dominant norms and a lack of desire to look into one's identity. Following this is an acceptance phase, a stage during which dominant group members internalize the identity imposed by the culture. In the third stage, redefinition, a reinterpretation of the dominant culture occurs and may be accompanied by attempts to openly challenge it. The fourth stage is integration, whereby white people connect themselves to a dominant culture that reflects an awareness of the special privilege accorded to them and an appreciation of the values of minority cultures. Of course, this final stage is frequently not achieved. Identity development may not necessarily follow a liner process, and the length of each stage may vary from person to person.

Reference

Hardiman, Rita (2001) 'Reflections on white identity development theory', in C. L. Wijeyesinghe and J. B. Bailey (eds), *New Perspectives on Racial Identity Development: A Theoretical and Practical Anthology*. New York: New York University Press. pp. 12–34.

Further reading on identity development

Erickson, Erik H. (1980) *Identity and the Life Cycle*. New York: W. W. Norton & Co.

Theory in Practice

IDENTITY DEVELOPMENT THROUGH ADOLESCENCE

Psychologists often regard adolescence as a period of self-identity and growth, particularly in relation to the physical and social changes that teenagers go through during this time. Social identities are activated through self-categorization, particularly through comparison of oneself with others. Some scholars believe that during adolescence young people undergo the stages of identity development. Tanti and colleagues (2011: 556) argue that 'in most Western cultures, adolescents generally experience significant change in their social world during two major transitions that are clearly afforded by the prevailing social-cultural milieu': transition from primary school to secondary school, and transition from secondary school to university or work. Both of these transitions involve a marked period of discontinuity in the adolescent's social world. They may confront more diverse and heterogeneous social situations, and different roles, responsibilities, and expectations from the different groups with which they are associated. All these experiences give rise to the possibilities of new social group memberships and identities. In their study, Tanti et al. (2011) found that the stages of identity development of adolescents are shaped by the stereotyping of the groups they belong to as well as of the groups they do not belong to.

Questions to take you further

How can each of Hardiman's (2001) stages of identity development be illustrated during adolescence? How do these stages work as social identity changes across situations?

Reference

Tanti, Chris, Arthur A. Stukas, Michael J. Halloran and Margaret Foddy (2011) 'Social identity change: shifts in social identity during adolescence', *Journal of Adolescence*, 34(3): 555–567.

Further reading on identity development during adolescence

Tarrant, Mark, Adrian C. North, Mark D. Edridge, Laura E. Kirk, Elizabeth A. Smith and Roisin, E. Turner (2001) 'Social identity in adolescence', *Journal of Adolescence*, 24(5): 597–609.

Critical thinking...

Ageism, as an example of negative stereotyping of older people, is manifested in daily life, such as 'baby talk' – a condescending form of addressing older people adopted by younger people. Do you think all older people have negative views about 'baby talk'? Why or why not? Give some examples of other groups where stereotypes affect the way people address each other.

Ingroups and outgroups

For individuals in any culture, there are groups to which they belong, called membership groups, and the groups to which they do not belong, or non-membership groups. Membership groups can be involuntary (like age, race, sex), or they can be voluntary (like political affiliation, religion, or occupation). *Ingroups* represent a special class of membership group characterized by internal cohesiveness among members. An ingroup's norms, aspirations, and values shape the behaviour of its members. When the ingroup is salient, members are concerned about each other's welfare and are willing to cooperate without demanding equitable returns. Ingroups are characterized by some shared experiences (sometimes via the mass media) and an anticipated shared future, so that they create a sense of intimacy, solidarity, and trust.

Like membership groups, non-membership groups can be voluntary or involuntary. An *outgroup* is a non-membership that is salient to the ingroup. An outgroup is seen as distinct from the ingroup or sometimes standing in the way of the accomplishment of the ingroup's goals (Jandt, 2007). Outgroups comprise people whose welfare we are not concerned about, and groups with whom we require at least an equitable return in order to cooperate (Neuliep, 2012). Attributions made about ingroup and outgroup members are typically biased in favour of the ingroup. Ingroup bias occurs on the dimensions on which we compare ingroups and outgroups (e.g., intelligence, language proficiency), even though any real difference may be on another dimension altogether (e.g., national origin). We tend to see outgroups as homogeneous, but to see more variability in ingroups (see Chapter 4).

Different cultures ascribe different meanings to ingroup and outgroup relationships. In individualistic cultures, such as that of the United States and the Netherlands, people are considered as independent, and fewer and less sharp distinctions are made between ingroups and outgroups. In collectivistic cultures like Greece and Nigeria, people are more group-oriented and individuals are considered as interdependent and hence very close to their ingroups. As survival of both the individual and society is more dependent on the group, sharper distinctions are made between ingroups and outgroups. Distinctions between ingroups and outgroups lead to a sense of belonging, security, and trust. We often treat strangers or outsiders with suspicion and control them carefully while deciding if we can trust them or not. We tend to be more tolerant of the behaviour of ingroup members than of outsiders, creating a distinction between what is known as '*inside* morals' and '*outside* morals'. The reach of morals is called the scope of justice. Coleman (2000: 118) states: 'Individuals or groups within our moral boundaries are seen as deserving of the same fair, moral treatment as we deserve. Individuals or groups outside these boundaries are seen as undeserving of this same treatment.'

It is important to remember that social identities, and indeed our group memberships, are not fixed. As our memberships or the social context changes, we need to reconstruct or renegotiate our social identities. The Indian feminist scholar Chandra Talpade Mohanty vividly illustrated this point by drawing upon her own experience (Mohanty, 2003: 190):

Growing up in India, I was Indian; teaching in high school in Nigeria, I was a foreigner (still Indian), albeit a familiar one. As a graduate student in Illinois, I was first a 'Third World' foreign student, and then a person of color. Doing research in London, I was black. As a professor at an American university, I am an Asian woman – although South Asian racial profiles fit uneasily into the 'Asian' category – and, because I choose to identify myself as such, an antiracist feminist of color. In North America I was also a 'resident alien' with an Indian passport – I am now a US citizen whose racialization has shifted dramatically (and negatively) since the attacks on the World Trade Center and the Pentagon on September 11, 2001.

Critical thinking...

Think about a time when you were treated as an outgroup member. What was done by others that made you feel like an outgroup member? How did you react to being excluded? When have you treated other people as outgroup members, rather than as individuals? How has this changed your own behaviour? What has their reaction been?

THEORY CORNER

IDENTITY NEGOTIATION THEORY

Identity negotiation theory, proposed by Stella Ting-Toomey (2005a), emphasizes particular identity domains as influential to our everyday interactions. Individuals acquire and develop their identities through interaction with others, as it is in this way that we acquire values, beliefs, norms, and styles governing communication behaviour. There are many possible identities available or ascribed to us, including those of social class, sexual orientation, age, race, ethnicity, and culture. To become effective intercultural communicators, we have to understand both the cultural content and the salient issues of identity domains and how others view themselves in communication.

Identity negotiation theory posits identity as a reflective self-image constructed during the process of intercultural communication. The means of negotiating this identity is described as 'a transactional interaction process whereby individuals in an intercultural situation attempt to assert, define, modify, challenge, and/or support their own and others' desired self-images' (Ting-Toomey, 2005a: 217). Identity negotiation is present through all communication interactions as communicators simultaneously attempt to evoke their own desired identities and challenge or support others' identities. Intercultural communication requires the mindful process of attuning to self-identity issues, as well as being consciously aware of and attuning to the salient identity issues of others.

Reference

Ting-Toomey, Stella (2005a) 'Identity negotiation theory: crossing cultural boundaries', in W. B. Gudykunst (ed.), *Theorizing about Intercultural Communication.* Thousand Oaks, CA: Sage. pp. 211–233.

Further reading on identity negotiation

Qin, Desiree B. (2009) 'Being "good" or being "popular": gender and ethnic identity negotiations of Chinese immigrant adolescents', *Journal of Adolescent Research*, 24(1): 37–66.

Theory in Practice

IDENTITY NEGOTIATION FOR TOUR GUIDES

When people first meet and interact, they are likely to try to establish respective identities as well as projecting their own desired identity according to situational requirements. As Swann, Johnson and Bosson (2009: 81) write, 'The same woman, for example, may be warm with her children, chilly with her employees, and a mixture of both with her in-laws.' This can create a problem in communication when communicators on both sides are trying to predict what their counterpart will say or do and how she might react to what is said or done. This can particularly be an issue for tour guides, whose job requires them constantly to predict and appease the expectations of their customers.

Huang (2011) analysed the communication behaviours of tour guides in Yunnan Province in southern China. With growing tourism across China, it has become vitally important for tour guides to balance or negotiate identities in order to ensure that their communication with international tourists is appropriate and effective. As Huang argues, tour guides already have preconceived perceptions of themselves and their expected role; they may also have formed certain 'stereotypes' of tourists from different parts of the world. However, those pre-existing expectations of their customers and their own anticipated role as tour guides may not match. Huang's study revealed that tour guides from China place more emphasis on ethnic identity when interacting with foreign tourists than on professional identity or personal identity. Sometimes such expectations clash with the ways in which the tourists want themselves to be viewed. Therefore, identity negotiation has to take place during the initial communication between guides and tourists.

Questions to take you further

Why do you think ethnic identity is more important for Chinese tour guides than professional or personal identities? Are there other professions where this might be the same or opposite? Which aspect of your identity is most important to you and why?

References

Huang, Ying (2011) 'Identity negotiation in relation to context of communication', *Theory and Practice in Language Studies*, 1(3): 219–225.

Swann, William B., Russell E. Johnson and Jennifer K. Bosson (2009) 'Identity negotiation at work', *Research in Organizational Behavior*, 29: 81–109.

Further reading on identity negotiation
Pavelenko, Aneta and Adrian Blackledge (eds) (2004) *Negotiation of Identities in Multilingual Contexts*. Buffalo, NY: Multilingual Matters.

SUBGROUP MEMBERSHIPS AND IDENTITIES

The identities that mark the boundaries between the self and others, or those between ingroups and outgroups, explain a great deal about why people think and behave in the way they do. The following section discusses identities based on gender, ethnicity, religion, culture, and nationality.

Gender identity

Gender identity is a part of a personal as well as social identity. The term 'gender' entails social roles established for the sexes, while the term 'sex' refers to a biological category, usually determined at birth. Gender is a social interpretation of biological sex and its associated cultural assumptions and expectations. All cultures divide some aspects of human existence into distinct male and female roles, but the content of gender roles – the norms of behaviour, expectations, and assumptions associated with them – vary across cultures. These characteristics may or may not be closely related to the biological differences between males and females.

Further online reading The following article can be accessed for free on the book's companion website https://study.sagepub.com/liu2e: Stapleton, Karyn and John Wilson (2004) 'Gender, nationality and identity: a discursive study', *European Journal of Women's Studies*, 11(1): 45–60.

Children develop gender-identity constancy by 5–6 years of age (Lee, 2000). *Gender constancy* is the concept that a child born as a girl will always be female, will adopt female roles, and will grow up to be a woman; similarly, a child born as a boy will adopt male roles and grow up to be a man. However, these continuities are not completely clear, and they have to be learned (Dines and Humez, 1995). Piaget studied the development of gender identity by examining young children's everyday play interactions, and found that by age 5, children tend to play with gender-specific toys. For example, girls tend to play more with dolls, while boys play more with *Superman* and *Batman* toys: young boys play together in larger groups, while young girls prefer to play more in pairs and smaller groups. It is also during this period of early childhood that children become aware of stereotypical gender roles. For example, a girl may see her mother cook most of the meals at home, and thus learn that cooking is a woman's job; a boy may observe his father carrying out repairs around the house and from this observation start to perceive repairing things as a man's job. Early beliefs about gender roles reflect children's observations of what they see around them, in their family, and elsewhere in the social environment.

However, gender identity is not necessarily limited to male or female. In some societies, another gender identity is possible, culturally defined as a *third gender*. The Native American *berdache* is defined as an individual with two spirits, both masculine and feminine. The *berdache* is believed to have supernatural powers. The *hijra* of India are recognized as a special caste. They are born with male genitals, but do not accept specifically male or female gender roles; instead, they identify themselves as *hijra*. In the Islamic culture of Oman, males who wear clothing that mixes masculine and feminine characteristics and who engage in sexual relations with males are called *khanith* and are also defined as a third gender. The *fa'afafine* of Samoa, the *fakaleiti* of Tonga, and the *mahu* of Hawaii and Tahiti further illustrate that gender identity can be disconnected from gender roles. These people are males with a feminized gender identity; they dress in feminine styles and perform female-designated tasks. Importantly, these third-gender roles are defined and accepted not only by the individuals themselves, but also by the wider society in which they live. For example, Samoa's social acceptance of *fa'afafine* has evolved from the long tradition of raising some boys as girls. In families with all male children, or in which the only daughter is too young to assist with the women's work, parents often choose one or more of their sons to help the mother. These boys perform women's work and are raised and dressed as girls.

? Critical thinking…

With the supposed equality of women in Western countries, it is not uncommon to see 'stay-home dads', particularly in urban areas. How would people from your culture respond to this phenomenon? How might this custom affect the economic structure of a society?

It is society that defines the gender roles we know as feminine and masculine. Masculinity in the West was traditionally denoted by strength and rationality, whereas femininity was traditionally associated with physical weakness, emotion, and intuition. People perform their gender identities daily as a matter of routine. However, when we do not identify with the specific norms of our society, when our identity does not fit the dominant culture, or when we do not respond in socially-accepted ways to our assigned identity, then we may be disparaged or discriminated against. Resisting an assigned identity can be extremely difficult, since it takes place at a subconscious level. Moreover, mass media, school, religion, and other social institutions are creators of gender stereotypes, which reinforce the gender roles we are supposed to inhabit. For example, males are often shown on television as strong and brave, powerful, and dominant, whereas female characters sometimes appear as submissive, emotional, and primarily focused on romantic relationships. These media representations inform and influence our understandings and expectations of gender roles in the real world. As Western norms and stereotypes about gender change, as they have over the past several decades, our identities and social interactions change with them, and this process introduces new tensions in the enactment of gender identities. Today in the West, and increasingly in other societies as well, there are intergroup conflicts over the ways in which gender identities and roles should be constructed.

THEORY CORNER

GAY, LESBIAN, BISEXUAL, TRANSGENDER AND INTERSEX IDENTITIES

Identity based on sexual orientation is a complex issue. Often, the formation of such identities is a fluid process, particularly when considering the impact of cultural identity as well as social, emotional, and familial complexities (Telingator and Woyewodzic, 2011). Theories of sexual identity have traditionally focused on self-identification as a sexual minority (Morgan, 2013). Sexuality researchers in particular have adopted more inclusive and multidimensional conceptualizations of sexual identity that incorporate sexual attraction, fantasy, and behaviour, and romantic, emotional, and social preferences, in understanding sexual identity. Mass media, in addition, play a significant role in shaping our perceptions about identities based on sexual orientations. Telingator and Woyewodzic (2011) argue that the growing discourse and visibility of gay and lesbian role models in the media have challenged mainstream notions of what is considered 'normal' sexual orientations. One category that people may use to identify themselves and others is GLBTI, which stands for gay, lesbian, bisexual, transgender, and intersex individuals. There is a tendency, however, for people to categorize these individuals only as GLBTI, and this category can overpower other identifiers.

References

Morgan, Elizabeth M. (2013) 'Contemporary issues in sexual orientation and identity development in emerging adulthood', *Emerging Adulthood*, 1(1): 52–66.
Telingator, Cynthia and Kelly T. Woyewodzic (2011) 'Sexual minority identity development', *Psychiatric Times*, 28(12): 39–42.

Further reading on sexual orientation as identity

Savin-Williams, Ritch C., Kara Joyner and Gerulf Rieger (2012) 'Prevalence and stability of self-reported sexual orientation identity during young adulthood', *Archives of Sexual Behavior*, 41(1): 103–110.

Theory in Practice

THE PLIGHT OF GLBTI REFUGEES

Despite legislation to prevent discrimination against people based on sexual preferences or gender orientations, individuals who identify as GLBTI remain a target of exclusion in many parts of the world.

Several countries, including the United Arab Emirates and Malaysia, criminalize same-sex relations, with punishments ranging from fines to the death penalty. The situation can be even worse if the individuals in question are refugees. Many GLBTI refugees, who may have fled their home country either from persecution and abuse due to their sexual orientations or for other reasons, feel uncomfortable sharing their sexual preferences or gender identity with immigration officials. They fear discrimination or being barred from resettlement in the host country. In addition to social isolation, GLBTI refugees have been found to face physical and sexual violence in migration detention facilities (Tabak and Levitan, 2013). The prevailing stereotypes and prejudices against GLBTI people could undermine the impartiality of decision making about accepting the refugee or otherwise. As an attempt to resolve this problem, the United Nations High Commission for Refugees (UNHCR) issued a Guidance Note in 2008 hoping to improve decision makers' awareness about the specific issues and concerns that GLBTI refugees face (Türk, 2013). This note has now been superseded by new guidelines published in October 2012.

Questions to take you further

What challenges face community organizations that work with GLBTI people? Do those working for these community organizations need special training? Should sexual orientation be considered in the decision making of accepting refugees?

References

Tabak, Shana and Rachel Levitan (2013) 'LGBTI migrants in immigration detention', *Forced Migration Review*, 42: 47–49.
Türk, Volker (2013) 'Ensuring protection for LGBTI persons of concern', *Forced Migration Review*, 42: 5–8.

Further reading on GLBTI refugees

Rumbach, Jennifer (2013) 'Towards inclusive resettlement for LGBTI refugees', *Forced Migration Review*, 42: 40–43.

Ethnic identity

Ethnicity can be based on national origin, race, or religion (Gordon, 1964). Ethnicity is different from race, but as a concept is often used interchangeably with or in relation to race. However, race is based on biological characteristics, while ethnicity is based on cultural characteristics shared by people of a particular race, national origin, religion, or language. *Ethnic identity* refers to a sense of belonging to or identification with an ethnic group. Individuals associated with a particular ethnic group do not necessarily act in accordance with ethnic norms, depending on their level of ethnic identification. For example, many Australians identify their ethnicity based on the countries from which their ancestors came. Some Vietnamese refugees who came to Australia during the 1970s as adopted orphans may still identify themselves as Vietnamese, although they were brought up in Anglo-Australian culture and may not even have a Vietnamese name. Thus, ethnic identity has value content and and salience content (Ting-Toomey, 2005a).

Value content refers to the standards that individuals use to evaluate their behaviours (Ting-Toomey, 2005b). For example, individualism underlies the behavours of some cultural groups more than others. Gudykunst (2004: 81) states that 'It is the shared cultural characteristics that influence communication, not the biological characteristics associated with race.' For example, Greek Australians are known to be group-oriented, as they perceive their universe in terms of the ingroup over the outgroup, with outgroup members often being viewed with suspicion and mistrust (Cooper et al., 2007). This does not necessarily suggest that membership in an ethnic group automatically translates into identification. As Alba (1990: 22) notes, 'Individuals may be ethnic in their "Identities" and still consciously reject their ethnic backgrounds.' Tensions can exist between a person's physical attributes or ethnic origin and the values he or she cherishes.

The salience content of ethnic identity refers to the strength of affiliation people have with their ethnic culture (Ting-Toomey, 2005a). Strong identification reflects high identity salience whereas weak identification reflects low identity salience. Individuals who are associated with a particular ethnic group (e.g., identifiable by skin colour) may not behave in accordance with their ethnic norms (Ting-Toomey, 2005b). For example, they may not adhere to their ethnic traditions, customs, language, or way of living. Many scholars today agree that ethnic identity is therefore more of a subjective classification than an objective one. It is the extent to which group members feel emotionally bonded by a common set of values, beliefs, traditions, and heritage (Ting-Toomey, 2005a). Second- or third-generation immigrants are less likely to feel as close a bond to their ethnic traditions as first-generation immigrants, even though they share the same physical attributes and may even use the ethnic language at home.

Photo 6.2   Gondolas, a traditional Venetian row boat, are symbolic of Venetian identity.
Copyright © Zala Volčič. Used with permission.

Further online reading   The following article can be accessed for free on the book's companion website https://study.sagepub.com/liu2e: Sfard, Anna and Anna Prusak (2005) 'Telling identities: in search of an analytical tool for investigating learning as a culturally shaped activity', *Educational Researcher*, 34(4): 14–22.

THEORY CORNER

INTERPELLATION

We like to think that, as individuals, our thoughts, behaviours, and various other social attributes emerge from deep within the core of our being: that we make and create them. At the same time, we recognize that society itself can structure how we think and act; it can shape our hopes and dreams, and even our self-understanding. Imagine how different you would be if you were born in a different country and culture. You would still be you, but you might think about yourself very differently. Instead of thinking of yourself, say, as German, Indian, or Dutch, you would identify with a different country, with different values and priorities – and these values might well become your own. The French philosopher Louis Althusser (1971) describes the process whereby a society creates individuals as particular kinds of people as a form of 'interpellation' or 'hailing' (as when someone calls out to you, asking you to respond). For Althusser, cultures interpellate or hail particular types of subject. When we come to recognize ourselves as the type of subject being called, the interpellation has been successful. That is, we come to identify ourselves with this type of subject (or type of person), and in this respect our sense of identity comes not from within, but from the outside – our culture and society that are 'hailing' us.

Reference

Althusser, Louis (1971) 'Ideology and ideological state apparatuses', *Lenin and Philosophy and Other Essays*. New York: Monthly Review Press.

Further reading on identity construction

White, Richard (2001) 'Cooees across the strand: Australian travellers in London and the performance of national identity', *Australian Historical Studies*, 32(116): 109–127.

Theory in Practice

ACTING WHITE TO RESIST INTERPELLATION

Racial or ethnic characteristics are often used as the basis for interpellation in many societies. Historically, the racial discrimination against those marked as 'dark' gives rise to the well-known phenomenon of 'passing' or 'acting white'. This refers to a person's attempt to move out of the marked group into the majority or more powerful one, in order to enjoy the opportunities and privileges reserved for its members. Sasson-Levy and Shoshana (2013) did a cultural analysis of the practice of 'acting white' in Israel. In Israel, the phenomenon of ethnic passing is called *hishtaknezut* in Hebrew. The term refers to Mizrahim (Jews from North Africa and Middle Eastern countries) who adopt the practices associated with Ashkenazim (Jews of European origin). While Ashkenazim in Israel are not considered ethnic in everyday discourse owing to their whiteness, Mizrahim are generally marked as the Other, that is, of a disadvantaged ethnic group. In the Israeli context, acting white or passing refers to mimicking the behaviour of the dominant (European) ethnic group.

Based on their research, Sasson-Levy and Shoshana argue that the concept of *hishtaknezut* functions as a shaming interpellation. Passing as white in Israel entails a twofold sense of shame, over both one's ethnic origin and the concealment of that origin by mimicking another group. The prevalence of *hishtaknezut* illustrates the perpetuation of the ethnic order in Israel, which relies on a way of thinking and speaking that distinguishes between worthy social positions and unworthy ones from which one must escape to achieve social privileges.

Questions to take you further

Why is resisting interpellation difficult? Under what circumstances would people move from a hegemonic group to a marked one?

Reference

Sasson-Levy, Orna and Avi Shoshana (2013) '"Passing" as (non)ethnic: the Israeli version of acting white', *Sociological Inquiry*, 83(3): 448–472.

Further reading on interpellation in practice

Khanna, Nikki and Cathryn Johnson (2010) 'Passing as black: racial identity work among biracial Americans', *Social Psychology Quarterly*, 73(4): 380–397.

Religious identity

Religious identity is the sense of belonging based on membership of a religion. Religion is a powerful cultural institution (see Chapter 3). Religion interacts with economic, healthcare, political, and education institutions. The word 'religion' comes from the Latin word *religare*, which means 'to tie'. The implication is that religion ties members together to what is sacred. For many people worldwide, their religious traditions anchor them in the world. Although religious identity is closely related to religiosity, the two are not necessarily the same concept. Religious identity refers to religious group membership regardless of participation in religious activities whereas religiosity often refers to both the religious group membership and participation in religious events (Arweck and Nesbitt, 2010). Similar to ethnic groups, religious groups generally provide members with a repertoire of beliefs, values, and worldviews, as well as opportunities to socialize with ingroup members. Religion also provides a set of basic (ethical) principles for members to observe. For example, Buddha's four virtues teach people to strive for benevolence, compassion, joy in others' joy, and equanimity. In the past, it was believed that one's religious identity was a social and cultural given, not a result of individual choice. In the modern period, however, religion has become a matter of choice and training, not simply a fact of birth (Arweck and Nesbitt, 2010). Many religious groups have been very successful in educating individuals in the faith, whether through institutions such as the Catholic Church, spiritual leaders like Buddha, or the teachings of the Bible, to mention just a few. Religious beliefs, values, and worldviews shape an individual's self-concept.

Religious identity is often associated with a person's way of life. In many cultures, religious rituals, such as the rites of passage, are also important events in the life of the society. For thousands of years, people have relied on religion to explain the workings of the world, and in some cases the next world. They have always felt a need to look outside themselves to seek help when addressing questions about mortality and immortality, suffering, the nature of life and death, the creation of the universe, the origin of society and groups within the society, the relationship of individuals and groups to one another, the relation of humankind to nature, even natural phenomena like floods and droughts (Samovar et al., 2013). Religious traditions provide members with structure, discipline, and social participation in a community (Kimball, 2002). 'A shared religion reinforces group norms, provides moral sanctions for individual conduct, and furnishes the ideology of common purpose and values that support the well-being of the community' (Haviland, Prins, McBride and Walrath, 2011: 576).

The majority of research on identity formation tends to be devoted to ethnic, gender, and cultural identities; relatively less research has been conducted on religious identity. However, researchers in this area have investigated various factors that can affect the strength of one's religious identity over time, such as gender, ethnicity, and generational status. For example, Hirchman (2004) studied the religious identity of adolescents in immigrant families and found that immigrant youths reported higher levels of religious identity than adolescents from non-immigrant families. These findings support the argument that the emotional, social, and spiritual support from religious groups can help immigrants to overcome the stress associated with transition to a new cultural environment. Religious identity is perceived differently by different people. Some see themselves as belonging to a single community, which provides them with a firm direction in life; others live in situations where they see themselves as members of various groups. Religious people who have not been raised within a single religious tradition since childhood (converts or children of intercultural marriages) may have to deal with the complexity of identifying with more than one religious identity (Kimball, 2002). Religious conflicts and prejudice, if not managed properly, can lead to conflict and ethnic hatred.

Critical thinking...

Can a strongly-held religious faith be sustainable in the context of pluralism and multiculturalism? How can we construct religious identity so that it is strong, deeply felt, and well understood, yet not constructed against the 'Other'?

Cultural identity

Cultural identity refers to those social identities that are based on cultural membership; they are our identification with and perceived acceptance into a larger cultural group, into which we are socialized and with which we share a system of symbols, values, norms, and traditions. Cultural identity involves the emotional significance we attach to our sense of belonging to a larger culture (Ting-Toomey, 2005a). We are more aware of our cultural identities when we find ourselves in another culture than when we are in our own culture. Our cultural identity comprises elements such as physical appearance, racial traits, skin colour, and language, and is formed through socialization. The level of our cultural identification influences our behaviour. For example, Anglo-Australians who strongly identify with Australian culture may value freedom, a fair go, and independence more than those Anglo-Australians who only weakly identify with their culture.

Like ethnic identity, cultural identity also has value and salience content. Value content refers to the criteria that people hold to evaluate appropriate or inappropriate behaviour. In collectivistic cultures such as China, it is considered polite for a smoker to offer cigarettes to those he or she is with at the time, but in the United States, it is less common for a smoker to make such an offer. Also, in China a smoker might start smoking in a public place (where smoking is permitted) without asking for permission from the friends whom he or she is with but who are not smoking at the time; in the United States, such behaviour would be considered inappropriate. Behaviour that is perfectly acceptable in one culture may be considered as selfish and impolite in another.

Cultural identity salience refers to the strength of identification with a larger cultural group. A strong sense of affiliation indicates high cultural identity salience, whereas a weak sense of affiliation reflects low cultural identity salience. Cultural identity salience can be reflected consciously or unconsciously. For example, a person of Nigerian heritage may uphold strongly the commonly held collectivistic values of Nigerian culture, but he or she might not identify strongly as a Nigerian in public contexts. The more our self-concept is influenced by our cultural values, the more likely we are to practise them in communication. Although cultural identity is often defined by one's nation, it is important to note that it is different from national identity. Cultural identity refers to the sense of belonging to one's culture, whereas national identity refers to one's status in a specific nation (Ting-Toomey, 2005a).

National identity

National identity refers to a type of identity that is characterized by one's individual perception of himself or herself as a member of a nation. Smith (2007: 19) contends that national identity is a politically organized category, which is reproduced and reinvented through different 'symbols, values, memories, myths and traditions that compose the distinctive heritage of a nation, and the identification of individuals with the cultural elements of that heritage'. The national flag that hangs outside government buildings in every country represents a symbol of national identity, because the national flag symbolizes the distinctive character of the nation. Every nation also has a national anthem as a symbol of national identity.

Further online reading The following article can be accessed for free on the book's companion website https://study.sagepub.com/liu2e: Housley, William and Richard Fitzgerald (2009) 'Membership categorization, culture and norms in action', *Discourse and Society*, 20(3): 345–362.

National identity has two main features. First, it is based on a set of common characteristics that hold members of the nation together. These characteristics include a common descent, shared culture and language, common historical heritage, and a common legal and economic system (Smith, 1995). National identity creates feelings of national belonging – where you belong is where you feel safe, where you are recognized and understood, where you are 'among my own people – they understand me, as I understand them'; and this understanding creates within us a sense of national identity.

Secondly, national identity always implies difference – it involves not only awareness of the ingroup (people from the same nation), but also awareness of others from whom the nation seeks to differentiate itself. Like other identities, national identity suggests similarity, unity, and difference (Hobsbawm, 1983). In order to distance ourselves from other nations, we create distinctive national markers. For example, France promotes itself as culturally and historically based; the United States prides itself on being freed from historical ties.

National identity embraces both political and cultural aspects. The *political* relates to the presence of common political institutions, rights, and duties, while the *cultural* refers to people's sense

Photo 6.3 In front of the Macedonian state parliament in Skopje stand different statues from ancient times, representing Macedonian national identity and its ancient roots.
Copyright © Zala Volčič. Used with permission.

of belonging to a common cultural heritage (Hutchinson, 1987). A nation's history and myths of origin serve to reinforce the sense of national identity. For example, the Jewish myth is based on the notion of the 'Chosen People' and the story of Exodus; the Italians see themselves descending uniquely from Romans, and relate their identity to the history of Roman Catholicism; Greek identity is founded on the belief that they are the direct descendants of the Ancient Greeks; Indians see their roots in the stories of Mahābhārata and Rāmāyana; in Japan the myth of origin starts with the legend of Emperor Jimmu (Seton-Watson, 1977). The historical accuracy of all these myths can easily be challenged. Nevertheless, the power of myths helps to create a sense of national identity.

As in every nation-state today, there are debates about national identity, and about who has it, and who does not. For example, Sweden is currently undergoing two, somewhat contradictory, political processes: the increasing presence of non-white and non-Western migrants in the country, and the entry of the racist party Sweden Democrats (Sverigedemokraterna) into Parliament in September 2010. These developments have challenged two seemingly incompatible constructions of Swedish identity – 'the old Sweden' (conceiving of Sweden as a homogeneous country) and 'the good Sweden' (framing Sweden as an anti-racist and feminist country), which both ultimately constitute the 'double-binding power of Swedish whiteness' (Hübinette and Lundström, 2011: 43).

Critical thinking...

It is said that we all carry an 'invisible backpack' with us. In it we put our assumptions about people in different subculture groups. For example, the Dutch are very careful about money. Can you give some examples of the assumptions you have in your 'invisible bag'? How do these assumptions influence your behaviour towards people in your own and other cultures? Do you think your assumptions are correct? Why or why not?

IDENTITIES AND INTERCULTURAL COMMUNICATION

In his famous work 'Negotiating Caribbean identities', Stuart Hall (2001: 123) claims that 'Identity is a narrative; the stories that cultures tell themselves about who they are and where they came from.' Identities are externally and internally defined – we are created by ourselves and by others at the same time. Our perception of self and others influence how we communicate with others.

The role of identities in intercultural relations

Our appearance, values, dress, and language all reveal who we are, and subsequently influence our relationships with others. Theorists of intercultural communication have studied the dominant Western racial category of 'whiteness' in many different ways. They have analysed structural advantage, which is linked to (white) privilege, but is not equivalent to it. They have also examined cultural activities that mark white identity. To understand the factors underlying racial identity means to explore new ways of understanding racial identifications as complex social meanings, rather than as objective biological categories. This means that, although the existence of visible racial traits is relevant to racial identity, the significance of such traits is always embedded in specific socio-historical relations of power. For example, hair has a power to shape personal and collective identities in the lives of African-American women in the United States, as it represents a particular racial subgroup. Banks (2000) conducted interviews with over 50 black girls and women between 1996 and 1998 to explore the political complexities of African-American hair and beauty culture. Banks argues that hair shapes black women's identities and their feelings about race, gender, class, sexuality, and images of beauty. Since mainstream Western images of beauty do not include tight black curls, the decision of many African-American women to straighten their hair and to use pressing combs reflects a devaluation of their natural hair.

Identity conflicts may arise in intercultural situations if one is not treated in the way one expects. Argent (2003) writes that feeling or being made to feel different is a major issue for adopted children, particularly those from cultural backgrounds different from their parents or those with a disability. For an adopted child, the stigma of not living with the birth family, as well as living as a cultural minority, may require a long psychological and cultural adjustment. Many children adopted from minority groups have to conform to the demands of the dominant culture, which means internalization of dominant norms, assimilation into the dominant culture, and acceptance of its identity. Similarly, communication between those subgroups defined by socioeconomic class may present problems because the most basic class distinction is between the powerful and the powerless. If people from social classes with greater power attempt to retain their own positions in a culture, intergroup communication is unlikely to be successful.

Developing intercultural identity

Individuals who acquire an intercultural identity are willing to negotiate these differences. They are able to reach intercultural agreements, and they desire to integrate diverse cultural elements and achieve identity extension. In particular, they want to go beyond an 'unexamined identity', which is the stage of acceptance of dominant norms and lack of willingness to look into one's identity and reconstruct or negotiate it. One of the widely known approaches to develop intercultural identity is the *Developmental Model of Intercultural Sensitivity* (DMIS), created by Milton Bennett (1986, 1993) as a framework to explain people's reactions to cultural difference. Bennett's argument is that one's experience of cultural difference becomes more complex as one's competence in intercultural relations increases. He observed that individuals confront cultural difference in certain predictable ways as they learn to become more competent intercultural communicators. He organized these observations into six stages of sensitivity to cultural differences, moving from *ethnocentric*, which characterizes the first three stages, to *ethnorelative*, which characterizes the last three stages. Table 6.1 summarizes the characteristics of all six stages.

The DMIS has been used in constructing a competent intercultural identity that aims at understanding other cultures holistically. An open-minded intercultural communicator interacts actively with strangers and does not exclude other possibilities beyond the established cultural boundary. Effective intercultural communication requires both openness to culturally different others and willingness to negotiate differences. Thus, an intercultural person makes an attempt to abandon cultural stereotypes, prejudices, or ethnocentrism, and to engage in a dialogue with others. As cultural differences presuppose a need for coordination, intercultural identity negotiation should be interpreted as a process of informing, learning, and compromising in order to reach intercultural consensus. Only when difference is recognized can we start to reach out towards each other.

Table 6.1   Stages of Sensitivity to Cultural Differences

Sensitivity	Stages	Characteristics
Ethnocentric	Denial	One's own culture is experienced as the only real one. Other cultures are avoided by maintaining psychological and/or physical distance. Here, people are generally disinterested in other cultures.
	Defence	One's own culture is experienced as the only good one. The world is organized into 'us' and 'them', where we are superior and they are inferior.
	Minimization	Elements of one's own worldview are experienced as universal. People expect similarities, and they may insist on correcting others' behaviour to match their expectations.
	Acceptance	One's own culture is experienced as equal to others. Acceptance does not have to mean agreement – cultural difference may be perceived negatively, but the judgement is not ethnocentric. People are curious about and respectful of cultural difference.
	Adaptation	The experience of another culture replaces perception and behaviour appropriate to that culture. One's own worldview is expanded to include worldview constructs from others. People may intentionally change their behaviour to communicate more effectively in another culture.
Ethnorelative	Integration	One's experience of self includes the movement in and out of different cultural worldviews.

Sources: Bennett, Milton J. (1986) 'A developmental approach to training for intercultural sensitivity', *International Journal of Intercultural Relations*, 10(2): 179–195; Bennett, Milton J. (1993) 'Towards ethnorelativism: a developmental model of intercultural sensitivity', in M. Paige (ed.), *Education for the Intercultural Experience.* Yarmouth, ME: Intercultural Press. pp. 343–354.

SUMMARY

- Social categorization leads to the formation of ingroups and outgroups and group memberships based on gender, race, ethnicity, religion, culture, and nationality.

- Categorization helps us to understand the world by giving it structure; on the other hand, it creates and reinforces stereotypes of people, particularly those from outgroups.

- People live with multiple identities, and those identities change during the course of our lives. Identities can be studied at both individual and collective levels. Identity develops through several stages.

- The Developmental Model of Intercultural Sensitivity (DMIS), created by Milton Bennett, functions as a framework to explain the reactions of people to cultural differences.

- Intercultural identity can be developed through an openness to culturally different others and a willingness to negotiate differences. Today's world necessitates processes of identity construction and identity negotiation as opposed to the more traditional processes of taking on identity.

JOIN THE DEBATE

Is identity what we have or what we perform?

Some scholars argue that we act out different identities according to situational characteristics; hence identities are performance. Immigrants, for example, have to move between heritage and national cultures, and as they do so they take on different identities (e.g., Greek, Greek Australian, Australian). Others argue that the core of our identities remains stable across multiple contexts, although our behaviour may change. Our identities based on some categories, such as ethnicity, race, or physical characteristics associated with race or ethnicity or gender, are often considered stable across different contexts. However, research has found that people from ethnic minority groups can adopt the strategy of passing (e.g., acting white) in order for others to categorize them into the dominant group they would otherwise not belong to. This strategy may be permanent, but it can also change from one situation to another – acting white in public, but reverting to another identity at home with the family. In addition, nowadays people can choose to change hair and skin colour or even biological sex through means like surgery or hormone replacement therapy. Is identity what we have or what we perform? Can we always choose our identity? How can we resist the identities ascribed to us by others?

CASE STUDY

South African identity and apartheid in South Africa

The original inhabitants of southern Africa (from the Cape to the Zambezi) were the Khoi-San. Black people originally migrated into the region today known as South Africa from the north in two waves – migrants speaking Nguni moved down the east coast, and migrants speaking Sotho moved down through the interior and settled in the inland areas. The Dutch East India Company established a settlement at Cape Town in 1652. The Cape Colony at this time was settled by a mixture of Dutch, French, Germans, and Indonesians (who came to be called the Cape Malays) and from this ethnic mix emerged a new language called Afrikaans, meaning 'African'. The Khoi-San were gradually exterminated or displaced from the region by the black and white settlers. The largest surviving group descended from the Khoi was 'coloureds' – those of mixed Khoi and Indonesian descent. But some Khoi-San groups remained and survived in the desert regions of Botswana, Namibia, and north-western South Africa.

White settlers moving north and eastwards and black settlers moving south and westwards first encountered each other at the Fish River in the 1770s in what is still known today as the border region. Anglo settlers were first brought into this region in 1820, following British seizure of the Cape Colony some 14 years earlier. During the 1820s, Zulu King Shaka began a genocidal war, known as the Difaqane, which generated huge population movements across the whole region. Breakaway groups of Zulus, such as the Matabele, Shangaan, and Ngoni, migrated to the Highveld, Mozambique, Zimbabwe, and Malawi, where they attacked, subjugated, and displaced local people. Sotho people fleeing Zulu and Matabele *impis* (armies) relocated to western Zambia and Lesotho, leaving the Highveld depopulated. Afrikaners, fleeing British rule in the Cape, migrated to and settled in these Highveld areas during the mid-1830s. After inevitable Highveld battles between the Matabele and Afrikaners, the Matabele fled north and settled in western Zimbabwe, where they subjugated the Shona.

The British later established a colony in Natal in 1843, into which they imported Indian indentured labourers to work on their plantations. After defeating the Afrikaners during the Boer War, the British created a unified South African state in 1910. This state was set up to administer the new gold-mining-based economy developed by the British, and to police the cheap black labour system the British developed to run it. Living within this state were some 13 ethnic groups – white Anglos; white Afrikaners; Coloureds (mostly speaking Afrikaans); Indians (mostly speaking English); four Nguni-speaking groups, namely Xhosa, Zulu, Swazi, Ndebele; three Sotho-speaking groups, namely Sotho, Pedi, Tswana; plus two other black groups speaking Venda and Tsonga.

The construction of an Afrikaner identity became closely enmeshed with a battle to retain an identity separate from Anglos. After the Boer War, an enforced Anglicization programme in the schools served to greatly stimulate the growth of Afrikaner nationalism. Afrikaner nationalists came to see Anglicization pressures as a real threat to the survival of all that was Afrikaans, and thus sought to make Afrikaans a national language (alongside English) and create separate Afrikaans educational institutions.

From 1910 to 1948, Anglo South Africans dominated South Africa politically and economically in what has been dubbed a system of 'racial capitalism' – a system that revolved around a gold-mining industry reliant on cheap black labour imported from across Africa (especially Transkei, Zululand, Malawi, Mozambique, Botswana, and Lesotho). Racial capitalism created a society based upon the economic integration of different ethnic groups into one unified state, but which simultaneously deployed racial segregation to keep these ethnic groups separate when they were not engaged in labour. Thus, the Anglo-dominated South African state systematized and institutionalized a culture built around white supremacy.

When the Afrikaaner-dominated National Party (NP) came to power in 1948, their first actions were: (1) to enforce English–Afrikaans bilingualism in the civil service; (2) to create separate Afrikaans schools, colleges, and universities (i.e., remove Afrikaners from English-language institutions); and (3) to make the teaching of Afrikaans compulsory at English schools. Once the NP had achieved this, they turned their attention to the language use of black people. Afrikaner nationalists were unhappy about black people being Anglicized by an education system run by English missionaries. The NP opted to apply the same policy to black people as that being applied to Afrikaners, namely 'mother language' education for all ethnic groups as a vehicle to resist Anglicization pressures. They therefore closed the mission schools and created the Bantu education system. The state subsidized the codification of Afrikaans plus South Africa's nine black languages. The NP also created separate media systems in English and Afrikaans and in the nine black languages.

Afrikaner nationalists captured the South African state by winning the 1948 elections. The subsequent system of apartheid was motivated by two fears: (1) Anglicization, or being absorbed into white, English-speaking South Africa; and (2) being demographically swamped by black migrants. Afrikaner nationalists opposed an Anglo-ruled South Africa as they believed Anglo cultural imperialism would destroy their language and culture, and because they believed this state was assisting Anglo businessmen in importing cheap black labour. The National Party promised to end these perceived (British) threats to Afrikaner interests by implementing its apartheid policy. This involved trying to actively encourage the growth of Zulu nationalism, Xhosa nationalism, and Tswana nationalism in each of these new states. These separate nationalisms were intended to undermine black nationalism. At its heart, apartheid was a migration policy geared to stopping black migration and then reversing the flow, by sending blacks back to where they had come from. This was a real threat to Anglo businessmen and flew in the face of laissez-faire capitalism. As a result, Anglo liberals mounted opposition to apartheid, which continued and increased until apartheid was abandoned and majority rule adopted in the 1990s.

Reference

Personal communication with Eric Louw in the School of Journalism and Communication at the University of Queensland, Australia. Used with permission.

Questions for discussion

1. Who were the original inhabitants of southern Africa?

2. Why was Afrikaner identity created and what roles has it played in that particular historical context?

3. What does 'racial capitalism' refer to? What is its implication for both the ethnic majority and ethnic minority in South Africa?

4. What does this case tell us about the role language plays in creating and maintaining ethnic identity?

5. What did Afrikaner nationalists struggle for and why?

FURTHER READINGS

All articles listed next to the mouse icon below can be accessed for free on the book's companion website: https://study.sagepub.com/liu2e

Collective and personal identities

Cover, Rob (2012) *Queer Youth Suicide, Culture and Identity: Unliveable Lives?* Farnham, UK: Ashgate.

This book outlines some of the ways in which queer youth suicide is perceived in popular culture, media, and research. It highlights the ways in which we think about queer youth suicide as well as how views of this have changed over time. Some of the benefits and limitations of current thinking are highlighted. Drawing on approaches from queer theory, cultural studies, and sociology, the book explores how sexual identity formation, sexual shame, and discrepancies in community belonging and exclusions are manifested in our society; it offers explanations to why some groups are resilient while other groups are vulnerable and at risk of suicide. The book will be a useful reference for communication scholars who are more interested in the effects of popular culture and mass media on attitudes and behaviours.

Grimson, Alejandro (2010) 'Culture and identity: two different notions', *Social Identities*, 16(1): 61–77.

This article provides a clear, precise, conceptual distinction between 'culture' and 'identity', forming an essential precondition for analysing social processes. The anthropological concept of 'identity' has been built up over time and enriched by studies on inter-ethnic relationships, ethnic borders, and ethnicity. The article enriches our understanding of culture by incorporating decisive contributions from theories on the nation. Culture and nation are highly complex, both dealing with heterogeneous and conflictive entities. The author asserts that culture and identity allude to analytically different aspects of social processes. Therefore, it is necessary to analyse cultural and identity aspects separately.

Ethnic identity

Kidd, Warren, Alison Teagle and Alice Kessler-Harris (2002) *Culture and Identity* (2nd edn). Basingstoke, UK: Palgrave Macmillan.

This book explores the themes of culture and identity from a vast range of theoretical perspectives. It applies theories to a range of current and crucial sociological debates, such as youth cultures, gender and sexuality, ethnic and national identity, and the impact of social networking on identity formation. The practical and student-centred approach that the book has taken makes the reading enjoyable and engaging. The book also provides a series of skills-based activities, making it an ideal introductory tool for students and scholars new to the field of intercultural communication.

Sfard, Anna and Anna Prusak (2005) 'Telling identities: in search of an analytical tool for investigating learning as a culturally shaped activity', *Educational Researcher*, 34(4): 14–22.

This article attempts to operationalize the notion of identity to justify the claim about its potential as an analytic tool for investigating learning. The authors define identity as a set of reifying, significant, endorsable stories about a person. These stories, even if individually told, are products of a collective storytelling. Data were obtained from a study of the mathematical learning practices of a group of 17-year-old immigrant students from the former Soviet Union. They were newly arrived in Israel and were compared with a similar group of native Israelis. The authors argue that learning may be thought of as closing the gap between *actual identity* and *designated identity*. The two sets of reifying significant stories about the learner are also endorsed by the learner.

National identity

Housley, William and Richard Fitzgerald (2009) 'Membership categorization, culture and norms in action', *Discourse and Society*, 20(3): 345–362.

This article examined the extent to which membership categorization analysis (MCA) can inform an understanding of reasoning within the public domain where morality, policy, and cultural politics are visible. Through the analysis of three cases, the article demonstrates how specific types of category device(s) are a ubiquitous feature of accountable practice in the public domain where morality matters and public policies intersect. Furthermore, the authors argue that MCA provides a useful tool for analysing the mundane mechanics associated with everyday cultural politics and democratic accountability assembled and presented within news media and broadcast settings.

> *Man acts as though he were the shaper and master of language, while in fact language remains the master of man.*

Martin Heidegger, German philosopher, 1889–1976

7

VERBAL COMMUNICATION AND CULTURE

LEARNING OBJECTIVES

At the end of this chapter, you should be able to:

- Recognize the powerful influence of language on intercultural communication.

- Describe the components and characteristics of verbal codes.

- Explain how our language affects our attitudes and perceptions.

- Analyse communication styles and gender differences in verbal communication.

- Appreciate the influence of culture on verbal communication and identity.

INTRODUCTION

Language is an integral part of human lives and thus has a powerful influence on people's ability to communicate interculturally. The term 'language' may refer not only to spoken and written language, but also 'body language' (see Chapter 8). In this chapter, however, we will focus on verbal codes only. People use language to convey their thoughts, feelings, desires, attitudes, and intentions. We learn about others through what they say and how they say it; we learn about ourselves through how others react to what we say (Bonvillain, 2014). Verbal communication has been studied by scholars from a variety of disciplines, such as anthropology, psychology, sociology, political theory, and human geography, bringing diverse theories and perspectives into the study of communication and culture. Linguists are a key contributor to intercultural communication; they address the question of what is unique about human language in particular, sometimes along with aspects of the voice that accompany language. Noam Chomsky, a well-known linguist, wrote in his influential book *Language and Mind* (1968: 14): 'When we study human language, we approach what some might call the "human essence", the distinctive qualities of mind that are, so far as we know, unique to [humans].' Whether we speak English, French, Swahili, Dutch, German, Japanese, Hindi, Arabic, or any one of the numerous languages of the world, the important role language plays in communication holds true.

The language we speak defines our world and our identity. From childhood, we take for granted that our name describes who we are. A name connects us to our family origins and defines us as individuals. Many refugees or migrants have to change their names when they move into a new language community, and this may influence their identity. Moreover, language variations within cultures have an effect on how people communicate and how they categorize themselves. For example, people may use regional dialects to signify their identity as people from that region. The language or dialect we speak also influences the way we are perceived by others. The fact that someone speaks another language or speaks our language with a foreign or regional accent influences our social attitudes towards that speaker. Our language attitudes are also influenced by stereotypes and by the situations in which the language is used. Many people speak two or more languages, and may use these languages in different contexts and for different purposes (e.g., one language in public and another at home).

Language can also be a strong marker of our group or national identity. When Ireland, Israel, and Slovenia became independent nation-states, each country asserted its own distinct national language: Irish (Gaelic), Hebrew, and Slovene, respectively. In the case of Israel, a dead language, Hebrew, was brought back to life and modernized as a way of marking the new nation as distinctive; in Ireland, a language spoken by relatively few people (Irish) is now a required subject at school. The language we speak affects how we act in the world, because different languages and dialects are used in different contexts. For example, immigrants in Canada tend to use English in formal, public settings and their native language in informal, private environments. There are many symbolic resources necessary for the cultural production of identity, but language is the most pervasive resource (Fairclough, 2001).

In this chapter, we first explore the nature of verbal codes and the dynamic relationship among language, meaning, and perception. Next, we address the relationship between language and reality through the influential *Sapir–Whorf hypothesis* of linguistic relativity. This chapter then discusses communication styles across cultures, gender differences in verbal communication, discourse, and the role of language in constructing identities.

THE COMPONENTS AND CHARACTERISTICS OF VERBAL CODES

Verbal codes refer to spoken or written language. A verbal code comprises a set of rules governing the use of words in creating a message, along with the words themselves. We acquire or learn the rules and contents of our native language (or languages) as we grow up; thus, we can express our thoughts, emotions, desires, and needs easily in our first language. The study of language begins with identifying its components and how they are put together.

The components of human language

While studying human language, linguists focus on different aspects of the language system: sound, structure, and meaning. Lustig and Koester (2013) identified five interrelated components of language: phonology, morphology, syntax, semantics, and pragmatics. Collectively, knowledge of each aspect of the language system provides us with a holistic understanding of the nature of human language.

Phonology explores how sounds are organized in a language. The smallest sound unit of a language is called a phoneme. The phonological rules of a language determine how sounds are combined to form words. For example, the phonemes [k] and [au] can be arranged to form the word 'cow' [kau] in English. Mastery of any language requires the speaker to be able to identify and pronounce different sounds accurately. This may prove difficult for second language speakers, particularly those whose native language does not have a similar sound system to the new language.

Morphology refers to the combination of basic units of meaning, morphemes, to create words. For example, the word 'happy' consists of one morpheme, meaning to feel cheerful. The word 'unhappy' contains two morphemes: happy and the prefix 'un' meaning 'not' or the 'opposite'. Used together, they refer to a feeling akin to sadness. Morphemes, and the ways in which they are combined, differ across cultures. In the English language, prefixes or suffixes constitute morphemes as well as individual words, whereas in tonal languages such as Chinese, tones are morphemes and the meaning of units depends on the tone with which the word is pronounced.

Syntax concerns the grammatical and structural rules of language. We combine words into sentences according to grammatical rules in order to communicate. In English and other languages of the Indo-European family, people change the tense of a verb by adding a suffix or prefix or changing the morpheme, to describe past, present, and future events. In German, prepositions are often placed at the end of a sentence, whereas in French they are placed before nouns or noun phrases. Every language has a set of grammatical rules that govern the sequencing of words. Mastery of another language means knowing those grammatical rules in addition to building a stock of vocabulary.

Semantics refers to the study of the meanings of words, and the relationships between words and the things to which they refer. A command of vocabulary is an essential part of linguistic proficiency in any language. When we learn a second language, we devote much time to memorizing words and their meanings, concrete or abstract. However, just memorizing words and their dictionary meanings is often insufficient for successful intercultural communication, because meaning often resides in a context.

Linguists and social psychologists identify two types of meaning: denotative and connotative. *Denotation* refers to the literal meaning of a word or an object, and is basically descriptive. This is the kind of meaning we find in a dictionary. For example, a denotative description of a Big Mac would be that it is a sandwich sold by McDonald's that weighs a certain number of grams and is served with certain sauces. *Connotation* deals with the cultural meanings that become attached to a word or an object. The connotative meaning of a Big Mac may include certain aspects of American culture – fast food, popular food, standardization, lack of time, lack of interest in cooking. Because connotative meanings are often emotionally charged, we may make mistakes about the messages we think we are sending to others. In one class, students were asked to bring in an object that reflected them as people. One young woman brought a large seashell. She listed the attributes of the shell as beautiful, delicate, natural, and simple. Other students found different attributes in the shell: empty, brittle, and vacuous.

Language conveys meaning via its components, arranged according to rules. Morphemes combine with one another to produce the meaning of words, and words, in turn, combine to form sentences that yield additional meaning. Talk is achieved through the interdependent components of sounds, words, sentences, and meaning of a language (Bonvillain, 2014). Linguists have developed descriptive and explanatory tools to analyse the structure of language. The study of language based on the assumption that language is a coherent system of formal units, and that the task of linguistic study is to inquire into the nature of this systematic arrangement without reference to historical antecedents, is known as *structural linguistics*. The rise of modern structural linguistics came largely through the influence of the Swiss linguist Ferdinand de Saussure in the early twentieth century. Saussure compared language to a game of chess, noting that a chess piece in isolation has no value and that a move by any one piece has repercussions for all the other pieces. Similarly, the meaning of a unit in a language system can be discerned by examining the items that occur alongside it and those which can be substituted for it (de Saussure, 1983). Structural linguistics dominated twentieth-century linguistics, as opposed to much work in the nineteenth century when it was common for linguists (or philologists, as they were often called) to trace the history of words. But structural linguistics was also criticized for being too narrow in conception. For example, *generative linguistics*, begun by Noam Chomsky (see later sections of this chapter), argues that it is necessary to go beyond a description of the location of items to produce a grammar that reflects a native speaker's intuitive knowledge of language.

Critical thinking...

Do you know approximatxely how many people speak your native language? How does it make you feel when you hear a foreigner speak your language with a different accent? Have you been in a situation where people around you speak a language that you don't understand? How does that make you feel? What do you think are the consequences for intercultural communication?

THEORY CORNER

STRUCTURAL LINGUISTICS

Structural linguistics views language as a coherent system whereby every item acquires meaning in relation to the other items in the system. Ferdinand de Saussure (1857–1913) claims that meaning resides within the text (de Saussure, 1983). Within each language system, spoken or written words (the signifier) attribute meaning to objects, concepts, and ideas (the signified – mental pictures produced by the signifier) in the construction of reality. The relation between signifier and signified is based on convention. For example, the linguistic sign 'dog' (signifier) represents 'a four-legged, barking domestic animal' (signified). We recognize the meaning of the word 'dog' from its difference to other similar sounding words, such as 'hog' and 'cock', which produce different mental pictures. We also use the difference between 'dog' and similar concepts, such as 'cat' and 'rabbit', as well as opposing concepts, such as 'human', in comprehending meaning.

The structural approach dominated linguistics in the USA in the mid-twentieth century, when the prime concern of American linguists like Leonard Bloomfield was to produce a catalogue of the linguistic elements of a language and a statement of the positions in which they could occur. A central goal of many of these people was to record, analyse, and preserve indigenous languages that were losing speakers and threatened with extinction. Rules and signification are not the whole story, however. Critiques of de Saussure's model argue that abstract concepts like justice, truth, and freedom cannot be tied directly to the outside world, and they mean different things to different people. Hence, it is necessary to understand meaning beyond the text.

Reference

de Saussure, Ferdinand (1983) *Course in General Linguistics*, edited by C. Bally and A. Sechehaye, translated and annotated by Roy Harris. London: Duckworth.

Further reading on structuralism

Unger, Steven (2004) 'Saussure, Barthes and structuralism', in C. Sanders (ed.), *The Cambridge Companion to Saussure*. Cambridge: Cambridge University Press. pp. 157–173.

Theory in Practice

STRUCTURALISM AND 'COFFEETALK'

Structuralists argue that language exists in patterns, and certain underlying elements are common to all human experience. For example, we can examine the structure of a large number of coffee-house conversations (coffeetalk) to discover the underlying principles that govern their composition, narrative progression, and characterization. Coffee shops began to open with the rise of newspapers and magazines, and emerged to serve the growing and prominent bourgeois class of merchants and middle-range capitalists in European urban areas. Coffee houses have been imagined as eminently educational places, where bourgeois men explored their newly formed economic interests.

The practice of 'coffeetalk' is analysed in depth by Gaudio (2003), who used research methods including structural analysis of coffee-house corporations; informal interviews with coffee-house owners, employees, and patrons; and Gaudio's own observations as a 'native' participant in 'coffeetalk'. By situating 'coffeetalk' within its spatial, temporal, cultural, and social contexts, his analysis shows that conversations over coffee were inextricably implicated in the political, economic, and cultural-ideological processes of global capitalism, as well as in the culture rules of a society. This is poignantly symbolized by the increasingly ubiquitous Starbucks Coffee Company and the consequent Americanization of coffee houses and coffeetalk.

Questions to take you further

Using a specific structuralist framework, analyse the talk in your favourite coffee shops. How does this talk, as a narrative text, reflect the relationship between the text and the culture from which it emerged? What patterns and relationships in the text show that it is the product of a larger culture? How aware do you think the coffee drinkers are of these patterns?

Reference

Gaudio, Rudolf (2003) 'Coffeetalk: Starbucks and the commercialization of casual conversation', *Language and Society*, 32(5): 659–691.

Further reading on structuralism

Gutmann, Amy (1999) *Democratic Education*. Princeton, NJ: Princeton University Press.

Pragmatics is concerned with the impact of language on human perception and behaviour. It focuses on how language is used in a social context. Pragmatic analysis of language goes beyond its structural features and concentrates on the social and cultural appropriateness of language use in a particular context. For example, a fairly direct communication style is preferred for resolving interpersonal conflicts in South Africa or Germany; a more indirect approach tends to be favoured in South Korea, where the preservation of harmony is strongly valued.

Critical thinking...

Are there 'universal' rules governing the use of language? What difference do you think it makes for people to have only one native language (e.g., many British people) or several (e.g., many people in India)? What impact might this have on intercultural communication?

The characteristics of verbal codes

Language is uniquely a human system of communication. Because of their capacity for language, humans have become the most powerful living beings on earth. It is important to stress that communication is symbolic, but not all symbols are linguistic. In linguistics, symbols represent a subcategory of signs and, like signs, are not completely arbitrary. The symbol of justice, a pair of scales, could not be replaced by just any symbol, such as a chariot (de Saussure, 1983). Symbols such as gestures or cries may be shared with other animals. There are significant limits on the messages such symbols can communicate (Ritzer, 2004); those messages are mostly formed on the basis of a stimulus and are related to the present, without reference to past, future, or imaginary situations. However, the relationship between a linguistic symbol (such as the word 'cow') and its referent (a four-legged animal that gives milk) is completely arbitrary. There is nothing 'cowy' about the word 'cow'; the same referent is called 'vache' in French. There is no natural relationship between a word and its referent.

Although languages differ, there are some characteristics shared by all of them. Neuliep (2012) identified five common characteristics: (1) all languages have some way of naming objects, places, or things; (2) all languages have a way of naming action; (3) all languages have a way of stating the negative, constructing interrogatives, and differentiating between singular and plural; (4) all languages have a systematic set of sounds, combined with a set of rules for the sole purpose of creating meaning and communicating, with no natural or inherent relationship between the sounds and their accompanying alphabet; and (5) all languages have a set of formal grammatical rules for combining sounds and sequencing words to create meaning.

Photo 7.1   A café in Skopje, Macedonia, uses English, Italian, Macedonian, and Albanian to attract customers who speak different languages.
Copyright © Zala Volčič. Used with permission.

LANGUAGE, CULTURE, AND DISCOURSE

All normal children go through essentially the same process of language acquisition. As Dan Slobin (2000: 110) writes: 'Children in all nations seem to learn their native languages in much the same way. Despite the diversity of tongues, there are linguistic universals that seem to rest upon the developmental universals of the human mind.' Scholarly debates have centred on the issue of whether language is innately programmed, requiring only minimal environmental stimuli to trigger it, or whether language is actively learned through the general learning mechanisms present while children are growing up. We can divide the language acquisition debate into two contrasting views: nativists versus constructivists (Hoff, 2001).

Noam Chomsky's universal grammar

Noam Chomsky (1975) claims that all human languages share a universal grammar that is innate in the human species and culturally invariant. Just as humans are programmed to walk upright, so too are human minds equipped with a set of pre-programmed models that are triggered when exposed to the surrounding language. *Nativists*, such as Chomsky, argue that language acquisition involves triggering these models so that only the details of a particular language must be learned (Chomsky, 1980). Chomsky says that language is as much a part of the human brain as the thumb is a part of the human hand. One of the most remarkable features of any language's rule structure is that it allows speakers to generate sentences that have never before been spoken. Chomsky refers to this aspect of language as generative universal grammar. From a finite set of sounds and rules, speakers of any language can create an infinite number of sentences, many of which have never been uttered before. The commonalities between different languages are so strong that Chomsky and other linguists are convinced that the fundamental syntax for all languages is universal, and that particular languages are simply dialects of the universal grammar.

On the other hand, *constructivists*, grounded in the work of Piaget, oppose the idea that there is a universal grammar. They argue that language acquisition involves unveiling the patterns of language, and thus requires interaction with a structured environment (Piaget, 1977). A famous language acquisition debate

Photo 7.2   Samoan children learning language in St Mary primary school in Apia.
Copyright © UNESCO; photographer: Laura Berdejo. Used with permission.

between Chomsky and Piaget took place in 1975 at the Abbaye de Royaumont near Paris, nearly 200 years after 'the wild boy of Aveyron' was found in France. The boy lived his entire childhood in the forests, and lacked any language before he was found. Piaget saw the wild boy and his mind as an active, constructive agent that slowly inched forward in a perpetual bootstrap operation; Chomsky viewed the boy's mind as a set of essentially pre-programmed units, each equipped with its rules that needed only the most modest environmental trigger to develop. As Hoff (2001) points out, both sides are right, and indeed the line between nativists and constructivists is not clear-cut. Language may be natural behaviour, but it still has to be carefully nurtured. For this reason alone, in all cultures, language learning is an essential part of formal education.

The Sapir–Whorf hypothesis

Philosophical debates surround the question of the extent to which our perception is shaped by the particular language we speak. *Nominalists* argue that our perception of external reality is shaped not by language but by material reality. Any thought can be expressed in any language and can convey the same meaning (Louw, 2004a). *Relativists* believe that our language determines our ideas, thought patterns, and perceptions of reality (Hoff, 2001). A classic example to illustrate the relativists' view that language shapes our perception of reality is the existence of numerous words for 'snow' in the Inuit and other arctic indigenous languages, whereas in English there are fewer words for this concept. The relationship between language and thought is well captured in the Sapir–Whorf hypothesis, which proposes that language and thought are inextricably tied together, so that (in the original and strongest version of the hypothesis) a person's language determines the categories of thought open to the person. In his book *Language, Thought and Reality* (1956: 239), Whorf states that 'We cut up and organize the spread and flow of events as we do largely because, through our mother tongue, we are parties to an agreement to do so, not because nature itself is segmented in exactly that way for all to see.'

Edward Sapir (1884–1939), a famous linguist and anthropologist, taught at the University of Chicago and then at Yale University. Sapir published a paper that changed the face of the study of language and culture. He argued that the language of a particular culture directly influences how people think, and speakers of different languages see different worlds. In 1931, Benjamin Lee Whorf (1897–1941) enrolled in Sapir's course on Native American linguistics at Yale University. In his study of the Hopi language, Whorf learned that in Hopi, past, present, and future tense must be expressed differently from English, as the Hopi language does not have verb tense. This led Whorf to believe that people who speak different languages are directed to different types of observation of the world. Sapir and Whorf's ideas received great attention and became known as the Sapir–Whorf hypothesis.

Sapir and Whorf claim that a cultural system is embodied in the language of the people who speak the language. This cultural framework shapes the thoughts of the language's speakers. We think in the words and the meanings of our language, which in turn is an expression of our culture. The Sapir–Whorf hypothesis has two versions: strong and weak. The strong version of the hypothesis, or linguistic determinism, posits that the language one speaks determines one's perception of reality. The weak version of the hypothesis, or linguistic relativity, makes the claim that native language exerts an influence over one's perception of reality. The differences among languages are thus reflected in the different worldviews of their speakers.

Consider some examples of how language categorizes our world. In the Chinese language there are no single words that are equivalent to the English words 'uncle' and 'aunt'. Instead, Chinese has different words for one's father's elder brother, younger brother, mother's elder brother and younger brother, even different words for elder or younger brother-in-laws, and so forth. This diversity of terms may suggest that the interpersonal relationships involved between an individual and his or her extended family are more complex and perhaps more important in China than in English-speaking countries. Arabic has many words for 'camel', whereas English has few. The word 'moon' is masculine in German (*der Mond*), feminine in French (*la lune*) and neither masculine nor feminine in English (which does not use word gender for many nouns).

Language categorizes our experiences without our full awareness. Only when an individual learns a second language and moves back and forth between the first and second language does the person become aware of the influence that language has on perception. The Sapir–Whorf hypothesis does not imply that people of one culture cannot think of objects for which another culture has plentiful vocabulary (Neuliep, 2012). Rather, the fact that we do not think of certain concepts or objects in such specificity may mean that such distinctions are less important to our culture. It is worth noting that this same thing applies to the specialized languages of different professions. For example, medical doctors, lawyers, and academics have extensive vocabularies marking their areas of expertise; they learn these terms and the concepts and relationships underlying them as they learn their profession. Thus, the Sapir–Whorf hypothesis shows that language, thought, and culture (including professional and other types of subculture) are closely connected. Language, as a part of culture, affects how we perceive the world, and thus influences the meanings that are conveyed by words.

Critical thinking…

Write down three commonly used expressions in your language that suggest value orientations of your culture. Can you then explain the link between language and culture using your examples?

Discourse

In order to understand the importance of language in intercultural communication, one needs to explore the concept of discourse. *Discourse* refers not only to speech and writing, but 'embraces all systems of signification' (Laclau, 2006: 106). In contemporary societies, our lives are strongly governed by the state, the economy, different public and private institutions, and the media. Fairclough (2003) refers to the extension of these powers as a domination and colonization of people's lives by systems. These systems are carried out, in part, within the social order of discourse. Fairclough (2003: 124) states that discourses 'not only represent the world as it is (or rather is seen to be), they are also projective, imaginary, representing possible worlds which are different from the actual world, and tied in to projects to change the world in a particular direction'. Scollon, Scollon and Jones (2012) propose that we have been formally or informally socialized into various discourse systems. 'Discourse systems' contain 'ideas and beliefs about the world, conventional ways of teaching other people, ways of communicating using various kinds of texts, media, and "languages", and methods of learning how to use these other tools' (Scollon et al., 2012: 8). They also believe that we can only interpret the meanings of public texts like road signs, notices, and brand logos by considering the world that surrounds them. Thus, discourse is engaged and mediated in the situated actions of the everyday practices of social actors. Discourse acts as 'a regulating body' that establishes what can be said and what cannot be said in a given historical moment in a given society. For example, as Chouliaraki (2012) writes, the human rights discourse is one of the most important discourses today. At both the national and the global level, this discourse is itself a space of contestation, with issues about how we are to ensure human rights, how universal human rights might be achieved, and how culture must never become a shield for the denial of fundamental human rights.

THEORY CORNER

PIDGINS AND CREOLES

Pidgins are formed and used when two communities that do not share a common language come into contact and need to communicate. This is very common, especially in trade or other business activities. Common pidgins based on English, French, Spanish, and Portuguese are used in the East and West Indies, Africa, and the Americas. A pidgin has a simplified grammatical structure and reduced lexicon (vocabulary) and refers mainly to a small set of contexts – it is about situational use (McWhorter, 2003). For example, a line taken from a comic strip in Papua New Guinea is: 'Fantom, yu pren tru bilong mi. Inap yu ken helpim mi nau?' Its translation is: 'Phantom, you are a true friend of mine. Are you able to help me now?' Pidgin is not a native language to those using it, but a code system developed for a specific purpose.

However, when a pidgin is passed on to future generations who acquire it as a first language, it can develop and become a creole. A creole is a new language developed from the prolonged contact of two or more languages. It is a language that expands and regularizes its structural systems; and the next generation learns it as their first language. A creole develops a grammar, morphology, lexicon, phonetics, and phonology: English-based creoles contain words like 'banan' (banana), 'chek' (check), 'maket' (market). A creole is a full, linguistically complex language in its own right: examples include Hawaiian Creole English and Louisiana Creole French (McWhorter, 2003).

Reference
McWhorter, John (2003) *The Power of Babel: A Natural History of Language*. New York: Perennial/HarperCollins.

Further reading on pidgins and creoles
Mühlhäusler, Peter (2011) 'Language form and language substance: from a formal to an ecological approach to pidgins and creoles', *Journal of Pidgin and Creole Languages*, 26(2): 341–362.

Theory in Practice

CHINESE PIDGIN RUSSIAN

It is important to understand the social histories of the speakers of varieties of languages. Shapiro (2012) investigated the socio-historical development of Chinese pidgin Russian, its phonology, morphology, syntax, typology, and vocabulary. Initially developing on the Russian–Mongolian border around the trade city of Kyakhta, Chinese pidgin Russian later spread along the Russian–Chinese border. Shapiro analysed travelogues, newspapers, phrasebooks, dictionaries, and texbooks from the 1770s onwards. His findings showed that because the Chinese were adamant about not allowing foreigners to learn Chinese, they required Chinese businessmen and shop assistants in Kyakhta to learn Russian. However, the 'Russian' they taught and made their own material for was Russian written in Chinese characters! Russian merchants adapted to 'try to fit in with this broken speech known by the name of Kyakhta trade language' (2012: 6). In his analysis, Shapiro unravelled Chinese interpretations of Russian phonetics, semantics, and grammar, which were all written in Chinese characters; he also examined Russian interpretations of Chinese phonetics, semantics, and grammar, all of which was written in Cyrillic.

Questions to take you further
Do pidgins and creoles reflect language universals? What implications can the study of creoles have for second language acquisition? Can the kind of contact that leads to the formation of pidgins and creoles also be a source of loss of local knowledge?

Reference
Shapiro, Roman (2012) 'Chinese pidgin Russian', in A. Umberto (ed.), *Pidgins and Creoles in Asia*. Amsterdam and Philadelphia, PA: John Benjamins. pp. 1–58.

Further reading on pidgins and creoles in context
Gonçalves, Perpetua (2004) 'Towards a unified vision of classes of language acquisition and change: arguments from the genesis of Mozambican African Portuguese', *Journal of Pidgin and Creole Languages*, 19(2): 225–259.

CULTURAL VARIATIONS IN VERBAL COMMUNICATION

People from different social or cultural groups may experience similar events; however, there are vast differences in the ways in which they use language to interpret their experiences (Clark, Eschholz and Rosa, 1998). Cultural variation in verbal communication is reflected in language use and translation.

Further online reading The following article can be accessed for free on the book's companion website https://study.sagepub.com/liu2e: Carbaugh, Donal, Michael Berry and Marjatta Nurmikari-Berry (2006) 'Coding personhood through cultural terms and practices: silence and quietude as a Finnish "natural way of being"', *Journal of Language and Social Psychology*, 25: 203–220.

Communication styles and culture

Successful communication not only depends on what is said but also on how the message is communicated. *Communication style* refers to how language is used to communicate meaning. Two leading researchers from communication studies, William Gudykunst and Stella Ting-Toomey (1988), describe four communication styles identified by communication theorists: direct/indirect, elaborate/succinct, personal/contextual, and instrumental/affective. Recognizing the differences in communication styles can help us to understand the cultural differences underpinning the verbal communication process.

Direct/indirect communication styles

A *direct communication style* is one in which the speaker's needs, wants, desires, and intentions are explicitly communicated. Conversely, an *indirect communication style* is one in which the speaker's true intentions or needs are only implied or hinted at during the conversation. Although both styles are to some extent universally used in communication, research indicates that indirect styles are more likely to be used in collectivist or Asian cultures, such as in Japan, China, South Korea, and Hong Kong, where harmony is considered important for maintaining good interpersonal relationships. Indirect communication styles are also more likely to be used in high-context cultures, where meaning is communicated through context rather than explicitly conveyed in words. By comparison, Western cultures generally prefer a direct communication style. As an example, an American student asked his Nigerian friend to give him a lift on an evening when the Nigerian had made a commitment to babysit his niece so that his sister could go to work. However, instead of saying 'Sorry I cannot do it', the Nigerian replied by talking about how his sister perhaps could make alternative arrangements or stay home instead of working that night. The American student felt confused as to what his Nigerian friend was trying to say. In American culture, if such a request for a lift is inconvenient, one would simply respond by saying 'Sorry, I can't do it'. However, in collectivistic cultures like Nigeria, it is not considered polite to say 'no' to a friend – but it is the responsibility of the person who made the request to figure out it is not appropriate to ask for the favour. Differences in expectations for appropriate communication styles can lead to misunderstandings between speakers.

Elaborate/succinct communication styles

This dimension is concerned with the quantity of talk a culture values, and reflects a culture's attitudes towards talk and silence (Martin and Nakayama, 2001). The *elaborate style* involves the use of rich, expressive, and embellished language in everyday conversation. For example, rather than simply saying that someone is thin, a comment such as 'she is so thin that she can walk between rain drops without getting wet' embellishes and colours the statement. Arab, Middle Eastern, and African-American cultures tend to use metaphorical expressions in everyday conversation. In the *succinct communication style*, simple assertions and even silence are valued. The use of either an elaborate or a succinct style is closely related to Hall's high- and low-context cultures (see Chapter 5). Elaborate style tends to characterize low-context cultures, in which meaning is conveyed through verbal codes. Conversely, in high-context cultures, where meaning is more often conveyed by nonverbal and contextual cues, silence rather than talk can be used to maintain control in a social situation. For example, in Europe, the Finns place a high value on silence, and it is not unusual to pass a companiable evening in Helsinki with virtually no words exchanged at all (Carbaugh et al., 2006).

Personal/contextual communication styles

This dimension is concerned with the extent to which the speaker emphasizes the self as opposed to his or her role. Gudykunst and Ting-Toomey (1988) define *personal style* as one that amplifies the individual identity of the speaker. This style is often used in individualistic cultures, which emphasize individual goals over those of the group. Person-centred communication tends to be informal and is reflected by the use of the pronoun 'I'. On the other hand, *contextual communication style* is oriented by status and role. Formality and power distance are often emphasized. Contextual style is often seen in collectivistic cultures where one's role identity and status are highlighted. For example, instead of using 'you' for all persons, as is the case in English, in Japanese there exists an elaborate system of linguistic forms used to communicate respect to people of different ranks or social status.

Instrumental/affective communication styles

Instrumental style is goal-oriented and sender-focused. The speaker uses communication to achieve an outcome. *Affective communication style* is receiver-focused and process-oriented (Gudykunst and Ting-Toomey, 1988). Speakers using affective communication are more concerned with the process of communication than the outcome. For example, in an organization where the boss explicitly tells a subordinate what to do and why, communication is instrumental. Instrumental and affective communication styles can also be related to individualism–collectivism and high- and low-context cultural dimensions. In collectivistic cultures, people are more conscious of the other person's reactions, and attempt to sense meaning by situational cues, so that an affective style tends to be preferred. An instrumental style, on the other hand, is often seen in business and other professional contexts, particularly in Western cultures where verbal explicitness is valued.

Gender and communication

In her seminal work *Language and Woman's Place*, Robin Lakoff (1975) argues that women and men speak differently because boys and girls are socialized separately. Deborah Tannen (1990), a discourse analyst, further claims that men and women express themselves differently because they have different cultures. In her influential 'two-cultures' theory, she states that men usually use verbal communication to *report* about the world. A report is a specific way to communicate in order to maintain independence and status in a hierarchical social order. Women, however, use verbal communication for *rapport*, in order to establish a human connection. It is a way of establishing connections and negotiating relationships. Moreover, on the question of who talks more, the usual stereotype is that women are *talkers*, men are *doers* (Mohanty, 2003). On the other hand, academic research shows that men tend to speak more often in public, and they tend to speak longer in meetings (Tannen, 1994).

....

Further online reading The following article can be accessed for free on the book's companion website https://study.sagepub.com/liu2e: Mucchi-Faina, Angelica (2005) 'Visible or influential? Language reforms and gender (in)equality', *Social Science Information*, 44(1): 189–215.

....

Gender differences in verbal communication are a complex and controversial combination of biological differences and socialization. Many linguists argue that language defines gender. Think of words such as 'businessmen', 'chairman', and 'mankind', in which there is a generic male implication. In subtle ways like this, language reinforces social stereotypes (Ardizzoni, 2007). For example, women are often defined by appearance or relationships; the use of the titles 'Miss' and 'Mrs' designates a woman's marital status. On the other hand, men are more commonly defined by activities, accomplishments, or positions. In general, it is gender-studies scholars who explore issues of sexuality, power, language, and marginalized populations and point to the increasingly complex and murky binary oppositions between male and female language.

Critical thinking...

How does language help to constitute masculinity and femininity? Can you give some examples from your own culture? When and why do men and women move away from this kind of stereotyped language?

THEORY CORNER

GENDER-NEUTRAL LANGUAGE

In neutral gender languages such as English, there is no grammatical marking for most nouns, whereas in grammatical gender languages, such as French and German, a gender is assigned to every noun. While arbitrary in the case of inanimate objects, the grammatical gender assigned to animate beings does match the biological gender in most cases (for instance, in German, *der Lehrer* as masculine and *die Lehrerin* as feminine, male and female teacher). If a group has a mixed or unknown composition, the masculine form usually prevails. This generic use of grammatically masculine words also exists in English (e.g., he and man), but is far less widespread than in languages with grammatical gender.

Gender-neutral language is a verbal communication style that adheres to certain rules originally suggested by feminist language reformers in universities during the 1970s. These rules discourage various common usages which are thought of as sexist, such as the generic use of masculine pronouns in referring to persons of either sex. Consequently, a number of new words have been coined, such as 'chairperson', 'spokesperson', as substitutes for the older male-oriented words in common usage. Feminists hope that by paying attention to gendered details in language, the language of the whole society can gradually be reformed, and people will develop more positive attitudes towards equality between the sexes (Gauntlett, 2002). The term 'gender-neutral language' is also called 'inclusive language', 'gender-inclusive language', 'gender generic language', and 'non-discriminatory language'.

Reference
Gauntlett, David (2002) *Media, Gender and Identity*. New York: Routledge.

Further reading on language and gender
Mucchi-Faina, Angelica (2005) 'Visible or influential? Language reforms and gender (in)equality', *Social Science Information*, 44(1): 189–215.

Theory in Practice

ATTITUDES TOWARDS GENDER-NEUTRAL LANGUAGE

Sarrasin, Gabriel and Pascal (2012) compared attitudes to gender-neutral language in three contexts: (1) where gender-neutral language had consistently been implemented for a long time (the United Kingdom); (2) where gender-neutral language had only recently been implemented (the German-speaking part of Switzerland); and (3) where such language was still under debate (the French-speaking part of Switzerland). They examined the relationships between three forms of sexism (modern, benevolent, and hostile) and two components of attitudes towards gender-neutral language (attitudes towards gender-related language reforms and recognition of sexist language) across different contexts. A questionnaire was distributed to students in the UK and in two (French- and German-speaking) regions of Switzerland (N = 446). The study found that, across all contexts, modern and hostile sexist beliefs were indeed related to negative attitudes towards gender-related language reforms. Recognition of sexist language was significantly related to modern sexism. Most importantly, British students were found to express more positive attitudes towards gender-neutral language than Swiss students.

Questions to take you further
Would you agree that all cultures should establish gender fairness in language use? If gender-neutral language use were promoted, would humiliation of women disappear? What examples can you give of this kind of language?

Reference
Sarrasin, Oriane, Ute Gabriel and Pascal Gygax (2012) 'Sexism and attitudes toward gender-neutral language: the case of English, French, and German', *Swiss Journal of Psychology/Schweizerische Zeitschrift für Psychologie*, 71(3): 113–124.

Further reading on attitudes to gender-neutral language
Crawford, Mary (1995) *Talking Difference: On Gender and Language*. London: Sage.

Translation and interpretation

Even when cultures speak the same language, as do Australians and Britons, there can be vocabulary and semantic differences. When cultures that speak different languages come into contact, translation is critical but always imperfect. *Translation* refers to the process of converting a source text, either spoken or written, into a different language. For example, ethnic shops often put up signs in both the host language and their native language to attract ethnic customers. *Interpretation* refers to the process of verbally expressing what is said in another language. Interpretation can be simultaneous, with the interpreter speaking at the same time as the original speaker, or consecutive, with the interpreter speaking only during the breaks provided by the original speaker (Lustig and Koester, 2013). Cultural differences

Photo 7.3   Names of popular tourist places in Beijing, like Silk Street, have been translated into English. However, 'silk' – the English translation – is a rough sound equivalence of the Chinese name (*Siu Shui*), not a concept equivalence.
Copyright © Shuang Liu. Used with permission.

in word usage make translation a difficult task, and two translators rarely agree on the exact translation of any given source text. Translation and interpretation raise issues of authenticity and accuracy, as well as the subjective role of the translator or interpreter.

It is very difficult, if not impossible, to translate an entire text word-for-word from one language to another, because different languages may convey views of the world in different ways. Problems of translation arise owing to lack of equivalence in vocabulary, idiomatic expressions, connotational meaning, experience, and concepts (Jandt, 2007). Word-for-word translation can result in awkward (sometimes hilarious) expressions that puzzle people from both sides. Here are examples of some awkward translations:

- On the menu of a Swiss restaurant: 'Our wines leave you nothing to hope for'.

- In a Copenhagen airline office: 'We take your bags and send them in all directions'.

- Outside a Hong Kong tailor shop: 'Ladies may have a fit upstairs'.

- On the box for a toothbrush at a Tokyo hotel: 'Give you strong mouth and refreshing wind'.

In addition to lexical equivalence, experiential equivalence can cause problems in translation. If an experience does not exist in a culture, it is difficult to translate words or expressions referring to that experience in that culture's language. For example, the literal translation of an expression in Hong Kong is 'Touch the nail on the door'. It actually means 'No one was home when you went to the house'. The meaning of this expression dates back to ancient China when upon leaving their houses, people would hammer a nail on the door instead of locking it. Thus, if a visitor touched the nail when trying to knock on the door, the visitor would know that no one was home. The literal meaning of 'touch the nail on the door' would not be easily understood by people from another culture in which this practice has never existed. To translate into another language, the translator has to offer an explanation either by using a word-for-word translation or by using a different set of words to capture the meaning. Translation problems like these raise the issue of the role of translator or interpreter.

We tend to consider translators or interpreters as 'intermediaries', simply rendering the source text into the target language (Martin and Nakayama, 2001). The assumption is that anyone who knows two languages can act as a translator. The example of 'touch the nail on the door' shows that language proficiency alone does not make a good translator. Knowledge of history and culture plays a significant role in how well or accurately a message from one language is rendered into another. Translation involves more than finding linguistic equivalence; conceptual, idiomatic, and experiential equivalence are also key factors in comprehending messages, particularly in intercultural situations.

Critical thinking...

In your opinion, is an original text like a book, a poem, or a play (or an email or SMS) fixed and complete once it is written, or is it incomplete and unstable, and thus subject to change? Do you believe that the perfect translation of a text which is culturally bound is possible? What do you think about authors who feel they must rewrite their texts in a new language rather than translating them?

LANGUAGE AND IDENTITY

Language defines our identities, as we use it to mark our social, ethnic, and national boundaries. As a Czech proverb goes, 'Learn a new language and get a new identity'.

Language and national identity

The sense of national unity is concerned with the integrity of the national language, territory, and religion. A contemporary interest in linguistic homogeneity is often traced to the eighteenth-century German philosopher Johann G. Herder, who claims that language expresses the inner consciousness of the nation, its ethos, its continuous identity in history, and its moral unity. Nationalists defend their national language against foreign 'pollution' in the belief that moral degeneration will follow. For example, language is seen as one of the most important markers of Serbian national identity, since it is understood as preserving, bearing, and passing down memories over the centuries (Volčič, 2005). Interestingly, majority groups in multicultural societies such as the United States and Canada can become threatened by other languages, so that significant groups have asserted the dominance of their languages through English-only (in the US) and French-only (in Quebec) movements (Barker et al., 2001).

Other scholars of language, nationalism, and nation-states argue that, as we are living in multicultural societies, 'There is no need for all citizens of a nation to be native speakers of a single language, and absolutely no need for a nation's language to be clearly distinct from others' (Barbour, 2002: 14). The fact remains that every nation faces some kind of language dilemma. For example, Louw (2004a) writes extensively about *Afrikaans*, the first language of 5.9 million people, mostly in South Africa and Namibia. But by the end of the twentieth century, English replaced Afrikaans as the dominant state language. With the ending of apartheid in 1994, Afrikaners became a South African minority group, marginalized within a political process geared to 'black empowerment'. Westernized black South Africans have deployed English as a language of state administration and lingua franca, further marginalizing Afrikaans. Today, only three of South Africa's languages are important print media languages, namely, English, Afrikaans and Zulu. A number of South Africa's languages are spoken in neighbouring countries, such as Tswana in Botswana; Sotho in Lesotho; Swazi in Swaziland; Tsonga in Mozambique; Venda (which is a dialect of Shona), the dominant language in Zimbabwe; Ndebele in Zimbabwe; and Afrikaans in Namibia. Nearly all South Africans are multilingual – being fluent in at least the two main languages of their area, but often understanding many more. In this way, South Africa is similar to the highly multilingual country of India, which has 22 official languages (including English), but literally thousands of languages and dialects (Sachdev and Bhatia, 2013). It is uncommon for an Indian not to speak several languages, yet communication across regions can still be problematic.

In Sweden, the national identity has for a long time been perceived by many as a monolingual and homogeneous one (Godin, 2006). Throughout the centuries, the Swedish language has played a major role in the unification of the country and the creation of a sense of national identity. However, twentieth-century globalization led the homogeneous Swedish society to welcome immigrant workers and refugees among its citizens, people from different cultures who did not share the same native language as the majority. Even as the newcomers tried to integrate themselves into their new society, Sweden had to adapt to its changing demography. Godin argues that it is not a surprise to find questions regarding language at the centre of national identity in the public sphere in Sweden.

There is a strong desire in many parts of the world to retain and enhance local or regional language that may once have been common but are now spoken only by a few people; this is a good example of glocalization (local and global at the same time). A key concern is that, because language encodes so much of culture, when the language is lost the culture goes with it. Today, entire institutes – the School of Oriental and African Studies in London and the Mercator Institute in the Netherlands are European examples – are devoted to researching on minority and endangered languages in order to preserve them. Similarly, people in many countries are taking political and social actions to enhance the status of local languages, including reinstating the teaching of these languages at school (Everett, 2002). For example, speakers of Welsh and Irish have mobilized over the past decades to achieve higher status for their languages, and have been successful to a significant extent. The indigenous language, Welsh or Irish, is now a required subject in schools, along with English and other languages. As a result, the number of speakers of these languages is increasing, and the languages themselves are adapting new vocabulary and structure to accommodate the modern world.

This same desire to retain and enhance regional languages spoken by only a few people is common throughout Europe. For example, regional languages in Spain, such as Catalan and Basque, now have institutional status and are taught in schools. In the Netherlands, the Frisians have taken an innovative approach to maintaining the indigenous language and yet teaching young people to live in the modern world. In Friesland (the northwest province of the Netherlands), schools conduct all subjects in Dutch for two days each week, in Frisian for two days, and in English for one day; only other languages (like French or German) are exempt. Thus, children learn not only language, but science, mathematics, literature, music, and craft in all three languages, with the aim of teaching them to be well-rounded people in their own as well as the national and most common foreign languages. It remains to be seen whether this approach produces the hoped-for results, but it is an interesting example of building culture through language.

Critical thinking…

Should knowledge of the national language be a criterion for citizenship? Is national identity necessarily dependent on a shared language? Is competence in the national language primarily a discriminatory requirement for citizenship, or a right that would contribute to making the life of immigrants and refugees easier?

Language and ethnic identity

Language is a vital aspect of any ethnic group's identity. Often, immigrant groups maintain their cultural heritage and identity by using their native language in their new cultures and teaching them to their children. Identity based on ethnic language also hinges on the assumption that one's linguistic community is acceptable in a number of ways. The degree of prestige, acceptability, and importance attached to a group's language is known as *ethnolinguistic vitality*. When you are faced with an ethnic or cultural group obviously different from your own, this encounter may be brief and unpleasant if you have the feeling that your ethnic or cultural group is being put down. Since language is one of the most clear-cut and immediate ways by which groups are identified, it is quite easy to see how your confidence can suffer if your language is disparaged.

Further online reading The following article can be accessed for free on the book's companion website https://study.sagepub.com/liu2e: Pantos, Andrew J. and Andrew W. Perkins (2013) 'Measuring implicit and explicit attitudes toward foreign accented speech', *Journal of Language and Social Psychology*, 32(1): 3–20.

Considerable evidence indicates that speech patterns, dialect, and accent serve as cues that cause listeners to assign certain attitudes or characteristics to another person. Dodd (1998) related an anecdote illustrating the relationship between language and identity: When a student who came from a rural area of the United States entered a large North American university, his mass media professors told him that his rural accent was inappropriate for broadcasting. This student adapted to the 'standard' speech to meet the norms favouring standard American patterns of speech. When he went home for Thanksgiving, his mother would not let him into the house because when he knocked and called out, she did not recognize his voice. Her response was that he had to start 'talking right' or he would not be allowed entry. This dilemma, common for people who participate in two or more different cultures or subcultures, is illustrative of how important our language is as an aspect of our identity and of our group membership.

SUMMARY

- Language comprises a set of symbols shared by a community to communicate meanings and experiences. Children learn the rules of their language and are productive and creative in their language acquisition.

- The language we speak influences how we perceive and categorize the world around us. The Sapir–Whorf hypothesis highlights the close connections between language, thought, and culture.

- Communication styles can be broadly categorized along four dimensions: direct/indirect, elaborate/succinct, personal/contextual, and instrumental/affective.

- Gender differences are reflected in the use of language. The preference for gender-neutral or inclusive language may depend on the cultural context.

- Language is an integral part of our personal, social, ethnic, and national identities, because the language we speak marks our cultural and social boundaries.

JOIN THE DEBATE

'Do the limits of my language mean the limits of my world?'

Ludwig Wittgenstein (1889–1951) played a key role in twentieth-century analytic philosophy and language studies. His work continues to influence current philosophical thought in topics as diverse as logic and language, perception, ethics and religion, aesthetics, and culture. In one of his most influential works, *Tractatus Logico-Philosophicus*, Wittgenstein (1922/2001) writes: 'The limits of my language are the limits of my world' ('Die grenzen meiner sprache sind die grenzen meiner welt'). This statement invites different interpretations. How do you understand his argument? One way to construe it would be to think of how your own world is limited by your language. Language shapes our perception of reality, our attitudes towards others, and others' perceptions of us. Would you agree here that we know what we know because we have words for it in the language we speak? If you agree, what limits do you think this places on our thinking? If you disagree, how do you think we can have knowledge without appropriate words?

CASE STUDY

How is politeness expressed across cultures?

Politeness is defined by many as the practical application of nice manners or behaviour (Félix-Brasdefer, 2006). It is a culturally invented phenomenon: what is considered polite in one cultural context can be viewed rude, strange, or simply eccentric in another cultural context. While the aim of politeness is to make verbal communication easy and comfortable, these culturally created norms of behaviour can sometimes be changed or manipulated. Linguistic politeness is an interesting concept because it encompasses how a particular language works in particular speech acts, as well as how speech acts dynamically create and are created by particular sociocultural contexts (Okura Gagné, 2010). During the course of communication acts, communicators engage in a negotiation of face relationships and employ diverse strategies to express a series of communicative acts in conversation, such as complaining or refusing.

Since its emergence over two decades ago, Brown and Levinson's (1987) innovative universal theory on linguistic politeness (or face theory) offered many arguments on the role of language in performing politeness. As a topic for linguistic analysis, they contributed significantly to theorizing the ways of understanding linguistic politeness in human speech interactions across the social sciences. As a result, it offers a powerful argument for a universal politeness theory as a possible way of understanding the cultural function of language use. Central to Brown and Levinson's theory is the universal applicability of the notion 'face'. Face, for them, is the 'positive social value a person effectively claims for himself', which is interactionally and symbolically defined through 'approved social attributes' (Brown and Levison, 1987: 61). Brown and Levinson saw this concept as a way to build a bridge between the micro and macro levels of analysis by highlighting the dynamic quality of face, as it can be lost, maintained, given, and enhanced in social interaction.

They identified two kinds of politeness, borrowing from Erving Goffman's concept of face. They define negative face as 'the basic claim to territories, personal preserves, right to non-distraction, i.e. to freedom of action and freedom from imposition', or 'the want of every competent adult member that his actions be unimpeded by others'. Positive face is defined as 'the positive consistent self-image or "personality" ... claimed by interactants', or furthermore 'the want of every member that his wants be desirable to at least some others' (Brown and Levinson, 1987: 61–62). On the one hand, negative politeness can be expressed through language in making a request that is less intrusive, such as 'If you don't mind...' or 'If it isn't too much trouble...'. On the other hand, positive politeness aims to establish a positive and connected relationship between communicators: respecting one's needs to be appreciated, liked, and understood.

According to their theory, linguistic politeness is highly contextual, in that a communicator chooses a linguistic action in accordance to particular face wants. For example, a speaker might adopt negative politeness practices to satisfy the hearer's negative face (and vice versa) depending on their respective 'social distance', 'power distance', and 'the weight of imposition' of a particular request (Okura Gagné, 2010: 125). For example, we are inclined to speak to our social equals differently from the way we speak to those who hold higher or lower status than our own in a given situation. If a professor is working in a public library and the people next to her are being very loud and disruptive, she will go over and tell them to be quiet – and she will employ different words depending on who it is making noise. If they are students, she will use more direct language, allowing for no confusion in what she is asking: 'Stop talking so loudly, please!' If they are colleagues, she will claim common ground with them using the positive politeness strategy: 'I'm writing a book and it's really hard to concentrate with all this noise.'

Brown and Levinson (1987: 245) also argue that one can distinguish between 'positive politeness cultures' and 'negative politeness cultures'. The former features a lower weight of imposition and a relatively smaller power distance (USA and New Guinea), and the latter emphasizes a greater weight of imposition and relatively larger power and social distance (the UK and Japan). Brown and Levinson acknowledge that the expression of face varies across cultures. Nevertheless, they argue that it is a universal social fact that all cultures have the concept of face, which individuals use to shift and adjust their public self-image to positive and/or negative face wants in society (Okura Gagné, 2010).

A range of researchers have tested Brown and Levinson's theory regarding the universal applicability of linguistic politeness. For example, Félix-Brasdefer (2006) investigated the linguistic strategies employed by male native speakers of Mexican Spanish to maintain the equilibrium of interpersonal relationships in the course of refusal interactions in formal and informal situations. He writes that linguistic politeness may be realized by means of both formulaic and semi-formulaic utterances. Formulaic utterances are linguistic expressions that are used in ritualized forms of verbal interaction and comprise forms of address and expressions commonly used in specific speech acts, such as thanking, apologizing, or refusing. Semi-formulaic expressions are, he writes, conventionalized forms that 'carry out indirect speech acts appropriate to the politic behaviour of a social situation' (Félix-Brasdefer, 2006: 2166), and may include linguistic forms that internally modify a speech act to soften the force of a statement ('I don't think', 'maybe', 'probably'), solidarity markers that support mutual knowledge of the participants ('you know'), and sentential structures containing specific modal verbs ('May I ask you to open the door?'). He suggests that although no linguistic expressions are inherently polite or impolite, some expressions may be open to a polite or impolite interpretation in a given cultural context.

References

Brown, Penelope and Stephen Levinson (1987) *Politeness*. Cambridge: Cambridge University Press.

Félix-Brasdefer, César J. (2006) 'Linguistic politeness in Mexico: refusal strategies among male speakers of Mexican Spanish', *Journal of Pragmatics*, 38(12): 2158–2187.

Okura Gagné, Nana (2010) 'Reexamining the notion of negative face in the Japanese socio-linguistic politeness of request', *Journal of Language and Communication*, 30(2): 123–128.

Questions for discussion

1. Politeness is interpreted and evaluated differently across cultures and between persons. How do you interpret politeness?

2. Do you use 'positive face' during verbal communication? What are the strategies people can adopt to avoid 'negative face'? When might 'negative face' be appropriate?

3. Would you argue that your culture is a 'positive politeness culture' or a 'negative politeness culture'? Why?

4. Do you agree that linguistic politeness depends on a specific context? Give some examples.

5. Give some examples of how politeness is expressed in your culture through verbal communication.

FURTHER READINGS

All articles listed next to the mouse icon below can be accessed for free on the book's companion website: https://study.sagepub.com/liu2e

Language and discrimination

Fairclough, Norman (2003) *Analysing Discourse: Textual Analysis for Social Research*. London: Routledge.

This book is about how language works to maintain and change power relations in contemporary society, and how understanding these processes can enable people to resist and change them. It is a critical introduction to discourse analysis as it is practised in a variety of different disciplines today, from linguistics and sociolinguistics to sociology and cultural studies. The author shows how concern with the analysis of discourse can be combined, in a systematic and fruitful way, with an interest in broader problems of social analysis and social change. Fairclough provides a concise and critical review of the methods and results of discourse analysis, discussing the descriptive work of linguists and conversation analysts as well as the more historically and theoretically oriented work of Michel Foucault.

Pantos, Andrew J. and Andrew W. Perkins (2013) 'Measuring implicit and explicit attitudes toward foreign accented speech', *Journal of Language and Social Psychology*, 32(1): 3–20.

Research on explicit language attitudes has shown that listners determine a speaker's social identity based on accent. This paper reported a study that examined language attitudes to foreign and US-accented speech. A total of 165 undergraduate students from an American university participated in the study. Implicit attitudes were measured by using an implicit association test that incorporated audio cues as experimental stimuli. Explicit attitudes were measured through self-reported questionnaires. Results showed that participants' implicit attitudes favoured the US-accented speaker over the Korean-accented speaker. However, they showed a pro-foreign accent bias on explicit measures. The authors concluded that implicit and explicit attitudes are separate constructs. Because explicit attitudes are more controllable, listeners can hypercorrect implicit attitudes, if they suspect those attitudes could reflect a socially unacceptable bias.

Rusi, Jaspala and Adrian Coyleb (2010) 'My language, my people: language and ethnic identity among British-born South Asians', *South Asian Diaspora*, 2(2): 201–218.

This study explores how a group of second-generation Asians (SGAs) understood and defined language, focusing upon the role they perceived language to have played in their identity. Twelve SGAs were interviewed, and the data were subjected to qualitative thematic analysis. Four superordinate themes are reported, entitled 'mother tongue and self', 'a sense of ownership and affiliation', 'negotiating linguistic identities in social space', and 'the quest for a positive linguistic identity'. Participants generally expressed a desire to maintain continuity of self-definition as Asian, primarily through the maintenance of the heritage language (HL). An imperfect knowledge of the HL was said to have a negative impact upon psychological well-being. There were ambivalent responses to the perception of language norms, and various strategies were reported for dealing with dilemmatic situations and identity threat arising from bilingualism.

Variations in language use

Kramsch, Claire (1995) 'The cultural component of language teaching', *Language, Culture and Curriculum*, 8(2): 83–92.

Despite the advances made by research in the spheres of the intercultural and the multicultural, language teaching is still operating on a relatively narrow conception of both language and culture. Language continues to be taught as a fixed system of formal structures and universal speech functions, a neutral conduit for the transmission of cultural knowledge. Culture is incorporated only to the extent that it reinforces and enriches, not that it puts in question traditional boundaries of self and other. The theoretical framework the author proposes for teaching culture through language suspends the traditional dichotomy between the universal and the particular in language teaching. It embraces the particular, not to be consumed by it, but as a platform for dialogue and as a common struggle to realign differences.

Kress, Gunter and Theo van Leeuwen (2001) *Multimodal Discourse: The Modes and Media of Contemporary Communication*. London: Arnold.

Multimodal Discourse offers a theoretical framework for the study of communication in the modern world of multimedia. The book helps students of linguistics, cultural studies, and communication, as well as journalists, photographers, designers, and others who work practically in the field of communication and design, to understand and differentiate the distinct levels of mass communication and their interaction. The authors also give an overview of the development of communication and discourse and show how this development is influenced by overall changes in society and social life. Linguists have shown that discourse is not only used and expressed in and/or by language; Kress and van Leeuwen also apply the term of 'discourse' to music, architecture, and many other domains of culture.

Words are a wonderful form of communication, but they will never replace kisses and punches.

Ashleigh Brilliant, British author and cartoonist, 1933–

8

NONVERBAL COMMUNICATION AND CULTURE

LEARNING OBJECTIVES

After this chapter, you should be able to:

- Define nonverbal communication.
- Identify characteristics and functions of nonverbal communication.
- Evaluate different types of nonverbal code.
- Explain the influence of culture on nonverbal communication.

INTRODUCTION

Broadly speaking, nonverbal communication can be defined as communicating without using words. In this chapter, the term *nonverbal communication* refers to the use of non-spoken symbols to communicate a message. Human communication frequently involves more than the use of a verbal code. Each of us uses nonverbal codes as a means of communicating with others, sometimes consciously and other times below the level of conscious awareness. Mehrabian (1982) estimates that 93 per cent of the meaning is carried through nonverbal communication channels (e.g., voice, body movement, facial expressions) and only 7 per cent of the meaning is carried through words. Mehrabian's numbers are not well supported by data, and other scholars dispute them. Nevertheless, all agree that a very significant amount of communication is nonverbal.

Many linguists, psychologists, and sociologists believe that human language evolved from a system of nonverbal communication. Humans possess a repertoire of non-linguistic ways to communicate with one another through the use of their hands, arms, faces, personal space, and so forth. Nonverbal behaviour reveals much about our attitudes, personalities, emotions, and relationships with others (Samovar et al., 2013). For example, there is a plethora of research in psychology studying the cues people give (or do not give) when they are lying, such as hands touching their face, throat, and mouth or scratching the nose – as it turns out, this is not easy to judge, but the clues that do exist are often culturally specific. Effective communication requires that we understand the central role of nonverbal behaviour as part of communication competence.

The study of nonverbal communication dates back at least to the time of Charles Darwin, who believed that facial expressions such as smiles and frowns are biologically determined. Although body language, as a form of communication, has been recognized since the time of Aristotle, and many thinkers in different cultures have written about it, it is the anthropologist Ray Birdwhistell who is recognized as the originator of the scientific study of body language – kinesics. In 1970, Birdwhistell published a book entitled *Kinesics and Context*, in which he argued that nonverbal communication, like spoken language, has its own set of rules. Ekman and Friesen's (1971) early research on facial expressions also illustrates the universality of many emotional expressions. For example, fear is indicated by a furrowed brow, raised eyebrows, wide-open eyes, partially open mouth, and upturned upper lip.

Based on subsequent research and observations, scholars have become convinced that, although all humans share basic emotions, such as fear, happiness, anger, surprise, disgust, and sadness, the rules governing the display of these emotions vary from culture to culture.

We learn display rules through socialization into our cultural context. For example, in Arab culture people express grief openly. Other people from, for example, Indonesia are more subdued in their mourning behaviour. Simple gestures of greeting also differ from culture to culture. Hindus greet one another by placing their palms together in front of their chest while bowing their heads slightly. Japanese greet each other by bowing their heads to show respect. Australians may tip their head slightly upward to signal 'hello'. In Oman it is not unusual for men to kiss one another on the nose after a handshake when greeting one another. An understanding of how nonverbal behaviours communicate messages in our own culture and in that of others can help us to appreciate the influence of culture on communication. As Ramsey (1979: 111) states:

> According to culturally prescribed codes, we use eye movement and contact to manage conversations and to regulate interactions; we follow rigid rules governing intra- and interpersonal touch, our bodies synchronously join in the rhythm of others in a group, and gestures modulate our speech. We must internalize all this in order to become and remain fully functioning and socially appropriate members of our culture.

This chapter focuses on nonverbal communication and how it influences intercultural communication. We explain similarities and differences between verbal and nonverbal codes, and describe the characteristics and functions of nonverbal codes. Different types of nonverbal codes, including body movement (kinesics), vocal qualities (paralanguage), the use of time (chronemics), space (proxemics), artefacts, dress, and smell (olfactics) are identified. Finally, this chapter shows the close link between culture and nonverbal communication. An understanding of how culture can influence behaviour and communication outcomes can improve intercultural communication competence.

Critical thinking…

Are there any nonverbal behaviours that people typically use in restaurants in your culture? What do these behaviours mean? Could they be misinterpreted in another culture? How?

CHARACTERISTICS AND FUNCTIONS OF NONVERBAL CODES

Characteristics of nonverbal codes

Verbal and nonverbal messages are inextricably intertwined to form the code systems through which members of any culture convey their attitudes, personalities, beliefs, values, thoughts, feelings, and intentions (Lustig and Koester, 2013). Verbal and nonverbal communication often takes place simultaneously. In the West, we tend to use verbal behaviour to convey the literal or *cognitive content* of a message (what is said), whereas the nonverbal component of the message communicates more of the *affective content* (feelings connected to the words). The affective content accounts for much of the meaning we derive from verbal communication, and hence can influence how a verbal message is interpreted. While we normally have some control over the words we say, we may inadvertently reveal our true feelings, which we would prefer to conceal, through nonverbal behaviour. Blushing, for example, is very hard to control. Other nonverbal cues may also be involuntary. On the other hand, some nonverbal behaviour is as easy to control as words, although we do not tend to believe this – that is, we can lie with our bodies as well as with our words. Nevertheless, if the nonverbal message contradicts the verbal one, we tend to believe the nonverbal message because we believe that nonverbal messages are less conscious and often more truthful.

However inseparably verbal and nonverbal codes are linked in a communication event, the difference between the two types of code is significant. Neuliep (2012) identified three ways in which verbal and nonverbal codes differ. First, the verbal language system is based primarily on symbols (things that stand for their referents, but are not part of the referents), whereas the nonverbal system is sign-based (parts of the referents that are used to stand for them) to a greater extent. A second way in which the nonverbal system differs from its verbal counterpart is that its sending capacity is more restricted. For example, it is difficult to communicate about the past or future through purely nonverbal codes. Likewise, it is hard to communicate nonverbally without seeing or hearing the other person (although devices like emoticons do some of this work). A third difference is that verbal codes have a formal phonetic (sound) system and syntax (structure and grammar) to govern usage, whereas there are fewer formal rules governing the use of nonverbal code systems. In fact, sign languages and semaphore communication are classified as verbal because they do have such formal rules. Different types of nonverbal behaviour can be categorized, but these categories are more loosely defined than those for verbal codes. The meanings of nonverbal behaviour are also usually less precise than those of verbal codes and are only made clear within a particular cultural and situational context. It is important to remember that these three differences are a matter of degree, rather than kind – for example, verbal codes are made up almost entirely of conventional symbols, whereas nonverbal codes are a mix of symbols and signs. This use of symbols and display codes in nonverbal as well as verbal behaviour, combined with the commonly-held belief that nonverbal behaviour is not learned but 'natural', creates the potential for misunderstanding both in the same culture and across cultures. This is especially likely in the latter case, where communicators may not share the interpretation of either verbal or nonverbal codes.

Further online reading The following article can be accessed for free on the book's companion website https://study.sagepub.com/liu2e: Hall, Judith A., Nora A. Murphy and Mast M. Schmid (2007) 'Nonverbal self-accuracy in interpersonal interaction', *Personality and Social Psychology Bulletin*, 33(2): 1675–1685.

THEORY CORNER

EXPECTANCY VIOLATION THEORY

Expectancy violation theory, developed by Judee Burgoon (1978), assumes that humans anticipate certain behaviour from the people with whom they interact. These expectancies may be general, pertaining to all members of a language community, or particularized, pertaining to a specific individual. When expectancies are violated, the violation can exert significant impact on the communicators' impression of one another and on the outcomes of their interactions. Based on evidence from various experiments, Burgoon concludes that people evaluate communication with others in either a positive or a negative way, depending on their expectation of the interaction and their evaluation of the communicator. Positive evaluation is often directed towards attractive, powerful, or credible others, while negative evaluation is more likely to be associated with unattractive or less powerful individuals. This theory was initially concerned only with spatial violations. But since the mid-1980s, it has been applied to other nonverbal behaviour, including facial expression, eye contact, touch, and body movement. The theory has also been used to explain emotional, marital, and intercultural communication.

Reference
Burgoon, Judee (1978) 'A communication model of personal space violation: expectation and an initial test', *Human Communication Research*, 4: 129–142.

Further reading on interpreting nonverbal codes
Elfenbein, Hillary A. and Nalini Ambady (2003) 'When familiarity breeds accuracy: cultural exposure and facial emotion recognition', *Journal of Personality and Social Psychology*, 85(2): 276–290.

Theory in Practice

EXPECTANCY VIOLATIONS IN SEXUAL RELATIONSHIPS

Expectancy violation theory has been applied in a range of communicative situations, including, but not limited to, rhetoric, visual appearance, and online versus offline interactions. One interesting example came from Bevan (2003), who applied expectancy violation theory to examine the link between sexual resistance and the violation of the resisted partner's expectations. Specifically, her study looked at the resisted individual's perception of sexual resistance message directness and relational context in terms of three aspects of expectancy violations: violation valence, violation importance, and violation expectedness. Data were obtained from 307 university students in the USA. Participants read eight sexual resistance scenarios and then judged the realism and frequency of occurrence of the scenario in their own close relationships and the messages' directness and strength. Findings indicate that participants view hypothetical sexual resistance from a long-term dating partner as a more negative and more unexpected violation than hypothetical rejection from a cross-sex friend. When a participant is hypothetically rejected by way of direct communication from his or her close relational partner, such a violation is perceived as more relationally important than indirect sexual resistance. Bevan argues that, as sexual encounters generally occur in situations with high levels of emotional sensitivity and vulnerability, partners' behaviour may be influenced by different sexual goals, with the result that each partner believes that their expectations have been violated. The prior history of an interaction, however, is likely to affect whether one partner decides the other's action is an expectancy violation, including implicit or contextual boundaries and nonverbal communicative clues.

Questions to take you further
What are the possible differences in effects of expectancy violation when comparing sexual partners in committed relationships with those in cross-sex friendships? Can you think of a scenario in which a 'breach' would be tolerated?

Reference
Bevan, Jennifer L. (2003) 'Expectancy violation theory and sexual resistance in close, cross-sex relationships', *Communication Monographs*, 70(1): 68–82.

Further reading on expectancy violation in intimate situations
Afifi, Walid A. and Judee K. Burgoon (1998) '"We never talk about that": a comparison of cross-sex friendships and dating relationships on uncertainty and topic avoidance', *Personal Relationships*, 5(3): 255–272.

Functions of nonverbal codes

Knapp and Hall (1997) identified six primary functions of nonverbal communication: *repeat* the message sent by the verbal code; *contradict* the verbal message; *substitute* for a verbal message; *complement* a verbal message; *accentuate* the verbal message; and *regulate* verbal communication.

Repeat a verbal message

We use nonverbal codes to repeat what has been said on another channel. For example, you may wave your hands while saying good-bye to a friend, as waving is a common nonverbal symbol for good-bye. Similarly, when someone asks us for directions, it is very likely that we would use our hands to point out the direction while explaining it in words. Verbal and nonverbal communication is usually largely redundant, which helps us greatly in understanding other people and in sending clearer messages ourselves.

Contradict a verbal message

Nonverbal messages may, however, contradict verbal ones. For example, imagine that your friend is proudly showing you a new dress she has bought. You think the dress is awful and unflattering on her, but do not wish to hurt her feelings. Unfortunately, while telling her you think the dress looks beautiful you may also inadvertently frown, or use your hands too abruptly. When verbal and nonverbal codes contradict, people tend to believe the nonverbal message because it is considered as less controlled and more revealing of our true feelings.

Substitute for a verbal message

Hand gestures in particular can be used to substitute for a verbal message in noisy places or in a situation when a common language is not shared. Police officers use nonverbal codes to direct the traffic flow. On tourist-populated marketplaces, sellers and buyers can use nonverbal symbols to bargain for goods if they do not speak the same language. In radio station recording studios, the director must use gestures to indicate to the speaker when to start speaking. In addition, some messages that are difficult to express in words can be communicated nonverbally. For example, you could keep looking at your watch to indicate to your visitor that it is time to go.

Complement a verbal message

A nonverbal message can complement the verbal message; that is, it can add information to the verbal message. For example, a man involved in a car accident may be able to use gestures to describe the accident to the police, while simultaneously conveying the same message in words. A student may jump up and down while saying how happy she is with an excellent grade received for her assignment. A mother may place a finger to her lips to tell her child to keep quiet in a puppet theatre.

Accentuate a verbal message

Although accentuating and complementing are similar, the former specifically increases or decreases the intensity of a message. For example, a manager may pound his fist firmly on the table to emphasize his feelings while saying 'No' to an unreasonable request for a pay rise from an employee. A child might say 'I love you' while giving you a kiss on the cheek. Alternatively, a colleague may use a neutral tone of voice to *lower* the intensity of negative words. In these cases, nonverbal codes accent the emotions conveyed by verbal messages because they add more information to them.

Regulate verbal communication

We can use nonverbal codes to tell others to do or not to do something. We use voice inflection, head nods, and hand movements to control the flow of conversation or to direct turn-taking. In fact, conversational speech is mainly regulated – in terms of who gets to speak, for how long, and when – by nonverbal behaviour in the voice (intonation, pausing) and body (forward lean, gaze, smiling).

Critical thinking...

How can power be communicated through body movement? In what ways can a senior manager in a company (within your cultural context) use nonverbal behaviour to communicate power relations during a conversation with a subordinate? How could the subordinate resist the manager's power displays, or go along with them, using nonverbal behaviour?

TYPES OF NONVERBAL COMMUNICATION

It is impossible to categorize all the different types of nonverbal behaviour. Not only are they too numerous, but often several types of nonverbal behaviour from seemingly different 'categories' can be used by the same person simultaneously. In this section, however, we examine the seven categories which are argued to be most relevant to intercultural communication: kinesics, proxemics, chronemics, haptics, physical appearance and dress, paralanguage, and olfactics.

Kinesics: body movement

Kinesics refers to gestures, hand and arm movements, leg movements, facial expressions, eye contact, and posture. Ekman and Friesen (1969) developed a system that organized kinesic behaviour into five broad categories: emblems, illustrators, affect displays, regulators, and adaptors.

....

Further online reading The following article can be accessed for free on the book's companion website https://study.sagepub.com/liu2e: Herzfeld, Michael (2009) 'The cultural politics of gesture: reflections on the embodiment of ethnographic practice', *Ethnography*, 10(1): 131–152.

....

Emblems are primary hand gestures that have a direct literal verbal translation; these gestures blur the boundary between verbal and nonverbal communication. Within any culture there is usually a high level of agreement about the meaning of a particular emblem. For example, making a circle with one's thumb and index finger while extending the other fingers is emblematic of the word 'OK' in the USA, but it stands for 'money' in Japan, and signifies 'zero' in Indonesia. In many Western cultures, beckoning people to come with the palm up is common, but in some Asian countries people only use such gesture to beckon dogs.

Illustrators are typically hand and arm movements that function to complement or accent words. Thus, illustrators serve a metacommunicative function; that is to say, they are messages about messages. For example, a person might describe the size of a crocodile she saw while using hand gestures to illustrate its length. Stewart and Bennett (1991) provide an interesting example of cultural differences in using illustrators. An American visitor to Mexico tried to convey the age of his young children to a Mexican by indicating their height. He held up his right hand, the palm open and facing down horizontally at the height of his children from the ground. The Mexican looked puzzled. Later, the American visitor learned that Mexicans would only use that particular hand gesture to indicate the height of a dog or some other animals; human height is indicated with the palm open and held vertical to the ground at the appropriate distance.

Affect displays primarily refer to facial expressions that communicate an emotional state. Through facial expressions we can communicate an attitude, or feelings of disgust, happiness, anger, or sadness. Some facial expressions are universal (e.g., a smile indicates pleasure and happiness in every culture), but the specific meaning attached to a facial expression or other affect display – even one as universal as smiling – must be linked to its cultural context. For example, a shop assistant may smile to customers to show friendliness and politeness; a mother may smile to her baby to show affection; a student unable to answer a question from the teacher may smile to cover her embarrassment. Besides facial expressions, posture – a person's bodily stance – also communicates feelings and emotions. For example, sitting with the soles of one's feet facing another person communicates disrespect in Thailand and Saudi Arabia, whereas in the United States, this posture just illustrates that the person feels relaxed.

Critical thinking…

What displays of emotion do you think are universal, and which ones are culturally learned? In what ways does culture have an impact on how its members display emotion?

Regulators include behaviours and actions that govern or manage conversations. We may use eye contact, silence, and head nodding during conversation to show interest and to indicate turn-taking. If a teacher asks a question and the student does not wish to respond, she can avoid direct eye contact to indicate her unwillingness to speak. However, it is worth noting that silence during a conversation may not always communicate disinterest (see Carbaugh et al.'s [2006] example of silence in Finland in Chapter 7).

Adaptors are kinesic behaviours used to satisfy physiological or psychological needs. For example, scratching an itch satisfies a physiological need, while adjusting one's glasses before speaking may satisfy a psychological need to calm down. These behaviours help people to adapt to their environment. The interpretation of any kinesic behaviour depends on its context and the other communication that takes place at the same time. For example, sitting with arms and legs tightly crossed may mean that the person is feeling cold (e.g., at a train station), defensive (e.g., during an argument), or nervous (e.g., waiting for a job interview).

Proxemics: the use of space

Proxemics refers to the use of space, including territory, which stands for the space that an individual claims permanently or temporarily. For example, it is very likely that you are sitting in the same seat in a lecture theatre where you sat at the beginning of the semester, even though you do not have assigned seating. If someone takes that seat before you, you may feel as if that person had taken 'your spot'. The study of proxemics includes three aspects of space: fixed features, semi-fixed features, and personal space

(Hall, 1966). The size of one's office, a fixed feature of space, communicates status and power, while semi-fixed features of space – the movable objects within an office, such as furniture and decorations – can communicate the degree of openness of the occupant, as well as status and power. Some people prefer to have their desk facing the door, which may make visitors feel welcome but may also communicate a barrier between the visitor and the resident of the office. Others prefer to put high bookshelves at the entrance to block the view in and out, which may make people feel the person is less accessible. Personal space refers to the distance within which people feel comfortable when interacting with others. We use space to communicate, and the size of such space is not only culturally determined, but also influenced by the relationship. People from Latin America or the Middle East often feel comfortable standing close to each other, while people from European countries or North America prefer a relatively greater distance. Lovers stand closer to each other during a conversation than do colleagues. Cultural norms and the relationship between the communicators determine the use of personal space in communication.

Further online reading The following article can be accessed for free on the book's companion website https://study.sagepub.com/liu2e: Molinsky, Andrew L., Mary A. Krabbenhoft, Nalini Ambady and Susan Y. Choi (2005) 'Cracking the nonverbal code: intercultural competence and gesture recognition across cultures', *Journal of Cross-Cultural Psychology*, 36(3): 380–395.

THEORY CORNER

THE MEANING OF SPATIAL RELATIONS

Edward Hall (1966) analysed North Americans' use of space and identified four zones of personal space that have meaning in communication. The first is the intimate zone (0–18 inches), which is used for intimate communication such as comforting, protecting, and love-making. The second is the personal zone (18 inches–4 feet), which is the distance that people commonly maintain in dyadic encounters. The third is the social zone (4–12 feet), which is the normative distance at social gatherings, in work settings, and during business transactions. The fourth zone comprises the largest distance between persons (12 feet and above). It is generally used in formal communication situations, such as public speaking. Different cultures may have different criteria for a 'comfortable' distance between speakers.

Reference
Hall, Edward T. (1966) *The Hidden Dimension*. Garden City, NY: Doubleday.

Further reading on proxemics
Burgoon, Judee K. and Stephen B. Jones (1976) 'Toward a theory of personal space expectations and their violations', *Human Communication Research*, 2(2): 131–146.

Theory in Practice

MAINTAINING PERSONAL SPACE IN COMMUNICATION

Personal space refers to the area or zone around an individual that generally should not be physically entered by another person. The personal space zone is usually reserved for close friends or family, and the actual distance will vary between individuals and cultures. Unwanted or unexpected intrusions often cause the 'invaded' individual to feel uncomfortable or even irritated. Khan and Kamal (2010) tested reactions to invasion of personal space in a group of postgraduate students in Pakistan. They compared different reactions from male and female students. The dominant reaction from affected individuals was to stare or glance at the invader, followed by pretending to use their mobile phone. The male participants tended to reach for their mobile phone more frequently than the female participants, though. In comparison, the female participants tended to display more compensatory behaviours after their personal space was invaded, such as moving away. Based on the findings from their study, the authors argue that the relationship between the two persons plays a significant role in how individuals react to personal space invasion. When an individual's personal space is invaded by a stranger or someone with whom he or she does not have a close personal relationship, the resulting effects are mostly negative.

Questions to take you further

What is the comfortable space that you prefer to maintain when you initiate a conversation with a stranger? How would it make you feel if someone came within that distance?

Reference

Khan, Anber Y. and Anila Kamal (2010) 'Exploring reactions to invasion of personal space in university students', *Journal of Behavioural Sciences*, 20(2): 80–99.

Further reading on personal space

Little, Kenneth B. (1965) 'Personal space', *Journal of Experimental Social Psychology*, 1(3): 237–247.

Chronemics: the use of time

Chronemics refers to the use of time. Our concept of time may influence our communication behaviour. A meeting in an African village does not begin until everyone is ready. A 45-minute wait may not be unusual for a business appointment in Latin America, but would probably be insulting to a North American businessman. Differences in the conception of time can cause frustration in intercultural communication. For example, a US American professor complained about the long staff meetings when he taught at a university in Hong Kong. Unlike his experience of staff meetings in the United States, those he attended in Hong Kong did not seem to follow the agenda items in a linear way. Oftentimes, even upon reaching the seventh item of the agenda, a question raised by someone could still bring the discussion back to the second item on the agenda. Decisions were not made by majority vote, but rather by consensus of people present at the meeting. Thus, each staff meeting commonly lasted for over two hours, which this American professor considered an inefficient use of time.

Different conceptions of time lead people to attempt only one task at a time, or to multi-task. Hall (1977) categorizes time orientations into monochronic and polychronic. People with *monochronic* time orientation, a characteristic of many Western cultures, view time as linear, much like a progressive path, having a beginning and an end. They also believe that this 'path' has discrete compartments; thus people should do only one thing at a time. To a Westerner, time can be bought, saved, spent, wasted, lost, or made up, and observing clock time is important. In contrast, *polychronic* cultures view time as cyclical and people attempt to perform multiple tasks simultaneously. To an Arab, observing clock time is irreligious, because only God can determine what will or will not happen. Offices in Arabic cultures may have large reception areas where several groups of people all conduct their affairs at the same time. To someone from a culture with a monochronic time orientation, this arrangement may appear counter-intuitive and confusing. Of course, the division between mono- and polychronic time orientations is not often clear-cut. People are capable of both orientations, depending on the context.

Photo 8.1   Mixed Gregorian and Buddhist calendar dates are shown on the wall of a building in Laos.
Copyright © Joan Burnett. Used with permission.

Another example of cultural differences in time conception is the use of calendar. While the Gregorian calendar is used universally, people from different cultures may also use their culture-specific calendars, such as the Chinese lunar calendar and the Buddhist calendar, to record their date of birth or to celebrate the New Year.

Haptics: the use of touch

Haptics refers to the use of touch, the most primitive form of communication. Touch sends a myriad of messages – protection, support, approval, or encouragement. As usual, when, where, and whom we touch and what meanings we assign to touch differ widely across cultures. The amount of touch also varies with age, sex, situation, and the relationship between the people involved. North American culture generally discourages touching by adults except in moments of intimacy or in formal greetings (e.g., hand shaking or hugging). Similar culturally defined patterns of physical contact avoidance are found in most cultures of Asia and Northern Europe. In so-called Mediterranean cultures, touch is extremely important, and people frequently use touch during a conversation or a meeting.

Hall (1966) distinguishes between high- and low-contact cultures. High-contact cultures are those that tend to encourage touching and engage in touching more frequently (e.g., Southern and Eastern Europe). Anglo-Celtic cultures are considered low contact. Even within a low- or high-contact culture, the cultural and social rules governing touch vary. People from Islamic and Hindu cultures typically do not touch with the left hand because to do so is a social insult. The left hand is reserved for toilet functions. Islamic cultures generally do not permit touching between genders, but touch between people of the same gender tends to be acceptable. In many Western cultures, touching between people of the same sex may be interpreted by others as a sign of homosexuality, but in other cultures this practice is normal for everyone.

Physical appearance and dress

Interpersonal communication is often preceded by the communicators' observations of each other's physical appearance. People can wear a particular type of clothes to communicate culture, religion, status, power, personality, self-esteem, and social identity. For example, Muslim women are often easily recognized by their headscarves, which are important symbols of religious faith. More religious or conservative Muslim women usually wear the *jilhah*, meaning 'outer-garment'. This is a long coat-like dress that covers the whole body except for the face and hands. Some Muslim men are identified by a long white robe and a hat.

In most cultures people consciously manipulate their physical appearance in order to communicate their identity. In ancient Chinese culture, women had to bind their feet at a young age, because small feet symbolized beauty. Plastic surgery is another example of using physical appearance to communicate messages. According to the American Society for Aesthetic Plastic Surgery (2006), there has been a 222 per cent increase in cosmetic procedures performed in the United States since 1997; 91 per cent of the cosmetic surgery was performed on young women (ASAPS, 2006). As Kathy Davis (1995) noted, in Western societies women are expected to look beautiful because they are considered 'to embody' beauty. Consequently, many women believe they must conform to society's notion of beauty, as it is reinforced as their 'role'.

Perceptions of beauty or physical attractiveness differ from culture to culture. More than three decades of extensive research on female gender portrayal in advertising offers a rich understanding of how beauty is constructed in different cultures (Frith, Shaw and Cheng, 2005). Frith and colleagues found that Western women appeared more frequently in clothing advertisements, whereas Asian models were more often used to advertise facial and beauty products. This is consistent with the idea that beauty in the East is related to a pretty face, while the predominant beauty ideal in the West relates to body as well as face. Beauty ideals and stereotypes put forth by advertisers can exert negative pressure on women of different races, and there are indications of a continued push in the West towards a white beauty ideal. While white women are pressured to be thin, women of colour may experience not only the societal pressure to be thin, but also that of an impossible expectation to be white.

Photo 8.2   Dressed in his traditional attire, a chief from the Baragam community in Papua New Guinea prepares to dance in his highland village.
Copyright © Alison Rae. Used with permission.

Paralanguage: quality and characteristics of the voice

Paralanguage refers to vocal qualities that accompany speech. It can be divided into two broad categories: voice qualities and vocalizations (Knapp and Hall, 1997). Voice qualities include elements like pitch, volume, tempo, rhythm, tone, pausing, and resonance of the voice. Vocalization includes laughing, crying, sighing, yelling, moaning, swallowing, and throat-clearing. Some scholars also include as paralinguistic vocalizations back-channel utterances such as *um*, *ah*, *ooh*, *shh,* and *uh*, although other scholars categorize these as verbal behaviour – once again, the boundary between verbal and nonverbal behaviour is blurred. Silence is also considered by some (but not all) to fall within the domain of paralanguage. People may use silence to show respect, agreement or disagreement, apathy, awe, confusion, contemplation, embarrassment, regret, repressed anger, sadness, and a myriad of other things. We interpret a speaker's feelings and emotions based partly on our perception of the variations in vocal quality. The same words said with different vocal qualities convey different meanings, as illustrated in the example below:

Mark, you are going to marry Hillary. (A declarative statement of a fact)

Mark, you are going to marry *Hillary*? (A question to convey that I thought you were going to marry someone else)

Mark, you are going to marry Hillary! (An exclamation to express excitement)

Mark, are *you* going to marry Hillary? (A question to express surprise, e.g., I thought someone else was going to marry her)

Mark, *are* you going to marry Hillary? (A question to get confirmation; I thought you just liked her, not loved her)

Cultural differences are reflected in people's use of paralanguage. Speaking loudly indicates strength and sincerity to Arabs, authority to Germans, but impoliteness to Thais, and loss of control to the Japanese. The Lebanese proverb 'Lower your voice and strengthen your argument' also emphasizes the value that this culture places on controlling one's voice in a conversation. The use of vocal segregates (e.g., *um, uh*) may communicate interest, uncertainty, attention, acceptance, or hesitation, and their meanings vary across cultures. In China, people may use 'um' or 'hai' (for Cantonese speakers) to indicate 'yes' or 'I see' while the other person is speaking. This vocal segregate is used to encourage the other speaker to continue talking, rather than to suggest a change of turn. The appropriateness of vocal qualities is also judged based on gender. For example, laughing loudly is common and acceptable for American women, but it might not be considered as such in Thailand. In ancient China, women had to cover their mouth with a handkerchief when they were laughing to indicate good manners and politeness.

Olfactics: the use of smell, scent, and odour

Olfactics refers to human perception and use of smell, scent, and odour. Compared with other types of nonverbal code, the study of olfactics has received less academic attention. Research evidence shows that there is a universal preference for some scents that may have biological and evolutionary roots. For example, the fragrances of jasmine, lavender, and roses tend to communicate a soothing and pleasant feeling to people; the perfume industry makes billions of dollars a year by capitalizing on these scent preferences.

Smell can also be used to communicate position, social class, and power. Anthony Synnott (1996) claims that odour is used to categorize people into social groups of different status, power, and social class because the meanings attributed to a specific scent give it social significance. Synnott argues that perceived foul odours are one of the criteria by which negative identities are attributed to some social or ethnic groups. If a well-dressed man carrying a briefcase and smelling of a high-quality aftershave gets into the lift of an office building, others in the lift are more likely to think he is someone who holds a management position, rather than as an ordinary office worker. Nevertheless, people's smell preferences are not universal, but vary across cultures. For example, the Dogon people of Mali find the scent of onions very attractive, and young men and women rub fried onions all over their bodies (Neuliep, 2012); the smell of onion from a person's mouth is considered bad breath in many other cultures.

Further online reading The following article can be accessed for free on the book's companion website https://study.sagepub.com/liu2e: Johnson, Richard R. and Jasmine L. Aaron (2013) 'Adults' beliefs regarding nonverbal cues predictive of violence', *Criminal Justice and Behavior*, 40(8): 881–894.

INFLUENCE OF CULTURE ON NONVERBAL COMMUNICATION

People hold expectations about the appropriateness of others' nonverbal behaviour. These expectations are learned and, thus, vary across cultures. Interactants from different cultural backgrounds have to learn each other's expectations regarding appropriate nonverbal behaviour. Lustig and Koester (2013) identified three cultural variations in nonverbal communication. Firstly, cultures differ in their specific repertoire of behaviours. Body movements, gestures, posture, vocal qualities, and spatial requirements are specific to a particular culture. For example, shoulder shrugging is commonly used by Westerners when something is not understood, whereas in some Asian cultures this body movement is almost never used; the same feeling is often expressed by shaking one's head. In Australia, people may snap their fingers or raise their hand in a restaurant to get a waiter's attention; in Malaysia people can get a waiter's attention by making a sound with their mouth. In Slovenia, guests wave at the waiter as well, not using verbal communication.

Photo 8.3 Dim sum at a Chinese *yum cha* place.
Copyright © Shuang Liu. Used with permission.

Another example is *yum cha* – an important part of Chinese culinary culture, particularly for people from Hong Kong and Guangdong province. In *yum cha* etiquette, it is customary for one person (people at the table take it in turns) to pour tea into other people's cups before filling their own. The nonverbal behaviour to thank the person who has poured tea into your cup is to tap the table with three or two fingers. Finger tapping is also known as finger *kou-tou*; this is a gesture to thank someone in the traditional Chinese style. A story has it that the historical significance of this gesture can be traced to the Qing Dynasty. When visiting south China on an incognito inspection visit, the emperor went to a teahouse with his companions and guards. To disguise his identity, the emperor joined others at the table in taking turns to pour tea. His companions could not kneel down and kowtow to show gratitude for this great honour, because doing so would reveal the identity of the emperor. Instead, they tapped three fingers on the table to represent their bowed head and their prostrated arms. Times have changed, and there is no longer an emperor to whom people should kowtow. However, tapping one's fingers remains the ritual expression of gratitude to someone when being served tea. Nowadays it is more common to see people using two fingers (index and middle fingers) to tap the table, instead of three fingers.

The second cultural variation identified by Lustig and Koester (2013) is that all cultures have display rules which govern when and in what context certain nonverbal expressions are required, permitted, preferred, or prohibited. Display rules govern such things as how far apart people should stand during a conversation, where and whom to touch, when and with whom to use direct eye contact, how loudly one should speak and how much one should show his or her feelings. A good place to observe cultural variations in display rules is the arrival terminal of an international airport. Westerners tend to greet their loved ones with hugs and kisses, whereas Asians tend to be more reserved and may hug each other but will generally not kiss each other in public places. To illustrate this point, think of any kind of public space and observe how different people, from different walks of life (different gender, class, race, etc.) display their nonverbal communication.

The third cultural variation identified by Lustig and Koeter (2013) is that the meanings attributed to particular nonverbal behaviours differ from culture to culture. In Western countries, it is common to see people smile at strangers or passers-by in the neighbourhood, while this facial expression may be interpreted as strange in Singapore or other Asian countries where people do not often initiate conversations with strangers. On one occasion in China during the peak travel time (before the Chinese New Year), posters were displayed in railway stations advising travellers not to speak to strangers. In Australian universities, it is very common to see students wearing thongs in the classroom; in China, shoes that look like slippers are regarded as improper footwear in the classroom. Interestingly, pulling down on your lower eyelid with one finger means 'my eye' in English (and French) – that is, 'I don't believe you', but the same gesture, *Chashm* (my eye) in Farsi, means 'I promise'.

Culture and nonverbal behaviour are inseparable. Unlike verbal codes, however, there is little grammar for nonverbal codes that foreigners can learn to make intercultural communication easier. Members of a particular culture learn the norms for appropriate and inappropriate nonverbal behaviour through the process of socialization. In addition, the application of these rules usually occurs outside conscious awareness. We become aware of our culture's rules and norms mainly when we see them broken. Consequently, when we communicate with people whose repertoire of nonverbal codes differs from our own, misunderstandings are almost certain to occur. Violation of nonverbal rules or misinterpretations of nonverbal codes can lead to negative attitudes or even conflict. It is important, therefore, for us to be alert to differences in nonverbal codes in intercultural communication, to monitor our own use of nonverbal codes, and to be observant of rules governing the use of nonverbal codes of other people.

Further online reading The following article can be accessed for free on the book's companion website https://study.sagepub.com/liu2e: Marsh, Abigail A., Hillary A. Elfenbein and Nalini Ambady (2007) 'Separated by a common language: nonverbal accents and cultural stereotypes about Americans and Australians', *Journal of Cross-Cultural Psychology*, 38(2): 284–301.

SUMMARY

- Unlike verbal codes, there is no formal grammar governing the use of nonverbal codes. These rules are learned as part of a culture's socialization process.

- Nonverbal communication often takes place simultaneously with verbal communication; however, if the messages from the two contradict one another, people tend to believe the nonverbal communication because it is believed to be less controlled and thus more likely to reveal the true feelings of the speaker.

- Nonverbal codes are used to: repeat the message sent by the verbal code; contradict the verbal message; substitute a verbal message; complement a verbal message; accentuate the verbal; and regulate verbal communication.

- There are seven major types of nonverbal code system: kinesics, proxemics, chronemics, haptics, physical appearance and dress, paralanguage, and olfactics, which have different functions and are culture-specific.

- Although there is evidence that some nonverbal codes have universal meanings (e.g., facial expressions of fear or anger), how behaviour is displayed and the circumstances where it is appropriate vary from culture to culture.

- Nonverbal codes send powerful messages, influencing our perception of others and how we are perceived by others. Nonverbal communication skills, therefore, are an important component of intercultural competence.

JOIN THE DEBATE

Can we lie with our body language?

Low-context cultures, like many Western cultures, tend to place greater emphasis on verbal codes; but of course nonverbal behaviours, which often accompany verbal communication, can 'speak' volumes in a very powerful way. When we lie, for example, our body language sometimes gives away our true feelings and intentions, irrespective of the content of our words. Nonverbal specialists often apply the concept of norming when analysing videotapes to detect differences between what is being spoken and what the speaker really means; in other words, whether the nonverbal cues are consistent with the verbal content. These specialists believe that there are always tell-tale signs when someone is lying, no matter how good they think they are; this is often referred to as 'nonverbal leakage' or 'hot spots'. Eye contact, blinking, shoulder movement, posture, crossing and uncrossing ankles, and tapping feet are all indicators that can give away even the most accomplished liar. However, the mere presence or absence of these behaviours does not necessarily indicate lying, and nonverbal cues vary across individuals. Indeed, detection of lying through nonverbal cues is not always accurate, even when the observers are highly trained (e.g., specialist police). Some scholars (e.g., Levine, 2010) argue that, with the exception of a small number of people who give themselves away, it is extremely difficult to detect lying in interpersonal communication by any means. Can you give examples where you have successfully lied by using body language? What behaviour did you use? Have you ever been able to detect others who were lying, by using their nonverbal behaviour? How did you do it? Were there important features of the context (e.g., how important the lie was, how much independent evidence you had) that helped you or hindered you? Is it possible to lie with our body language?

CASE STUDY

Nonverbal expressions in politics—the case of Vladimir Putin

Using the appropriate and effective nonverbal codes to communicate is important for all politicians, especially in public speaking, networking, media appearances, and fund-raising activities. Nonverbal communication is extremely effective in creating a particular type of desirable political image, and this has an important role in international and national politics. That 'we do not communicate by words alone' is an important first lesson for politicians: facial expression, voice, accent, silence, colour, body movements, posture, touching, smell, use of objects, sense of place and time, dress, accessories used, and walking style are all included in the nonverbal communication codes that politicians employ. When voters are evaluating political leaders they make use of information other than the content of the politicians' speeches, and this information is often obtained from nonverbal communication. Politicians learn that the same words uttered in different tones of voice, with variations in loudness, pitch, pause, and tempo, can have different effects on audience. Populist politicians from Berlusconi in Italy, and Sarkozy in France, to Putin in Russia use nonverbal communication very cautiously. They learn how important it is to know when to look or not to look at each other, when to stand close or further apart, when to face each other more or less directly, and when to move their bodies. Sometimes, they know they need to touch and in that way they appear more connected to voters (Foxall, 2013).

Research has identified three main dimensions of nonverbal behaviour among politicians: a positiveness dimension, a responsiveness dimension, and a potency or status dimension. These are very basic dimensions that we use constantly in interpersonal and intergroup judgements, and they have been extensively studied in many contexts since the 1950s. Concrete behaviours within these dimensions emerge at several nonverbal communication levels. For example, politicians can use their voice, gestures, or body movements to be perceived as friendly, interested, competent, compassionate, powerful, or superior. One can demonstrate sympathy towards another person on the positiveness dimension by smiling, nodding, or touching that person. Responsiveness is related to nonverbal communication that demonstrates the other's importance for the politician. Keeping an eye contact, for example, is a concrete behaviour on this dimension that politicians use frequently. Finally, nonverbal behaviour indicating potency or status is used to demonstrate social control. Politicians expand their size and presence, and take up a lot of space, by using gestures or body movements or by speaking with a loud voice (Tavanti, 2012). What happens in political spaces, and the way it happens, can have great importance for the development of political culture. Both sports and politics have become places where it is legitimate to show aggressive feelings, within culturally-prescribed limits. It is generally accepted as 'not masculine' if a male sports player begins to cry, whereas women players are regarded as feminine if they cry (but female politicians might be regarded as weak).

One of the leading politicians in the world, Vladimir Putin, is famous for his effective use of nonverbal communication. He appears very much in control of his 'brand' image of masculinity: strong, fashionable, with decisive looks, charismatic posture, and confident walk (Foxall, 2013). He was elected Russian President in March 2000. Despite being seen as mishandling the *Kursk* submarine disaster in 2000 and there being an increase in Chechen terrorist attacks in Russia (including the Nord-Ost theatre siege in Moscow in 2002), Putin was re-elected President for a second term in March 2004 (with 71.9 per cent of the vote). After serving as Prime Minister between 2008 and 2012, Putin was again elected President in March 2012 (with 63.6 per cent of the vote). As the President (2000–08 and 2012–present) and a former member of the KGB (translated into

English as Committee for State Security, which was the main security agency for the Soviet Union from 1954 until its collapse in 1991) between 1975 and 1991, he is widely seen as the authoritarian face of Russia in the 'New Cold War' (Foxall, 2013). When he stood down as President in April 2008, owing to the Russian Constitution forbidding more than two consecutive terms, Putin enjoyed approval ratings of 84 per cent. Putin is not just influential and popular in Russia; he was named 'Person of the Year' by *Time Magazine* in 2007, the world's most influential person by *Vanity Fair* in 2008, and the world's second most powerful person by *Forbes* in 2011. He has been named as Russia's 'James Bond' or 'Action Man'. Putin is marketed and branded by the Kremlin as a Russian strongman and smart action hero – 'He is, if you like, our James Bond', claims the Russian journalist Vladimir Solovyov (Foxall, 2013: 139). Putin's popularity in Russia also means that his name and image are used in commercials – among the Putin-branded products are *Putinka* vodka, *PuTin* brand canned food, and *Gorbusha Putina* caviar (Foxall, 2013).

Putin offers a rich case for exploring how nonverbal communication is used to convey masculinity and power. Putin uses nonverbal communication and his body, in particular, is an element in building his cult of personality. Putin is an expert judo player, and frequently poses in front of the cameras dressed in his judo outfit and his black belt. Putin's holiday photographs are regularly published by the Kremlin, and he is often photographed semi-naked while on holiday. Other politicians use this same behaviour; there were pictures of the UK Prime Minister Tony Blair talking on the phone wearing swimming trunks in 2002 and 2006, and a bare-chested Barack Obama (then Senator of Illinois) body surfing in Honolulu in 2008 (Foxall, 2013). The Australian Prime Minister, Tony Abbott, is frequently photographed running along the beach in a very brief swimming costume, accompanied (with obvious physical difficulty) by his staff members, security personnel, and journalists. Other photos of Putin show him dressed in fatigues, fingerless gloves, a bush hat, and chic sunglasses, riding horses, rafting down a river, fishing for grayling, and off-roading in a sport utility vehicle. These photographs of Putin help to reflect and perpetuate the stereotypically masculine discourse about what it means to be a leader in contemporary Russia – how to use the body to perform strong politics.

Putin appeared as a true hero in 2008, when, reportedly using a tranquillizer gun, he rescued a Russian television crew that had moved too close to a Siberian tiger (Foxall, 2013). Some of Putin's other public performances include flying a Tupolev Tu-160 (Blackjack) strategic bomber to test a new conventional cruise missile in 2005; test driving a Renault Formula One car in 2010; taking part in an archaeological excavation of an ancient Greek port on the Taman Peninsula in 2011; and attempting to bend a frying pan with his bare hands during a visit to the summer camp of the pro-Kremlin youth group 'Nashi' at Lake Seliger in 2011 (Foxall, 2013).

Some commentators claim that Putin uses his body very openly during his public performances. He uses the centre of his chest, which is an important nonverbal gesture to indicate that we are openly expressing what we think. His arm gestures also accentuate his verbal message. His crossed fingers to express a stressful, tense situation, and the gesture of putting his finger or an object into his mouth (for example, pen) reflects a need for confidence (Tavanti, 2012). A close analysis of his nonverbal communication shows a distinctive nonverbal behaviour (with a high amount of aggressiveness) when he addresses topics related to the domestic financial crisis, in comparison to the other topics. Putin's hand gestures are also used very differently in speeches about the financial crisis, in comparison to the other topics (Tavanti, 2012). Thus, Putin is able to convey nuanced – but always masculine – attitudes to different topics and in different contexts.

References

Foxall, Andrew (2013) 'Photographing Vladimir Putin: masculinity, nationalism and visuality in Russian political culture', *Geopolitics*, 18(1): 132–156.

Tavanti, Marco (2012) 'The cultural dimensions of Italian leadership: power distance, uncertainty avoidance and masculinity from an American perspective', *Leadership*, 8(3): 287–301.

Questions for discussion

1. What are the effects of politicians' different nonverbal behaviour styles on their image?

2. Do you agree that the appearance of both the speaker and the surroundings are vital to the successful conveyance of a message?

3. Body language, and particularly facial expressions, can provide important information that may not be contained in verbal communication. Can you think of any examples about the nonverbal behaviour of particular politicians?

4. Politicians' clothing style can demonstrate their mood, levels of confidence, interests, age, authority, values/beliefs, and their sexual identity. Do you think clothing is an important aspect of nonverbal communication? How does it function?

5. Do you think that the position of the feet may also transmit interest or disinterest to the communicated person?

FURTHER READINGS

All articles listed next to the mouse icon below can be accessed for free on the book's companion website: https://study.sagepub.com/liu2e

Nonverbal communication in general

Manusov, Valerie L. and Miles L. Patterson (eds) (2006) *The SAGE Handbook of Nonverbal Communication*. Thousand Oaks, CA: Sage.

This handbook provides a comprehensive collection of essays by some of the best minds in the field of nonverbal communication. The text is divided into four sections covering a range of topics. Firstly, scholars discuss the foundations of nonverbal communication, including a history of the field and methods for studying nonverbal communicative behaviours. The second section examines factors influencing nonverbal communication styles, including culture, biology, age, and personality. The third section covers different functions of nonverbal communication, and includes chapters that deal with nonverbal communication in a range of situations, including intimate relationships, dominance, and deception. Finally, the text reveals the importance of context when studying nonverbal communication and consequences of using (and misusing) nonverbal communication.

Segerstråle, Ullica and Peter Molnár (1997) *Nonverbal Communication: Where Nature Meets Culture*. Englewood Cliffs, NJ: Lawrence Erlbaum Associates.

This book presents a complex picture of human communicative ability as simultaneously biologically and socioculturally influenced. Some capacities are apparently more biologically hard-wired than others: face recognition, imitation, emotional communication, and the capacity for language. The book also suggests that the dividing line between nonverbal and verbal communication is becoming much less clear-cut. The book is divided into sections dealing with, respectively, human universals, evolutionary and developmental aspects of nonverbal behaviour within a sociocultural context, and finally, the multifaceted relationships between nonverbal communication and culture.

Specific nonverbal behaviours and their interpretations in cultural contexts

Demir, Müge (2011) 'Using nonverbal communication in politics', *Canadian Social Science*, 7(5): 1–14.

This article discusses the effect of nonverbal communication in voter perceptions of political rhetoric. In addition to rhetoric, when a community is evaluating political leaders they resort to some other information. This information is usually obtained from nonverbal communication. Tone of voice, dress style, accessories, body posture, and facial expressions, among other aspects of nonverbal communication, are argued to be much more effective, easier to recall, and more persuasive than the written communication of political leaders' messages. This article addresses the question: How do political leaders use nonverbal communication to effectively create their political image and make an impact?

Johnson, Richard R. and Jasmine L. Aaron (2013) 'Adults' beliefs regarding nonverbal cues predictive of violence', *Criminal Justice and Behavior*, 40(8): 881–894.

This study seeks to identify which nonverbal cues adults perceive as being associated with imminent violence. Data were collected from 178 participants, who were university students with ages ranging from 17 to 30 years, with a relatively even split between male and female participants. A questionnaire containing the same, interpersonal conflict scenario was presented to each participant, followed by questions about 23 nonverbal cues that may be associated with impending violence. Findings indicate that the participants identified body language, including boxing stance, invading personal space, and clenched fists, to be associated with imminent violence, whereas rapid eye blinking, crying, and avoiding eye contact were rarely perceived to indicate violence. Further analyses by sex and race found only minor differences, suggesting these perceptions may be innate rather than cultural.

Newlin-Canzone, Elizabeth T., Mark W. Scerbo, Gayle Gliva-McConvey and Amelia Wallace (2011) 'Attentional and mental workload demands in nonverbal communication', *Proceedings of the Human Factors and Ergonomics Society Annual Meeting*, 55(1): 1190–1194.

This study applied assumptions of attention and working memory theories to tasks involving nonverbal communication. Thirty-six undergraduates were interviewed for a job, and both the types of interview (rote and improvisational) and the types of observation (passive and active) were manipulated within groups. Against expectation, participants detected fewer nonverbal behaviours and reported higher mental workload when required to simultaneously participate in an interview and observe the interviewer, and particularly when they needed to improvise responses. These findings suggest that the ability to observe and possibly assess another's nonverbal behaviours may be compromised when being engaged in an active conversation.

> *'Recognize yourself in he and she who are not like you and me.'*

Carlos Fuentes, Mexican writer, 1928–2012

9

IMMIGRATION AND ACCULTURATION

LEARNING OBJECTIVES

At the end of this chapter, you should be able to:

- Understand immigration as a major contributor to cultural diversity.

- Explain culture shock and reverse culture shock.

- Identify acculturation models and acculturation orientations.

- Analyse factors that influence cross-cultural adaptation.

- Design communication strategies to facilitate cross-cultural adaptation.

INTRODUCTION

It goes without saying that our society is becoming more culturally and ethnically diverse by the day. An important contributor to cultural diversity is immigration. Advances in technology, modern transportation facilities, telecommunications, and international business transactions make it much easier for people to travel, work, and live in another country. Globalization not only redefines the movements and mobility of people in contemporary societies, but also delineates new parameters for interpreting immigration. Historically, immigration was conceptualized as restricted cross-border movements of people, emphasizing permanent relocation and settlement of usually unskilled, often indentured or contracted labour, or people who were displaced by political turmoil and thus had little option other than resettlement in a new country. Today, growing affluence and the emergence of a new group of skilled or educated people have fuelled a new global movement of migrants who are in search of better economic opportunities, an enhanced quality of life, greater freedom, and higher expectations. Those people form an integral part of the immigrant population today – skilled migrants. Relocated into the legal and political institutions of the host culture, migrants aspire to a higher quality of life, good education for themselves or their children, the freedom to be their own boss, autonomy in their choice of work, and prosperity.

Although the reasons for migration vary, all immigrants face the same task of moving between their home culture and the mainstream culture of their new country. Acculturation, a process through which immigrants are integrated into the host cultural environment, is essential to being able to move between the two cultures effectively as circumstances and situations demand. This capability not only involves a mental reconciliation of sometimes incompatible pressures for both assimilation into the mainstream and differentiation from it, but also is important for immigrants' economic survival in the host country. Ien Ang (2001: 34), a cultural studies scholar, argues that while migrants derive a sense of belonging from their identification with their homeland, they are also fully aware that 'This very identification with an image [of] "where you're from" is also a sign of, and surrender to, a condition of actual marginalization in the place "where you're at".' Immigrants' ability to achieve a sense of place in the host country, where they feel somewhat 'out of place', at least upon arrival, is crucial to their psychological well-being.

Living in a multicultural society is a long educational process, in which tensions between host and home cultures are constantly evident. In order to maximize the benefits of cultural diversity, a country that embraces a multicultural policy must still be aware of the potential threats such a policy poses to cultural uniqueness. Around the world, host nationals express concerns about the threat that incoming ethnic cultures pose to mainstream cultural values, the existing political and economic power structure, and the distribution of employment opportunities. Migrants everywhere, on the other hand, form associations to maintain their ethnic and cultural heritage and promote the survival of their languages within mainstream institutions. For example, in both Germany and France, there is growing anxiety about the withdrawal of immigrant groups into their home cultures and their increasing unwillingness to integrate into the host culture. Situations like this raise the question for all multicultural nations: Does multiculturalism pose a threat to cultural identity? Our understanding of what multiculturalism means influences our acculturation strategies.

This chapter concentrates on immigration and acculturation. We firstly define and explain the terms diaspora, migrancy, and transnationalism. Current practices in relation to transnationalism, migrancy, immigration, and identity are reviewed so as to explore the concepts and analyse their strengths and weaknesses. Next, we discuss the concept of multiculturalism and its differentiated benefits for host nationals and immigrants. We explain culture shock and reverse culture shock. The concept of acculturation is defined and key acculturation models are introduced. This chapter identifies a range of personal, social, and political factors that shape acculturation outcomes. Finally, it concludes by a discussion on communication strategies for facilitating cross-cultural adjustment.

MIGRATION AND CULTURAL DIVERSITY

Human migration is more than 1 million years old and continues in response to complex human cultural and existential circumstances. The concept of migration contains emigration and immigration, both of which involve spatial and social transformations. In modern times, profound changes in the world political and economic order have generated large movements of people in almost every region. Viewed in a global context, the total world population of immigrants, that is, people living outside their country of birth or citizenship, is huge. Massey and Taylor (2004: 1) wrote that if these people, estimated at some 160 million, were united in a single country they would 'create a nation of immigrants'.

Critical thinking...

Immigration can be voluntary and involuntary. Would the adjustment in the host country be easier for voluntary migrants – for example, skilled migrants who choose to live permanently in a new country where they believe their skills will be recognized? Or do you think the experience of adjusting to a new culture would be the same regardless of reasons for migration?

Trends of migration: past, present, and future

Geographical mobility has consistently characterized the lives of populations in all historical eras. For example, following the lifting of restrictions on race-based immigration in the 1950s and 1960s, Asians and Africans began to migrate in large numbers to North America, Australasia, and Europe. There has also been substantial migration from Latin America into the United States, and significant labour migration into newly industrialized nations such as Korea, Malaysia, and Singapore during the 1970s and 1980s (Brubaker, 2001). In Europe, the countries with the highest emigration rates until 1960 were Italy, Spain, Portugal, former Yugoslavia, and Greece (Vukeljic, 2008).

There is a widespread consensus among migration scholars that it was not until the 1980s that migration came to be one of the most important factors of global change (Castles, 2000). According to a report from the International Organization for Migration (2006), the number of international migrants is thought to have reached between 185 and 192 million in 2005, an upward trend that is likely to continue. Most countries are affected by a range of migratory phenomena, such as labour migration, refugees, and permanent settlement. A salient feature of the Asia Pacific system is the increasing scale and significance of female migration (Ehrenreich and Russell-Hochschild, 2002). For example, the massive economic development of Malaysia that began after the implementation of the New Economy Policy (NEP) in the 1970s provided wide opportunities for employment for local and foreign workers (Chin, 2003). The higher wage and status of industrial work attracted many Malaysian women to the workforce, which creates problems in household labour. To resolve this problem, Malaysians hire low-wage female domestic workers from other countries, such as the Philippines and Indonesia. Consequently, the number of foreign maids increased from a few hundred in the 1970s to around 228,000 by 2010 (Asrul Hadi, 2011). Migration affects not only the migrants themselves, but also the receiving societies.

Further online reading The following article can be accessed for free on the book's companion website https://study.sagepub.com/liu2e: Bjarnason, Thoroddur (2009) 'London calling? Preferred emigration destinations among Icelandic youth', *Acta Sociologica*, 52(2): 149–161.

Diaspora, migrancy, and transnationalism

The term *diaspora* is based on the Greek terms *speiro*, meaning 'to sow', and the preposition *dia*, meaning 'over'. The Greeks used diaspora to mean migration and colonization. In Hebrew, the term initially referred to the settling of scattered colonies of Jews outside Palestine after the Babylonian exile, and came to have a more general connotation of people settled away from their ancestral homeland. The meaning of diaspora has shifted over time and now refers not only to traditional migrant groups, such as Jews, but also to much wider communities composed of voluntary migrants living in more than one culture. For example, there were an estimated 5 million Philippine citizens living in over 160 countries in 2000 (Ehrenreich and Russell-Hochschild, 2002). Diasporas are not temporary; they are lasting communities. They differentiate themselves from their new environment, identify themselves with other members of diasporas through networks of symbols and meanings, and form an 'imagined community' (Anderson, 1983). Such a community maintains the identification of members outside the national borders of space and time in order to live within the new environment (Clifford, 1997).

The concepts of migrancy and transnationalism are intertwined. *Migrancy* highlights movement, so that greater attention is paid to movement in both space and time in transnational practices. Basch and colleagues (1994) define *transnationalism* as the process by which migrants forge and sustain multi-stranded social relations that link together their societies of origin and settlement. Many immigrants today build social networks that cross geographic, cultural, and political borders. For example, ethnic business entrepreneurs in Australia maintain close ties with their ethnic group because bonds of solidarity within the ethnic community provide resources for business operations as they establish and develop businesses (Dyer and Ross, 2000). In addition, ethnic communities may be a source of intangible assets, such as values, knowledge, and networks upon which ethnic business people may draw (Liu, 2011). However, clientele from the ethnic community alone is insufficient to sustain ethnic businesses. To survive in a competitive market in the host country, ethnic businesses have to expand their target customers to the mainstream group. Those who present themselves well in both cultural contexts can reap the financial reward from drawing upon a wider clientele. Immigrants who develop and maintain multiple relationships spanning borders – familial, economic, social, organizational, religious, and political – are referred to as *transmigrants*.

Further online reading The following article can be accessed for free on the book's companion website https://study.sagepub.com/liu2e: Elsrud, Torun (2008) 'Othering through genderization in the regional press: constructing brutal others out of immigrants in rural Sweden', *European Journal of Cultural Studies*, 11(4): 423–446.

Sociologists generally focus on the receiving end of immigration, while anthropologists tend to work at both ends of the immigration process, beginning in the country of birth and asking what prompts individuals to leave particular communities, what happens to them in their receiving country, and how they remain connected to their former homeland. While sociological and anthropological approaches appear to differ in their methodologies, they do not differ in their outcomes; both fields have developed 'push-and-pull theories' in an attempt to explain the reasons, selectivity, flow, and scope of migration (Kearney, 1995). For example, predominant push factors include economic stagnation, decline in living standards, reduction of national resources, low personal income, unemployment, political and other discrimination, political persecution, alienation, and natural disasters. On the other hand, the principal pull factors are economic prosperity, education, appropriate employment, and higher income.

As Østergaard-Nielsen (2003) observed, immigration is no longer considered as a one-way or two-way journey. Instead, immigrants bridge here and there by continuously coming or going, or by engaging economically, socially, or politically in their home country while residing abroad. In essence, sociological and anthropo-

Photo 9.1   On the first of Syawal in the Muslim calendar, the Muslim community in Brisbane gather for prayer after fasting for a whole month in Ramadhan.
© Abdul Lattif Ahmed. Used with permission.

logical approaches appear to agree that immigrants do not make a sharp break with their homeland; for example, they continue to observe ethnic festivals or religious practices while living in the host culture.

It's important to look at how migrants maintain contacts across international borders, and how their identity is not necessarily connected to a unique home. One implication is that migrants continuously negotiate identities between 'old' and 'new' worlds, creating new configurations of identification with home in both places. One interesting example of this is Salih's (2003) research on Moroccan women living in Italy. Writing about their cooking practices, Salih shows how these women fuse elements of both countries' cuisines to symbolize their double identities in homes 'here' and 'there'. When in Italy, the women mix traditional Italian recipes with imported Moroccan ingredients to enliven the dishes; and conversely, returning to Morocco for holidays, Italian goods are used in the preparation of local Moroccan meals. Rather than seeing the women's identities in relation to specific homes as mutually exclusive, Salih demonstrates how the meaning of home is defined through interactive transnational identifications with homes stretched across geographically remote places.

Identity reconstruction for immigrants

Migrancy and transnationalism necessitate the reconsideration and reconstruction of identity. The difficulty that confronts immigrants in terms of how they reconstruct their identity in order to fit into the new society has been extensively researched and commented on in the scholarly literature. For example, the *melting-pot* ideal used to be the dominating discourse of immigrant identity in Australia and the United States. People with this ideal take the view that national identity should be the amalgam of the cultures – a melting pot – so that differences between 'us' and 'them' are reduced, in the hope that 'we' become more like 'them', and 'they' see us as less alien and more like them (Zubrzycki, 1997). Over time has come the realization that a multitude of ethnic cultures can co-exist in a given environment, retaining their original heritage while functioning in the mainstream culture. This has led to a change of perspective from the melting pot to the *salad bowl* to depict contemporary American society (Ogden, Ogden and Schau,

2004). Similarly, Canada has been described as a mosaic of cultural groups, to reflect the distinguishable constituent parts of the multiple cultures there. The survival of ethnicity has directed scholars' attention towards understanding how immigrants integrate into the host society. When immigrants interact with people from host cultures, they move not only between languages, but also between cultures. Central to this culture-switching process is the presentation of the self in terms of their relationships to the ingroup (their ethnic group) and outgroup (the mainstream cultural group). Connectedness to either their own ethnic group or the larger cultural group is not merely affiliation between the self and others, but also entails fundamental differences in the way the self is construed under different circumstances (Triandis, 1989). As Waters (1995: 3) states, migrancy and transnationalism are the 'social process in which the constraints of geography and social and cultural arrangements recede and in which people become increasingly aware that they are receding'. In this process, the boundaries used to define one's identities also recede.

Critical thinking...

The host country environment plays an important role in influencing immigrants' adaptation. Think of the differences between the melting pot and the salad bowl metaphors when talking about immigrant identity. What are the positives and negatives of each conception? If you were (or if you are) a migrant, which would you prefer? Why?

DIVERSITY AND MULTICULTURALISM

The increase in cultural diversity has led to the promotion of multiculturalism, which 'aims to achieve social cohesion through an environment where diverse cultures are recognized and valued' (Department of Premier and Cabinet, 2000: 4). The concepts of multiculturalism and diversity have captured the imagination of the public and scholars alike, suggesting a reconfiguring of economic arrangements, adjusting of political systems, and a recasting of cultural identities.

Further online reading The following article can be accessed for free on the book's companion website https://study.sagepub.com/liu2e: Bygnes, Susanne (2013) 'Ambivalent multiculturalism', *Sociology*, 47(1): 126–141.

Attitudes towards diversity and multiculturalism

Multiculturalism stresses the importance of recognizing cultural diversity within a given social and political environment. On the one hand, it promotes multi-ethnic or multicultural co-existence; on the other hand, it can lead to group distinctions (Brewer, 1997) and threaten social cohesion (Berry, 2001). Berry and Kalin (1995) argue that groups are more in favour of multiculturalism when they see advantages for themselves. The *ideological asymmetry hypothesis* (Sidanius and Pratto, 1999) suggests that hierarchy-attenuating ideologies such as multiculturalism appeal more to low-status groups than to high-status groups because the existing status hierarchy tends to be more beneficial for members of high- than low-status groups. For minority and lower-status groups, multiculturalism offers the possibility of maintaining their own culture and at the same time obtaining higher social status in society. Majority group members, on the other hand, may see ethnic minorities and their desire to maintain their own culture as a threat to mainstream cultural identity and their higher-status position. Thus, multiculturalism has more to offer to less powerful groups than to more powerful ones.

Multiculturalism holds that a multitude of ethnic cultures can co-exist in the mainstream or host culture and yet retain their original ethnic cultural heritage (Tadmor and Tetlock, 2006). The question remains: to what extent can immigrants maintain their access to ethnic language, religion, customs and traditions, and ethnic organizations without posing a threat to the overall political unity of the host society? Studies conducted with Asian immigrants in Australia show that they tend to view multiculturalism as a greater benefit than do Anglo-Australians, who see it as more of a threat (Liu, 2007). The perceived threat to one's own culture from another culture is one of the greatest stumbling blocks in intercultural relations (Stephan, Ybarra and Bachman, 1999). Such fears interfere with diplomatic relations, business cooperation, and interpersonal relations between members of different cultures, and can even lead to wars between nations. Such fears may also lead to prejudice by people in one culture against another. According to the *multicultural hypothesis*, confidence in one's cultural identity involves a sense of security, which is a psychological precondition for the acceptance of those who are culturally different (Berry, Kalin and Taylor, 1977). When people feel their cultural identity is threatened, they reject others. The extent to which members of the majority tolerate ethnic culture maintenance plays an important role in the construction of a truly multicultural society.

THEORY CORNER

INTEGRATED THREAT THEORY

A significant amount of research indicates that perception of threat plays an important role in prejudice towards outgroups in general and immigrants in particular. Integrated threat theory, advanced by Walter G. Stephan and his associates (1999), identifies four domains of threat: realistic, symbolic, negative stereotypes, and intergroup anxiety. Realistic threat concerns threat to the political and economic power and well-being of the ingroup. Immigrants are likely to evoke such a threat as they need jobs and may also require additional resources from the host society. Symbolic threat concerns group differences in values, beliefs, morals, and attitudes, which may lead to prejudice against members of outgroups. Negative stereotypes serve as a basis for negative expectations concerning the behaviour of members of the stereotyped group. For example, when migrant group members are perceived to be untrustworthy, mainstream group members may feel threatened when interacting with them. The fourth type of threat, intergroup anxiety, refers to people's feeling of being personally threatened in intergroup interactions because they are concerned about negative outcomes for themselves, such as being embarrassed, rejected, or ridiculed. Interacting with immigrants is often difficult for people from the host culture because of differences in language and cultural values, and this adds to intergroup anxiety in interaction.

Reference
Stephan, Walter G., Oscar Ybarra and Guy Bachman (1999) 'Prejudice toward immigrants', *Journal of Applied Social Psychology*, 29(11): 2221–2237.

Further reading on integrated threat theory
Rohmann, Anette, Arnd Florack and Ursula Piontkowski (2006) 'The role of discordant acculturation attitudes in perceived threat: an analysis of host and immigrant attitudes in Germany', *International Journal of Intercultural Relations*, 30: 683–702.

Theory in Practice

MUSLIMS IN WESTERN EUROPE

Following a number of terrorist attacks in the early twenty-first century, including the September 11 attacks in the USA, the 2002 nightclub bombings in Bali, and the 2005 bombings in London, Muslims have increasingly become the targets for hostility across the world. Croucher (2013) studied the effects of growing Muslim populations in the United Kingdom, France, and Germany, where Muslims are increasingly becoming 'victims of prejudice and hate' (pp. 50–51). He applied Stephan's four domains of threat in integrated threat theory to examine the relationship between host nationals' perceptions of Muslims' motivation to fit into the host culture and the level of perceived threat from them. Firstly, he found that when members of the host culture feel a threat, either real or symbolic, they are more likely to believe that the immigrant group does not want to integrate. Secondly, the research revealed that there is increasing nationalism among host nationals across Europe, expressed particularly by intensifying ethnic or linguistic pride. Finally, Croucher's findings showed that the economic and political context strongly affected the perceived level of threat from migrants. Muslim immigrants are considered a higher threat, both symbolic and real, in the United Kingdom and France, where both unemployment and anti-Muslim rhetoric is high. People in Germany, on the other hand, see Muslims as less of a threat.

Questions to take you further
How are Muslim immigrants viewed in your country? How about Chinese or Indian immigrants? If there is a perceived threat, do you think the threat is real or symbolic?

Reference
Croucher, Stephen M. (2013) 'Integrated threat theory and acceptance of immigrant assimilation: an analysis of Muslim immigration in Western Europe', *Communication Monographs*, 80(1): 46–62.

Further reading on integrated threat theory and immigration
Tausch, Nicole, Miles Hewstone and Ravneeta Roy (2009) 'The relationships between contact, status and prejudice: an integrated threat theory analysis of Hindu–Muslim relations in India', *Journal of Community and Applied Social Psychology*, 19(2): 83–94.

Critical thinking...

Does multiculturalism pose a threat to our cultural uniqueness? How do we locate a cultural home while living in a multicultural society?

Challenges faced by host nationals and immigrants

The arrival of immigrants as new settlers brings changes to the host cultural environment. As pointed out by Sayegh and Lasry (1993: 99), it is difficult 'to imagine a host society which would not be transformed after immigrants have been accepted as full participants into the social and institutional networks of that society'. Thus, both the immigrant group and host nationals undergo psychological and sociocultural adjustment as a result of the presence of culturally distinctive others (Ward and Kennedy, 2001). Under some circumstances, psychological adjustment for members of the majority may be even more difficult than that experienced by immigrants. The reason is that immigrants, in many cases, are aware of the need to adjust to their host cultural environment as soon as, if not well before, they set foot in the host country. People in the majority group, however, are not likely to be so well-prepared to accept or adjust to the changes in their

Photo 9.2 Names of visitors from different parts of the world were painted in one street of Ubud in Indonesia – a symbol of multiculturalism. © Joan Burnett. Used with permission.

lives brought about by the immigrant population. Hence, in discussing multiculturalism, it is important to take into consideration both ethnic minorities and the majority group or groups, because the lack of accommodating attitudes in either group may hamper the realization of a positively diverse and equal society.

Significant debate has surrounded the question of how immigrants should live in their host societies. In some countries, immigrants are increasingly seen as a source of social disturbance and economic burden, and opinion polls show unease with the growing visibility of foreign cultures. There seems to be no consistent framework for immigrant ethnic minorities to participate in the political and social life in European countries. Some European countries, like Germany, see immigrants mainly as temporary labour, whereas the traditional countries of immigration, including the United States and Canada, see immigrants as permanent settlers (Hargreaves, 1995). Governments differ in the degree of cultural diversity they are ready to accept. The 2004 French law banning the wearing of religious insignia in schools, for instance, has over time led to many hot public debates about the issue of the role of religion in the public sphere. In Western European countries such as the Netherlands and France, young Muslim women wearing the *hijab*, a headscarf that fully covers the hair and neck of Muslim women, have become the symbols of controversy (Vivian, 1999). Thus, the presence of visible multicultural symbols, such as ethnic shops and clothing, is not an indicator of a truly multicultural society unless there is both mutual acceptance and equal societal participation by all groups.

> ## Critical thinking...
>
> What do you believe that immigrants should do to acculturate into the host country? Do host nationals and immigrants share the same understanding of what the immigrants should do to adapt into the host culture? For example, should immigrants abandon their traditional dress in favour of the dress of the host culture?

CULTURE SHOCK AND ACCULTURATION ORIENTATIONS

Culture shock and reverse culture shock

Culture shock refers to the feelings of disorientation and anxiety that a sojourner experiences when entering a new culture. It occurs in social interactions between sojourners and host nationals when familiar cultural norms and values that govern behaviours are questioned in the new cultural environment (Furnham and Bochner, 1982). Adler (1975) notes that culture shock is a psychological and social process that progresses through several stages. For some people, it may take several weeks to overcome psychological stress; for others, the frustration of culture shock may last as long as a year. Symptoms of culture shock include depression, helplessness, anxiety, homesickness, confusion, irritability, isolation, intolerance, defensiveness, and withdrawal, all indicators of psychological stress.

The most widely known model is the *U-curve model*. The initial stage of culture shock, usually called the *honeymoon stage*, is characterized by intense excitement associated with being somewhere different and unusual. The new arrival may feel euphoric and excited with all the new things encountered. The second stage is called *disintegration*, when frustration and stress begin to set in owing to the differences experienced in the new culture. The new environment requires a great deal of conscious energy that is not required in the old environment, which leads to cognitive overload and fatigue. Communication difficulties may occur. In this stage, there may be feelings of discontent, impatience, anger, sadness, and feelings of incompetence. The third stage of culture shock is called the *reorientation* or adjustment phase, which involves reintegration of new cues and an increased ability to function in the new culture. Immigrants start to seek solutions to their problems. A sense of psychological balance may be experienced, which initiates an evaluation of the old ways versus the new. The fourth stage of culture shock is labelled the *adaptation* stage. In this stage, people become more comfortable in the new culture as it becomes more predictable; they actively engage in the culture with their new problem solving and conflict resolution tools, with some success. The final stage is described as *biculturalism*, where people are able to cope comfortably in both the home and new cultures. This stage is accompanied by a more solid feeling of belonging as people have recovered from the symptoms of culture shock.

The literature on the classical U-Curve hypothesis suggests that there is an association between the length of time spent in the host country and the cross-cultural adaptation experience. This and other similar models are not without criticism, because they seem to simplify cross-cultural adaptation and fail to reflect the range of factors at play (Ward, Okura, Kennedy and Kojima, 1998). Furthermore, numerous studies have not found support for claims about the U-Curve (e.g., Kealey, 1989). Nevertheless, intercultural scholars do recognize that the culture shock models significantly contribute to the theoretical understanding of the study of cross-cultural adaptation processes. For instance, in a longitudinal study on the cross-cultural adaptation of 35 international students studying in New Zealand, Ward and colleagues' (1998) found that psychological and sociocultural problems were greatest at the beginning of their sojourn. In a more recent study of 500 Korean immigrants residing in the United States, Park and Rubin (2012) reported that longer residence was associated with better adaptation. The longer the sojourners stay in the new culture, the more likely they are to develop sociocultural and linguistic competence as they become more experienced in dealing with their lives in the new culture.

Further online reading The following article can be accessed for free on the book's companion website https://study.sagepub.com/liu2e: van der Zee, Karen and Jan P. van Oudenhoven (2013) 'Culture shock or challenge? The role of personality as a determinant of intercultural competence', *Journal of Cross-Cultural Psychology*, 44(5): 928–940.

Culture shock can also be experienced by people who return to their home country after an extended stay in a foreign culture. Such an experience is referred to as *reverse culture shock*. In fact, in early work, Gullahorn and Gullahorn (1963) extended the U-curve hypothesis to account for reverse culture shock, in the *W-curve*. This type of culture shock may cause greater distress and confusion than the original shock experienced in the new culture. In reverse culture shock, the home culture is compared adversely to the admired aspects of the new culture. Research indicates that no one wants to admit that he or she is having difficulty readjusting to the home culture, so the re-entry process often involves suffering in silence. Upon first returning home, there is a sense of relief and excitement about being back in familiar surroundings, seeing old friends and family, and eating familiar food. However, to the surprise of everyone, especially the returning expatriate, a sense of depression and a negative outlook can follow the initial re-entry cycle. Several factors contribute to the downturn phase. Firstly, upon re-entry to the home culture, there is a feeling of a need to search for identity. Secondly, the home culture may look so negative at times that the re-entering person longs for the 'good old days' in the host country where she or he lived for the previous period. Thirdly, the old values, beliefs, and ways of thinking and living, with which the person was once familiar, may have changed, resulting in a sense of loss or ambiguity. Finally, people too may have changed over the intervening years; resuming deep friendships with old friends may not be automatic or easy. For example, Chiang (2011) conducted a study of 25 young Taiwanese who emigrated to Canada and New Zealand with their parents at a young age in the 1980s and 1990s, but who had returned to Taiwan. The findings showed that although these returnees were born and raised partly in Taiwan, they reported encountering reverse culture shock during their adaptation process. More than half of the participants interviewed would like to move back to the place to which they had emigrated for a better living environment and for their children's education in the future.

Critical thinking…

Can you list some factors that contribute to culture shock? What about reverse culture shock? Can you give an example to explain why reverse culture shock tends to cause greater distress and confusion than the culture shock the person first experienced in the new culture?

Acculturation models

Acculturation refers to the changes that cultural groups undergo after being in contact over a period of time (Berry, 1986). Acculturation is often marked by physical and psychological changes that occur as a result of the adaptation required to function in a new and different cultural context. The most widely applied model of acculturation was developed by John Berry (1980). According to his model, immigrants are confronted with two basic issues: maintenance of their heritage culture and maintenance of relationships with the host society. On this continuum, acculturation orientations range from a positive value placed on both the heritage and the new culture (integration), a negative value to the old and a positive value to the new (assimilation), a positive value to the old and a negative value to the new (separation), and a negative to both cultures (marginalization). For example, individuals who wish to maintain their ethnic traditions and at the same time to become an integral part of the host society are *integrationists*. *Marginalization* refers to individuals devaluing their cultural heritage but not having significant psychological contact with the host society either. Marginalized people may feel as though they do not belong anywhere or, in a variant of this orientation, they may reject ethnic identity altogether as a valid source of self-esteem (Bourhis et al., 2007, refer to such people as *individualists*). *Assimilation* and *separation* both refer to rejecting one culture and living exclusively in the other. Many immigrants move between these orientations and over time gravitate to one – most commonly integration or assimilation. People adapting to new cultures face changes in diet, climate, housing, communication, roles, social networks, norms, and values. The stress associated with such changes is called *acculturation stress*.

A shortcoming of Berry's original model is that it places the emphasis in acculturation on minority or immigrant groups, on the assumption that immigrants have the freedom to pursue the acculturation strategy they prefer in the host society. In reality, host-culture attitudes can exert a strong influence on how immigrants experience the acculturation process (Kosic, Mannetti and Sam, 2005). Like immigrants, members of a host society also develop acculturation attitudes (Rohmann, Florack and Piontkowski, 2006). For them, acculturation centres on whether they want immigrants to maintain their heritage culture and whether they value intergroup contact. Their acculturation attitudes, in a model analogous to Berry's but referring to the host culture, are referred to as integration, assimilation, segregation, and individualism (Bourhis et al., 1997). Discordance between majority and minority acculturation attitudes leads to negative outcomes such as stereotyping, prejudice, and discrimination (Zagefka and Brown, 2002). To overcome the limitations of the original model, Berry (2005) proposed a three-dimensional model, including cultural maintenance, contact and participation, and the power to decide on how to acculturate. With the promotion of cultural diversity and multiculturalism, immigrants are more welcome to integrate into the host culture while maintaining ties with their own ethnic heritage.

Integration offers immigrants the opportunity to keep their ethnic cultural practice while maintaining a positive relationship with the host society. Integration probably benefits immigrants most, as among other advantages it gives them an opportunity to raise their lower social status. An important assumption of social identity theory is that membership in a high-status group is desirable because it contributes to positive social identity (Hogg and Abrams, 1988). To maintain a positive self-concept derived from a satisfying social identity, individuals who belong to a group of subordinate status may either strive for a higher status by leaving their low-status group or try to upgrade the status position of their group as a whole (Tajfel, 1978). In the case of immigrants, it is difficult, if not impossible, for them to upgrade the status position of their whole ethnic group. Efforts to achieve a positive social identity are therefore often focused on integrating into the host group rather than remaining as a member of the foreign outgroup. Evidence from previous research also indicates that the integration strategy is linked to good psychological adjustment, a sense of belonging, and a feeling of acceptance.

Critical thinking…

Immigrants across the world are subject to various stereotypes. Why are some immigrant groups subject to more prejudice and negative stereotypes than others? What factors do you think make people most resilient in the face of such prejudice?

THEORY CORNER

BICULTURAL IDENTITY INTEGRATION

Many people are now exposed to more than one culture and become bicultural or multicultural. These bicultural/bilingual individuals may be international students, expatriates, business people, immigrants, refugees, foreign-born migrants, or children of interracial marriages. As a result, biculturalism and bilingualism have been attracting increasing attention in research in the field of cross-cultural psychology and intercultural communication. One influential theoretical concept in this field is bicultural identity integration (BII), developed by Benet-Martínez and colleagues. Bicultural individuals differ in how they combine and negotiate their two cultures. Benet-Martínez and Haritatos (2005) conducted a study using a sample of Chinese American biculturals to unpack the construct of BII, that is, the degree to which a bicultural individual perceives his or her two cultural identities as 'compatible' versus 'oppositional'. The BII measure has two components: distance (versus overlap) and conflict (versus harmony) between one's two cultural identities or orientations. A high BII person is one who identifies with both heritage and mainstream cultures, sees them as compatible and complementary, and sees themselves as part of a combined, blended cultural being (e.g., 'I keep Chinese and American culture together and feel good about it'); a low BII person also identifies with both cultures, but they are more likely to feel caught between the two cultures and prefer to keep them separate (e.g., 'I feel conflicted between the Chinese and American ways of doing things'). Benet-Martínez and Haritatos's study also found that the perceived cultural distance and conflict have distinct personality, acculturation, and sociodemographic antecedents.

Reference
Benet-Martínez, Verónica and Jana Haritatos (2005) 'Bicultural identity integration (BII): components and psychosocial antecedents', *Journal of Personality*, 73: 1015–1050.

Further reading on bicultural identity integration
Nguyen, Angela-Minh Tu D. and Benet-Martínez, Verónica (2013) 'Biculturalism and adjustment: a meta-analysis', *Journal of Cross-Cultural Psychology*, 44(1): 122–159.

Theory in Practice

SHIFTING BETWEEN CULTURAL IDENTITIES

Bicultural individuals engage in a process called cultural frame switching, where they shift between their two cultural interpretive frames in response to cues in the social environment. However, although extensive research has investigated the differences between cultural groups, relatively less is known about cultural switching processes within multicultural or bicultural individuals. For example, how do bicultural individuals organize and move between their various cultural orientations without feeling disoriented? Cheng, Lee and Benet-Martínez (2006) conducted a study to examine how the valence of cultural primes affects the cultural frame switching of individuals with high and low levels of bicultural identity integration (BII), using a sample of 179 first-generation and 41 second-generation Asian–American biculturals. They used an implicit word-priming task that included one of four types of words: (a) positive words associated with Asians, (b) negative words associated with Asians, (c) positive words associated with Americans, or (d) negative words associated with Americans. The findings indicate that when exposed to positive cultural cues, biculturals who perceive their cultural identities as compatible (high BII) respond in culturally congruent ways, whereas biculturals who perceive their cultural identities as conflicting (low BII) respond in culturally incongruent ways. The opposite was true for negative cultural cues. These results confirmed that the cultural frame switching process is different depending on one's level of BII, and that both high and low BIIs can exhibit culturally congruent or incongruent behaviours under different situations.

Questions to take you further
What kind of factors can contribute to positive bicultural experiences for individuals? What kind of individual differences can also shape the positivity of one's bicultural experiences, and in turn influence the level of BII?

Reference
Cheng, Chi-Ying, Fiona Lee and Verónica Benet-Martínez (2006) 'Assimilation and contrast effects in cultural frame switching (CFS): bicultural identity integration (BII) and valence of cultural cues', *Journal of Cross-Cultural Psychology*, 37: 742–760.

Further reading on biculturalism in practice
Love, Julia A. and Raymond Buriel (2007) 'Language brokering, autonomy, parent–child bonding, biculturalism, and depression: a study of Mexican American adolescents from immigrant families', *Hispanic Journal of Behavioral Sciences*, 29(4): 472–491.

CROSS-CULTURAL ADAPTATION

Regardless of their reasons for calling the new country home, all sojourners have to adapt to an unfamiliar cultural terrain. *Cross-cultural adaptation* refers to the process of increasing one's level of fitness in a new cultural environment (Kim, 1988). A number of factors influence the level of anxiety, distress, and frustration experienced by sojourners or new immigrants, and thus influence cross-cultural adaptation outcomes.

Further online reading The following article can be accessed for free on the book's companion website https://study.sagepub.com/liu2e: Crippen, Cheryl and Leah Brew (2013) 'Strategies of cultural adaption in intercultural parenting', *Family Journal*, 21(3): 263–271.

Factors influencing the cross-cultural adaptation process

Similarity between host and home cultures

The degree of similarity between the host and the home cultures of immigrants can predict the acculturation stress experienced by immigrants. For example, Sudanese immigrants in Australia exhibit significantly larger psychological and cultural distance as compared to those from New Zealand. In addition to physical appearance and language, cultural traits such as beliefs and values may also be used to set one group of immigrants apart from others. The early Chinese settlers in Australia in the 1840s were resented because they were efficient, hardworking, and economically competitive, and were therefore viewed as a threat to the livelihoods of the European migrants (Ang, 2000). Increasing cultural distance encourages immigrants to remain psychologically located within their ethnic groups. This creates a challenge, particularly for ethnic business people who need to be accepted by both the co-ethnic and the mainstream groups if they are to sustain businesses and clientele.

Ethnic social support

Immigrants extend their connection to their home culture through various types of ethnic association, including religious groups. Ethnic community networks provide valuable support for immigrants in adjusting to the new culture. For example, previous research identifies social networks as a critical part of the entrepreneurial activities of immigrants in many countries (Light and Gold, 2000). When immigrants relocate from the home country, they bring with them significant attachments to their home culture. They also extend this attachment in the host country by connecting to ethnic social networks, which provide an initial cushion for negotiating a sense of place, as evidenced in ethnic residential concentration in certain areas. Ethnic social support can therefore create a space where immigrants can bridge cultural distance and gradually build connections with the mainstream culture.

Photo 9.3 Translation services provided by the Chinese community in Brisbane aim to support Chinese migrants in settling in the host country. © Shuang Liu. Used with permission.

Personal characteristics and background

Demographic factors such as age, native language and education, personal experience such as previous exposure to other cultures, and personality characteristics such as extraversion may all influence cross-cultural adaptation outcomes. Younger migrants generally adapt more easily than older ones, particularly when they are also well-educated. However, there are studies that did not find age a significant predictor of acculturation outcomes (Park and Rubin, 2012). The ability to speak the language of the host culture certainly facilitates one's ability to adapt and function in the new culture and therefore reduces acculturation stress. Scholars argue that the lack of host language proficiency is one of the main barriers that sojourners face during cross-cultural adaptation, especially in terms of developing quality and quantity of contact with host members (e.g., Berry, 2005). Previous exposure to other cultures also better prepares a person psychologically to deal with the stress and frustration associated with settling in a new culture. For example, international students cope with the settling-in process better if they have travelled to other countries where they cannot use their native language to communicate.

Effect of mainstream media

As an institution of culture and an influential shaper of cultural thought, mass media influence the consciousness of the public through the symbolic environment they create and sustain (McLuhan and Fiore, 1967). This symbolic environment is commonly referred to as symbolic social reality (Adoni and Mane, 1984). When an ethnic group is portrayed in the mass media, that particular symbolic social reality becomes a common category utilized by others to identify members of that ethnic group (Potter and Reicher, 1987). Because of this naturalizing effect on the materials they present, mass media can serve as a contributor to perpetuating or diminishing racial stereotypes (Mastro and Greenberg, 2000). This role of the mass media in activating and perpetuating racial stereotypes is particularly significant when the audience either has little direct experience of the group or lacks other sources of verification (Khan et al., 1999). For example, Lee and Wu (2004) found that exposure to negative images associated with Asian Americans create doubts and ambivalence about them among other racial groups. When negative stereotypes are perceived to be real, prejudice is a likely outcome. An ethnic group's perception of how they are portrayed in the mass media will affect their attitudes to the host culture and, subsequently, their desire to integrate into the host society (Liu, 2006).

Effects of ethnic media

In addition to exposure to mainstream media, ethnic minorities or immigrants also have access to ethnic media, such as newspapers printed in their native language published in their host countries. Ethnic media have both intragroup and intergroup functions. As an intragroup function, ethnic media promote ethnic group cohesion not only through their news stories but also via the ethnic language they use (Ward and Hewstone, 1985). For example, Chinese ethnic groups in Australia, like other groups, value their own language as a tool in maintaining their cultural identity (Luo and Wiseman, 2000). Ethnic media also serve to help immigrants to broaden and deepen their knowledge about the unfamiliar host culture via their familiar language. Past studies have found that ethnic minorities, especially during the early stages in the new culture, may avoid interpersonal encounters when they can instead use less personal mass media, such as newspapers printed in their native language, as alternative and less stressful sources of learning about the host environment (Adoni and Mane, 1984). Ethnic media, therefore, play a positive role in affecting immigrants' cross-cultural adaptation.

Intergroup contact

The amount of interpersonal contact between immigrants and host nationals can influence the process of cross-cultural adaptation. Contact between groups has long been considered to be an important strategy for improving intergroup relations. Pettigrew (1997) examined the responses of over 3,800 majority group members from France, Great Britain, the Netherlands, and Germany, and found that intergroup contact played a critical role in reducing bias. Appropriate and friendly intergroup contact may translate into more positive perceptions and may also strengthen ingroup identification by creating positive feelings about it.

Potentially negative stereotypes created by the mass media may also be reduced by more frequent contact. For example, Hartmann and Husband (1972) demonstrated that among adolescents living in low immigration areas, the tendency to define race relations in the terms used by the mass media was greater than among those living in high immigration areas. Intergroup contact or intercultural friendships can facilitate immigrants' cross-cultural adaptation.

Political and social environment

The host culture's political and social environment has a major impact on adjustment to new cultural surroundings. Specific outgroups are more (or less) welcome in a culture. Negative attitudes towards immigrants and sojourners can demonstrate a rejection of a minority group and establish impermeable social boundaries (Bourhis et al., 1997). Giles, Bourhis, and Taylor (1977) argue that the extent to which an immigrant or minority group is supported in the host society (captured by the numerical and political strength of the group, support for its language and culture, and support from institutions in the larger society like the media) is a strong predictor of resilience of the language and culture in the new society and a marker of discrimination as well. The higher the support (which they call ethnolinguistic vitality), the more resilient the ethnic group is and the lower the discrimination will be. Numerous studies have found that perceived discrimination is significantly associated with acculturative stress and psychological adaptation. For instance, Liebkind and Jasinskaja-Lahti (2000) compared the experiences of discrimination on psychological distress among a large sample of 1,146 immigrants representing seven ethnic groups (Russian, Ingrian/Finnish, Estonians, Somalis, Arabs, Vietnamese, and Turks) in Finland. They found that, across the sample, self-reported experiences of discrimination were highly predictive of psychological well-being. Factors affecting the degree of tolerance of particular outgroups include the social or political policies of the mainstream culture, such as political representation, citizenship criteria, language requirements, and employment opportunities.

THEORY CORNER

THE STRESS–ADAPTATION–GROWTH MODEL

Communication scholar Young Y. Kim (2001) explains the intercultural adaptation process in a new culture in her stress–adaptation–growth model. According to this model, adaptation is a progressive series of positive and negative experiences, rather than a smooth, continuous process. This process can be pictured as a coiled spring, which stretches and grows but is pulled back by its own tension. Kim argues that acculturation is an interaction between the stranger and the host culture. Personal and social communication, the host environment, and individual predisposing factors are the central features of the acculturation process. Personal communication refers to the individual's ability to use verbal and nonverbal codes to communicate in the host environment. Social communication refers to the interaction between the newcomer and host nationals. The environment includes: the degree to which the host culture is receptive to strangers; the extent to which host nationals exert pressure on newcomers to conform to their culture's values, beliefs and practices; and ethnic group strength. Predisposing factors include how much people know about their new culture, their ability to speak the language, the probability of employment, their understanding of the cultural institutions, and the characteristics that newcomers have regarding orientation change and personal resistance.

Reference

Kim, Young Y. (2001) *Becoming Intercultural: An Integrative Theory of Communication and Cross-Cultural Adaptation*. Thousand Oaks, CA: Sage.

Further reading on cross-cultural adaptation

Miglietta, Anna and Stefano Tartaglia (2009) 'The influence of length of stay, linguistic competence, and media exposure in immigrants' adaptation', *Cross-Cultural Research*, 43(1): 46–61.

Theory in Practice

MEASURING ADAPTATION OF REFUGEES FROM POST-CONFLICT ZONES

Refugees constitute a special category of migrants. Often, they have been through traumatic experiences, such as persecution, or substantial discrimination amounting to a gross violation of their human rights in their home countries. They have to flee their home country to seek refuge and protection in a foreign country. Many of them suffer from distress, anxiety, or mental illness after arrival in the destination country. The loss of social networks, separation from family members, lack of language proficiency of the settlement country, fear of repatriation, and the situation in the home country, among other factors, play a role in perpetuating psychiatric symptoms, particularly depression.

Shoeb, Weinstein and Mollica (2007) conducted ethnographic interviews with 60 Iraqi-born refugees in Detroit, a city which is home to the oldest, largest, and most visible population of Arabs in North America, to inform the development of the Iraqi version of the Harvard Trauma Questionnaire (HTQ). The individual life stories of the participants revealed their life in Iraq, the decision to escape, the circumstances of their flight, the escape journey and transition in refugee camps, conditions surrounding their acceptance for resettlement in the United States, their early experiences in America, and the nature of their current social participation within the Iraqi community and the larger society. The in-depth data provided rich resources for developing culture-specific items used in the HTQ. The findings from this study also painted a vivid picture of the ordeal and challenges refugees may face in resettlement and integration into the host culture.

Questions to take you further

What level of support do you think a receiving country should provide for refugees arriving in its land? How can refugees contribute to their receiving country?

Reference

Shoeb, Marwa, Harvey Weinstein and Richard Mollica (2007) 'The Harvard Trauma Questionnaire: adapting a cross-cultural instrument for measuring torture, trauma and posttraumatic stress disorder in Iraqi refugees', *International Journal of Social Psychiatry*, 53(5): 447–463.

Further reading on short-term adaptation to host cultures

Laban, Cornelis J., Hajo B. P. E. Gernaat, Ivan H. Komproe, Ingborg van der Tweel and Joop T. V. M. De Jong (2005) 'Postmigration living problems and common psychiatric disorders in Iraqi asylum seekers in the Netherlands', *Journal of Nervous and Mental Disease*, 193(12): 825–832.

Developing strategies for cross-cultural adaptation

Immigration invariably means having to live in both the home culture and the host culture. Consequently, migrants engage in communication with three types of audience: members of the mainstream culture, people from the home country, and their children who have grown up in the new culture. Firstly, migrants have to learn how to communicate with members of the dominant culture in the host country. This involves learning about a new culture and the practices and discourses of this host culture. They face a choice of how to respond to the new culture they encounter, allowing themselves to be assimilated into the new culture (assimilation), opting to minimize their engagement with the new culture by withdrawing into an ethnic enclave (separation), developing the skills of functioning simultaneously in two different cultures and of effectively moving between cultures (integration), or withdrawing from both the host and home cultures (marginalization). Secondly, immigrants must relearn how to communicate with people from the home country. Engaging with the home culture can take the form of remaining as a part of it by keeping in regular contact with people from the home country. Some immigrants, for example Vietnamese refugees who arrived in Australia in the 1970s, may lose touch with the old country owing to the prevailing conditions there. If this happens, they will eventually only have a historical understanding of the 'home' country, and they will lose the ability to move between the two cultures. Thirdly, immigrants have to learn to 'translate' between their old culture and their children's hybridized culture (Liu and Louw, 2009). Learning to cope with their children's hybrid culture is a part of the daily routine of older generations of immigrants, as dealing with their parents' and grandparents' different culture is a part of the daily life of second- or third-generation immigrants.

This myriad of relationships requires immigrants to adopt strategies to integrate into the host country. Learning as much as possible about the new culture is the first step of acculturation. Successful cross-cultural adaptation is related not only to the psychological and social well-being of the immigrants, but also to their economic survival. Part of the process of acculturation is learning survival skills, including how to use banking services, where to go shopping, when to eat, how to work and rest, how to use public transport, among other things essential to daily life. Building intercultural friendships can be helpful as it not only gives immigrants local guidance, but also increases the opportunity for intergroup contact, hence promoting mutual understanding. It is not uncommon to find many immigrants remaining within a network of their own ethnic group, not being aware that the best way to become acquainted with another culture is to establish relationships with members of that culture. Further, cross-cultural adaptation also requires immigrants to learn to accept differences.

As intercultural communicators, we should try to understand and interpret the things we experience as they are within a particular cultural context, rather than using our own cultural norms as the only judgement criteria. Regardless of how well we have prepared ourselves before entering a new culture, there will always be moments when we experience culture shock, encounter difficulties, or feel frustrated at our own incapability to accomplish our goals. Therefore, a positive attitude towards the new culture is something we should carry with us throughout the cross-cultural adaptation process.

SUMMARY

- The cultural diversity that immigrants bring to the host country also means changes for mainstream cultural beliefs, values, and identities. Thus, diversity creates challenges for both sides. It is not only the immigrant group but also the host nationals who need to undergo psychological and sociological adjustment as a result of the presence of culturally distinctive others.

- The concepts of migrancy and transnationalism are intertwined. The transnational movement associated with migrancy is no longer a one-way journey. Many immigrants today build social networks across geographic, cultural, and political borders, hence engaging in the process of transnationalism.

- All people moving to a new culture experience culture shock, the process of which can be divided into several stages. Returning migrants may experience reverse culture shock, too.

- Orientations to heritage and host cultures can result in four acculturation orientations: assimilation, integration, separation, and marginalization.

- Acculturation processes can be influenced by a range of personal, social, cultural, and environmental factors.

JOIN THE DEBATE

To what extent should migrants be encouraged to maintain their heritage culture?

People move to other cultures for different reasons, including joining family, undertaking further study, or seeking humanitarian protection or employment opportunities. For example, almost 1.5 million migrants over the age of 15 have settled in Australia since 2000. As the global number of migrants increases, the debate over the maintenance of heritage culture remains at the forefront. A melting pot versus a salad bowl is a commonly used metaphor when discussing managing diversity in multicultural societies. While we enjoy the benefits of cultural diversity and encourage migrants to keep their heritage, cultural traditions, and practices (particularly language and customs), and pass these on to future generations, we also hope that the endorsement of diversity will not create a threat to the uniqueness of our own culture. The question is: To what extent should we encourage migrants to maintain their heritage cultural practices without creating a threat to the unity of the mainstream culture? What difference does context (e.g., public versus private) make? What other factors make a difference, and what difference do they make?

CASE STUDY

The Cronulla riots

Alcohol, the Australian flag, and raw racism fuelled a violent demonstration by thousands of young people in Sydney, Australia. The demonstrators were singing and waving the national flag as they 'reclaimed' Cronulla, a beachfront suburb of Sydney, in December 2005. The incident was known as the Cronulla riots – a series of confrontations between white Australian youths and Middle Eastern Australian youths. Fuelled by drink, the crowd of white youths became a mob, beating up anyone who looked Middle Eastern. That night and the next, carloads of young men of Middle Eastern descent headed for the beach suburbs to launch similarly random and savage acts of revenge.

In the lead-up to the riot, allegations circulated around the local area that groups of Middle Eastern youths had asked white women on the beach wearing bikinis to 'cover up'; a 23-year-old man was stabbed in the back outside a golf club by what police described as a group of males of Mediterranean or Middle Eastern appearance; and three off-duty lifeguards from north Cronulla were assaulted by youths of Middle Eastern origin. It was believed that these alleged incidents, among others, prompted retaliation by Cronulla locals.

On Sunday, 11 December 2005, approximately 5,000 people gathered on the Cronulla beach to protest against the reported incidents of assaults and intimidating behaviour by people, most of whom were identified in earlier media reports as Middle Eastern youths from the suburbs of Western Sydney. The crowd initially assembled without incident, but violence broke out after a large group chased several men of Middle Eastern appearance into a nearby hotel. As the crowd moved along the beach and foreshore area, a man on the back of a utility vehicle began to shout 'No more Lebs!', a chant picked up by the group around him. A small number of demonstrators wore clothing bearing racist slogans such as 'We Grew Here, You Flew Here', 'Ethnic Cleansing Unit', 'Aussie Pride', 'Save Nulla', 'Lebs Go Home', and 'No Lebs'. Through the remainder of the day, several more individuals of Middle Eastern appearance were allegedly assaulted, including several people who were not ethnic Arabs (among them Turks, a Jewish boy, and a Greek girl). Police and ambulance workers who were leading the victims away from the riots were also assaulted by groups of people throwing beer bottles. Several dozen people were treated for minor cuts and bruises, while six individuals were evacuated under police escort for medical care. In some cases, police cars were swamped and stomped on as they tried to move from one violent flare-up to another.

The police employed riot equipment, including capsicum spray, in order to subdue several of the attackers. Local police at Cronulla had earlier commented that they were sufficiently prepared to deal with any anticipated violence at Cronulla beach, but they appeared to be overwhelmed by the sheer

Photo 9.4 On 11 December 2005, crowds gathered at North Cronulla amid Australian flags and anti-Lebanese fanfare (Sydney, Australia). Copyright © Warren Hudson. Used with permission.

number of people who arrived. A call for reinforcements was placed to police stations in other suburbs. The following nights saw several retaliatory assaults in the communities near Cronulla and an unprecedented police lock-down of Sydney beaches and surrounding areas. Political spokespeople attributed the state of conflict to years of disagreements and simmering hatred between the two main ethnic groups involved in these incidents: white Australians and Middle Eastern Australians. In the years after the September 11, 2001 attacks in New York City, many began to feel a sense of fear created by terrorism and a perceived threat of Islamic terrorists. This has heightened public awareness of Arab-Australian communities in Sydney and their ongoing differences with non-Muslim Australians.

ABC's *Four Corners* programme interviewed some of the participants – young Anglo-Australians who joined the seething mob at Cronulla on 11 December 2005 and Middle Eastern men who took part in revenge attacks. The report exposed a strong perception of threat among white Australians in the suburb. The white Australian youths expressed their desire for the government to stop appeasing people who follow Islam, for fear that those people would 'out-breed white Australians'. 'Once they get the numbers', one of the youths remarked, 'they can vote their members into parliament. And once their members are in parliament, they can pass laws, like they've already tried to get the Islamic law into Australia a few times.' To many Arab Australians, the Cronulla riot represented an attack on their entire community. A comment from one youth who twice joined the revenge convoy was: 'When I watched the TV, it hurt me, it hurt everyone ... they hit our innocent people ... so why not, may as well do the same thing.'

The aftermath of the riots on the economy in the local area was enormous. Many of the small businesses in the nearby beachside suburbs reported a significant downturn in trade following the main incident of 11 December 2005, normally a busy time of the year. On 22 December, the BBC reported that some beachside businesses indicated a slump in takings of up to 75 per cent since the riots. Authorities in Britain, Canada, and Indonesia issued warnings to their citizens visiting the area to be on guard for possible continuing racial violence. Subsequently, the New South Wales state government announced an AU$250,000 (at the time, approximately US$183,000) campaign to bring tourists back to Sydney beaches, including advertisements featuring well-known sports stars, assuring tourists that it was safe to visit the area.

References

Jackson, Liz (2006) 'Riot and Revenge' [online]. Accessed 12 May 2008 at: www.abc.net.au/4corners/content/2006/s1588360.htm.

Kennedy, Les and Damien Murphy (2005) 'Racist Furore as Mobs Riot' [online]. Accessed 12 May 2008 at: www.theage.com.au/news/national/racist-furoe-as-mobs-riot/2005.

Questions for discussion

1. What were the causes of tension between white Australian youths and Lebanese Australian youths? How common do you think these tensions are between immigrant and host communities elsewhere?

2. What characteristics of culture can you identify based on the Cronulla riot?

3. What problems does this case reveal about co-existence of different cultural groups in the host country?

4. What challenges can you identify from this incident regarding promoting multiculturalism in our society?

5. How can we prevent such incidents from happening again in our society?

FURTHER READINGS

All articles listed next to the mouse icon below can be accessed for free on the book's companion website: https://study.sagepub.com/liu2e

Acculturation orientations and strategies

Crippen, Cheryl and Leah Brew (2013) 'Strategies of cultural adaption in intercultural parenting', *Family Journal*, 21(3): 263–271.

This article discusses the potential issues arising when intercultural couples raise children. Twenty-one participants were interviewed regarding their parenting experiences as part of an intercultural couple, where each member of the couple had different sociocultural heritages with distinct cultures of origin, as identified by the participants. All couples identified that either they or their parents were born and raised in a different country of origin from that of their partner. The study identified the diverse strategies that were used by intercultural parents to negotiate diversity based on their cultural differences, and their degree of mutual acculturation emerged to support this model. These strategies of adaptation included assimilation, cultural tourism, cultural transition, cultural amalgamation, and dual biculturalism.

Culture shock

van der Zee, Karen and Jan P. van Oudenhoven (2013) 'Culture shock or challenge? The role of personality as a determinant of intercultural competence', *Journal of Cross-Cultural Psychology*, 44(5): 928–940.

This paper provides a theoretical basis for the empirical link between traits and intercultural success indicators relying on the A (affect) B (behaviour) C (cognition) model of culture shock. With respect to affect, the authors argue that intercultural traits can be differentiated according to whether they predispose individuals to be (in)sensitive to either threat or challenge. Whereas stress-related traits (emotional stability, flexibility) are linked to a lower tendency to perceive an intercultural situation as threatening, social-perceptual traits (social initiative, open-mindedness) may predispose individuals to perceive its challenging aspects and respond with positive affect. As a behavioural consequence, stress-buffering traits may protect against culture shock, whereas social-perceptual traits may facilitate cultural learning. Finally, the ABC model defines cognitions in terms of associated cultural identity patterns. Whereas stress-related traits may help individuals refrain from sticking to one's own culture, social-perceptual traits reinforce identification with new culture.

Factors influencing cross-cultural adaptation

Bjarnason, Thoroddur (2009) 'London calling? Preferred emigration destinations among Icelandic youth', *Acta Sociologica*, 52(2): 149–161.

The preferred emigration destinations of adolescents reflect images and stereotypes of other countries that continuously emerge in a multitude of local and global discourses and from other concrete experiences with other countries. This study found that, if they wish to leave Iceland, female adolescents are more likely to move to other Nordic countries, particularly Denmark. Male adolescents, on the other hand, preferred

English-speaking countries that have a reputation for economic or military power, such as the United States or the United Kingdom. The study also found that Icelandic adolescents who are proud of their Icelandic nationality and have more highly educated parents are more likely to prefer to emigrate to Europe for study or employment opportunities, whereas adolescents who actively wish to leave Iceland are more likely to move to North America.

Gudykunst, William B. and Young Yun Kim (eds) (1988) *Cross-Cultural Adaption: Current Approaches*. Newbury Park, CA: Sage.

This multidisciplinary volume considers the cross-cultural adaptation process from psychological, sociological, anthropological, and communication perspectives. Using diverse case examples, it integrates theoretical and empirical research and presents studies of both long- and short-term adaptation. Reflecting these multidisciplinary and multi-societal approaches, this collection presents 14 theoretical or research-based essays dealing with the cross-cultural adaptation of individuals who are born and raised in one culture and find themselves in need of modifying their customary life patterns in a foreign culture. Papers in the collection include the adjustment of sojourners, the psychological acculturation of immigrants, and the issues around cross-cultural adaptation.

Multiculturalism

Bygnes, Susanne (2013) 'Ambivalent multiculturalism', *Sociology*, 47(1): 126–141.

Multiculturalism is a fiercely debated subject, and this article argues that ambivalence is a central feature of people's perspectives on societal diversity. Focusing on interviews with leaders of three Norwegian social movement organizations, the study found that despite the leaders' very different organizational and political vantage points, they share a common ambivalence towards multiculturalism. This perspective on political and organizational leaders' views on diversity provides an important supplement to analyses aimed at classifying specific political preferences on multiculturalism. Ambivalent multiculturalism, the author argues, is key to understanding those elements of public debate that are not 'either/or'.

> '*It takes a lot of experience of life to see why some relationships last and others do not. But we do not have to wait for a crisis to get an idea of the future of a particular relationship. Our behaviour in little every incident tells us a great deal.*'

Eknath Easwaran, Indian scholar and author, 1901–1999

10

DEVELOPING RELATIONS WITH CULTURALLY DIFFERENT OTHERS

LEARNING OBJECTIVES

At the end of this chapter, you should be able to:

- Define the nature and characteristics of human relationships.

- Identify the stages of relationship development.

- Compare and contrast theories on intergroup and intercultural relationships.

- Evaluate the influence of culture on human relationship development.

INTRODUCTION

Initiating and maintaining personal and social relationships with others is an essential part of human life. We are connected to others in a variety of ways – through social groups, ethnic communities, friendships, family, organizations, and online social networks – and we define ourselves and evaluate others through these relationships. William Schutz (1966) claims that we satisfy three basic needs through interaction with others: inclusion, affection, and control. *Inclusion* is a sense of belonging or of being involved with others, as well as of including others in our activities. We are members of different groups, and maintaining relationships with others in different groups gives us a sense of personal identity, because it is in groups that our individuality is recognized (Madder and Madder, 1990).

Control refers to our ability to influence others, our environment, and ourselves, along with our desire to be influenced by others (or not). We can gain control by initiating ideas, supporting others, showing disagreement, resolving conflicts, or giving orders, and we can ask for this control from others through questions and supportive statements. The various roles we play can also satisfy our need for control (Chen and Starosta, 2005). For example, the father of an Indian family often has the power to make decisions regarding the career path his child is to follow.

Affection refers to emotions, and to showing love to and being loved by others. We all need, to a greater or smaller extent, to share emotions with other people (friends, colleagues, family members). Affection fosters passion, commitment, care, and intimate relationships. In sum, we engage in initiating, maintaining, or terminating relationships with others throughout our lives, and we mutually satisfy our social needs through these relationships.

The way we perceive and fulfil social needs is influenced by culture. People from different cultures may meet each other's needs for inclusion, control, and affection differently. For example, in some cultures, a man will open the door for a woman to show masculinity and courtesy; in other cultures, a woman is expected to walk a few steps behind a man in deference to masculinity. The influence of culture on developing and fostering relationships with others is the focus of this chapter. We define the nature and characteristics of human relationships and describe the stages of relationship development. Several theories of human relationships, including social exchange theory, similarity attraction paradigm, and anxiety/uncertainty management theory, are introduced. We then discuss the influence of culture in human relationships, drawing on views from different cultures regarding friendship, family, and romantic relations. This chapter also examines cyberspace as a site for developing intercultural relations. Finally, we suggest some ways for improving intercultural relationships.

(?) Critical thinking...

Can you list some important relationships you develop with others throughout your life? What are their most important features? Are any of these people from cultures different from your own? What challenges or problems have you had with the relationship? How have you addressed these problems?

DIMENSIONS AND CHARACTERISTICS OF HUMAN RELATIONSHIPS

A *human relationship* can be defined as an interactional process of connecting ourselves with others in the network of social needs (Chen and Starosta, 2005). Some connections occur because of kinship, family, or marriage; other connections exist owing to group membership, such as religion, class, ethnicity, and political affiliation. Still others are made because of shared interests or goals, such as relationships between colleagues, friends, or people in an online social network community. Relationships can be organized along several dimensions.

Further online reading The following article can be accessed for free on the book's companion website https://study.sagepub.com/liu2e: Ferrin, Donald, Michelle Bligh and Jeffrey Kohles (2007) 'Can I trust you to trust me? A theory of trust, monitoring, and cooperation in interpersonal and intergroup relationships', *Group & Organization Management*, 32(4): 465–499.

Dimensions of social relationships

Triandis (1977) suggests four universal dimensions of social relationships: association–dissociation, superordination–subordination, intimacy–formality, and overt–covert, as summarized in Table 10.1.

Table 10.1   Four Dimensions of Social Relationship

Dimension	Behaviours
Association–dissociation	*Association* behaviours include helping friends, cooperating with colleagues, and supporting others' ideas or actions, whereas *dissociation* behaviours are illustrated in verbal or nonverbal behaviours such as fighting or avoiding the other person.
Superordination–subordination	Examples of *superordinate* behaviours are a supervisor giving orders to workers; *subordinate* behaviours, in contrast, involve employees obeying orders from above.
Intimacy–formality	*Intimate* behaviours can be seen in a person's self-disclosure, such as revealing personal attitudes and feelings, touching, and expressing emotions; *formality* behaviours include sending written invitations or other formal communication behaviour.
Overt–covert	*Overt* behaviours are visible to others, such as touching, whereas *covert* behaviours are not visible (e.g., evaluating the behaviours of others).

Source: Triandis, Harry C. (1977) *Interpersonal Behavior*. Monterey, CA: Brooks/Cole.

Triandis (1984) argues that, although these four dimensions are universal, the degree to which they are manifested varies across cultures. For example, Nigerian families generally are more associative, subordinate, formal, and covert than US American families. Traindis also relates these four relationship dimensions to cultural dimensions identified by Hofstede (1980), and to Kluckhohn and Strodtbeck's (1961) value orientations (see Chapter 5). *Associative* behaviours are more important in cultures that consider human beings as inherently good, while *dissociative* behaviours are more important in cultures where human beings are viewed as inherently evil. *Superordination–subordination* behaviours can be linked to Hofstede's power distance dimension. In high power-distance cultures like Japan and Arab countries, subordination and superordination are viewed as natural and acceptable. However, in low power-distance cultures like Austria, Denmark, and Sweden, where equality between people is treasured, superordination and subordination are seen as a function of the differentiated social roles of individuals. In general, individuals in subordinate cultures are deferential to those in power. This is expressed, for example, in the bowing customs observed in Asian nations such as Japan and Thailand; one bows deeply to a superior, who may merely nod in return. By contrast, the Western custom of handshaking only connotes a greeting and signifies equality on the part of those engaged in the handshake.

The *intimacy–formality* dimension refers to the degree of contact people in a given culture desire. Edward Hall (1966) called cultures that display a high degree of affiliation 'high-contact cultures' and those that display a low degree of affiliation 'low-contact cultures' (see Chapter 8). In high-contact cultures, people stand closer and use more touching when interacting than in low-contact cultures, where people may feel more comfortable standing farther apart during a conversation.

The *overt–covert* dimension, as Triandis (1984) suggests, relates to the level of tightness or looseness in a culture. Cultures towards the tight end of the continuum are characterized by more role-bonded relationships; an example is the social hierarchy observed in India. Tight cultures tend to be more collectivistic and high-context. On the other hand, cultures at the loose end of the continuum are characterized by fewer role-bonded relationships. Loose cultures tend to be more individualistic and low context. Triandis (1984) claims that more overt behaviour is seen in loose cultures and more covert behaviour in tight cultures. One explanation is that contextual cues play a greater role in communication between tightly bonded people than between loosely bonded people.

? Critical thinking...

A frequent complaint by Asian business people about their US American counterparts is that in business negotiations, American business people are more money-minded than people-oriented. How would you explain this complaint in terms of the model discussed? What might the Americans complain about their Asian negotiating partners? How might the partners address these issues?

Dimensions of interpersonal relationships

Lustig and Koester (2013) identify three dimensions of interpersonal relationships: control, affiliation, and activation. *Control* (like the control dimension in Schutz's theory) involves power: the level of control we have over others, ourselves, and the environment is dependent on the amount of power we have to influence the people and events around us. For example, we have more control over our financial status if we have a good source of income and knowledge of financial planning. In a different form of power, when guests are present in a home, a mother may use eye contact to control her children's behaviour. We also give control to others by the way we address them. For example, we tend to address doctors by their title and last name, whereas we might call our local butcher by his first name.

Similar to Schutz's (1966) needs for inclusion and affection, Lustig and Koester (2013) define *affiliation* as the degree of friendliness, liking, social warmth, or immediacy that is communicated between people. Affiliation between speakers engaged in a conversation can be expressed through eye contact, close physical proximity, touching, smiling, and a friendly tone of voice. People from high-contact cultures, such as those of the Mediterranean region and Latin America, tend to show affection more openly by touching more frequently, standing closer to each other during a conversation, and using more emotional expressions.

Activation in this model refers to the ways people react to the world around them. Some people seem very energetic, excitable, and quick; others value and exude calmness, peacefulness, and a sense of inner control (Lustig and Koester, 2013). What constitutes an acceptable or appropriate level of activation in communication also varies from culture to culture. For example, Germans mostly value order and control. They compare themselves to a symphony orchestra because of its emphasis on rules, regularity, and punctuality. Italians use opera as a cultural metaphor to define themselves because of its emphasis on emotion, drama, and the lyrical use of language. Italians tend to engage in more animated conversations by using expressive hand gestures and vivid facial expressions. By comparison, Chinese tend to be more reserved. Some Westerners comment that they do not know what the Chinese are thinking in a conversation because the Chinese do not reveal their feelings through facial expressions and tend to use neutral words. This is also true for other Asian cultures, such as Malaysian or Thai. Asian people are taught to avoid extremes in communication; being neutral is considered a virtue. How a particular trait is perceived or displayed in a specific culture, therefore, must be interpreted against the beliefs, values, norms, and social practices of that culture.

Characteristics of human relationships

Human relationships comprise individuals' connection to others. The key characteristic of a human relationship is *interdependence*. For example, your friend may depend on you for acceptance and guidance, and you may need support and respect from your friend. We learn about ourselves and others through interpersonal relationships (Pearson and Nelson, 1997). Sometimes our self-concept is strengthened by the confirmation we receive from others, but at other times our self-perception is at variance with others' perception of us. Interpersonal relationships assist us in understanding others and allow us to test our stereotypes about others, particularly people from outgroups whose cultural or social norms we are not familiar with.

In another model, Chen and Starosta (2005) identify five characteristics of human relationships. Firstly, human relationships are *dynamic*. They develop and are transformed through communication. Secondly, human relationships are *hierarchical*. Based on the level of intimacy or closeness, human relationships can be arranged in a hierarchical order ranging from strangers to intimate friends. The required degree of inclusion, control, and affection varies depending on the hierarchical order of the relationship. Thirdly, human relationships are *reciprocal*. Reciprocity occurs when individuals in a relationship network can satisfy each other's social needs. Fourthly, human relationships are *unique*; they are rule-governed, with different rules for different types. Fifthly, human relationships are *interdependent* and *irreplaceable*. Individuals in a human relationship network connect to each other, and share emotions with each other. Moreover, human relationships are irreplaceable, in that one person's place in the relationship network (e.g., loss of one friend) is not replaceable by another person (e.g., another friend).

People in relationship networks, particularly interpersonal relationships, continually try to maintain balance amid changing circumstances and seemingly opposing needs (Lustig and Koester, 2013). Leslie Baxter (1988) refers to the basic contradictions in human relationships as *relationship dialectics*, using a term first used by Hegel in the nineteenth century. She identifies three dialectics, or points of tension, that lead to growth in interpersonal relationships; in turn, these have implications for intercultural relations (see Table 10.2).

Table 10.2   Dialectics in Interpersonal Relationships

Dialectics	Definition	Cultural implication
Autonomy–connection	The extent to which individuals want a sense of separation from others (autonomy) or a feeling of attachment to others (connection).	Culture teaches its members the appropriate range of autonomy and connection when communicating with others (e.g., individualistic versus collectivistic cultures).
Novelty–predictability	The dynamic tensions between people's desire for change (novelty) and stability (predictability) in their interpersonal relationships.	The level of uncertainty avoidance in culture suggests the range of desired novelty and predictability.
Openness–closeness	The extent to which individuals want to share (openness) or withhold (closeness) personal information.	Collectivistic cultures encourage openness to ingroup members but closeness to outgroup members.

Source: Baxter, Leslie (1988) 'A dialectical perspective on communication strategies in relationship development', in S. W. Duck (ed.), *Handbook of Personal Relationships: Theory, Research, and Interventions*. New York: Wiley. pp. 257–273.

THEORY CORNER

SOCIAL EXCHANGE THEORY

Social exchange theory aims to explain the development of interpersonal and intercultural relationships. Developed by John Thibaut and Harold Kelley, the basic assumption of this theory is that individuals establish and continue social relations on the basis of their expectations that such relations will be mutually beneficial (Kelley and Thibaut, 1978). When we enter a relationship, we usually evaluate the rewards we are likely to gain and the costs we are willing to pay. If the calculated rewards are greater than the costs, we will continue to develop the relationship. If not, we may leave the existing relationship and seek a new one. The rewards of human relationships can be expressed in the form of satisfaction, happiness, self-esteem, acceptance, and friendship. The costs may involve money, time, unhappiness, dissatisfaction, losing face, and frustration. Our culture provides an implicit theory about what is considered as important in what types of relationship. For example, studies in East Asia have reported that social forces such as power and status are important in the development of business relations.

Reference
Kelley, Harold H. and John W. Thibaut (1978) *Interpersonal Relations: A Theory of Interdependence*. New York: Wiley.

Further reading on social exchange theory
Muthusamy, Senthil K. and Margaret A. White (2005) 'Learning and knowledge transfer in strategic alliances: a social exchange view', *Organization Studies*, 26(2): 415–441.

Theory in Practice

UNDERSTANDING RELIGIOUS BEHAVIOUR AS SOCIAL EXCHANGE

Social exchange theory is based on the assumption that all individuals are rational beings, and human decisions are made based on the consideration for the highest net benefit in the circumstances. Corcoran (2013) applied social exchange theory to explain religious behaviour, arguing that individuals make choices about religious behaviour based on their evaluation of the maximum benefits, and religious behaviour can be understood as social exchange. These exchanges can be between an individual and his or her God(s), usually through an intermediary such as a religious representative or institution. Corcoran (2013: 342) believes that the benefits or rewards from these exchanges are largely 'other-worldly'. In other words, the reward received is not necessarily immediate or tangible, but often deemed in an afterlife context. People tend to seek assurance of these rewards before committing themselves. This assurance reduces uncertainty and increases the likelihood of participation in religious exchanges. A range of personal, social, and cultural factors can affect the levels of certainty (e.g., the likelihood of receiving the promised reward), and subsequent religious exchange behaviour (e.g., donation to the religious institution).

Questions to take you further

Do you think religious behaviour is largely determined by rational choices about perceived rewards and costs? How could social exchange theory be used to explain the strong emotional commitment of religious people to their faith?

Reference

Corcoran, Katie E. (2013) 'Divine exchanges: applying social exchange theory to religious behavior', *Rationality and Society*, 25(3): 335–369.

Further reading on social exchange theory and religion

Barrow, Katie M. and Katherine A. Kuvalanka (2011) 'To be Jewish and lesbian: an exploration of religion, sexual identity, and familial relationships', *Journal of GBLT Family Studies*, 7(5): 470–492.

Further online reading The following article can be accessed for free on the book's companion website https://study.sagepub.com/liu2e: Cropanzano, Russell and Marie S. Mitchell (2005) 'Social exchange theory: an interdisciplinary review', *Journal of Management*, 31(6): 874–900.

STAGES OF HUMAN RELATIONSHIP DEVELOPMENT

Berger and Calabrese (1975) propose that relationships develop in three phases. In the *entry* phase, communication is governed by a set of social norms. The communication patterns in this stage are structured, and the content focuses mostly on demographic information. Our interactions with strangers or those whom we meet for the first time are examples of this entry phase. The second phase is *personal*. Communication content in the personal phase goes beyond the superficial (e.g., the weather or sharing demographic information), and may include information on personal problems, attitudes, and opinions. The relationship between interactants becomes more intimate, and the communication styles they use are often more informal and relaxed. The third stage of relationship development is the *exit* phase. In this phase, the relationship begins to deteriorate and the frequency of interaction decreases. Interactants are no longer interested in maintaining the relationship and tend to avoid communicating.

Like Berger and Calabrese, Irwin Altman and Dalmas Taylor (1973) proposed social penetration theory to explain the development of relationships through exchange of information. This theory states that, as an interpersonal relationship develops, the interpersonal exchange of information moves from superficial and impersonal to intimate and personal. The depth of information exchange reflects one of four stages of relationship development: orientation, exploratory affective exchange, affective exchange, and stable exchange. The *orientation* stage is characterized by superficial information exchange about weather or demographic information. The *exploratory affective* stage involves exchange of information on the periphery of our personality, such as who you are and how you evaluate yourself (e.g., intelligent or hardworking). In the *affective exchange* stage, people feel more comfortable exchanging opinions and attitudes, such as 'I think Jenny is too bossy and arrogant'. At the *stable* exchange stage, an intimate relationship is developed and people freely express their true feelings. The frequency and amount of interaction also increase as the relationship develops. A key concept in the social penetration theory is *self-disclosure*, which refers to the process of revealing personal information that another person would be unlikely to discover through third sources.

Critical thinking...

How much do friends self-disclose to each other in your culture – a lot or only a little? What could be some potential consequences if a violation of the expected level of self-disclosure occurred between two communicators?

Although self-disclosure is used in almost all cultures as a means of developing relationships, cultural norms and values govern the degree to which it is acceptable in interpersonal relationships. For example, US Americans generally feel comfortable sharing family problems or tensions with colleagues. In Chinese culture, self-disclosure about family problems is only expected to take place between close friends or relatives. As Xi describes (1994: 155): 'For Americans, self-disclosure is a strategy to make various types of relationships work; for Chinese, it is a gift shared only with the most intimate relatives and friends.' On the other hand, cultural norms govern what content is considered private and what is public (or appropriate for self-disclosure). For example, in Hong Kong, it is common to ask and to disclose information of one's income and age, even when meeting for the first time; in England, however, people are hesitant to reveal such private information – in this case, norms about self-disclosure are reversed.

The emergence of the internet has opened a new context for disclosing the self to others. Researchers have begun to study gender effects on self-disclosure in online environments, and have reported gender differences in self-disclosure in cyberspace. Most studies indicated that women include more intimate information than men. Women are far more likely than men to include statements about their outlook or philosophy on life. However, Trammell, Tarkowski, Hofmokl and Sapp's (2006) quantitative content analysis of 358 Polish blogs found both gender differences and similarities in self-disclosure. Their results showed that women tend to provide a record of the day, discuss a memory, and communicate feelings or thoughts more often than men, whereas men discuss hobbies or interests more often than women. Men and women are similar in providing information about current events in society, current projects, feelings and thoughts towards or about something, family/friends, intimate details about life, and expressions of gratitude to readers.

CULTURE AND HUMAN RELATIONSHIP DEVELOPMENT

Cultural beliefs, values, and norms regulate relationship development. In this section, we introduce Yum's (1988) relationship model and discuss relationship practices across cultures.

Yum's model of human relationships

The five types of relationship identified by Yum (1988) have been widely applied in intercultural communication research. They are: particularistic versus universalistic, long term versus short term, ingroup versus outgroup, formal versus informal, and personal versus public relationships.

Particularistic versus universalistic relationships

The subject of particularistic relationships was raised by John Condon, an intercultural communication scholar, in the 1970s. Condon (1977) notes that in a culture where *particularistic relationships* are desired, people maximize differences in age, sex, and status, and encourage mutuality and interdependency between cultural members. Particularistic societies tend to be more hierarchically structured, and human relationships are established in accordance with the levels of hierarchy accepted by the society. Communication is governed by specific cultural rules concerning whom to talk to, what to talk about, and when and how to talk about it in specific social contexts. Yum (1988) found that particularistic relationships are practised more in East Asian countries. For example, in Singapore people tend to develop friendships with people of similar social status. Similarly, because marriage in collectivistic cultures like China implies an alliance of two families, couples usually come from a similar social class. The Chinese metaphor 'Bamboo door matches bamboo door and wooden door matches wooden door' illustrates this, implying that the matching couple need to come from 'matching doors' (status and family background).

In contrast, in cultures where *universalistic relationships* are desired, people establish interpersonal relationships based on rules of fairness and equality. Yum (1988) found that universalistic relationships are practised by North Americans. To them, the development of an interpersonal relationship relies on the principle of equality, not hierarchy. The rules governing ways of addressing people, for example, illustrate the level of hierarchy in a society. Employees in Australia may address their bosses using first names, whereas such a practice is not common in companies in Malaysia. People in universalistic societies, such as Canada, Sweden, Denmark, and Norway, believe that laws and regulations are written for everyone to follow and must be respected all the time. Relationships should follow rules as well. In contrast, for people in particularistic societies, such as China, South Korea, Venezuela, and Russia, the nature of the particular relationship in a given situation will determine how you will act in that situation. The relationship might be more important than following the rules.

Long-term versus short-term relationships

Long-term relationships are preferred in East Asian cultures, where a social reciprocity is viewed as centrally important. People in these cultures tend to feel indebted to others (Chen and Starosta, 2005). For example, the Chinese always try to return a favour from friends with much more than they received, as expressed in the Chinese adage, 'One should return a drop of kindness received with a fountain of kindness'. This practice is intended to maintain the existing relationship over a long period of time or permanently. When friends go out for a meal, often one person pays the bill for the whole group – the shared understanding is that, as friendship is considered long-lasting, there will be many opportunities in the future for each person to reciprocate in like manner. The same friendship practices are characteristic of Slavic cultures; friends pay for everyone in a friendship circle, and each person paying only for himself or herself seems rude. The Anglo-Celtic custom of 'shouting' in pubs – each person buying a round of drinks – has some similarities, but in this case the expectation is that everyone will buy a round in turn on the same occasion (which, of course, can result in far too much to drink); in this case, there is less expectation of permanence in the relationships, but the same expectation of reciprocity and generosity.

Yum (1988) found that short-term and symmetrical reciprocity is more characteristic of North Americans' interpersonal relationships. Commitment to a long-term interpersonal relationship is not considered as so important. In cultures where short-term relationships are commonly practised, people consider freedom and independence as important, and the flexibility to initiate or terminate relationships as an individual choice is treasured. Hence, it is a common practice for North Americans to split the bill when having a meal with friends. The value placed on long-term versus short-term relationships is also reflected in communication styles. For example, Australians are usually direct when they need to say 'No' to friends – although they usually give an excuse or reason for refusal, and are not as direct as Dutch or German people. However, the Japanese tend to say 'Maybe' or 'That would be somewhat hard' instead of a direct 'No'.

Ingroup versus outgroup relationships

The boundary between ingroups and outgroups is very clearly drawn in East Asian cultures (see Chapter 6). To East Asians, ingroup membership ties suggest similarity, trust, and affinity, ultimately leading to the development of close interpersonal relationships. On the other hand, the boundary between ingroup and outgroup members is less clearly defined for North Americans, British, and other Western Europeans, who establish relationships to fit specific contexts. They feel comfortable being affiliated with a relatively large number of groups, even though relationships based on these affiliations are often brief (Condon and Yousef, 1975).

The boundary drawn between ingroups and outgroups can create challenges for managers in the business context, particularly in workplaces comprising ethnically diverse employees and where group work is required. From an organizational perspective, managers realize that employees need to work in groups in order to make use of scarce resources, increase work productivity, reduce absenteeism, and thus increase competitive advantage. For example, the mobile phone company Motorola depends highly on workgroups to produce innovative mobile phones (Katzenbach and Smith, 2003). However, evidence suggests that a diverse group encounters difficulties in functioning due to differences such as culture, religion, and ethnicity. Research showed that similarities, rather than differences, in demographic backgrounds 'strengthen in-group prototypes, identification and thus adherence to group norms' (Hogg and Terry, 2000: 127).

Critical thinking...

You probably have experiences of working on group assignments. Think of the last assignment group you were in. Were the members from the same or different cultural or ethnic backgrounds? Were there 'groups' within the group? How were the roles of group members allocated? Was this experience satisfactory or not? Why?

Formal versus informal relationships

The practice around formal and informal relationships in a society depends on the hierarchical structure of the society. In vertical cultures like those of East Asia, relationship development is more formal than in horizontal cultures like North America. East Asians are more comfortable with initiating a relationship using a third party as a go-between. This can also avoid embarrassment or loss of face if the other party does not desire to enter into the relationship. Germans are also formal when introducing and meeting others, and reserve informality for close friends and family.

The form of address used in social interactions reveals the desired formality. For example, Japanese, Slavic, and Arabic language systems contain many pronouns and grammatical tags used to indicate the degree of formality and relationship intimacy between interactants (Condon and Yousef, 1975), whereas English is less specific in this area. Directly initiating a relationship characterizes horizontal cultures, where interactions are usually less formal. For example, it is common for Autralians at social functions to approach strangers and introduce themselves by saying, 'I'm …', unlike in Hong Kong, where more commonly a go-between would say, 'Let me introduce my friend to you …'. Even so, in less formal cultures this kind of introduction can be a source of great tension. For example, Australians (and people from other cultures with informal relationship structures) at a business gathering in Hong Kong might be in great doubt about whether it is appropriate to introduce themselves to someone they want to meet.

Photo 10.1   Chinese and Australians at a gathering. Initiating relationships with others tends to be more formal in Chinese culture. Copyright © The Chinese Consulate in Brisbane. Used with permission.

Personal versus public relationships

Yum notes that an overlap between personal and public relationships characterizes East Asian cultures. For example, a Chinese business person about to embark on negotiations would start the conversation with small talk, asking questions about the other person's family. Gift-giving is also a common practice in Chinese business culture – it is not a sign of bribery, as some Westerners view it, but an attempt to build trust and a good relationship so that smooth and cooperative transactions in the future can be expected. Because of the blurred boundary between personal and public relationships in Asian cultures, people tend not to separate the issue from the person. Thus, if someone criticizes a suggestion made by a manager, the manager may view the criticism as a personal attack. At meetings, therefore, people in Asian organizations are cautious about bringing up negative comments about managers or leaders.

In contrast, an emphasis on privacy, individualism, autonomy, and self-reliance encourages Westerners to keep public and personal relationships separate. Colleagues are less important as a source of friends for Americans than for Asians. Westerners may argue with or criticize each other at a meeting, but laugh and chat over drinks after the meeting; they separate the issue from the person. A frequent complaint by Chinese business people about their Western counterparts is that, in business negotiations, Westerners are more 'money-minded' than 'people-oriented'. The reason for this is cultural; Westerners tend to be issue-focused and to start business negotiations by going immediately to the business at hand, without showing interest or concern in their Chinese counterpart's personal life. Moreover, gift-giving is not a tradition among Western business people. Together, these behaviours may make the Chinese business partners feel that they are not respected or have not been 'given face'.

Friendship, romantic relationships, and family

Friendship is one of the most important interpersonal relationships people develop with others, and it usually involves high levels of intimacy, self-disclosure, and involvement. We choose our friends based on shared interests, goals, and liking. Because friendship is voluntary, it usually occurs between people who are similar in important ways.

Critical thinking...

What do you consider are important characteristics of friendship? What do you consider are important aspects for choosing a friend? What do you look for in a friend? How many of your preferred qualities do you think are determined or influenced by your culture?

Although friendship is universal across cultures, our interpretation of the term varies from culture to culture. Thais are likely to view a person as a whole, and a friend is accepted either completely or not at all. The Chinese have a more conservative definition of friends than Westerners do. Chinese expect friends to be involved in all aspects of each other's lives, to anticipate each other's needs, and to provide advice on various matters when needed. Family members of friends tend to know each other as well. Condon (1985) notes that the language people use to describe their friends can reflect underlying cultural values about the meaning and importance attached to the friendship. For example, among Mexicans, friends are referred to as a brother or a sister, suggesting collectivistic cultural values and a lasting bond. In Australia, friends are referred to as 'mates', but not as brothers and sisters.

Romantic relationships are another important interpersonal relationship that is influenced by culture. There are enormous differences in cultural beliefs, values, norms, and social practices about love, romance, dating, and marriage. Casual dating for romance among Americans is not viewed as a serious commitment that will necessarily lead to marriage (Lustig and Koester, 2013). If the lovers choose to get married, it is because of their love for each other, not because of any external cultural commitment or obligation. Although family members may be consulted before a final decision is made, the choice to marry is primarily made by the couple themselves. In Norway, marriages are supposed to be romantic love matches between two individuals with similar values and perspectives. Marrying for economic, social, or political reasons seems improper to most people. When King Harald, then the crown prince, wished to marry a commoner in 1968, rather than seeking a bride among the royal families of Europe, the nation approved. In Italy, in the past, marriages were arranged and women brought a dowry to the marriage. However, there were ways to help one's parents arrange marriage with the right person. Divorce was forbidden until recently. In India, casual dating relationships for romantic expression among unmarried individuals are still not common. Marriage is usually arranged by the parents with the consent of the couple. For example, an Indian speech pathologist who works in Sydney asked his mother in India to find him a wife. His mother compiled a list of 14 women that she believed would be suitable, and the son went back to India for three days and picked one from the list. After consent had been obtained from the girl's parents, a wedding ceremony was held in India. At that point, the couple knew very little about each other; it was not until nine months after the marriage when the wife joined her husband in Sydney that the couple began to get to know each other and develop affection. Similar patterns of familial arrangement can also be found in Muslim cultures, in which marriages are seen as alliances between families. In both Indian and Muslim cultures, romantic love is believed to be something that develops after marriage, not before.

THEORY CORNER

SIMILARITY ATTRACTION PARADIGM

The similarity attraction paradigm was proposed by Byrne (1971). The basic premise of this paradigm is that, if we perceive that our attitudes are similar to some people, we are attracted to them, because the similarity in attitudes validates our view of the world. However, actual similarities in attitudes and self-concept may not be related to our attraction to another person; rather, we are attracted to others based on perceived similarity. Think about the similarities you have with your ethnic group that make you want to form relationships with them, and how lack of perceived similarity with members of other ethnic groups influences your communication with them. In the initial stages of getting to know strangers, we tend to focus on general attitudes and opinions. As we get to know them, we search for similarities in central concepts, such as worldviews or core values. The similarity attraction paradigm and social identity theory have been applied by intercultural scholars like William B. Gudykunst and Young Y. Kim to study identities and intergroup relations.

Reference
Byrne, Donn (1971) *The Attraction Paradigm*. New York: Academic Press.

Further reading on interpersonal relationship in a management context
Clausen, Lisbeth (2007) 'Corporate communication challenges: a "negotiated" culture perspective', *International Journal of Cross-Cultural Management*, 7(3): 317–332.

Theory in Practice

SIMILARITY ATTRACTION IN SPEED-DATING

Research applying the similarity attraction paradigm has found consistent support for the proposition that people are more likely to be attracted to strangers whom they perceive have similar traits to them. In a speed-dating session, participants only have a few minutes to learn about their potential new romantic partner before moving on to the next potential partner. This scenario provides an excellent context for examining the effects of actual and perceived similarity simultaneously during an initial face-to-face encounter.

Tidwell, Eastwick and Finkel (2013) applied the similarity attraction paradigm to examine this effect, using a sample of 187 college students who attended one of the eight dating sessions. Actual and perceived similarity for each pair was calculated from questionnaire responses obtained before the event and after each date. Overall, the study found no evidence that actual similarity predicted romantic liking. However, participants who perceived similarity, both trait-specific and general, with their speed-dating partners indicated strong levels of romantic liking. This study demonstrates that actual similarity is a weaker and less consistent indicator of romantic attraction in a speed-dating setting than perceived similarity.

Questions to take you further
Why might perceived similarity be a stronger indicator of romantic attraction in face-to-face initial interactions than actual similarity? How might this compare with other romantic settings, such as online dating or traditional dating? What do you think predicts the success (or failure) of a blind date?

Reference
Tidwell, Natasha D., Paul W. Eastwick and Eli J. Finkel, (2013) 'Perceived, not actual, similarity predicts initial attraction in a live romantic context: evidence from the speed-dating paradigm', *Personal Relationships*, 20(2): 199–215.

Further reading on the similarity attraction effect
Montoya, R. Matthew and Robert S. Horton (2012) 'A meta-analytical investigation of the processes underlying the similarity-attraction effect', *Journal of Social and Personal Relationships*, 30(1): 64–94.

Critical thinking...

What is your view on 'love by arrangement'? What are the advantages and disadvantages? How would you feel about marrying someone to look after your family's interests? How would you feel about marrying someone of whom your family disapproved?

With the increasing cross-border movement and intercultural contacts, the number of interracial couples has dramatically increased since the later decades of the twentieth century in the Americas, East and South-East Asia, Europe, Australia, and New Zealand. For example, the number of interracial marriages in the USA increased by more than 1000 per cent between 1960 and 2002 (Zhang and Kline, 2009). One notable world trend is the frequency with which people of Chinese ancestry are marrying people from other cultural groups. This has been attributed to the large diaspora of Chinese people throughout the world, and the notable excess of young Chinese men relative to young Chinese women (Jones and Shen, 2008). Intercultural couples often struggle to resolve different cultural beliefs about what constitutes a good relationship, and how partners need to communicate in a good relationship. Cross-cultural scholars argue that individualism–collectivism is a key cultural dimension that influences interpersonal behaviour (Bond, 2009). The notion of romantic love can be seen as meeting the individualistic needs of self-expression and discovery, in that it provides romantic partners with the opportunity to explore their emotional selves. However, it has been argued that there is less need for love and intimacy within couple relationships in collectivistic societies, as these are shared across the broader family network (Lewinsohn and Werner, 1997). Moreover, the mutual absorption and disregard of others' views that characterize romantic love in individualistic societies are regarded as dysfunctional in collectivistic societies, in which group needs are prioritized over personal desires (Dion and Dion, 1993).

Family relationships are also characterized by cultural variations. Among members of European cultures, family life is primarily confined to interactions between parents and children. Members of the extended family rarely live together in the same household or take an active part in the daily lives of the nuclear family members. In China, the family is the primary means through which a person's social life is extended. For example, Chinese children's first friendships are usually with the children of their parents' colleagues or friends. In Australian culture, families are often peripheral to the social networks that people establish, although school networks are a strong source of friendships and often include partners and children. Moreover, the roles of family members are more clearly defined in Asian cultures. Gender roles, for example, are well defined in South Asian cultures; men make major decisions, provide for the family, and are the head of the family. Women are expected to take care of the family and perform household duties, although nowadays more and more women join the workforce and work side by side with male colleagues. Due to the change in tradition and the effects of globalization, arranged marriage is not as common now, but there is still significant pressure on couples not to divorce, as to do so reflects badly upon the whole family. Similarly, in India, conflict between married couples is an issue for members of the extended family. In a traditional method of mediation, male elders consider the conflict between the couple, and decide who is wrong and how that party should change in order to fix the problem and maintain the marriage.

Culture is also reflected in family relationships. While individualistic cultures emphasize family members' independence, autonomy, and self-sufficiency, collectivistic cultures emphasize interdependence of family members throughout the lifespan. For example, US spouses have been found to desire stronger boundaries around their relationship (less sharing of information and acceptance of advice from others), reflecting the US perception of the couple as a separate system. In contrast, in China the marital relationship is considered a continuation of the parents' family, rather than a separate system. The term 'extended family' is not used in many collectivistic cultures, as all relatives are considered part of the family. In addition, network members' approval and the belief that a potential partner will support one's parents have been found to have more influence on Chinese than American marital intentions and relationship commitment (Zhang and Kline, 2009). The importance of family relationships to collectivistic couples' functioning is further demonstrated by research findings that indicate that relationships with significant others are ranked among the most important dimensions of marriage by Hong Kong Chinese (Chan and Rudowicz, 2002).

The power of decision making in the family is influenced by cultural values and constraints. In collectivistic cultures, such as Japan, Korea, India, and China, families play a pivotal role in making decisions for children, including the choice of university, profession, and even of marital partner. For example, in the movie *Bend It Like Beckham*, the Indian girl's (Jess) parents felt they should decide which career path their children would follow. Thus, they wanted Jess to go to university to study medicine, even though it was her personal desire to become a professional football player. In individualistic cultures, children are taught from early years to be independent, to make their own decisions, and to plot their own career paths. The parents' role is to support their children in achieving their goals, although once again, this can be a source of great tension if the parents do not approve of the child's career choice. In Chinese families, it is not uncommon to see grown-up children, even after they are married, still living in the parental home. Some parents encourage their married sons to live with them so that they may take better care of them. In contrast, children in Western cultures are encouraged to move out of the family home when they become adults.

Further online reading The following article can be accessed for free on the book's companion website https://study.sagepub.com/liu2e: Marshall, Tara C. (2008) 'Cultural differences in intimacy: the influence of gener-role ideology and individualism–collectivism', *Journal of Social and Personal Relationships*, 25: 143–168.

DEVELOPING INTERCULTURAL RELATIONSHIPS

Today, it is more likely than ever that we live with culturally different others in our own cities and countries. Hence, developing good intercultural and intergroup relations becomes an important part of our life.

Awareness of cultural norms governing relationships

Relationship development is governed by cultural norms and values. People's knowledge of what constitutes appropriate or acceptable behaviours regarding a certain relationship varies across cultures. Moreover, people's interpretation of the same type of relationship also varies across cultures. For example, friendship is universal to all cultures, but who can be called a friend and what a friend means differ depending on the culture. In Australia, the term 'friend' can be used to refer to neighbours or colleagues, or even someone whom a person has just met. The boundaries between the ingroup and outgroup in Australia may not be as hard to cross as they are in some collectivistic cultures. For collectivistic cultures like the Greek culture, the line between ingroups and outgroups is much sharper. Cultural differences are also reflected in what is considered as private or intimate information. In Hong Kong, it is perfectly appropriate to ask a married acquaintance about his wife; in the United Arab Emirates, this would be considered a major breach of social etiquette. In Bosnia and Herzegovina, people like to say that they 'breathe' politics and political discussions. In Korea, however, similar topics would be avoided. In Taiwan, discussion about income and religion among colleagues is acceptable; in Slovenia, the United States, and in many other parts of Europe such information is only shared with close friends or family members.

Cultural differences in reliance on contextual cues can create difficulty in intercultural relationships. Take the example of interracial marriage. When one partner comes from an individualist culture and the other from a collectivist one, collectivist partners can misinterpret individualist spouses' remarks, assuming they mean more than they say explicitly, whereas individualist partners who are not sensitive to indirect cues can miss their collectivist partners' messages altogether. Furthermore, collectivist partners' indirect communication (e.g., 'Are you thirsty?' 'Shall we get something to drink?') might be seen as manipulative by individualist spouses, while individualist spouses' explicit statements of wants and needs (e.g., 'I want an orange juice') may appear demanding, rude, and selfish to collectivist partners. In a similar vein, when conflicts arise in relationships comprising an individualist and a collectivist partner, partners are likely to engage in different conflict resolution strategies based on different cultural expectations. Based on previous scholars' work, Chen and Starosta (2005: 133) emphasized the importance of developing 'cultural synergy', or a third culture, whereby people from different cultures negotiate their cultural differences and build common ground for communication. Such a process requires interactants to adapt to each other's cultural differences. Developing successful intercultural relationships requires us to understand the meanings different cultures attribute to different types of human relationship, and the cultural rules governing interaction between people involved in different types of relationship.

THEORY CORNER

ANXIETY/UNCERTAINTY MANAGEMENT THEORY

Anxiety/uncertainty management theory was developed by William B. Gudykunst (2004), and is based on the uncertainty reduction theory proposed by Berger and Calabrese (1975). The theory posits that effective interpersonal and intercultural communication is a function of how individuals manage the anxiety and uncertainty they experience when communicating with others. Uncertainty refers to individuals' ability to predict and/or explain others' feelings, attitudes, and behaviour. The reduction of uncertainty leads to an increase in both the amount of communication and the level of interpersonal attraction. If the amount of uncertainty present in initial interactions is not reduced, further communication between the people is unlikely to occur.

Anxiety is the affective equivalent of uncertainty. It stems from feeling uneasy, tense, and worried about what might happen, and is based on a fear of potentially negative consequences. Because intercultural communication involves people from dissimilar cultures, there is always the possibility of anxiety and uncertainty. To behave both appropriately and effectively in an intercultural encounter, one must make an accurate assessment of a range of information about people, the message, the context, and cultural norms, so as to reduce uncertainty/anxiety to optimize effective communication outcomes.

References

Berger, Charles R. and Richard J. Calabrese (1975) 'Some explorations in initial interaction and beyond: toward a developmental theory of interpersonal communication', *Human Communication Theory*, 1: 99–112.

Gudykunst, William B. (2004) *Bridging Differences: Effective Intergroup Communication* (4th edn). Thousand Oaks, CA: Sage.

Further reading on uncertainty reduction in intercultural communication

Miller, Ann and Jennifer Samp (2007) 'Planning intercultural interaction: extending anxiety/uncertainty management theory', *Communication Research Reports*, 24(2): 87–95.

Theory in Practice

INFLUENCE OF ANXIETY AND UNCERTAINTY IN INTER-JOURNALISTIC DISCOURSE

Public discourse between journalists usually takes place in the form of casual conversations between colleagues or formal interviews of journalists by other journalists. For example, while pre-planned conversations or interviews may not reveal a journalist's underlying ethnic prejudices, in crisis reporting, the chaotic and unpredictable situation can create anxiety, uncertainty, and fear for journalists, which can result in ethnocentric and stereotypical thinking. As anxiety/uncertainty management theory assumes, anxiety, uncertainty, and fear give rise to ethnocentric thinking and encourage reliance on stereotypes.

Johnson and colleagues (2010) conducted a critical discourse analysis on transcripts of on-air conversations between journalists in national and cable television news broadcasts made during the second week after Hurricane Katrina devastated New Orleans in 2005. The 65 news programmes contained inter-journalistic discourse about African Americans in New Orleans. The findings showed that unfamiliarity with the African-American community created anxiety and uncertainty for reporters covering the post-Katrina devastation. The stressful nature of covering the crisis and the unfamiliar cultural terrain gave rise to ethnocentric, dichotomous, and stereotypical thinking expressed in talk between journalists. These findings provide support for anxiety/uncertainty management theory, which proposes that exposure to unpredictability and unfamiliar settings can cause individuals to think in ethnocentric, dichotomous (us–them), and stereotypical ways.

Questions to take you further
How can journalists overcome the anxiety and uncertainty that occur when they report on crises? What kinds of training programme can we design to enhance journalists' ability to cover racial and other intergroup matters in an unbiased way?

Reference
Johnson, Kirk A., John Sonnett, Mark K. Dolan, Randi Reppen and Laura Johnson (2010) 'Interjournalistic discourse about African Americans in television news coverage of Hurricane Katrina', *Discourse & Communication*, 4(3): 243–261.

Further reading on anxiety and uncertainty in intercultural relationships
Samochowiec, Jakub and Arnd Florack (2010) 'Intercultural contact under uncertainty: the impact of predictability and anxiety on the willingness to interact with a member from an unknown cultural group', *International Journal of Intercultural Relations*, 34(5): 507–515.

Cyberspace as a site of intercultural relationship development

Communication technologies allow us to initiate relationships with other people via the internet. Cyberspace provides an arena for intercultural communication, where people across the world can connect in social networks. Indeed, the growth of social networking sites, such as Facebook and Myspace, is of great interest to scholars of intercultural communication because of the opportunity they provide to maintain and expand such networks independent of spatial constraints. For example, online dating services allow subscribers from different countries to build profiles of themselves and to contact or be contacted by other users in view of developing romantic relationships. While forms of internet communication make international phone calls less expensive, they require a relatively high level of engagement. Online social network sites, by contrast, allow for the maintenance of extended networks at a relatively low intensity of engagement; people can add contacts and keep in touch at their convenience. Rather than having to track down new phone numbers and addresses, such sites allow for constant con-

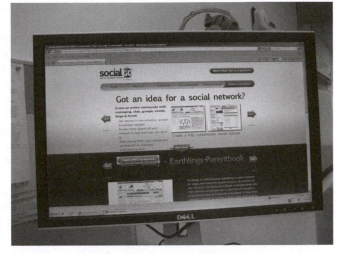

Photo 10.2   Social networking sites have become an important arena for culturally different others to meet and communicate. Copyright © Shuang Liu. Used with permission.

tact, even if contacts have moved or are travelling. Individuals who travel abroad, for example, can collect online social contacts and easily stay in touch with them when they return home. Internet technology helps to de-territorialize extended social networks by transposing them into cyberspace, where geographic distance is collapsed. Online social networking sites, therefore, are also an important site for intercultural communication insofar as the ability to maintain extended social networks raises the issue of cultural norms and practices.

Critical thinking...

How has internet communication technology affected your relationships with friends or family? How are Facebook friends different from (or similar to) face-to-face friends? What is your view on developing online romantic relationships? Could you suggest some strategies for dealing with deception online?

Facebook ushers in new forms of communication practices for which new norms need to be established: What is appropriate to include in status updates? How does one manage self-presentation in a context in which many different groups of social contacts mingle – parents, close friends, professional colleagues, and so forth? In this regard, Facebook represents an example of 'glocalization': the customized local uptake of a global phenomenon. Particular cultural groups customize their use of Facebook's standard template according to their own cultural values. Facebook comes to reshape their forms of communication and is, in turn, shaped by how they decide to use it. Moreover, Facebook allows for cross-cultural interfaces in which the individual and groups need to figure out what type of behaviour is acceptable or desirable in interactions with people internationally and interculturally. This process will both import existing sets of values and lead to the creation of new forms of standardized global communication, along with a range of other increasingly global communication practices, including texting, Twitter, and email (Miller, 2011).

However, there are issues we need to address when developing relationships with others via online social networking sites like Facebook. Although various types of social networking site serve to increase opportunities for communicating with culturally different others who may be located in another place, online social networking also creates the possibility of deception, an issue that has received scholarly attention in recent years. In Caspie and Gorsky's (2006) study of chat room users, for example, over 60 per cent of the respondents reported that deception online is widespread. With the emergence of profile-based social networking sites, including online dating sites, online self-presentation is no longer limited to text-based descriptions; instead, the profile photograph becomes a critical component for relational success (Hancock and Toma, 2009). Hancock and Toma found that female online daters, compared to males, are more likely to use profile photographs as a tool to showcase their physical attractiveness. Another problem is cyber-bullying, which can have a serious negative effect on the victim, even leading to suicide. Nevertheless, online social networking, although not without problems, facilitates contact with people that transcends geographic and cultural confines, and thus has become an arena for developing intercultural relations.

Further online reading The following article can be accessed for free on the book's companion website https://study.sagepub.com/liu2e: Chan, Darius K. S. and Grand H. L. Cheng (2004) 'A comparison of offline and online friendship qualities at different stages of relationship development', *Journal of Social and Personal Relationships*, 21(3): 305–320.

SUMMARY

- Humans develop different kinds of relationship to fulfil the needs for inclusion, control, and affection.

- Social exchange theory, social penetration theory, the similarity attraction paradigm, and anxiety/uncertainty reduction theory are used to explain intercultural relationship development.

- People from different cultures may have very different interpretations of various types of relationship and the rules governing appropriate behaviour in them.

- Yum's work identifies five dimensions on which differences between East Asians and North Americans (and members of other cultures) can be compared in terms of interpersonal relationships.

- Culture influences various types of interpersonal relationships, including friendships, romantic relationships, and families.

- With the advancement of internet technologies, cyberspace has become an arena for developing intercultural relationships. However, there are also problems associated with cyber-bullying and online deception.

JOIN THE DEBATE

Does communication technology bring us closer or set us further apart?

Communication technologies, such as the mobile phone and the internet, have become an inseparable part of our daily lives. These were celebrated at the time of their invention as being able to overcome geographical boundaries and time constraints, hence bringing people across the world together. But has this happened? The digital divide, or the gap between those who have access to communication technologies and those who do not, continues to grow. While this concept is generally applied to developing versus developed countries, it is also of concern within the same country across different regions or communities, and even between generations. With so much of our communication now being dependent on mobile phones and internet-enabled computers or tablets, older people, those in regional or remote areas, or people of lower socioeconomic status may be at a significant disadvantage. On the other hand, those of us who have easy access to the all-powerful modern communication gadget – the mobile phone – become very reliant on it: we take our mobile phone to restaurants, meetings, the dinner table at home, the bedroom, and even the bathroom; we check messages or text contacts on the train, at the airport, and in shops, sometimes instead of talking to people. Even when we set aside some time to catch up with friends face to face, we might be 'phubbing' (snubbing someone in a social setting by looking at our mobile phone instead of talking to them). Does communication technology bring us closer together, or set us more apart?

CASE STUDY

Love by arrangement in India

India is the world's second most populated country, approaching a total of 1 billion people. It is a country of extreme diversity, with multiple languages, religions, castes, and classes. Arranged marriages have a long tradition in Indian society. There is no greater event in an Indian family than a wedding, and it is not uncommon for middle- or upper-class weddings to have a guest list of over 500 people. Arranging and conducting weddings is a complex process, from match-making and engagement to the actual wedding (which can last up to five days). Marriage is deemed essential for virtually everyone in India. A Hindu marriage joins two individuals for life, so they can pursue *dharma* (duty), *artha* (possessions), *kama* (physical desires), and *moksa* (spiritual release) together.

For an Indian, marriage is a great watershed in life, marking the transition to adulthood. Generally, this transition occurs as a result of the efforts of a whole community. Arranging a marriage is a critical responsibility for parents and the extended families of the bride and groom. Marriage alliances entail a redistribution of wealth as well as building and restructuring social relations. Some parents begin marriage arrangements at the birth of their child. In the past, Indians were likely to marry at a young age; in smaller communities, such as Rajasthan, children under the age of 5 could be united in marriage. Legislation which mandates minimum marriage ages has been introduced over past decades, but such laws have had limited effects on actual marriage practices.

An arranged marriage begins with the parents discussing their expectations with their sons/daughters before they embark on the search for a match. The following elements are usually important in a quest for compatibility:

- Values and personal expectations: should match.
- Age and height: the girl should generally be younger and shorter than the boy.
- Looks: should be acceptable to the partner.
- Religion: should be the same.
- Mother tongue and caste: preferably the same.
- Diet (vegetarian or not; use of alcohol and cigarettes): may differ, but only if acceptable to the partner.
- Education: similar level.
- Astrological signs and attributes: should be compatible, if the two families believe in astrology.

India's dominant wedding traditions are difficult to categorize, especially on the basis of religion. Essentially, India is divided into two large regions with regard to Hindu kinship and marriage practices: the north, and the south. Additionally, various ethnic and tribal groups in the central, mountainous north, and eastern regions follow a variety of other practices. Broadly, in the Indo-Aryan-speaking north, a family seeks marriage alliances with people to whom the family is not already linked by blood ties. On the Indo-Gangetic Plain, marriages are contracted outside the village, sometimes even outside the wider collection of villages, but with members of the same caste. Thus, in most parts of north India, the Hindu bride goes to live with strangers in a home she has never visited. In contrast, marriages between cousins (especially cross-cousins, i.e., the children of a brother or sister) and even between uncles and nieces (especially a man and his elder sister's daughter) are common in south India. Among Muslims in both the north and the south, marriage between cousins is encouraged.

In many communities throughout India, a dowry has traditionally been given by a bride's kin at the time of her marriage. In ancient times, the dowry was considered a woman's wealth – property due to a beloved daughter who had no claim on her natal family's estate – and typically included portable valuables such as jewellery and household goods that a bride could control throughout her life. Over time, the larger portion of the dowry has come to consist of goods and cash payments given directly to the groom's family. Throughout much of India in the late twentieth century, dowry payments escalated, and a groom's parents sometimes insist on compensation for their son's higher education and even for his future earnings, to which the bride will presumably have access. Some of the dowries demanded are quite oppressive, amounting to several years' salary in cash as well as items such as motorcycles, air conditioners, and expensive cars. Among some lower-status groups, large dowries are currently replacing traditional bride-price payments. The dowry is becoming an increasing burden for the bride's family. Anti-dowry laws exist but are largely ignored, and a bride's treatment in her marital home is often affected by the value of her dowry.

Pre-wedding ceremonies include engagement and the arrival of the groom's party at the bride's residence, often as a formal procession. The specific rituals may vary across religious groups. For example, in an Indian Christian community known as Syrian-Christians, the bride-to-be is given milk – a symbol of fertility. This tradition is probably borrowed from the Hindus. The post-wedding ceremonies involve welcoming the bride to her new home. The wedding rituals themselves vary, based on family traditions.

Photo 10.3 In a pre-wedding ceremony of the Indian Christian community, the bride-to-be is given milk – a symbol of fertility. Copyright © Pradip Thomas. Used with permission.

Reference

A Short Hindu Wedding Ceremony [online]. Accessed 16 July 2009 at: http://aprendizdetodo.com/wedding.

Questions for discussion

1. What does a wedding generally signify in Indian culture?

2. How has the concept of dowry changed over time? What is your view of this practice?

3. Some cultures and religions (e.g., Jewish and Hindu) place people under a lot of social pressure to marry within the culture, but many individuals nevertheless find love across cultural boundaries. What can you learn from the case study about out-of-culture marriages?

4. What are some reasons for choosing not to date interculturally? Are there any reasons (apart from romance itself) for choosing to date interculturally?

5. What beliefs, thoughts, feelings, and attitudes do couples have in common? What differences are there between couples? What conflicts do you think might occur in intercultural marriage?

FURTHER READINGS

All articles listed next to the mouse icon below can be accessed for free on the book's companion website: https://study.sagepub.com/liu2e

Human relationship development

Johnson, Amy, Elaine Wittenberg and Michel Haigh (2004) 'The process of relationship development and deterioration: turning points in friendships that have terminated', *Communication Quarterly*, 52(1): 54–67.

The conceptualization of relationship development and deterioration has been a key area in interpersonal communication research. Traditional views perceive relationships as developing linearly to a very intimate level. Either relationships are maintained satisfactorily in this state, or they begin to become less intimate, and ultimately end. This article examines why friendships end and identifies both linear and non-linear trajectories of friendship development and deterioration. Turning points for both friendship development and friendship deterioration include participating in activities together, shared living quarters, hanging out with mutual friends, or shared common interests. In particular, this study demonstrates that some friendships reach the highest level of closeness early in a relationship, rather than working towards a maximum point of closeness.

Intercultural relationships

Marshall, Tara C. (2008) 'Cultural differences in intimacy: the influence of gener-role ideology and individualism–collectivism', *Journal of Social and Personal Relationships*, 25: 143–168.

This article reported two studies that examined emotional intimacy in European Canadians and Chinese Canadians in romantic relationships. The researchers hypothesized that cultural differences in gender role ideology and invividualism–collectivism would have different contributions to self-disclosure and intimacy. Study 1 found that Chinese Canadians' lower level of intimacy relative to that of European Canadians was mediated by their gender–role traditionalism, rather than by their orientations to individualism or collectivitism. However, Study 2 revealed that greater gender-role and traditionalism was associated with lower self-disclosure, and in turn lower intimacy. Results also showed that Chinese Canadians' lower intimacy was related to lower relationship satisfaction.

Neville Miller, Ann and Jennifer A. Samp (2007) 'Planning intercultural interaction: extending anxiety/ uncertainty management theory', *Communication Research Reports*, 24(2): 87–95.

This article reported a study which applied theories of anxiety/uncertainty management and planning to examine the notion of mindfulness in inter- and intracultural interactions and how self-monitoring and tolerance for ambiguity influence planning, attributional confidence, and interaction anxiety. Participants were 108 female Caucasian American college students who responded to a videotape of either an American or a Korean confederate with whom they believed they would be holding a conversation. The prediction by the researchers was that participants who anticipated interacting with someone from their own culture would differ from those who anticipated interacting with someone from a different culture in terms of content and complexity of their pre-interaction plans. Interestingly, this study found that there was no significant difference in the complexity of plans prior to conversational engagement between inter- and intracultural situations.

Online relationship and social networking

Chan, Darius K. S. and Grand H. L. Cheng (2004) 'A comparison of offline and online friendship qualities at different stages of relationship development', *Journal of Social and Personal Relationships*, 21(3): 305–320.

This article compares online and offline friendship qualities at different stages of relationship development. A sample of 162 Hong Kong internet users was asked to think of two friends, one they knew through face-to-face interactions and one they knew through the internet, and then describe the qualities of their offline and online friendships. Results revealed that offline friendships involved more interdependence, breadth, depth, understanding, commitment, and network convergence than online friendships. Although the qualities of both online and offline friendships improved as the duration of the relationship increased, the differences between the two types of friendship diminished over time. These results suggest that the influence of the structural and normative constraints typically found in face-to-face interaction may be different in the online setting.

Social exchange theory

Cropanzano, Russell and Marie S. Mitchell (2005) 'Social exchange theory: an interdisciplinary review', *Journal of Management*, 31(6): 874–900.

Social exchange theory is one of the most influential conceptual paradigms for understanding workplace behaviour. One of the basic tenets is that relationships develop and strengthen over time. To do so, however, it requires participants to abide by unspoken norms of reciprocity and negotiated rules. This article provides a comprehensive review of social exchange theory, including highlighting key components of the theory, a typology of relationships and exchange mechanisms, and the need for mutually beneficial transactions and relationships.

> *If we have no peace, it is because we have forgotten we belong to each other.*
>
> Mother Teresa, a humanitarian and advocate for the poor and helpless, 1910–1997

11

MANAGING INTERCULTURAL CONFLICTS

LEARNING OBJECTIVES

At the end of this chapter, you should be able to:

- Identify the different sources of intercultural conflicts.

- Describe the stages in the conflict process.

- Compare and contrast different conflict styles.

- Recognize the influence of culture on conflict management.

- Develop communication strategies to manage intercultural conflicts effectively.

INTRODUCTION

The growth in intercultural contact increases the opportunities for understanding, but also the possibilities of misunderstanding between people, groups, communities, organizations, and nations. If misunderstanding or miscommunication goes unmanaged, it can result in conflicts. The word 'conflict' has Latin roots: *con* meaning 'together' and *fligere* meaning 'to strike'. To 'strike together' the conflict parties have to be linked in an interdependent manner. This chapter adopts Putnam and Poole's (1987: 552) definition, which conceptualizes *conflict* as 'the interaction of interdependent people who perceive opposition of goals, aims, and values, and who see the other party as potentially interfering with the realization of these goals'. This definition highlights three key elements of conflict: incompatible goals, interdependence of the parties involved, and communication.

Conflict permeates all social relationships. Just as relationship development occurs at different levels, so too does conflict. At the individual level, conflict occurs between two (or several) persons when they are disagreeing with each other, or competing for something (often scarce resources); such conflict is defined as *interpersonal conflict*. For example, two co-workers competing for the title of 'model worker', which is available to only one person in the same workshop, where each believes that the other person does not deserve the title, may engage in interpersonal conflict. *Intergroup conflict* occurs when two cultural or social groups perceive disagreements over resources, power, territory, and the like (Gudykunst, 2004). In an organization, conflicts may occur between aggregates of people, for example, between the sales and supplies departments or between management and unions. *Interorganizational conflict* involves disputes between two or more organizations; in this case, the organizations themselves enter intergroup disputes. For example, different energy suppliers may engage in interorganizational conflict when they are competing for a larger market share. *International conflicts* refer to disputes between nations. In the context of intercultural encounters, *intercultural conflict* involves perceived or actual incompatibility in goals, interests, resources, values, expectations, processes, or outcomes between two or more people from different cultures (Ting-Toomey, 1994). For example, in a Sino-American joint venture operating in southern China, the Chinese manager prefers an authoritarian leadership style, whereas the American manager likes democratic and participatory decision making. Conflict occurs when the two managers have to cooperate to accomplish a project. As culture influences communication at all levels, intercultural conflict can be interpersonal, intergroup, interorganizational, or international.

Although conflict is pervasive in all societies, our view of conflict and our conflict management styles are culture-bound. Individuals from different cultural groups bring with them diverse and complex value assumptions, expectations, verbal, and nonverbal communication rules and norms that govern the conflict process. Similarly, communities with different cultural patterns and belief systems create their own distinctive norms to govern their behaviour. Hence intercultural conflict involves perceptions filtered through our cultural lenses. For example, cultures that emphasize individualism and competition, like the Netherlands and Belgium, view conflict positively, whereas collectivistic cultures that emphasize collaboration, cooperation, and conformity, like Greece and Turkey, generally see conflict as negative. In short, intercultural conflict is a conflict between persons, groups, or nations of different cultures over perceived incompatible values, norms, face orientations, goals, scarce resources, processes, and/or outcomes. The pervasiveness of conflicts and the importance of managing them constructively give the study of intercultural conflict great significance.

This chapter first describes potential sources of intercultural conflict, and identifies different stages in the conflict process. We then discuss the influence of culture on conflict management styles. Conflict styles are made up of communicative behaviours, because communication is the means by which conflicts are socially defined and conducted, and the instrument through which influence is exercised. As culture acts as guide and predictor of communication behaviour, conflict in intercultural settings must be viewed in terms of culture and communication (Liu and Chen, 1999). A lack of cultural awareness and appropriate intercultural responses results in unrealistic expectations, frustration, anger, and failure to establish friendly social relationships (Dodd, 1998). This chapter concludes by suggesting some ways to effectively manage intercultural conflicts.

Critical thinking...

How and why do you think a conflict generally occurs? Do you think that more collaborative and cooperative cultures expect less conflict during intergroup interactions? What strategies do you usually employ to deal with interpersonal conflict? What about intergroup conflict (such as between teams, project groups, etc.)?

POTENTIAL SOURCES OF INTERCULTURAL CONFLICT

Whether communication is cooperative or competitive depends on what is shared, perceived, and experienced between the communicators – individuals, groups, organizations, and so forth. Cooperative behaviour builds a sense of trust, and leads to the sharing of beliefs and attitudes and a desire for both sides to be satisfied in the relationship or interaction (Fisher-Yoshida, 2005). However, when the communication space shrinks or even closes because of perceived or real differences, conflicts may occur. The sources of intercultural conflict are myriad: differences in beliefs and values, incompatible goals, bias and prejudice, ethnic and racial prejudice, historical grievances and hatred, and political, territorial, and economic disputes.

THEORY CORNER

TYPES OF CONFLICT

Conflicts can be categorized as affective, cognitive, and goal-oriented (Amason, 1996). Affective conflict arises from interpersonal tension and is largely emotional in nature. When affective conflict arises, disagreements over personal, individually oriented matters become detrimental to personal and group performance, and emotions seem incompatible. Cognitive conflict arises from the perceived disagreements between the two parties about viewpoints, attitudes, and opinions. These conflicts are common and usually result from individual incompatibility. Disagreements among individuals are bound to occur, since they bring different ideas, opinions, and perspectives to the table. Cognitive conflict, some argue, is beneficial because it requires individuals to engage. For example, in experiencing cognitive conflict as a result of being part of a team in a workplace, team members learn from one another's ideas, opinions, and arguments. In goal-oriented conflicts, people disagree about preferred goals and ends. African Americans in the 1960s in the USA, for example, wanted at least a desegregated society with equal rights, but this was not what was preferred by many white Americans. Parties in conflict generally have two types of goal: (1) a preferred future, where conditions, relationships, and needs must be met, and (2) expectations about the behaviour of their opponent(s).

Reference

Amason, Anne C. (1996) 'Distinguishing the effects of functional and dysfunctional conflict on strategic decision-making: resolving a paradox for top management teams', *Academy of Management Journal*, 39: 123–148.

Further reading on conflict styles

Parayitam, Satayanarayana and Robert S. Dooley (2009) 'The interplay between cognitive and affective conflict and cognition- and affect-based trust in influencing decision outcomes', *Journal of Business Research*, 62(2): 789–796.

Theory in Practice

GOAL-ORIENTED CONFLICTS IN TURKEY

Cafnik (2010) explored goal-oriented conflict in Turkey. With the slow decline of the Ottoman Empire at the end of nineteenth century, and later on with the occupation of Ottoman regions by the Allies in the aftermath of the First World War, internal conflicts about the future of the Ottoman Empire started. A Turkish national movement was established and fortified. It led to the war of independence and finally to the establishment of the Republic of Turkey in 1923. Mustafa Kemal Atatürk, a distinguished military commander, became Turkey's first president. This transformation in leadership and politics changed more than 600 years of monarchical rule based on Islamic beliefs and laws. Turkey went through many conflicts and adjustments in the first years of its existence as a secular state. While some changes were welcomed and desired, others had to be demanded. In this way Mustafa Kemal Atatürk and his supporters enacted modernity as a desired future. That meant that Atatürk was fighting for specific goals, one of them being for Islam to be officially removed from the state. After this goal had been achieved, other reforms followed. All educational institutions were put under direct state control, and religious courts were abolished. The call to prayer was ordered to be in the Turkish language instead of Arabic, imams were ordered to preach in Turkish only, the Qur'an was translated into Turkish, and the Arabic alphabet was substituted with the Latin alphabet. Because the countryside did not change dramatically, soon two parallel cultures started to exist inside the new country: one was a Westernized, secular, urban culture with a small but powerful elite, and the other was a local, traditional culture connected to Islam. According to Cafnik, this division soon became evident at the level of state politics.

Questions to take you further

How would you explain goal conflict? Can you give more examples? How would you explain the conflicts and dilemmas around women wearing a veil (*hijab* or *niqab*) in the context of conflicting goals?

Reference

Cafnik, Petra (2010) *The Veil which Shows and Hides: Turkish Women between Modernity and Tradition.* Nova Gorica, Slovenia: University of Nova Gorica.

Further reading on conflict resolution

Morgan, Michael C. and Abby McLeod (2006) 'Have we failed our neighbor?', *Australian Journal of International Affairs*, 60(3): 412–428.

Critical thinking...

The *hijab* (headscarf) was discouraged by Atatürk when the Turkish Republic was founded. In 1980, the 'Dress and Appearance Regulation' prohibited employees, while on duty in public agencies, offices, and institutions, from wearing, in the case of men, moustaches, beards, and long hair, and in the case of women, mini-skirts, low-necked dresses, and headscarves. What kinds of conflicts might this regulation lead to? Would you describe this conflict as political or religious?

Globalization and the rise of racial violence

Although large parts of humanity lived in stateless political systems until the nineteenth century, imperial expansion (e.g., Russia), Western colonialism, and the internal colonialism of independent nation-states all over the world have led to a situation where almost everyone now belongs to a state. Many intercultural communication scholars believe that globalization today is experienced unevenly around the world (Harvey, 2001). On the one hand, information technology can be used to empower marginalized communities like those in developing countries to engage in global knowledge sharing. On the other hand, large populations that do not have the resources to connect to the new types of global systems have been further marginalized. Thus, while different international networks of production and consumption are expanding, we are witnessing increasing racial violence and crime against vulnerable groups, such as migrants, asylum seekers, and refugees in all parts of the world. According to Dupuy and Peters (2010), as of 2008, the total number of refugees was estimated at 10 million, and the number of internally displaced persons at 26 million – many of them children and young people.

Moreover, young people are also major participants in armed conflicts, with ultra-young combatants (i.e., child soldiers) being especially active in African conflicts. Racial violence like this is defined as a complex and enduring social problem that exists in many forms at institutional, interpersonal, and individual levels. Racism can be broadly defined as a phenomenon that maintains or exacerbates unfair inequalities in power, resources, or opportunities. Indeed, hostilities against ethnic and religious minorities in the world are on the rise everywhere (e.g., conflicts against Roma in Europe, Muslims in India, Christians in the Arab world, Tutsis in Rwanda, Kurds in Iraq, Baha'is in Iran, and so forth). Based on a report released by the Heidelberg Institute for International Conflict Research (HIICR, 2007), the number of conflicts observed per year has risen from 81 in 1945 to approximately 300 in 2006. Most of these conflicts are *low-intensity conflicts*, i.e., they involve the use of military armed forces by at least one party.

The number of *high-intensity conflicts*, i.e., those involving a series of intense, complex battles between conventional military forces or even the use of nuclear weapons, also rose from seven in 1945 to 41 in 2004. The all-time high was 49 high-intensity conflicts in 1992, shortly after the collapse of the Soviet Union. Jitpiromsri's (2006) study of the conflicts in Thailand's south and southern border provinces provides an example of violent intercultural conflicts. Jitpiromsri explored the history of these provinces, which were annexed to Thailand in the 1900s, and which are plagued by political, religious, and cultural conflicts. More than 80 per cent of the population in these provinces are Malay Muslims who now demand independence. Since the new resurgence of violence in 2004, roughly 3,071 people have been killed and 4,986 injured (Jitpiromsri, 2008). At this time, when the number of violent conflicts on different scales around the globe is increasing, it is more important that we realize the potential role that intercultural communication can play in understanding and transforming conflicts.

Further online reading The following article can be accessed for free on the book's companion website https://study.sagepub.com/liu2e: Peters, John D. (2001) 'Witnessing', *Media, Culture & Society*, 23(6): 707–723.

Ingroup/outgroup bias and prejudice

Ingroup and outgroup bias has been one of the major sources of intercultural conflict in all societies through-out history. As earlier chapters explain, all of us categorize people into ingroups and outgroups and develop perceptions of 'us' versus 'them' in our identifications. Origin and ancestry myths reinforce the sense of unity among ingroup members by suggesting that they share a common history and a way of being that captures the uniqueness of their group or nation. Every nation has a narrative that explains its origin and distinctiveness and, in one way or another, justifies the nation's contemporary state. Many of the myths and stories, although inspiring and largely accepted by the people and supported by the state, are challenged by other groups in society. Indeed, often these stories do not have a strong foundation in historical events. For example, Italians see themselves as descending uniquely from the Romans and relate their identity to the history of Roman Catholicism; Greek identity is founded on the belief that they are the direct descendants of the Ancient Greeks. The historical accuracy of all these myths can easily be challenged.

The strength of origin and ancestry myths lies instead in that they form points of consensus around which a sense of national unity can be developed and maintained. Such myths are understood as the sites of social memory. They are used by members of an ethnic or national group to draw boundaries around ingroups and outgroups. The unfavourable attitudes and exclusion of outgroups based on origin and ancestry myths often lead directly to intercultural conflict (Lévi-Strauss, 1962). As an example, Mostar is a city in Bosnia and Herzegovina, famous for its ancient bridge. The elegant bridge was designed by the Ottoman (Turkish) architect Mimar Hayruddin and was completed in 1566. In 1993, during the Bosnian war, it was destroyed by the Croatian army as a way of destroying part of Bosnia's Muslim history. Today, the city remains divided between Croats (mainly Catholics) and Bosnians (mainly Muslims).

In a society where different groups exist, more often than not there is an uneven distribution of power among the groups. Consequently, the group in power has greater influence over the ingroup/outgroup dynamics in their society. It is important to note that processes of inclusion and exclusion result from interaction, or the lack of it, between social agents (i.e., individuals and groups) and social institutions (e.g., educational institutions, media, regulatory bodies, government agencies, and law enforcement agencies). If the attributes of the social agents are seen to support the state and nation, the interaction results in social inclusion, and access to resources will be granted. However, if the agents' attributes are not deemed to be relevant and useful to the system, then exclusion and conflict are likely to follow. For example, Louw (2004b) describes the story of twentieth-century South Africa as an example of exclusion, with racial conflicts and apartheid. Apartheid, a racial policy which was constructed by the ethnic white minority and which dominated South Africa until 1992, served to maintain the political and economic supremacy of the white ethnic minority. Louw indicates that apartheid was premised not only

Photo 11.1   The historical bridge in Mostar divides Croats (mainly Catholics) and Bosniaks (mainly Muslims).
Copyright © Zala Volčič. Used with permission.

upon the notion of white supremacy, but also on political partition. It was a strategy constructed by the powerful minority in order to hold on to political power. Such a racial policy, based on ingroup and outgroup bias and prejudice, led to many inter-ethnic and interracial conflicts in South Africa.

Historical grievances and inter-ethnic hatred

Although everyday intercultural conflicts are often based on cultural ignorance or misunderstanding, some intercultural conflicts are based on hatred and centuries-old antagonisms, often arising from long-standing historical grievances. For example, tensions between Muslims and Orthodox Christians in the Balkan region have been ongoing since the Turks conquered Serbia and the rest of the Balkans in the fourteenth century (Colovic, 2002). The defeat of the Christian armies in the famous Battle of Kosovo in 1389 has been perceived as the epitome of Serbian sacrifice; the theme of the Serbs defending Christian Europe against Islamic expansionism has been appropriated into Serbian history. This was evident in the prism of victimhood through which the military conflicts in Bosnia and Kosovo in the 1990s were often represented – as Serbs defending themselves, the Serbian nation, Yugoslavia, and/or Christianity. Today, the conflicts in Bosnia still persist largely because of historical grievances (Erjavec and Volčič, 2007).

Intercultural conflicts due to historical hostility, hatred, and grievances are also illustrated in the disputes between the Mexican government and Mexican Indian farmers, known as Zapatistas (Zapatista National Liberation Army) after the nineteenth-century agrarian leader Emiliano Zapata. Few international events over the last decade have captured the global imagination as much as the Zapatista uprising in Chiapas, Mexico, in 1994. The impoverished Indian farmers, led by the rebel leader, Subcomandante Marcos, advocated a rebellion against the Mexican government, with minimal violence, to change their oppressive economic and political conditions. At that time, the Mexican government was creating an image of the country as socially and economically stable, but the Zapatistas argued that poverty, landlessness, inadequate heathcare, illiteracy, and governmental corruption were ruling Mexico. They fought for land, justice, democratic reforms, and the end of Mexico's one-party state (McCowan, 2003).

In this case, historical antagonism between poor Mexican Indian farmers and the Mexican government led to new forms of hostility and hatred.

Another international conflict that has only slowly attracted international attention was violent conflict in Rwanda. Between March and April 1994, around 1 million ethnic Tutsis were slaughtered by the other main ethnic group, Hutus. The genocide in Rwanda was the most brutal and devastating since the Holocaust during the Second World War, and has received much media, scholarly, and international attention. The failure of the United Nations to protect unarmed civilians has been the subject of academic and policy debates, and has led to the doctrine of 'Responsibility to Protect', which was invoked later in the Libyan revolt. However, the situation of the Rwandan women who survived the genocide but were brutally exposed to sexual violence has never received such attention. Rape was used in Rwanda, as in other war-torn societies, as a weapon of war (Simic, 2010).

Critical thinking...

How can the international community help to prevent international violent conflict? What should other nations do when there is a violent ethnic or civil war? Do conflict prevention agencies have the power, or the right, to move a country or region along the continuum from ongoing conflict to durable peace? How might communication help or hinder this process?

Inter-ethnic hatred as a result of cultural ignorance is illustrated clearly by the continuing practice of anti-Semitism. *Anti-Semitism* refers to a negative perception of Jews (Office for Democratic Institutions and Human Rights [ODIHR], 2008). Historically, rhetorical and physical manifestations of anti-Semitism have been directed towards Jewish individuals or their property, Jewish community institutions, and their religious facilities. Examples of contemporary anti-Semitism can be found in the media, in schools, in the workplace, and in the religious sphere. According to the Anti-Semitism Worldwide Report (2007), anti-Semitic manifestations have become an increasingly pervasive phenomenon in European countries.

The Anti-Semitism Worldwide Report also introduces the term *Islamophobia*, which refers to expressions against anything Muslim (Said, 1994). Over the last 20 years or so, in various countries, including Afghanistan, Turkey, Algeria, Singapore, the Netherlands, the United Kingdom, Bosnia, and Canada, Islamic female clothing and the interpretation of Islamic law have become the focus not only of political debates and legal battles, but also of political aggression. For example, the Netherlands is known as one of the most tolerant nations in the world, but the murder of the extreme right-wing Dutch filmmaker Theo van Gogh in 2004 by a Muslim immigrant of Moroccan origin, Mohammed Bouyeri, challenged this image (Buruma, 2007). At the time of the murder, van Gogh collaborated with Ayaan Hirsi Ali in making the film *Submission*, which attempted to demonstrate that the Quran considers women to be fundamentally inferior to men. Ayaan Hirsi Ali is a Somali refugee and former Muslim, who argued against Islam in the name of women's emancipation. Following the murder of van Gogh, a number of mosques were assaulted with racist symbols, and an Islamic school was burnt down. Although the intensity of the incidents decreased soon afterwards, the sense that ethnic/religious conflict existed in this multicultural country remained. Dutch opposition to Muslims living in the Netherlands was on the rise. Similarly, in April 2007, the local imam and his pregnant wife in Kostroma, Russia, who were both dressed in traditional Muslim clothing, were approached, pushed, and beaten in the street by two youths who demanded that they leave Russia. Crimes of this kind are sometimes justified by their perpetrators through historical grievances and inter-ethnic hatred.

Further online reading The following article can be accessed for free on the book's companion website https://study.sagepub.com/liu2e: Schulz, Markus S. (2006) 'Transnational conflicts: Central America, social change, and globalization', *International Sociology*, 21(2): 425–427.

THEORY CORNER

ORIENTALISM

Edward Said is a well-known Palestinian scholar and author of a highly influential book, *Orientalism* (Said, 1994). The book offers the classical framework for understanding relationships between the 'West' and the 'Rest' – Muslims in the Middle East. Based on his analysis of the works of painters, historians, linguists, archaeologists, travellers, and colonial bureaucrats, Said demonstrates the links between knowledge and power in the context of the relationship between Western and Muslim societies. Said argues that European domination is not only about political and economic interests, but also about cultural power. He created the term 'Orientalism', which refers to a specific kind of discourse that fosters the difference between the familiar (Europe, the West, 'us', the democratic and civilized) and the strange (the Orient, the East, 'them', the uncivilized and barbaric).

Orientalism, Said contends, rests upon four dogmas. Firstly, the Orient is undeveloped and inferior, while the West is rational, developed, humane, and superior. Secondly, the Orient lives according to rules inscribed in its sacred texts, rather than in response to the changing demands of life. Thirdly, the Orient is eternal, uniform, and incapable of defining itself, thereby justifying the vocabulary used by the West to describe it. Finally, the Orient is either something to be feared (e.g., Islamic terrorism) or something to be controlled by pacification, occupation, or development. Said's theory is particularly illuminating when one examines the Western media's negative representations of the Middle East, Arabs, and Islam.

Reference
Said, Edward (1994) *Orientalism*. New York: Vintage Books.

Further reading on Orientalism
Cooper, Melinda (2008) 'Orientalism in the mirror: the sexual politics of anti-Westernism', *Theory, Culture & Society*, 25(4): 25–49.

Theory in Practice

THE ROLE OF CINEMA IN REPRESENTING SPAIN'S INTERNAL OTHER

Scholars have applied Said's theory of Orientalism to explain how this discourse creates stereotypes and how politics is significantly intertwined with discourse. One illustration is the use of films to highlight the construction of 'us' and 'them' in Spain. According to Loxham (2014), Spain has a diverse regional make-up of 17 autonomous communities enshrined in the constitution of 1978, and also faces a dilemma of how to deal with the legacies of Franco's dictatorship (1939–1975). In practice, some regions have a strongly separate national/regional identity based on customs, traditions, fiestas, sport, regional variations in food, and a strong sense of affiliation to local traditions and specific geographical sites. Those identities, which have been violently suppressed or marginalized at various points during Spain's history, have been manifested through cultural production to interrogate what it might mean to be Spanish or the Other, and, specifically, as a way of dealing with (continuing) conflicts and the traumatic past.

A good example of a representation of the cultural identities and conflicts between different regions in Spain is the work of the Catalan filmmaker Bigas Luna, and the films he made in the 1990s: *Golden Balls* and *The Tit* and *The Moon*. In Catalonia, the strength of feeling towards a separate and distinct Catalan identity is manifested in its language, its political movements, and its cultural production of films. All of Bigas Luna's films present a humorous and sometimes extreme challenge to the notions of hegemonic national identity. National Spanish identity was propagated during the Franco dictatorship and has been repeated by a succession of governments in an attempt to ensure the national unity of Spain and in the hope of nurturing a sense of national unity. Thus, films as cultural forms can highlight the ways in which the nation is constructed and the problems and paradoxes in this construction.

Questions to take you further

Do you consider cinema as having the potential to trigger public debates about violence and intercultural conflict? Can you think of a film that powerfully represents violent conflict? Can the mass media be used to represent political conflicts and tensions? If so, how?

Reference

Loxham, Abigail (2014) *Cinema at the Edges: New Encounters with Julio Medem, Bigas Luna and José Luis Guerín*. New York: Berghahn Books.

Further reading on the role of cinema in dealing with conflict

Ruby, Jay (1991) 'Speaking for, speaking about, speaking with, or speaking alongside – an anthropological and documentary dilemma', *Visual Anthropology Review*, 7(2): 50–67.

Critical thinking…

The process of 'dealing with the past' for a conflict-ridden country usually needs to happen on a number of different levels, from the micro-level of an individual to the macro-level of national, regional, and international political bodies. Can you identify some challenges that a country might face in 'dealing with the past'?

Political, territorial, and economic disputes

Intercultural conflict can arise from political disputes over territory, economic control over resources, inequalities, and cultural disputes over language and religion. For example, the violent conflict in Palestine represents a political dispute over territory. Historically, the most fundamental bonding among various Jewish groups was the Zionist dream of building a Jewish state in Palestine, the Promised Land, as the traditional saying of 'Next year in Jerusalem' shows (Hestroni, 2000). Zionists began buying land and settling throughout Palestine in the late nineteenth century and continued doing so after the establishment of Israel in 1948. Zionists thought of Palestine as desolate, despite the fact that Palestinians lived there. This point is especially important in understanding the continuing conflict between Jews and Arabs over this land, with each side seeing it as their people's homeland. The conflict did not cease with the establishment of Israel in 1948, but still continues today, and is the basis for a great deal of intercultural conflict throughout the region. Meanwhile, the land has become a central component in Jewish identity and the Israeli national identity.

In addition to territorial claims, international and intercultural conflict can occur as a result of prohibiting people from speaking their own language. For example, the rise in the status and usage of the English language in Wales coincided with the gradual disappearance of the Welsh language, a policy that was supported by state institutions. In one instance, Welsh children were forced to speak English at school and were punished for speaking Welsh. In recent times, a movement for the resurgence of the Welsh language, accompanied by Welsh nationalism, has reversed this decline to some extent. Today, the number of speakers of Welsh as a first language is rising. The devolution of political power in the UK has meant that Welsh now has a higher status and is supported by state institutions in Wales, which has also helped in the revival of Welsh. Now cultural icons like Bryn Terfel and Katherine Jenkins promote Welsh identity throughout the world, demonstrating the possibility of a peaceful rather than violent reclaiming of cultural status.

Photo 11.2.   Both Arabs and Jews claim the old city of Jerusalem as 'theirs'.
Copyright © Helga Tawil-Souri. Used with permission.

Economic issues can also underlie intercultural conflicts. Such conflicts are often expressed through cultural differences and through blaming minorities (e.g., immigrants) for economic pressure in a society. The prejudice and stereotypes that lead to such intercultural conflict frequently result from perceived economic threat and competition. In a study conducted in Australia, Anglo-Australians were found to view cultural diversity and equal societal participation as more of a threat than a benefit, as compared with the ratings on the same items by Asian immigrants (Liu, 2007). In particular, Asian immigrants were viewed by Australians more than by Asian immigrants as a burden to the economy of the host country and a threat to host nationals in a competitive job market.

Political, territorial, and economic disputes begin when a society fails to provide reasonable equality for various groups of citizens. Towards the end of the last century, scholarly works in the area of intercultural and international conflicts became prominent in addressing the relationship between conflict and concepts such as identity, culture, history, and the nation-state. Many of them addressed these relationships in the aftermath of the immense social changes in the world at the end of the twentieth century. For example, the fall of the Berlin Wall, the collapse of the Soviet Union, the end of apartheid in South Africa, and the civil war in the Balkans signified the end of an era marked by high tensions between nations advocating different concepts of social order and development. Today, more than ever before, there are claims for the recognition of ethnic and cultural identities in the rapidly changing international cultural environments, fuelled by increasingly complex flows of cultural and economic goods (Erjavec and Volčič, 2007).

CONFLICT STAGES AND CONFLICT MANAGEMENT APPROACHES AND STYLES

Stages in the conflict process

Individuals, groups, or nations do not move suddenly from peaceful co-existence to conflict. Rather, as Louis Pondy (1967) indicates, people move through stages as conflict develops and subsides (see Table 11.1). According to Pondy, the first phase, *latent conflict*, involves a situation in which the conditions are ripe for conflict because incompatibilities and interdependence exist between the two parties. The second phase, *perceived conflict*, occurs when one or more of the parties believe that incompatibilities exist. It is possible to have latent conflict without perceived conflict. For example, two ethnic groups have different value orientations about the relationship between humans and nature. This difference in worldviews may not be an issue for either group, unless there is a need for them to reach a consensus about how to conquer drought: to pray for rain or to use cloud-seeding technology. During the third phase, *felt conflict*, the parties begin to formulate strategies about how to deal with the conflict, and to consider outcomes that would or would not be acceptable. These strategies and goals are enacted in communication during the *manifest phase*. Finally, the last phase discussed by Pondy is *conflict aftermath*, which emphasizes that conflicts can have both short-term and long-term consequences. Even after a manifest conflict is concluded, the conflict can change the nature of the interactants' relationship and functioning in the future.

An illustration of the development of a conflict is the dispute between German nudists and Polish puritans on the Baltic Sea island of Usedom (Boussouar and Mailliet, 2008). Straddling the border between Germany and Poland, Usedom is divided into German and Polish parts. For over 50 years, nudist beaches have been the norm on the German side, as naked bathing is not considered unusual in Germany (latent conflict). However, the removal of border controls between Germany and Poland as part of the Schengen agreement in January 2008 has enabled Polish people to stroll along the leafy coastal paths to nearby German towns, so that they notice the nudist beaches (perceived conflict). Many are shocked by what

Table 11.1   Stages of the Conflict Process

Stages	Characteristics
Latent conflict	Conditions are ripe for conflict because incompatible goals and interdependence exist between parties.
Perceived conflict	One or more parties believe incompatible goals and interdependence exist.
Felt conflict	Parties begin to focus on conflict issues and formulate strategies to deal with the conflict.
Manifest conflict	Conflict and conflict strategies are enacted through communication between parties.
Conflict aftermath	Conflict seems 'settled'. However, it has short-term or long-term effects on the relationship between the conflicting parties.

Source: Pondy, Louis R. (1967) 'Organizational conflict: concepts and models', *Administrative Science Quarterly*, 12: 296–320.

they see (felt conflict). For the Polish people, nude sunbathing where people go walking is unacceptable. Poland is approximately 80 per cent Catholic, which has influenced their views on nudist bathing; a Polish national remarked: 'It's horrible, we would never bathe naked, we are Catholic.' While nude bathing can lead to a fine in Poland, for Germans of all ages who enjoy swimming and sunbathing on naturist beaches, the disapproving glances from Polish walkers are incomprehensible and intrusive (manifest conflict). Hence, the island of Usedom has become a site of a culture clash – the centre of a conflict of values. Both Poles and Germans cheered in December 2007, when the barbed-wire border was dismantled as part of the Schengen agreement; the cultural walls, however, are more difficult to demolish. As a temporary resolution, authorities plan to put up signs marking the boundaries of the nudist beach in both German and Polish (conflict aftermath). Clearly, if this conflict is not managed properly, in the long term it may have international repercussions.

Further online reading   The following article can be accessed for free on the book's companion website https://study.sagepub.com/liu2e: Sameeksha, Desai, Zoltan J. Acs and Utz Weitzel (2013) 'A model of destructive entrepreneurship: insight for conflict and post-conflict recovery', *Journal of Conflict Resolution*, 57(1): 20–40.

Conflict management approaches

Two major approaches are evident in the literature on intercultural conflict. The first is *conflict as normal*. This approach views any type of conflict as an opportunity to grow and as a chance to develop and build relationships. Advocates of the conflict-as-normal approach believe that working through conflicts provides potential benefits, including acquiring new information about other people or groups, and increasing the overall integrity and cohesiveness of the parties involved. Therefore, conflict can be understood as a renegotiation of contracts, and should be celebrated. With this in mind, individuals should be encouraged to think of creative solutions to conflict situations. The most desirable response is to recognize and work through conflict in an open and constructive manner. The second approach is *conflict as destructive*. This approach views conflict as unproductive, negative, destructive, and dangerous for relationships. Ting-Toomey (1994) suggests that the conflict-as-normal orientation grows from an attempt to protect an individual, while the conflict-as-destructive orientation arises from a higher value being attributed to maintaining harmony in relationships and saving another's face. She differentiated two basic concerns in managing conflict: concern for one's own face and concern for the other's face. These dimensions describe the motivational orientations of individuals or groups. Augsburger (1992) summarizes four main assumptions underlying each approach (see Table 11. 2).

Table 11.2   Assumptions Underlying Conflict Approaches

Approach	Assumptions
Conflict as normal	Conflict is normal and useful.
	All issues are subject to change through negotiation.
	Direct confrontation is valuable.
	Conflict always represents a renegotiation of contract, a release of tensions, and a renewal of relationships.
Conflict as destructive	Conflict is a destructive disturbance to peaceful situations.
	The social system should not be adjusted to the needs of its members, but rather, members of a society need to adapt to the established values.
	Confrontations are destructive and ineffective.
	Agents involved in a conflict should be disciplined.

Source: Augsburger, David (1992) *Conflict Mediation across Cultures*. Louisville, KY: Westminster/John Knox Press.

The Amish, for example, see conflict not as an opportunity for individual growth, but as a distress to their community. Legal and personal confrontations tend to be avoided because the use of force is discouraged in the Amish culture. Similarly, in Chinese culture, harmony in social relationships (interpersonal, intergroup, interorganizational, or international) is valued. A Chinese saying, 'Everything prospers in a harmonious family', reflects the belief that conflict should be reduced, if not avoided, as it disturbs harmony. Cultural groups that view conflict as destructive often avoid direct confrontation in a conflict situation and may instead seek to use a third party in order to avoid direct confrontation and save face. Third-party intervention may be informal, such as when a friend is asked to intervene, or formal, such as when legal or expert assistance is sought. This 'peacemaking' approach to conflict values harmony and protection of face in conflict resolution.

Conflict management styles

The way conflicts are addressed can vary considerably from culture to culture. These differences relate to the degree to which disagreement is acceptable; the extent to which conflict is tolerated; the preferred means of dealing with conflict; and the moment when intervention is needed. Conflict management styles are strategies people adopt to handle a conflict. The application of different conflict strategies leads to different outcomes. Blake and Mouton (1964) first classified five conflict management styles: avoiding, competing, accommodating, compromising, and collaborating. *Avoiding* is the physical withdrawal or refusal to discuss the conflict. *Competing* is linked to the use of power to gain one's objectives, even though it means ignoring the needs of the opponent. Competing is highly assertive and does not require cooperation. The outcome of this strategy is that you win and the other person loses. *Accommodating* refers to behaviours that conceal or play down differences by emphasizing common interests. If you chose to apply an accommodating strategy, you would sacrifice your own interest to satisfy that of the other party; that is, you lose and the other party wins. *Compromising* aims to find a midpoint between the opposing parties – both parties involved in a conflict try to work out a solution so that everyone gets something, although no one party may get everything. Compromising involves both assertiveness and cooperation, and is a popular way to resolve conflicts because neither side wins or loses. In the *collaborating* strategy, conflict agents are encouraged to find a solution where both sides can win. It is considered the ideal way to handle conflict in most situations, but it is not often used because it requires much time, a willingness to negotiate, assertiveness, and cooperation, and not all conflicts have win-win solutions.

Here is an example to illustrate the application of the five conflict strategies in resolving an interpersonal conflict. Imagine that your boss has informed you that your advertising firm has just signed a contract to produce a television commercial for a toy manufacturing factory. You and one of your colleagues need to work on Saturday in order to get the draft proposal ready for a meeting with your client on Monday. However, neither you nor your colleague wants to work on the weekend because you both have other plans. If you want to maximize your own interest, you could exercise your power as the project team leader to force your colleague to work long hours on Saturday, while you stay home fulfilling your personal commitments (a competing strategy). On the other hand, if you wish to sacrifice your own interest in order to show concern for your colleague, who has a birthday party scheduled over the weekend, you could come to the office to work instead of your colleague (an accommodating strategy). Finally, you could talk with your colleague to see whether you could each work for half a day or evening and free some time over the weekend to accomplish the task, which might (or might not) allow you both to complete your personal plans as well (a compromising or, if you are lucky, collaborating strategy). The application of different conflict styles requires different levels of assertiveness and cooperation from the conflict parties.

Critical thinking...

Do you focus on your face or others' face when you communicate with others in a conflict situation? What is your preferred conflict management strategy, and why? Which strategies are likely to have the most serious consequences? Which are the most likely to be effective in resolving intergroup conflicts?

INFLUENCE OF CULTURE ON CONFLICT MANAGEMENT

In any conflict there are different levels of engagement, as well as different aspects that are elevated; thus determining what gets acknowledged and what gets resolved is the first step in conflict management (Fisher-Yoshida, 2005). Culture shapes perceptions and choice of alternatives, and influences conflict outcomes (Pedersen and Jandt, 1996). Understanding how culture influences conflict management strategies helps us to achieve better outcomes.

Further online reading The following article can be accessed for free on the book's companion website https://study.sagepub.com/liu2e: Mae-Li, Allison and Tara Emmers-Sommer (2011) 'Beyond individualism–collectivism and conflict style: considering acculturation and media use', *Journal of Intercultural Communication Research*, 40(2): 135–152.

Cultural dimensions and conflict management

Photo 11.3   Protestors in Bil'in, Palestine, march on the separation barrier during a weekly protest against ongoing Israeli development. Copyright © Alison Rae. Used with permission.

Ting-Toomey (1994) identified the individualism–collectivism dimension (also see Chapter 5) as one of the key cultural variables in the management of intercultural conflict. In individualistic cultures, independence, freedom, privacy, and self-esteem are considered important (Triandis, 1995); thus, conflict strategies tend to be goal-oriented, focusing on problem solving, and communication is direct. On the other hand, in collectivistic cultures people are willing to sacrifice some personal interest in order to maintain good relationships with others during conflict, and may choose accommodating or avoiding communication styles. Okabe (1983) found that Americans tend to use explicit words like 'certainly', 'absolutely', and 'positively' in interactions, whereas Japanese prefer to use implicit and less assertive expressions, such as 'maybe', 'perhaps', and 'somewhat'. In conflict management, people from individualistic cultures therefore tend to state their own position directly, defend their ground, and justify their decisions. People from collectivistic cultures, by contrast, tend to express their views indirectly (e.g., 'Maybe what I said is incorrect, but …'; 'Perhaps we could do it this way …'; 'Let's not consider this for the time being…'). In such situations, it is up to the other party to work out the underlying meaning and intention of the speaker.

Critical thinking…

In individualistic cultures, conflict is likely to occur when individuals' expectations of appropriate behaviours are violated. Conflict in collectivistic cultures is more likely to occur when the group's normative expectations for behaviours are violated. What adjustments do individualists have to make to manage conflicts successfully with collectivists, and vice versa?

Cultural context and mediation

Conflict management strategies are not meaningful unless they are understood in the context of culturally learned expectations (Liu and Chen, 2002). It is important to interpret behaviour in terms of its intended expectations and values, consistent with its context, because context stimulates, sustains, and supports behaviour. Conflict strategies that are not sensitive to each culture's unique context are not likely to succeed. Merry (1989) describes how mediation practices across cultures are dependent upon context, where the process rather than the substance of agreement becomes the focus. In every culture, there are 'conflict transformers' who help disputants to think in new ways about the conflict in an atmosphere of mutual respect. For example, an elder or the chief of a village may be brought in to resolve a dispute between two villages or between two villagers. Mediation also occurs between two nations. The promise of a Palestinian nation, for instance, was 'born' at the signing of the Oslo Accords on 13 September 1993 (Oslo I) – a pledge of peace between Israel and the Palestinians – as a result of mediation by the international community. Subsequently, between then and the outbreak of the Second Intifada seven years later, state-building and development efforts were significant in the territories. This example illustrates the potential positive outcome of mediation in a conflict situation.

Cultural values and negotiation

Conflict management, to a certain extent, is negotiation in order to reach a solution that satisfies both sides. Lewicki et al. (2003) identified eight aspects through which cultural values can exert influence on the effectiveness of negotiation: (1) the way the negotiation is defined; (2) the parties at the negotiating table; (3) the protocol that is followed; (4) the style of communication; (5) the time frame; (6) the perception of risk; (7) whether the negotiation is group or individual; and (8) the way the agreement is shaped and enforced. These factors highlight the intricacies of addressing conflicts when the parties involved frame the conflict according to different cultural values. For example, in individualistic cultures, conflicts can be resolved directly through face-to-face negotiations. In more collectivistic cultures, this may not be possible. Rather, a third party may need to perform a type of shuttle diplomacy between the conflicting parties, guiding them towards a resolution. It is worthy of mention that third-party intervention is employed in both individualistic and collectivistic cultures, but the nature and role of the third party is different. In more individualistic cultures, the third party is usually a neutral mediator who guides the resolution process without adding his or her own beliefs. In collectivistic cultures, the mediator is more likely to be a known and trusted person who is expected to recommend the desired course of action.

THEORY CORNER

TRANSITIONAL JUSTICE AND INTERCULTURAL CONFLICT

Transitional justice refers to a range of approaches that cultures undertake to deal with legacies of widespread or systematic human rights abuses as they move from a period of violent conflict or oppression towards peace, democracy, the rule of law, and respect for individual and collective rights. It also refers to the short-term and often temporary judicial and non-judicial mechanisms that address the legacy of conflicts during a specific culture's transition away from conflict or authoritarian rule.

In making a transition towards peace, cultures must confront the painful legacy of the past in order to achieve a holistic sense of justice for all citizens, establish or renew civic trust, reconcile people and communities, and prevent future abuses (Simic and Volčič, 2013). All stakeholders in the transition process must be consulted and participate in the design and implementation of transitional justice policies. The approaches to transitional justice are based on a fundamental belief in universal human rights. The major approaches to transitional justice include: domestic and international prosecutions of perpetrators of human rights abuse; determining the full extent and nature of past abuses through truth-telling initiatives; providing reparations to victims of human rights violations, including compensatory, rehabilitative, and symbolic reparations; promoting reconciliation within divided communities; and constructing memorials and museums to preserve the memory of the past.

Reference

Simic, Olivera and Zala Volčič (2013) *Transitional Justice and Civil Society in the Balkans*. New York: Springer.

Further reading on transitional justice

Orentlicher, Diane (2007) '"Settling accounts" revisited: reconciling global norms with local agency', *International Journal of Transitional Justice*, 1(1): 10–22.

Theory in Practice

TRANSITIONAL JUSTICE IN THE SOLOMON ISLANDS

In late 1998 the Solomon Islands was plunged into a period of violent civil conflict, precipitated by a complex web of grievances, injustices, ethnic tensions, and economic insecurities. The conflict continued until the middle of 2003, leaving some 200 people dead, more than 20,000 displaced from their homes, and numerous others subjected to torture, rape, fear, and intimidation. On 24 July 2003, the Australian-led Regional Assistance Mission to the Solomon Islands (RAMSI) arrived in the capital Honiara. In an attempt to restore law and order, RAMSI facilitated the arrests of more than 700 individuals who were accused of committing serious offences, including murder and human rights violations. Jeffery (2013) examined this case, which sheds a unique light on the debates surrounding transitional justice.

Despite the fact that RAMSI's actions created the initial impression of swift justice for human rights violations, questions emerged regarding whether the mission had in fact contributed to a new set of tensions between the 'rule of law' approach and the 'reconciliation' approach. The 'rule of law' approach is a top-down approach that favours the strengthening of key state institutions and the pursuit of accountability through criminal justice. The 'reconciliation' approach is a bottom-up method of post-conflict justice that is preferred by large sectors of the local community. In the Solomon Islands, those localized traditional practices were routinely implemented by community groups, women's organizations, and the churches throughout the post-conflict recovery period. Jeffery's study shows that in the absence of a formally planned transitional justice process those two approaches came into serious tension. Supporters of prosecution argued that reconciliation processes limited the possibility of achieving accountability, whereas supporters of reconciliation argued that the nature of the criminal justice system did not resolve tension or help recovery.

Questions to take you further

Do you think transitional justice should be directed from above or it should be encouraged to emerge from the grassroots? Why?

Reference

Jeffery, Renee (2013) 'Enduring tensions: transitional justice in the Solomon Islands', *Pacific Review*, 26(2): 153–175.

Further reading on transitional justice in practice

Subotic, Jelena (2009) 'The paradox of international justice compliance', *International Journal of Transitional Justice*, 3(3): 362–382.

Effective management of intercultural conflict

Culture influences how conflict is perceived and interpreted; effective intercultural conflict management therefore requires intercultural awareness and sensitivity (Chen and Starosta, 2005). In *Managing Cultural Differences*, Harris and Morgan (1987: 257) proposed a five-step method of managing intercultural conflict, based on their study of British and American business people. The five steps are: (1) describe the conflict in a way understood in both cultures; (2) analyse the conflict from both cultural perspectives; (3) identify the basis for the conflict from two cultural viewpoints; (4) resolve the conflict though synergistic strategies; and (5) determine if the solution is working interculturally. For example, American culture values hard work, competition, personal achievement, and determination. From an American perspective, British business people can appear to lack an aggressive approach and the ability to engage in competition. From the British perspective, however, American business people seem impatient and too eager to prove themselves to their superiors. To sacrifice the quality of their life simply to be more efficient may not seem worthwhile to the British. This conflict may best be resolved through the use of synergistic strategies, which refer to 'a dynamic process in which the opposing parties combine their actions by adapting and learning different viewpoints through empathy and sensitivity' (Chen and Starosta, 2005). This will involve becoming more aware of the other culture's values and the priorities set on them.

Critical thinking...

What role can mediation, healing, reconciliation, and forgiveness potentially play in enabling communities to transform their attitudes and behaviours towards other cultures? Do you think building trust and creating a safe space in which people are able to express their emotions are also a crucial part of conflict management?

Ting-Toomey (1994) provides specific suggestions for effective conflict management in individualistic and collectivistic cultures. For people from individualistic cultures operating in a collectivistic cultural context, Ting-Toomey provided seven suggestions to help manage conflict effectively: (1) understand the opponent's face-maintenance assumptions in order to keep a balance between humility and pride and between shame and honour in communication; (2) save the opponent's face by carefully using informal consultation or a go-between to deal with low-grade conflicts before they fall irrevocably into face-losing situations; (3) give face to opponents by not pushing them into a corner with no leeway for recovering face; (4) avoid using too much verbal expression, and learn how to manage conflicts by effectively reading implicit and nonverbal messages; (5) be empathetic by listening attentively and respecting the opponent's needs; (6) put aside the explicit and direct communication skills practised in the West and learn to use an indirect communication style; and (7) tolerate the opponent's tendency to avoid facing the conflict by being patient, thereby maintaining a harmonious atmosphere and mutual dignity. These strategies have been widely applied in academic research and practice.

Communication is the means through which conflict is defined, managed, and resolved. Based on the literature, we propose the following communication strategies.

Focus on common ground and reduce disagreement. Intercultural conflict occurs because of the incompatibility of goals, interests, resources, values, expectations, processes, or outcomes. Our attempts to establish and maintain intercultural relationships sometimes fail because others dislike what we like, or vice versa. One way to restore balance in the relationship is to seek commonalities by emphasizing a shared goal of accomplishing a task, or a common desire to restore peace or get a fair share of the resources. Emphasis on common ground fosters positive attitudes which, in turn, can ease tension and reduce negative feelings or stereotypes.

Practise relational empathy. Relational empathy refers to seeing the issue from the perspective of the other party. Relational empathy skills, such as active listening, form the starting point for the conflict management process (Dodd, 1998). Mindful listening involves the process of interpreting the attitudes, emotions, and values underpinning spoken messages. To understand our own and others' deeply held cultural values and to engage those values in a culturally appropriate way are important in effective conflict management.

Develop a positive communication climate. Conflict is more likely to be resolved effectively in a positive communication climate. During the process of conflict negotiation, both parties should avoid emotional presentations such as angry or insulting remarks. Another way to build a good communication climate is to deal with one issue at a time. Although intercultural conflicts can be the result of historical grievances and long-standing hatred, bringing up too many unresolved issues at one time may obscure the present question or escalate the conflict.

SUMMARY

- There are several potential sources of intercultural conflict: racial violence, ingroup/outgroup bias, historical grievances and ethnic hatred, and political, territorial, and economic disputes.

- Communication is the means by which conflicts are defined and resolved. Intercultural miscommunication lies at the heart of intercultural conflict management.

- Intercultural conflict occurs at multiple levels – interpersonal, intergroup, interorganizational, interethnic, and international. The intensity of an intercultural conflict can range from individual acts of disrespect, localized, short-lived riots, and group violence up to large-scale violence and war.

- There are five conflict management styles: avoiding, competing, accommodating, compromising, and collaborating.

- It is important to recognize the impact of the cultural context in which a conflict is situated, and to develop culturally appropriate strategies for managing conflict effectively.

- As conflict is pervasive in all social relationships, we need to identify potential sources of intercultural conflict and apply appropriate strategies to resolve conflicts.

JOIN THE DEBATE

When can conflict lead to productive and positive outcomes in workplaces?

Generally, we view conflict in the workplace as negative. Common sources of conflict include poor communication, resource ambiguity, personality clashes, structural problems, and poor leadership. However, when properly addressed and managed, conflict can provide positive results in the workplace. Productive conflict, also known as meaningful conflict, is important for problem solving and for developing positive workplace relationships. For example, members of a workgroup may hold different opinions on how to increase productivity without increasing the number of workers in the group. If they can engage in open and constructive discussion about different options, they may arrive at creative solutions to the problem. Overall, meaningful conflict helps to identify problems and foster creative solutions, enables issues to be prioritized, and makes people aware of the positive outcomes as a result of individual differences. Meaningful conflict can also help to identify potential future leaders – people who are willing to state their argument, justify their position, and demonstrate leadership ability to get their messages across in clear and persuasive ways. If everyone agreed with each other all the time, there would be no innovation and no new ways of doing things. How can managers and employees create a climate for conflict to lead to positive outcomes? How can managers reward meaningful conflict results?

CASE STUDY

Hollywood celebrity activism in war-torn societies

There is a current debate on the suitability of using celebrities for humanitarian activism, in a post-conflict context, although this idea is not new (Yrjölä, 2011). Goodwill Ambassadors have been used by the United Nations (UN) for more than 50 years. UNICEF appointed Danny Kaye, an American actor, singer, and comedian, as its first Goodwill Ambassador in 1953, and the UN agency has since recruited celebrities such as Whoopi Goldberg, Ricky Martin, Jackie Chan, and David Beckham, among others, as international ambassadors and advocates for its causes. When Kofi Annan was appointed UN Secretary General in 1997, he was particularly interested in recruiting Hollywood celebrities as Goodwill Ambassadors, in order to promote the UN's diplomatic agenda and to draw attention to development causes. His decision to employ more than 400 UN Goodwill Ambassadors by 2007, and to create a new type of celebrity activist programme, *Messengers of Peace*, signalled a new era for the UN. This era was heavily reliant upon popular trust in celebrity culture, amounting to a kind of a public relations revolution within international diplomatic spaces. Annan's hope was that celebrities would possess the power to help end violent conflicts or, at the very least, shape international public opinion in support of UN missions, to draw attention to its activities, and to raise awareness about the suffering of others during different conflicts (Wheeler, 2011).

Celebrity and global fame were Angelina Jolie's primary qualifications for being appointed to the United Nations High Commission for Refugees (UNHCR) as a celebrity diplomat in 2001 (Cooper, 2008). Jolie is both a Hollywood sex symbol and a globally famous figure. Throughout her career, Jolie's image has been transformed from that of a Hollywood wild woman, to an internationally credible celebrity peace ambassador. She was reported to be personally committed to 'saving the world' and has been heavily involved in celebrity activism in Africa, Cambodia, Pakistan, Ecuador, and Bosnia (Repo and Yrjölä 2011). If in 2001, Jolie still played the sexy action hero Lara Croft in *Tomb Raider*, she decided, ten years later, to become a passionate and emotional witness of human suffering. Endorsing diverse international campaigns and causes, she also directed the widely acclaimed 2011 film, *In the Land of Blood and Honey*, which is about war rapes in Bosnia and Herzegovina. Despite the mixed reviews of the film, Jolie has repeatedly said that her intention was to create a visual explanation of what happened during the Balkan wars.

Today, many celebrities have become well-recognized global activists in helping to bring peace to war-torn regions. In Bosnia and Herzegovina, for example, during and after the 1990s war, Bono, Richard Gere, Bianca Jagger, Princess Diana, and Mia Farrow, among others, used their celebrity to campaign for peace there. Wheeler (2011: 58) suggests that this 'celebritization of international politics' has led to celebrities becoming more politically active, linking 'high politics with a more populist approach to cultural citizenship'. The value of celebrities as activists is drawn from their public and media image, with the symbolism of their value as a 'media star' easily transferred to diplomacy, and vice versa. For example, Arnold Schwarzenegger seamlessly moved from movie star to a governor in the USA; and Peter Garrett moved from singer to politician in Australia (Pleios, 2011). It is not just the personification and familiarization of celebrities that lend them credibility and power across many societal fields; the channel through which they promote themselves and their ideas, the mass media, also play a vital role.

Research on the role of celebrity activism is growing, but remains highly diverse. On the one hand, diplomacy scholars such as Cooper (2008) argue that celebrity diplomats have become enormously successful in mobilizing attention, channelling support, and influencing international public policy. For Cooper, celebrity diplomats employ innovative practices and are a part of unofficial public diplomacy during and after conflicts. On the other hand, critical scholars see the emergence of celebrity activism as being linked to the emergence of a post-democratic order in which politics is transformed into a media spectacle that is only to be performed in front of an audience, while public opinion is reshaped and manipulated (Moyo, 2009). According to these accounts, the celebrity holds a false promise of the power of the individual to influence social change, and thereby reinforces a reductionist, individualist, and post-political politics. Scholars point to celebrity activism's impulse to reduce complex problems of development into forms of mediated entertainment. These scholars see celebrity activism as not promoting peace, or any other cause, but only the celebrities themselves.

References

Cooper, Andrew F. (2008) *Celebrity Diplomacy*. London: Paradigm.

Moyo, Dambisa (2009) *Dead Aid*. New York: Farrar, Straus and Giroux.

Pleios, George (2011) 'Fame and symbolic value in celebrity activism and diplomacy', in L. Tsaliki, C. A. Frangonikolopoulos and A. Huliaras (eds), *Transnational Celebrity Activism in Global Politics: Changing the World?* Bristol: Intellect. pp. 249–262.

Repo, Jemima and Yrjölä, Riina (2011) 'The gender politics of celebrity humanitarianism in Africa', *International Feminist Journal of Politics*, 13(1): 44–62.

Wheeler, Mark (2011) 'Celebrity politics and cultural citizenship: UN Goodwill Ambassadors and Messengers of Peace', in L. Tsaliki, C. A. Frangonikolopoulos and A. Huliaras (eds), *Transnational Celebrity Activism in Global Politics: Changing the World?* Bristol: Intellect. pp. 45–61.

Yrjölä, Riina (2011) 'The global politics of celebrity humanitarianism', in L. Tsaliki, C. A. Frangonikolopoulos and A. Huliaras (eds), *Transnational Celebrity Activism in Global Politics: Changing the World?* Bristol: Intellect. pp. 175–191.

Questions for discussion

1. What is your view on celebrity activism? Are there any unintended consequences of celebrity activism?

2. The challenge of rebuilding societies after conflict is much more complex and difficult than the task of putting an end to fighting. What measures can we take to prevent violent conflicts from happening?

3. One comment often heard in post-conflict contexts is that 'Law and order is here but peace is not in our hearts'. Do you think peace agreements can help stop violent conflicts? Do you have any examples to illustrate your points?

4. Who should be the focus of justice efforts: the perpetrators or the victims?

5. What communication strategies can be employed to help people in post-conflict regions to 'forgive and forget'? Or should we restore peace and order by criminal prosecutions? What role can mass media play in helping to restore peace and order in post-conflict regions?

FURTHER READINGS

All articles listed next to the mouse icon below can be accessed for free on the book's companion website: https://study.sagepub.com/liu2e

Conflict management strategies

Chouliaraki, Lilie (2006) *The Spectatorship of Suffering*. London: Sage.

This book is about the relationship between the spectators in the countries of the West and the distant sufferer on the television screen – the sufferer in Somalia, Nigeria, Bangladesh, India, Indonesia, but also from Paris, New York, and Washington, DC. How do we relate to television images of the distant sufferer? How do we understand mediated violence? The questions touch on the ethical role of the media, conflicts, and resolutions in public life today. The book addresses the issue of whether the media can cultivate a disposition of care for, and engagement with, the far-away Other: whether television can create a global public with a sense of social responsibility towards the distant sufferer.

Sameeksha, Desai, Zoltan J. Acs and Utz Weitzel (2013) 'A model of destructive entrepreneurship: insight for conflict and post-conflict recovery', *Journal of Conflict Resolution*, 57(1): 20–40.

The research on entrepreneurship as an economic phenomenon often assumes its desirability as a driver of economic development and growth. However, entrepreneurial talent can be allocated among productive, unproductive, and destructive activities. This allocation has important implications in the developing world, particularly for countries hosting conflict or recovering from conflict. The allocation of entrepreneurship is theorized as being driven by institutions. The authors developed a model of destructive entrepreneurship and identified four key propositions on the nature and behaviour of destructive entrepreneurship. They also suggested research agendas in relation to conflict and post-conflict recovery.

Intercultural and international conflict

Goodman, Amy and Denis Moynihan (2012) *The Silenced Majority: Stories, Uprisings, Occupation, Resistance, and Hope*. New York: Haymarket Books.

The authors, both journalists and media scholars, provide a vivid record of the international events, conflicts, and social movements shaping our society today. They give voice to ordinary people standing up to corporate and government power around the world. Their writing and daily work at the grassroots public TV/radio news hour *Democracy Now*, which is carried on more than 1,000 stations globally and at democracynow.org, casts in stark relief the stories of the silenced majority and major conflicts taking place today: the Afghanistan war, climate change, racism, class conflicts. These stories are set against the backdrop of the mainstream media's abject failure, with its small circle of pundits, who know so little about so much, attempting to explain the world to us and getting it so wrong.

Kunkeler, Josjah and Krijn Peters (2011) 'The boys are coming to town: youth, armed conflict and violence in developing countries', *International Journal of Conflict and Violence*, 5(2): 277– 291.

This article analyses violent youth conflicts in (West) African and Latin American cities, extrapolating findings to the case of Freetown, Sierra Leone. Drawing on ethnographic research, the authors suggest that much of today's urban youth violence, particularly in third-world cities, should be interpreted (conceptually) as armed conflict. Those conflicts are characterized by high levels of organization and are the product of the socioeconomic marginalization of young people. The authors indicate that young people are major participants in contemporary intra-state armed conflicts. Since the end of the Cold War there has been a trend to portray these as criminal violence for private (economic) ends, rather than as politically or ideologically motivated. Hence, the perception of young people's role has moved from 'freedom fighters' to 'violent criminals'. The authors conclude that urban and rural youth violence in developing countries cannot be separated from its political roots.

Peters, John D. (2001) 'Witnessing', *Media, Culture & Society*, 23(6): 707–723.

In this article, Peters deals with questions of conflict, trauma, media, communication, and witnessing. Witnessing is a common but rarely examined term in both the professional performance and academic analysis of media events and conflicts. His article explores the practice of witnessing in general to clarify such problems in media studies as veracity, reliability, responsibility, trauma, and historicity. The long history of puzzlement and prescription about proper witnessing that developed in oral and print cultures is a rich resource for reflection about some of the ambiguities of audiovisual media. Peters traces the genealogy of the different discursive domains through which witnessing has been historically constituted – law, theology, and atrocity – and makes a critical distinction that enables 'bearing witness' to be distinguished from 'eye-witnessing'.

> *'The media is the most powerful entity on earth. They have the power to make the innocent guilty and to make the guilty innocent, and that's power. Because they control the minds of the masses.*

Malcolm X, American black leader, 1925–1965

12

MASS MEDIA, TECHNOLOGY, AND CULTURAL CHANGE

LEARNING OBJECTIVES

At the end of this chapter, you should be able to:

- Describe the impact of globalization on mass media in the digital age.

- Explain how mass media shape our thinking, doing, identities, and communication.

- Understand the influence of social media on traditional media and cultural change.

- Analyse the relationship between media and culture.

INTRODUCTION

Mass media are all around us, playing a significant role in producing and representing our cultures. Almost all aspects of our everyday life – from food to clothing, housing, education, entertainment, and transportation – are affected by the mass media. Media not only bring us news, but also function as sources of education, entertainment, and identity construction. McLuhan (1964) states that as the hammer extends our arm and the wheel extends our legs and feet, the mass media extend our connection to parts of the world where our physical bodies cannot reach. Mass media shape our thinking, doing, and being. For example, we often judge others by the types of media they consume – the newspapers they read, the movies and television programmes they watch, and the internet sites they visit. By extending our connections to the rest of the world, mass media can promote better understanding, appreciation, and connections between different cultures and facilitate intercultural communication. Mass media can also achieve the opposite: increasing misunderstanding, fear, and antagonism through the repetition of negative stereotypes about ethnic origin, age, gender, sexuality, and religion.

Questions about the reach and influence of media also link to wider global issues. For example, what happens when media cross national and cultural boundaries? What role do the mass media play in our seeing and understanding the world? What happens when a Western television programme is imported into a non-Western context? Becker (2004) studied the effects of mass media on teenage girls in Fiji. Before being introduced to television, the girls had little awareness of the Western 'ideal' thin body shape. However, after several months of viewing American television programmes and its representations of successful, attractive, and thin women, the Fijian girls began to feel that their body shape was too large to be successful and employable. This example shows that media representations of powerful foreign (in this case Western) ideals of beauty influence people's perceptions of themselves and others, even in a distant part of the world.

This chapter focuses on the role of mass media in intercultural communication. We first describe the impact of globalization on mass media in the digital age. We then explain how mass media function to construct our symbolic social reality, which in turn shapes our communication and identities. The role of social media and social networking is discussed as well as the influence of the media on cultural change. Based on this analysis, this chapter suggests ways to develop skills in understanding media and culture.

GLOBALIZATION, TECHNOLOGY, AND MASS MEDIA

Few would dispute that we live in a much more interconnected world today, and at the core of interconnectivity is globalization. Globalization is a complex process involving rapid social change that occurs simultaneously across a number of dimensions (economy, politics, communication, physical environment, culture). Each of these transformations interacts with the others. The functions of mass media in the digital age are shaped by globalization. Just think of social networking websites that have become an integral medium for communicating within and about intercultural relationships. Facebook has become ubiquitous, with over 1 billion active monthly users worldwide, including 74 per cent of adolescents and young adults (aged 12–24 years) (Miller, 2011). Among various social media, cell phones (or mobile phones) may be the most pervasive medium across the world today. A recent survey indicated that 85 per cent of American adults have a cell phone, while 75 per cent use the internet (Pew Internet, 2010). Thanks to cell phones' portability, people can satisfy their information needs anytime and anywhere.

Further online reading The following article can be accessed for free on the book's companion website https://study.sagepub.com/liu2e: Yesim, Kaptan (2013) 'We just know! Tacit knowledge and knowledge production in the Turkish advertising industry', *Journal of Consumer Culture*, 13(3): 264–282.

Globalizing the mass media

Mass media, even radio and film with their broad reach, were largely local and national until well into the twentieth century. Now, increasing connections and interdependencies among institutions and people around the world direct our attention to media globalization as a central phenomenon of the contemporary era. In particular, the rapid spread of digital media has been credited with many worldwide social, political, cultural, and economic changes. All societies are now part of a global system connected by a range of communication networks. The global media culture has manifested itself through a variety of signifiers, such as the Barbie doll, McDonald's fast food, Coca-Cola, MTV, Baywatch, YouTube, and even beauty contests such as 'Miss World'. The international reach of media has opened exciting new vistas of a global village. Television, satellite dishes, computers, and the internet open new borders around the world. Mass communication has become a vehicle for globally relevant media events. This feature testifies to the overwhelming success of the mass media, which allow people around the world to witness and experience the same event simultaneously: the Olympics, crises, famine, war, conflicts, earthquakes, and presidential elections.

The rise of global media is closely tied to technology. Two media technologies – radio and motion pictures – contributed very significantly to the rise of global media. As early as 1914, 85 per cent of the world film audience was watching American movies (Gupta, 1998). More recently, satellite broadcasting and the internet have reduced the geographic distance of mass communication. *Star-TV*, for example, is one of the most popular regional satellite and cable television operations in the world. Its coverage reaches from the Arab world to South and East Asia. It carries global US and British channels, as well as Mandarin and Hindi channels targeting regional audiences. The varieties of language and culture define a new type of geo-cultural television market that stands between the US-dominated global market and national/regional television markets. In 1995, *Star-TV* reached 53.7 million households in 53 countries, in English, Mandarin, and Hindi (Gupta, 1998).

However, media do not operate in a vacuum: they are always tied to political and economic systems. It is impossible to consider identities, communication, democracy, capitalism, nationalism, and the media as separate and autonomous. Their interaction is precisely what shapes the nature of the social order and daily lives. For example, Swedish, and Scandinavian films in general, are globally known for focusing on landscapes, a very slow pace of life, and melancholic feelings. In Australia, one popular television show that embraces multiculturalism through cooking is MasterChef Australia. The story follows a group of 'ordinary' Australians, often with multicultural backgrounds, who are brought together from around the country to live in a shared house in Sydney while vying to become Australia's leading amateur cook. In northern Nigeria, it is normal to watch films and television programmes in an open public or community space. Television ownership in many parts of Africa is still limited to the elite, so it is not surprising to see many people share one television set (Fair, 2003). Thus, the perception of globalization as a threat to nation-states and national culture is far too simplistic to account for the nature of interaction between the global and the local in the contemporary world.

Critical thinking...

Do you think that media continue to be involved in the reproduction of nationalism, despite the ongoing intensification of global media flows? What do you think is the role of social media in reporting or creating news around the world?

McQuail (2005) identifies two approaches to studying mass media: media-centric and society-centric. A *media-centric* approach attributes great autonomy and influence to the media, and concentrates on the impact of the media's own sphere of activity (e.g., the study of direct media effects). In contrast, a *society-centric* approach posits the media as the reflection of political and economic forces. For example, German media reflect the federal political system of the country. Each of the country's 16 regions regulates its own private and public broadcasting, and operates public television and radio services through a consortium representing the major sectors and groups, including political parties, churches, unions, and business organizations. Similarly, Turkey's media reflect larger Turkish society, dealing with the issues of secularization (should anchorwomen be veiled?) and the representation of minorities, such as the Kurds. Turkish Radio and Television Corporation (TRT) has four national, one regional and two international television channels. In Latin America, we find *telenovelas*, since Latin America is one of the world's largest producers of television serial melodramas. Televisa, Venevision, and Globo, the leading networks in Mexico, Venezuela, and Brazil respectively, distribute *telenovelas* all over the world, attracting a broad audience across nations, age, and gender. For much of the world, television remains the medium that most radically shapes social relations.

THEORY CORNER

CULTURAL STUDIES

The cultural turn in media studies dates back to the first half of the twentieth century. Cultural studies scholars are interested in the role culture plays in both preserving and transforming social relations. Whereas the study of art, music, or literature has a history of focusing on formal or aesthetic elements, the cultural studies approach is more interested in the relationship between cultural products (e.g., popular music, movies, and radio) and the societies that create and circulate them. Moreover, cultural studies scholars tend to focus on those popular cultural forms that are not traditionally studied in academic settings, such as popular TV shows, rap music, and romance novels (Turner, 2003). Examples of cultural studies projects are studies of the reaction of audiences in the Middle East and the Netherlands to the TV show *Dallas*, the reasons that women read romance novels, and the way reality TV portrays changes in the way we think about privacy. The Spanish version of *Big Brother*, for instance, has relentlessly sexualized female cast members. In addition, many scholars interrogate issues of gender, race, sexuality, and class.

Reference
Turner, Graeme (2003) *British Cultural Studies: An Introduction* (3rd edn). London: Routledge.

Further reading on cultural studies
Ang, Ien (1998) 'Doing cultural studies at the crossroads: local/global negotiations', *European Journal of Cultural Studies*, 1(1): 13–31.

Theory in Practice

REALITY TV AROUND THE WORLD

Cultural studies scholars who study reality TV attempt to place the reality TV trend within a broader social context, tracing its relationship to the development of a digitally enhanced, surveillance-based interactive economy and to a savvy mistrust of mediated reality in general. Reality TV shows like *Big Brother*, they suggest, promote an almost exhibitionist lifestyle in which work is living and living is work. Consumers-turned-producers actively participate in the process of production without having any control over the means of production. One of the crucial elements of reality TV is the way in which it has contributed to the diversity seen on television. Although reality TV offers more representations of gender, class, and religion than most other mainstream television, scholars have been quick to criticize the ways in which reality TV has reinforced existing gender, sexual, and racial stereotypes. For example, Banet-Weiser and Portwood-Stacer (2006) explored the complicated cultural work that female reality TV participants perform, not only in relation to beauty, femininity, nationhood, class, and race, but also in relation to sexuality. They argue that reality shows such as *The Swan* and *Extreme Makeover* are informed by cultural narratives about heterosexuality that equate happiness and success with normative ideals of sexual attractiveness.

Questions to take you further
Would you rather watch a reality TV show about people from your own culture or about people from another culture? How do you think reality TV reflects changing understandings of privacy in different cultures? Think about your favourite reality TV programme: does it encourage diversity or promote the norms of the majority? How?

Reference
Banet-Weiser, Sarah and Laura Portwood-Stacer (2006) 'I just want to be me again! Beauty pageants, reality television and post-feminism', *Feminist Theory*, 7(2): 255–272.

Further reading on reality TV
Andrejevic, Mark (2004) *Reality TV*. Boulder, CO: Rowman and Littlefield.

Political economy of mass media

Who owns and controls the mass media? What impact does this ownership and control have over media content and on the broader society? Where does the funding for the mass media come from, and where do the profits go? Does advertising affect journalists and editorial policy? Do mass media rely too much on information provided by the government or industry? These are some of the questions raised by media political economy scholars. The term 'political economy' in media research is often associated with questions about the domination of state or economic power in media spheres. Scholars in the political economy of media investigate processes of privatization, concentration, commercialization,

Photo 12.1   Television is the most popular medium in Istanbul, Turkey. Copyright © Zala Volčič. Used with permission.

and deregulation (where the market replaces the state). For example, they are interested in the conditions in which individuals can own many media corporations, and the consequences this has on democratic practices and media choices. These scholars claim that, globally, media are heavily dominated by a handful of gigantic media corporations and transnational corporations. The most important of these are Disney, TimeWarner, Viacom, and News Corporation. News Corporation's owner, the Australian-born American media mogul Rupert Murdoch, also owns Sky Television, which broadcasts all over the world. The so-called 'phone hacking scandal' that erupted in the UK in 2011 exposed illegal work practices among journalists from Murdoch's tabloid newspaper, *News of the World*. This incident has triggered worldwide debates about media ownership, journalistic ethics, respect for privacy, the problem of concentrated media ownership and its impact on the democratic public sphere, and tabloid culture in general.

Critical thinking...

What kind of consequences does concentrated media ownership have on democracy? Do media best serve a democratic society when a significant proportion of the media focuses less on profits and more on public interest? What evidence can you see of political or cultural bias in the news?

Scholars in media political economy have made consistent efforts to investigate the extent to which our view of the world is shaped by the concentration of power in certain media corporations, and the resulting impact this has on informed participation in our democratic societies. For example, the *Walt Disney Company* is now one of the six largest mass media corporations in the world, owning media production companies, studios, theme parks, television and radio networks, cable TV systems, magazines, and internet sites. Focusing on an image of magic, joy, and fun, its products are welcomed by parents, teachers, and children alike, and are a powerful force in creating children's culture. However, some commentators have raised concerns about the role of Walt Disney movies in constructing children's imaginary worlds (Wasko, 2001).

The issue of gender illustrates these concerns. The female characters in Disney movies often present a particular idealized version of femininity – highly sexualized bodies, coy seductiveness, always needing to be rescued by a male. *Snow White* cleans the dwarves' cottage to please them; Ariel gives up her voice in order to win the prince with her body in *The Little Mermaid*; Mulan almost single-handedly wins the war only to return home to be romanced; and *Beauty and the Beast*'s Belle endures an abusive Beast in order to redeem him. Of similar concern is the scarcity of genuine and realistic representations of race and ethnicity in Disney animated features. When they do appear, they tend to merely reinforce cultural stereotypes. For example, African Americans are presented as humans/orangutans in *Jungle Book* and are completely absent in *Tarzan*'s Africa; Latinos and African Americans are represented as street-gang thugs in *The Lion King*; Asians as treacherous Siamese cats in *Lady and the Tramp*; Arabs as barbarians in *Aladdin*; and Native Americans as savages in *Peter Pan* and *Pocahontas*. An important area for research is to study the way audiences in different cultures perceive these images, and the way they impact on their subsequent behaviour.

THEORY CORNER

THE FRANKFURT SCHOOL AND CRITICAL MEDIA THEORY

The Frankfurt School was formed by scholars working in different disciplines, from psychology to history: Max Horkheimer, Theodor W. Adorno, Herbert Marcuse, Leo Löwenthal, and Erich Fromm. Because of the Nazi regime they had to leave Germany for the USA. While in exile there, members of the Frankfurt School experienced the rise of media culture in film, popular music, radio, and television. They argued that media are largely commercially produced and controlled by big corporations, and thus by commercial imperatives in subservience to the system of consumer capitalism. They believed that media produce content in order to cultivate, maintain, organize, and utilize the audience as a product. The term 'critical media theory' is often associated with the Frankfurt School. Adorno (2001), a key critical media theorist from the Frankfurt School, developed the term 'culture industry' to call attention to the industrialization and commercialization of culture. Critical media theorists argue that the culture industry (media) aims to perform the dual task of attracting and sustaining the attention of the audience, while ensuring the audience continues to consume rather than critique the product.

Reference
Adorno, Theodor W. (2001) *The Culture Industry: Selected Essays on Mass Culture* (2nd edn). London and New York: Routledge.

Further reading on critical theory
Kellner, Douglas (1989) *Critical Theory, Marxism, and Modernity*. Cambridge and Baltimore, MD: Polity Press and Johns Hopkins University Press.

Theory in Practice

CRITICAL THEORY AND CYBER-BULLYING

Critical theory offers a very useful framework for studying cyber-bullying. Cyber-bullying generally refers to bullying using technology such as the internet and mobile phones (Perren et al., 2012). Cyber-bullying comes in diverse forms, such as sending insulting, rude, or threatening messages, spreading rumours, revealing personal information, publishing embarrassing pictures, or excluding someone from online communication. Critical theory researchers point out that cyber-bullying is part of a larger problem of the rise of violence. Studies reveal that boys and girls are differentially affected by cyber-bullying: girls are more likely to experience gender-based harassment, exclusion, having personal information about them posted online, and to be more negatively affected by the messages. Girls report with greater frequency that they feel their reputation is affected by the cyber-bullying they experience, that their concentration is affected, that bullying influences their ability to make friends, that it makes them want to bully back, and that it induces suicidal thoughts. The growth in ICTs around the world is also increasing offline risks, such as exposure to pornography and unwanted sexual solicitation. Recent studies have demonstrated that there is a significant overlap between traditional bullying and cyber-bullying, such that most young people who are cyber-bullied also tend to be bullied offline in more traditional ways (Perren et al., 2012).

Questions to take you further

Do you think that anonymous, bullying messages are worse than those from someone you know, or do you think that being cyber-bullied by someone you know is more damaging? What might motivate young people to cyber-bully others? Which prevention and intervention strategies would you recommend to counter the problem of cyber-bullying?

Reference

Perren, Sonja, Lucie Corcoran, Helen Cowie, Francine Dehue, D'Jamila Garcia, Conor McGuckin and Anna Sevcikova (2012) 'Tackling cyberbullying', *International Journal of Conflict and Violence*, 6(2): 283–293.

Further reading on cyber-bullying

Price, Megan and John Dalgleish (2010) 'Cyberbullying: experiences, impacts and coping strategies as described by Australian young people', *Youth Studies Australia*, 29(1): 51–59.

Homogeneity and heterogeneity of media content

There are two ways of conceptualizing the relationship between global and local media. One way posits that media flow from 'the West to the Rest', resulting in global homogeneity of products, lifestyles, cultures, identities, tastes, and attitudes. For example, television programming offers not only entertainment, but also reflects the sheer power and influence of global corporate culture. It shapes lifestyles and values, and replaces lost traditional institutions, communities, clans, family, and authority. The mass marketing of culture now takes place through satellite cables, mobile phones, social media and the internet, and DVDs. All over the world, people of all ages are exposed to the same music, sporting events, news, soap operas, and lifestyle. Young people in so-called 'third-world' countries are the largest consumers of this global culture. The success in sending global information may have possibly unintended, negative effects: the same media that inform globally also dominate globally. Some observers see media as a support system for one culture to dominate another culture – an uneven process called hegemony (Jandt, 2007). The argument is that mass media can unobtrusively influence the thinking and values of a specific society.

Global media flows bring about cultural hybridization (Kraidy, 2005). The process and impact of media convergence and globalization can be seen in a number of transnational television channels launched in the past few years. Many of these channels seek to target ethnic groups beyond their national borders. Examples include CBC TV, Greek Cypriot Satellite Television, which broadcasts in Greek; Zee TV, which broadcasts in Hindi across Asia; MED TV, which targets the Kurdish population in Europe; MBC, Al Jazeera, TRT, and Al Arabiya, which broadcast in Arabic across the Middle East and North Africa and are watched by Arabs around the world; and TRT-INT, which targets the Turkish population across Europe. While television channels can become the agents for a new global corporate vision, internet technology also contributes to the hybridization of culture by connecting people across the world. By the same means, the computer age also introduces subtle damage. Like video, film, and global entertainment, the internet has the potential to become a substitute for human interaction, community, and civic life, as adults and children alike spend increasing hours surfing, chatting, and shopping online. We live in a media-saturated world.

Internet technology and alternative media

In recent years we have seen many changes brought about by the internet in all layers of culture. Young people have especially benefited from these advances in the internet and in mobile phone technology – access to educational information, resources and collaborative learning networks, the development and maintenance of relationships and friendships with their peers, civic activity, and self-discovery – to name only a few. On the other hand, Brigitte Nacos (2007), a prominent scholar of media political communication, argues that not only can contemporary terrorists take advantage of a 24/7 news cycle, allowing for maximum exposure to violent acts, but also internet technologies have now enabled them to bypass mainstream media to communicate directly with individual citizens – even personally recruiting future members for their groups via the internet.

Internet technology has created a type of 'hybrid' media, called *alternative media*. One of the most used forms of alternative media is blogging, which provides space for online users to make their voices heard. Blogs are web pages on which content appears in reverse chronological order. According to the Nielsen/McKinsey company, the number of blogs reached over 181 million worldwide in 2011 (Nielsen Wire, 2012). Blogs do not require sophisticated technical knowledge to access or create, and they blur the boundaries between interpersonal, group, intercultural, and mass communication because they can serve as journal- or diary-type outlets and be shared with a large community of users around the world.

Further online reading The following article can be accessed for free on the book's companion website https://study.sagepub.com/liu2e: Khalil, Joe (2012) 'Youth-generated media: a case of blogging and Arab youth cultural politics', *Television & New Media*, 14(4): 338–350.

Blogs have assisted different political dissent movements to question and critique authoritarian regimes around the globe. For example, bloggers in Iran were extremely active during the 2009 elections, covering the street protests. In Zimbabwe, the democratic opposition has resisted Robert Mugabe's regime and its monopoly of information sources in rural regions by emailing daily news bulletins to other rural sites, where they were printed and distributed by children on bicycles. In Russia, the Netherlands, and Argentina, alternative media, such as *The Atlantic*, have surpassed many traditional news organizations by posting around-the-clock updates about global affairs. It is believed that alternative media are increasingly removing journalism from professionals employed by commercial organizations. This dramatic shift in news production and dissemination can provide the audience with platforms that foster dialogue rather than monologue. Blogs have excited both public and scholarly interest, with utopian claims that they can transform passive media users into active media producers. The desire to tell one's story to the world, write about one's personal experiences, or give one's opinions on world events through a blog site has been translated into a favourite media practice. In many ways, then, the internet has become as much about interaction with others as about accessing information. However, the power relations present in an offline world also appear online, and the dialogue, even though it is freer and more interactive, still resembles the rhetoric in most offline public spheres.

Internet technology and social media

The widespread use of social media has given rise to new forms of monitoring, mining, and aggregating strategies, which are designed to monetize the huge volumes of data such usage produces. Social media monitoring and analysis industries, experts, and consultancies have emerged, offering a broad range of social media intelligence and reputation management services. Such services typically involve a range of analytical methods (sentiment analysis, opinion mining, social network analysis, machine learning, natural language processing). An example of social media is Facebook, which started as a social networking site for students at Harvard University in 2004, where its co-founders attended university. It takes its name from the standard publication that is issued to incoming students at some universities that allow students to learn about one another (a university Facebook typically has a photograph of each incoming student and some basic information about where they are from and where they went to high school). The online version made this function interactive: people could find out about each other and post and share information about themselves. As a general rule, technologies that allow people to communicate with one another and socialize tend to be very successful, as indicated by the rise of emails, which had originally been almost an after-thought addition to the internet, but rapidly became one of its 'killer apps'. Something similar might be said of Facebook, which has had a phenomenal rate of growth: it took only eight years for the Facebook platform to attract over a billion registered users and it has become one of the most well-known sites on the internet (Miller, 2011). If it were a country, Facebook would be the third largest country in the world, which means that it already unites users from many parts of the world and serves as a new way of keeping in touch and extending social networks across large geographic spaces.

Similarly, YouTube – founded only a year after Facebook, in 2005 – rapidly turned into another internet phenomenon, allowing users to upload videos to share with others. As a convergence medium between the internet and TV, YouTube has highlighted a series of contradictions between traditional broadcasting and digital narrowcasting (Snikars and Vonderau, 2009). YouTube has influenced television, but at the same time, this new medium imitates the rules of the old media. The original goal was both to allow users to generate their own videos to show online and to find ways to share clips of videos by other users and by professional media organizations of one kind or another. YouTube has played a role in allowing media moments to 'go viral', as in the case of the video of *Britain's Got Talent* contestant Susan Boyle, whose rendition of 'I Dreamed a Dream' from the musical *Les Miserables* received tens of millions of hits and helped gain her international fame and million-dollar recording contracts.

Further online reading The following article can be accessed for free on the book's companion website https://study.sagepub.com/liu2e: Tan, Sabine (2012) 'Facts, opinions, and media spectacle: exploring representations of business news on the internet', *Discourse & Communication*, 5(2): 169–194.

YouTube is also credited with the discovery of pop idol Justin Bieber, and has created a tier of producers who are able to support themselves from the popularity of their online videos. At the same time, it has allowed for the international sharing of an eclectic mix of political events, disasters, popular music videos, and home videos (Snikars and Vonderau, 2009). Since its purchase by Google in 2006 for US$1.65 billion, it has worked hard to commercialize its content, and to address some of the concerns of copyright holders, who have sued the company for using their content without permission. As demonstrated by the most popular videos on the site, the most prevalent use is for short bites of entertainment: the music video for the pop song 'Gangnam Style' by South Korean artist Psy, for example. The most popular amateur user-generated video is called 'Charlie Bit My Finger,' showing two British toddlers playing with each other. The video, originally uploaded by the children's father to share with their godfather in the United States, has gone on to receive more than half a billion views. Thus, YouTube has helped create a new kind of international celebrity and allowed people from around the world to share videos with one another, whether for the purposes of politics, entertainment, or information.

Critical thinking...

Do you agree that YouTube and online video services have yielded new patterns of television watching? Do you believe that YouTube could serve as an intercultural video library? As commercial and non-commercial organizations alike seek to monitor, influence, manage, and direct social media conversations, and as global usage of social media expands, do you think we should question celebratory accounts of the democratizing, participatory possibilities of social media?

MASS MEDIA AND SYMBOLIC SOCIAL REALITY

In his book *Public Opinion* (1922), Walter Lippmann described an island where a handful of French, English, and Germans lived in harmony just before the First World War. A British mail steamer provided their only link with the outside world. One day, the ship brought news that the British and French had been fighting the Germans for over six weeks. For those six weeks the islanders, technically enemies, had acted as friends; as Lippmann put it, trusting 'the pictures in their heads' (their perceived reality). Lippmann's simple but important point is that we must distinguish between reality (the outside world of actual events) and social reality (our perception of those events), because we think and behave based not on what is, but on what is perceived to be. Three decades after Lippmann put forward his idea of 'pictures in our heads', genuine investigation began into how the pictures we receive and interpret from the media differ from the world outside. The importance of the mass media as sources for those 'pictures in our heads' leads us to question how closely the media world actually resembles the world outside.

Media and the construction of social reality

Photo 12.2   Thousands of reporters were at the Beijing 2008 Olympics.
Copyright ©Yang Xia. Used with permission.

Scholars now largely accept that reality is socially and culturally constructed, understood, and mediated. Mass media are one of the critical agents in this social construction of reality. Media content may be based on what happens in the physical world, but it singles out and highlights certain elements over others. Reality is necessarily manipulated when events and people are relocated into news or prime-time stories. In doing so, the media can emphasize certain behaviours and stereotype people. One of the most obvious ways in which media content structures a symbolic environment is simply by giving greater attention (e.g., more time, space, and prominence) to certain events, people, groups, and places than others. The media can thus be used to manufacture consent, legitimize political positions, or cultivate a particular worldview. This is defined as the 'CNN effect' – the ability of television pictures to influence people so powerfully that important military and political decisions can be driven by the pictures rather than by policies (Robinson, 1999). In some instances, a nation may decide to support a decision to go to war with another country where they have never been and about which they have very limited knowledge, except for what they have learned from the mass media. This is not new, as shown by the example of the Spanish–American war at the beginning of the twentieth century, which was propelled by an unsubstantiated US media report (from the then media mogul William Randolph Hearst) that the battleship *Maine* had been blown up by a Spanish mine in Havana (Robinson, 1996). Today, however, the potential for distortion is magnified by the mass media's greater reach and prominence.

Media mediation is also evident in the pervasiveness of celebrity coverage, which dominates magazines, televisions, and newspapers. Magazines and specialist 'insider' television programmes routinely present detailed information about celebrities' personal lives and everyday routines – romantic involvements, shopping habits, trips, leisure activities, and family issues – rather than their professional lives. In Brazil, for example, even though the fascination with celebrities is a relatively new phenomenon, the growing number of media outputs dedicated to fame, such as reality TV programmes, talk shows, websites, and magazines, has greatly increased the coverage of celebrities in the national market (Turner, 1994). Among Brazil's 15 weekly magazines in 2008, ten had mainly celebrity-oriented content. As such, media have a fundamental role in the construction of the famous: models, entertainers, athletes, hair stylists, fashion designers, as well as anyone directly related to them, such as spouses, children, and even pets.

The media play a crucial role in constructing reality, to which we have no direct access. Tuchman (1978) analysed the role of news in the construction of social reality. In her view, news is simultaneously a record and a product of social reality. The final news story contains only part of the actual event covered, but in the eyes of a reader, viewer, or listener it is timely and accurate. Had it not appeared in a news item, it might have no reality to the audience. At the same time, audiences make their own meaning, in order for a story to make sense to them. Thus, the news source is socially constructed as a reliable basis upon which assumptions of truthfulness are made. Dayan and Katz (1992) discussed the role of different media events in the creation of reality. *Media events* are large-scale interruptions of everyday life, when all media attend to one event and ceremonially mark it (e.g., coverage of the Olympic Games). In August 2008, television coverage of the Beijing Olympic Games broke all previous records for Olympics coverage. According to the International Olympic Committee, the Beijing Olympics attracted 21,600 accredited journalists, including 16,000 broadcasters and 5,600 writers and photographers.

Research on media effects

Research on media effects is central to understanding the role of the media in constructing social reality and in understanding how audiences make meanings out of different media products. When mass media emerged with full force at the beginning of the nineteenth century, questions about the impact of media on public opinion, individual beliefs, and political structures began. Concerns over the potential political and cultural power of the mass media, and the desire to quantify media effects on audiences and society, therefore are not only a product of recent globalization, but also have historically accompanied the phenomenon of the mass media (Couldry, 2000).

Audience analysis

Audience analysis deals with audience tastes, preferences, habits, and demographics. This type of research studies why we like particular radio programmes more than others, and why. One of the most commonly applied models for audience research is *uses and gratifications theory*, first formulated in the 1940s. Uses and gratifications studies ask the question 'What do people do with the mass media?' rather than 'What do media do to people?' Herzog (see Rubin, 1986) studied the gratifications that female listeners received from radio daytime serials, and drew the conclusion that there were three main categories: emotional release, wishful thinking, and advice seeking. Morley (2000) interviewed families about their television viewing to reveal the impact of gender on power over the remote-control, programme choice, viewing style, and amount of viewing. In his study, men and women offered different accounts of their viewing habits, in terms of their power to choose what and how much they

Photo 12.3   Advertisement in Singapore cleverly used Asian warrior characters to promote Australian Qantas Airways.
Copyright © Joan Burnett. Used with permission.

viewed and their viewing styles. Audience studies have been crucial in promoting the idea that audiences are not passive, but active, agents in media consumption.

Audience studies have also been highly influential in studying media effects on immigrants. Immigrants have always been quick to use mass media in order to reduce the geographic and spatial distances between the host country and their home country. While radio, video recorders, and films once served as the primary tool of maintaining contact with immigrants' culture of origin, it has now become common to find personal websites for immigrant communities (or diasporas), where images of the homeland are presented and important information about the homeland is relayed to family and friends. Kolar-Panov's (1997) research on the use of video letters among the Croatian and Macedonian communities in Australia showed the role of media in framing immigrants' cultures. News of the horrific events occurring in the former Yugoslavia, received by the immigrants through these diasporic channels, influenced the nature of their homeland connections. Naficy (1993) explored the ways in which Iranian refugees in Los Angeles make use of television programmes both to reflect on their existence in a new culture and to nostalgically remember the Iran they left behind. Robins (1996) studied second-generation Turks in Italy and found that they model themselves on neither the home nor the host culture, since they watch Turkish, German, European, and African television programmes.

Media effects on perceptions of social reality

At the beginning of the First World War, the image of the media as all-powerful gradually evolved in the assertion of their power to persuade citizens to do just about anything. The *magic bullet theory* claims that the mass media have a direct, immediate, and powerful effect on a passive mass audience. Other scholars argue that media influence masses of people indirectly, through a *two-step flow* of communication. The first stage is the direct transmission of information to a small group of people who stay well-informed (opinion leaders). In the second stage, those opinion leaders interpret and pass on the messages to less directly involved members of society (followers). The two-step flow model later evolved into a *multi-step flow model*, which claims that information-flows in a culture or group actually are filtered through a series of opinion leaders before reaching all other segments of the group or culture.

THEORY CORNER

CULTIVATION THEORY

George Gerbner's cultivation theory postulates a relationship between heavy television viewing and people's worldview. Specifically, he suggests that exposure to vast amounts of violence on the screen conditions viewers to view the world as an unkind and frightening place. For almost two decades, he headed an extensive research programme that monitored the level of violence on television, classified people according to how much TV they watched, and compiled viewers' perceptions of risk and other sociocultural attitudes. His cultivation explanation of the findings is one of the most cited and debated theories of mass communication (Griffin, 2006). Gerbner regards television as the dominant force in shaping modern society, and believes that television's power comes from the symbolic content of the real-life drama frequently broadcast on television. In his view, the TV set is a key member of the household, with virtually unlimited access to every person in the family. It dominates the symbolic environment, telling most of our stories most of the time.

Reference
Griffin, Erin (2006) *A First Look at Communication Theory* (6th edn). Boston, MA: McGraw-Hill.

Further reading on cultivation effects
Skeggs, Bev, Nancy Thumim and Helen Wood (2008) '"Oh goodness, I am watching reality TV": how methods make class in audience research', *European Journal of Cultural Studies*, 11(1): 5–24.

Theory in Practice

THE CULTIVATION OF FEAR OF SEXUAL VIOLENCE AMONG WOMEN

The relationship between violent narratives and fear of crime is a major focus of cultivation theory. It has been argued that the stereotypical representation of sexual crime and its victims on television may cultivate fear of crime and fear of sexual assault. Having a mediated experience with sexual violence (or being exposed to sexual violence on television repeatedly) may reinforce this fear among women. One study of the portrayal of women as victims of sexual assault on television was conducted by Custers and Van den Bulck (2013). They examined the relationship between television exposure and fear of sexual violence in women. Data were collected from 546 Flemish women in March 2010 by means of a standardized self-administered questionnaire. Findings showed that there was an indirect relationship between frequency of television viewing and fear of sexual violence. The level of fear of sexual violence was predicted by perceived risk, perceived control, and perceived seriousness. The authors criticized the excessive amount of sexual violence in television content for its possible effect on women's fear of crime in real life.

Questions to take you further
Do you agree that the relationship between exposure to television and perception of crime is stronger in women with direct crime experience than in women with no direct crime experience? In the television world, are women much more likely to be victimized than men? Why? What about in the real world?

Reference
Custers, Kathleen and Jan Van den Bulck (2013) 'The cultivation of fear of sexual violence in women: processes and moderators of the relationship between television and fear', *Communication Research*, 40(1): 96–124.

Further reading on violence against women
Yodanis, Carrie (2004) 'Gender inequality, violence against women, and fear: a cross-national test of the feminist theory of violence against women', *Journal of Interpersonal Violence*, 19(1): 655–675.

Media effects on agenda-setting

Researchers on *agenda-setting* propose that mass media focus our attention on certain aspects of life, and in doing so, set the agenda for us. Agenda-setting scholars claim that while the media definitely do not have the power to tell audiences specifically what to think, they are able to tell audiences what to think about (Newbold, 1995). As Robinson (1999) suggests, the most useful way to conceptualize the CNN effect is to view it as an agenda-setting agency. Muhamed Sacirbey, Bosnian ambassador to the United Nations, once remarked: 'If you look at how humanitarian relief is delivered in Bosnia you see that those areas where the TV cameras are most present are the ones that are the best fed, the ones that receive the most medicines. While on the other hand, many of our people have starved and died of disease and shelling where there are no TV cameras' (Seib, 1997: 90). When images of starvation, anarchy, and human misery appear on television screens, television becomes the *de facto* 'must-do-something' framework for everyone, including international policy-makers.

THEORY CORNER

AGENDA-SETTING THEORY

Maxwell McCombs and Donald Shaw (1972) proposed agenda-setting theory in the 1970s. They believe that mass media have the ability to transfer the salience of items on their news agendas to the public agenda. The theory has two interconnected points: it affirms the power of the press, while still maintaining that, ultimately, individuals are free to choose. Like the initial Erie County voting studies conducted by Paul Lazarsfeld and his team, the focus of agenda-setting is on election campaigns. The theory argues that there is a cause-and-effect relationship between media content and voters' perceptions. Although they did not use the largely superseded magic bullet conception of media influence, McCombs and Shaw ascribed to broadcast and print journalism the significant power to set the public's political agendas. Media may not exert a direct and instant influence on public opinion. However, news coverage of politics has been shown to have a wide range of subtle, but still powerful, effects on what the public thinks about important issues. As McCombs and Shaw suggested, the media may not be successful in telling people what to think, but there is much evidence to suggest that they are successful in telling people what to think about.

Reference

McCombs, Maxwell and Donald Shaw (1972) 'The agenda-setting function of the mass media', *Public Opinion Quarterly*, 36: 176–187.

Further reading on agenda-setting

Cho, Hiromi and Stephen Lacy (2000) 'International conflict coverage in Japanese local daily newspapers', *Journalism and Mass Communication Quarterly*, 77(4): 830–845.

Theory in Practice

THE MEDIA'S AGENDA AND THE PUBLIC'S AGENDA

Over the past decades, numerous empirical studies have been conducted to test the match between the media's agenda and the public's agenda. Some studies support the hypothesis. Kim et al. (2012) write on how South Korean president Roh in 2004 announced the New Capital Region Development Plan, which would in essence move the national capital from Seoul to another location. According to the plan, government and administrative functions would be relocated to a new city even though any sizable moving was not expected to happen until 2012. Right after the announcement, the plan was confronted with strong opposition, igniting nationwide controversy. Using this controversial topic in South Korea, Kim and colleagues explored how television news can influence the way the public evaluates the issue. They conducted content analysis of prime-time news programmes of the three major television networks in South Korea, examining which attributes of the issue were covered more prominently than others. Their findings support the idea that there is a significant link between salient issue attributes in the media and the agenda of attributes among the public. Findings from their study provide evidence that by placing different degrees of emphasis, news media influence the salience of certain attributes in the audience's minds.

Questions to take you further

How and why do you find agenda-setting theory useful? The Occupy Wall Street movement is an example of ordinary people setting the agenda in spite of the coverage of the mainstream media. Can you give another example like this one?

Reference

Kim, Sei-Hill, Miejeong Han, Doo-Hun Choi and Jeong-Nam Kim (2012) 'Attribute agenda setting, priming and the media's influence on how to think about a controversial issue', *International Communication Gazette*, 74(1): 43–59.

Further reading on agenda-setting in practice

Scheufele, Dietram and David Tewksbury (2007) 'Framing, agenda setting, and priming: the evolution of three media effects models', *Journal of Communication*, 57(2): 9–20.

Critical thinking...

Sometimes the opinion of a vocal minority can be taken as the representation of the majority. What are the conditions in which this is likely to happen? What role do the media play? What strategies might people use to make their voices heard?

Media effects on identity construction

Scholars have explored the important role of the mass media in the historical development of national cultures and identities (Morley and Robins, 1995). Media and cultural production have a key role in reconstituting national, religious, gender, and ethnic identities. The influential work of Anderson (1983) proposes that print capitalism is essential in promoting the creation of national imagined communities. The widespread dissemination of newspapers and novels creates an awareness of the 'steady, anonymous, simultaneous experience' of communities of national readers (Anderson, 1983: 31). The notion of simultaneity in time and a clearly defined national space is crucial to the construction of national consciousness today. Newspapers connect dispersed citizens with the land, people, and discourses of a nation. The ritual of reading the newspaper or watching the national news on TV continues to be an essential element in the construction of a national community.

Further online reading The following article can be accessed for free on the book's companion website https://study.sagepub.com/liu2e: Cho, Hiromi and Stephen Lacy (2000) 'International conflict coverage in Japanese local daily newspapers', *Journalism and Mass Communication Quarterly*, 77(4): 830–845.

In addition, most countries treat broadcasting as a national public resource with a unique responsibility to represent and support the national culture. A classic example is the British Broadcasting Corporation (BBC), known for its balanced and high-quality programming that reflects diversity of topic, equality in representation, and independence from outside governmental, religious, or commercial influence. However, the belief in a single national identity that is itself based on a culture, religion, and way of life that we all belong to is changing. Today, we belong to a world that is a vast cultural market from which we can pick and choose our preferences for music, fashion, food, and so on. We belong to many subcultural groups, and hence we have multiple identities. This is especially so because we live in a so-called 'digital culture' that denotes the multiple ways in which we engage with digital media and technologies in our daily lives in different cultural contexts.

> ## Critical thinking...
>
> Can you give an example to show the ways in which the mass media have shaped cultural identities? How have the media used national identity to place blame for a crisis inside or outside a particular nation?

MASS MEDIA AND CULTURAL CHANGE

That the reality presented by the media is socially constructed has two important implications: firstly, we can understand the media as a debating ground for our system of values and beliefs; secondly, we can think of media effects not as simple, direct effects, but as a much wider part of the cultural fabric (Dodd, 1998). Mass media influence cultural change through cultural learning.

Mass media and cultural learning

Media create awareness. The mass media serve an awareness function, creating interest in an event or idea through reporting about its existence (Dodd, 1998). Such was the case with the use of chemical weapons in Syria, which brought instant world attention and led to international condemnation.

Media set agendas. Agenda-setting is inevitable because the media must be selective in reporting news and other events. News outlets, as gate-keepers of information, make choices about what to report and how to report it. Thus, what the public knows about the current affairs at a particular time is largely a product of media gate-keeping. For example, the extensive coverage in the Australian media of the plight of struggling pensioners made this issue a public priority, and policy-makers had to address the ensuing public concern.

Media promote stereotypes. The media play a major role in constructing and maintaining stereotypes. They can create and reinforce stereotypes regarding old age, sexuality, religion, war, parenthood, and myriad other aspects of human life. News programmes can help to erase misunderstandings on issues vulnerable to stereotyping. Conversely, entertainment in movies, theatres, and television may inadvertently reinforce negative stereotypes. The representation of ethnic minorities has also been the subject of considerable attention because studies have found that when ethnic minorities are present in news reports, they tend to be linked to violence, gambling, crime, or alcoholism.

Media accelerate change. The mass media serve as accelerators for change, creating a climate in which change can more easily occur (Dodd, 1998). For example, what we regard as elements of a healthy lifestyle have changed considerably over the years, not least because of government-sponsored advertising campaigns against smoking and drink-driving, and on promoting healthy eating. In the same way, mass news coverage of issues like global warming, climate change, and the energy crisis has functioned as an accelerator for changes in people's behaviour, which is evident in the current concern for energy consumption and the preservation of natural resources.

Further online reading The following article can be accessed for free on the book's companion website https://study.sagepub.com/liu2e: Peck, Janice (1993) 'Selling goods and selling God: advertising, televangelism and the commodity form', *Journal of Communication Inquiry*, 17(1): 5–24.

Mass media and intercultural communication

By looking at examples of how media and culture interrelate, we can understand the importance of media in the intercultural communication context and be aware of the need to develop skills in understanding media and culture.

Be conscious of ways in which the media may have affected your perceptions of a particular group. We need to keep up to date about current events and understand the source of our personal feelings. This can assist you in your intercultural communication.

Use media as a tool for understanding culture. Mass media can open our eyes to what is considered important in a culture. We cannot personally experience some cultures fully, but we may have an opportunity to interact with people from those cultures. Learning about another culture can improve our understanding of that culture and hence assist us in interacting with its members. The mass media can play a significant role in culture-learning.

Broaden background knowledge. We need a broad knowledge of cultures other than our own. A common criticism of recent mass communication or journalism graduates is that they lack the background knowledge to carry out more than a superficial interview. Their articles will be superficial or incorrect, or even offensive, if they do not have an understanding of the influence of culture and context within which the reported events occurred. The same thing applies to everyone when they interact with another culture.

SUMMARY

- Advances in communication technologies and the rise of mass media have enabled the internationalization of media products, reducing the geographic distance between countries, people, and cultures.

- Media can promote social learning by giving prominence to certain issues, people, and places. On the other hand, media can promote stereotypes of disadvantaged groups, including women and ethnic minorities.

- The main approaches to the study of mass media and their role in intercultural communication are political economy, cultural studies, audience studies, media technology, media identity, and cultural change.

- Research on media effects is central to understanding the role of the media in constructing social reality and in understanding how audiences make meanings out of different media products.

- Media representation scholars study how the mass media that inform us of events across the world can also distort our perception of social reality.

JOIN THE DEBATE

Will the print media still maintain a place in the digital age?

The print media have traditionally played a primary role in informing citizens. In Italy, reading a newspaper in the morning is a very important cultural ritual, and print media continue to be Italians' first source of news. But as digital media came on the scene, print media are having a hard time surviving. The only print medium that is doing well is the business press, whose readers require international news and information. There is a falling readership of print media reported all over the world, and there is a corresponding fall in the number of different newspapers. It used to be common for small towns and cities to have multiple newspapers; today the trend is shifting towards having only one. How do newspapers stay in business? An important way for newspapers to stay in business is through advertising. Retailer advertising and classifieds spaces are where most of their revenue comes from, not subscriptions or sales. Advertising percentages are also taking away space from news stories. In the digital age, will advertisers still place their advertisements in print newspapers? Will newspapers still be able to play the roles they have traditionally fulfilled in terms of educating, informing, and entertaining their readers? Are print media going to be dead in the near future?

CASE STUDY

OhmyNews in South Korea

The online newspaper *OhmyNews* was set up by a journalist, Oh Yeon-Ho, in February 2000, and has since been very successful. It has been included in 'hybrid' types of media, meaning it incorporates print and electronic forms. While the South Korea of today is a democracy, most middle-aged Koreans have lived through dictatorships and years of political unrest. Rapid industrialization has changed South Korea into one of the world's fastest-growing economies; the embrace of new technologies, particularly the internet, has been phenomenal.

South Korea is the most connected society in the world today, with broadband connections in 83 per cent of households. Hence, the success of *OhmyNews* is its high level of connectivity. But there are other reasons for its success – both social and political.

The politics and media of South Korea are known for their relative conservativeness. For many years alternative news, opinion, and dissenting views were not tolerated, and dissenting journalists were imprisoned. While South Korean university students played a key role in opposing successive dictatorships, the regimes were supported with the aid of South Korea's key ally, the USA (which continues to maintain a large military base there), thus providing a formidable task for those who wanted political change. In 2002, two years after the establishment of *OhmyNews*, two school girls were run over by a US armoured carrier. While the mainstream media ignored the story, *OhmyNews* picked it up and called for popular protest. The anti-US protest became the largest in Korean history and, more importantly, the mainstream media were forced to pay attention to what had then become the key story in South Korea. Similarly, in December of that same year, presidential elections were held in Korea. While the mainstream media favoured the more conservative candidates, the more left-wing Millennium party candidate, Roh Moo-Hyun, was given less space, even though he came from the governing party at the time. *OhmyNews* strongly supported Roh Moo-Hyun's candidature, providing online space for discussions of the merits of South Korean politics, corruption, the role of industrial and media monopolies, and the need for social change in Korea. The platform that this online newspaper gave Roh Moo-Hyun inevitably contributed to his victory; he was strongly supported by younger voters, who are among the main consumers of *OhmyNews*. The first interview that he gave after his win was to *OhmyNews*.

Some of the achievements of *OhmyNews* are:

1. It has provided a platform for democratic dissent in a context in which dissent is frowned upon. The 'Net' is turned into a public space, available to all for discussion, debate, and popular action. It gives opportunities for ordinary people to write their version of the news, thus liberating and empowering ordinary people. More than 33,000 'netizens' contribute to *OhmyNews*. This type of participation enables people not only to contribute to news production, but also to play a role in deciding which news is important.

2. This empowerment has resulted in the beginnings of a potent social movement under 'anyone can be a journalist'. This is a recognition that new technologies, in particular the internet, have the potential to break down the barriers between professional journalists, who have been opinion makers, gatekeepers, and keepers of journalistic norms, and ordinary people, who were previously just consumers of news. *OhmyNews* has given the internet generation in Korea a new media choice. 'Our main concept is the citizen reporter', says Oh. 'Our second concept is: Please communicate in your style; if it is convenient for you, that's fine. Don't just follow the professional reporters.'

3. The existence of *OhmyNews* and other alternative news sources is a threat to controlled media monopolies and their power to censor those who are outside the political establishment. Today, *OhmyNews* is among the six most influential media outlets in Korea. It has helped its readers to recognize that they have the power to make their elected representatives, public servants, and industrial houses accountable. It has contributed to making Korean politics transparent, with thousands of netizens now having the opportunity to discuss the latest corruption scandal or government action.

4. It has added to the credibility of news and helped it to strike a chord with the younger generation who have been, to some extent, ignored by mainstream media. Young people in South Korea often resent established media structures and practices. They appreciate the freedom that *OhmyNews* gives them and use it to their own advantage.

5. *OhmyNews* is an example of new media blazing a new trail. It is an alternative to old media, and some would say that it has helped to diminish print media (e.g., newspapers), whose circulation the world over is in decline. In this sense, *OhmyNews* is the future.

Reference

OhmyNews International [online]. Accessed 25 October 2013 at: http://english.ohmynews.com.

Questions for discussion

1. Do you believe that you must be in mainstream journalism in order to speak with credibility to the public, or do you think one needs to join alternative types of media to successfully reach an audience?

2. Do you think *OhMyNews*, as a type of hybrid media, will eventually take over traditional media like the print newspaper?

3. What are the cost and benefits of technologies in bringing change to the media industry?

4. Do you believe that a project like *OhMyNews* would be successful in your society? Why or why not?

5. Do you regularly read blogs or alternative media sources, such as *OhMyNews*? How would you evaluate the credibility of such media outlets?

FURTHER READINGS

All articles listed next to the mouse icon below can be accessed for free on the book's companion website: https://study.sagepub.com/liu2e

Globalization, homogenization, and hybridization

Yesim, Kaptan (2013) 'We just know! Tacit knowledge and knowledge production in the Turkish advertising industry', *Journal of Consumer Culture*, 13(3): 264–282.

This article focuses on a broad understanding of the knowledge production processes in the advertising industry during a period of rapid globalization in Turkey. Drawing on interviews with advertisers in three Turkish advertising agencies, this paper analyses the knowledge production practices of these agencies in order to understand how tacit knowledge has become the main source of differentiation for survival in the advertising sector. Relying on Pierre Bourdieu's definition of common sense and Alfred Schutz's social theory of knowledge, Kaptan argues that the production of implicit or tacit knowledge – nonverbal or otherwise unarticulated and intuitive forms of knowledge – is understood not merely as a business strategy and a battleground within and between agencies, but also as a socially constructed form of power. Thus, tacit knowledge, as a practical strategy, is employed for the purposes of improvisation and invention within the structured social order of the advertising field.

Internet technology and social media

Andrejevic, Mark (2013) *Infoglut: How Too Much Information is Changing the World*. London: Routledge.

This book is an analysis and critique of new media interactivity. Andrejevic argues that the rhetoric of interactivity, as a form of empowerment providing largely open exchange of information, fails to reflect its reality. The reality is one of increasing surveillance and information gathering by corporations and the state via new media technologies. The book focuses on interactive technologies and how the information they produce is or could be used for social control. Most consumers and citizens are aware that their information is being collected when they use a mobile phone, an internet search engine, or a credit card, but are ignorant of what information is gathered, by whom, and how it is used. The book explores the connections between these wide-ranging sense-making strategies for an era of information overload and the new forms of control they enable.

Clark, Schofield Lynn (2012) *The Parent App: Understanding Families in a Digital Age*. Oxford: Oxford University Press.

This book investigates how digital and mobile media are both changing and challenging parenting for all families. Based on a ten-year study of hundreds of parents and children, Clark provides practical advice for parents on what works for both parents and kids when it comes to social media and new technologies. More families report that technology makes life with children more challenging as parents today struggle with questions previous generations never faced: Is my 13-year-old responsible enough for a Facebook page? What will happen if I give my 9-year-old a cell phone? Clark interviewed scores of parents, identifying their various approaches. The book tackles a host of issues, such as family communication, online predators, cyber-bullying, sexting, gamer drop-outs, helicopter parenting, and technological monitoring.

Khalil, Joe (2012) 'Youth-generated media: a case of blogging and Arab youth cultural politics', *Television & New Media*, 14(4): 338–350.

This article is about contemporary Arab youth, cultural politics, and public life, as demonstrated through 'youth-generated media', which is famous in connection with protests in Tunisia, Egypt, and elsewhere in the Arab world. These include, but are not restricted to, Facebook, Twitter, blogs, graffiti, videos, songs, and other forms of communication developed and circulated by young people, with or without the support of adults. Khalil examined the contemporary configuration of youth cultural politics through self-expressive artefacts, probing in the process the changing mediascape in the Arab world. The article discussed the relationship between youth and media, focusing on the way young people develop and circulate their own messages outside corporate, religious, and state institutions.

Media representation and media effects

Tan, Sabine (2012) 'Facts, opinions, and media spectacle: exploring representations of business news on the internet', *Discourse & Communication*, 5(2): 169–194.

In the digital age, the way business news is mediated has become radically different from the structured, predominantly text-based representations that one finds in respectable broadsheets. Tan argues that in the twenty-first century, the field of business and finance has become a media spectacle. Not only have advances in technology changed the ways in which audiences engage with business information: the pervasiveness of internet and cable television networks has led to the emergence of new hybrid forms of business news discourse, blending verbiage, images, graphics, audio, and video clips. This article explores the multiple ways in which business news are mediated on the internet by continuous 24-hour business news networks such as Bloomberg, CNBC, FOX Business, and Reuters.

'*We ought to think that we are one of the leaves of a tree, and the tree is all humanity. We cannot live without the others, without the tree.*'

Pablo Casals, Spanish cellist and musician, 1876–1973

13

BECOMING AN EFFECTIVE INTERCULTURAL COMMUNICATOR

LEARNING OBJECTIVES

At the end of this chapter, you should be able to:

- Identify global and local dimensions of culture.

- Explain the dialectic of homogenization and fragmentation of cultures.

- Describe contributors of cultural diffusion, convergence, and hybridity.

- Suggest strategies to develop intercultural competence.

INTRODUCTION

One of the challenges facing intercultural scholars is a shifting understanding of cultural boundaries in societies characterized by emerging forms of economic and cultural globalization. The 'global village' described by McLuhan in the 1960s represents only a partial social reality of the world we inhabit today. As Adams and Carfagna (2006: 23) write: 'Globalization is making the world truly round because it is bringing all of humanity into a single eco-system of embedded, overlapping networks. Borders, boundaries, delineations, and walls of any kind are slowly giving way to the compelling force of integration and interdependence.' Indeed, our global village is becoming increasingly interconnected at political, economic, cultural, social, and even personal levels.

Yet, as Skalli (2006) points out, all these interconnections are embedded in a system of inherent differences. At one end of the economic scale, cosmopolitan elites work and study in several different countries, mastering multiple languages and moving seamlessly between cultural contexts. At the other end, ethnic minorities and refugees are trying to find ways to preserve elements of their own cultural practices while adjusting to the cultures of their host countries. In the internet era, media content, once subject to limits imposed by both legal regimes and transportation technology, now circulates around the globe at the speed of light. Mass cultural products, such as Latin American *telenovelas*, Egyptian melodramas, Nigerian cinema, Arab reality TV, and televised Hindu epics, have generated passionate global debates about politics, international wars, religious conflicts, same-sex marriage, climate change, women's emancipation, and possibilities for cultural hybridity. Social media everywhere are transforming professional journalism by providing a platform for audiences to publish their views on the internet. And the speed of the real-time revolution raises significant challenges and opportunities for journalists and their publishers. Global trends of homogenization and local processes of fragmentation suggest multiple ways in which global and the local cultural realms are connected.

Global employment of media technologies has enormous potential to facilitate cultural, social, and political communication and understanding. For example, transnational media corporations create programming templates that can be customized to individual countries. The internationally successful TV show 'franchises', such as *Biggest Loser*, *Who Wants to Be a Millionaire?*, or *X Factor* add local interest to standard formats by recruiting cast members from the countries in which they are broadcast. As an example of this type of 'glocalization', the TV show *Temptation Island* was filmed on the same island in shifts – each shift was devoted to a different country and its associated cast members. Furthermore, many aspects of everyday life, particularly food and food products, stay linked to local identities and sentiments. Even the products of highly standardized global brands, such as McDonald's, are being adjusted to local demands. Thus, the globalization of the current era does not mean that cultural differences are being eradicated and that the whole world is being subsumed into one global culture. On the other hand, they do mean that cultures circulate in new and different ways, and that people are likely to reflect more and more about their similarities to and differences from one another. This is a time in which *cultural hybridization*, a new cultural form that combines elements of other cultures to one's own, is proliferating. It is also a time when an understanding of intercultural communication is even more important, but is becoming increasingly complicated.

This chapter addresses the various challenges we face in an increasingly globalized society. We firstly explain the dialectic of homogenization and fragmentation of cultures and the effects of these processes. The chapter then presents arguments about how to understand the global through local context and how local cultures challenge, negotiate, and adjust to globalization. A description of factors that influence cultural convergence and hybridization is provided. Finally, components of intercultural competence are identified and strategies to improve intercultural communication are suggested. Along with the rest of the book, this chapter aims to equip you with the knowledge and skills to become a more effective intercultural communicator.

HOMOGENIZATION AND FRAGMENTATION

There are two countervailing tendencies associated with globalization: the overcoming of cultural or economic differences, known as *homogenization*, and new forms of cultural *fragmentation* and innovation. The dialectic between them is reflected by cultures themselves, as well as by people living in culturally diverse societies.

Critical thinking...

What evidence of cultural diversity do you routinely experience as part of your day-to-day life? What effects does globalization have on you (e.g., watching a TV programme or reading a textbook in a second language)? Do you feel that globalization poses a threat to your cultural identity? Why or why not?

Homogenization and fragmentation of cultures

Globalization generally refers to an accelerated interconnectivity in the economic, social, political, cultural, and even personal aspects of life. Today, almost everywhere we see familiar signs of an interdependent economy (Lustig and Koester, 2013). It is hard to avoid products from international locations. However, the suggestion that the spread of Western globalization means we need to be less attuned to cultural differences is misguided. On the one hand, the forms of isolation and insulation that once nurtured cultural uniqueness are being eroded, thanks to increasing economic and political interdependence and the spread of transport and communication technologies that shrink space and transmit culture. On the other hand, these same tendencies generate unique and culturally distinctive responses and enhanced opportunities for the expression and circulation of culture-specific products. Satellite television, for example, enables people around the world to remain in instantaneous contact, so that viewers in one hemisphere can watch real-time events unfolding in the other. At the same time, new information and communication technologies (ICTs) make it possible for indigenous cultures to create their own media outlets and products, to circulate them widely, and to create connections with other Indigenous peoples who may share the same political and social concerns. These same ICTs also make it possible for diasporic communities to maintain close ties with their countries of origin, even if they are living at the heart of their new cultures.

The dialectic of homogenization and fragmentation can be described as engagement versus isolationism, or globalism versus nationalism (Lustig and Koestger, 2013). Economic interdependence sustains engagement and globalism. For example, in almost every country, we can find signs of McDonald's, KFC, Pizza Hut, Toyota, Sony, Nestlé, and Coca-Cola, all contributing to globalism and the homogenization of cultures. Nevertheless, the desire to preserve cultural uniqueness promotes isolationism and nationalism. Nations take measures to protect their local economies from foreign products. For example, when tropical cyclone Larry destroyed many banana plantations in Australia in 2006, the price of bananas increased greatly owing to the local shortage of bananas. In spite of this, to safeguard the local economy, regulations were issued to prohibit the importation of cheap bananas from overseas. One method that countries use to protect their trade is to enact tariffs, which are taxes levied on imported goods. This immediately raises the price of the imported goods, making them less competitive when compared to locally produced goods. This may work especially well for a country which imports a lot of consumer products, like the USA. However, in the long run it can make the country, and the industries it is trying to protect, less competitive in the global market.

Nations may also protect their people from the perceived effects of the beliefs, values, norms, and social practices coming from exposure to 'outside' cultural products. An example of this type of isolationism is illustrated by the concern shown over the celebration of 'foreign' religious and cultural festivals in China. Some Chinese scholars in China worry about the growing popularity among younger Chinese generations' celebrations of Western festivals, not just Christmas, but also St Valentine's Day, Halloween, Thanksgiving, and more (Ye, 2010). Ye suggests that the popularity of Western festivals in China reflects the fading of Chinese cultural identity, and that cultural protection should be in place in the era of globalization to 'counter such kinds of cultural colonization in avoidance of the dissolution of our 5000-year Chinese tradition' (Ye, 2010: 157).

Concern about the impact of foreign products is pervasive. There is worry in many countries in particular that American media products will erode local cultures and local languages, and there is an element of truth in this. Nevertheless, most of the world remains bi- or multilingual, and new online translation devices (like Google Translate) may ultimately encourage people to operate and publish more in their native language. Furthermore, there is little evidence that the American accent is creeping into other native English dialects, in spite of the great concern about this. There is some evidence of the internationalization of vocabulary in English, including American words entering other dialects and vice versa, but accents seem much more resistant. In an interesting example of this phenomenon, many people in England are worried that the Australian accent will creep into their language because of the popularity of Australian soap operas – yet there is very little evidence of this in a country which is now highly multicultural, and where all native English accents are routinely heard.

Different countries may add their own innovations to mass cultural products as a way of preserving their national characteristics. For example, music is readily marketed as a commercial product across cultural borders, but it is adapted, modulated, and transformed as it travels around the world. Rap music, which started in African-American neighbourhoods in the United States, has been taken up in a variety of countries, such as Japan, Germany, France, and South Africa, with each culture adding its own innovations to the original style. Globalization then works *dialectically*: on the one hand, there is a growing interconnectedness; on the other hand, there is a rise in deep-seated xenophobia and nationalistic sentiments.

? Critical thinking...

Arts and culture strategies reveal and enhance the unique meaning, value, and character of the physical and cultural form of a community, and give a community a sense of place. What do you think urban planners and municipal governments need to consider in urban planning in order to articulate the historic, cultural, and economic context of the community? How can they best preserve the local culture, yet take advantage of international developments in urban planning?

Homogenization and fragmentation of people

We find ourselves living in a world of increasing cultural mobility. Modern means of transportation and technology make travel faster and easier. As Edwards and Usher (2008: 16) note: 'What in the past would have taken months to move around the globe now takes hours or even seconds.' Moreover, thanks to the internet, people find themselves moving among different cultures without leaving home, or staying immersed in their home cultures even after they have geographically located elsewhere. At the same time, the uneven diffusion of technology and the uneven characteristics of Western globalization may create new forms of social and cultural stratification between those who participate in an increasingly transnational economy and those who still live and work under more traditional conditions. Mutual cultural exposure does not necessarily imply mutual benefits, acceptance, or harmony. Cultural exposure can highlight and exacerbate differences between groups or nations. Just as those living in traditional communities may feel shocked and threatened by the products of contemporary consumer culture, those living in the capitals of consumerism may find their own values and practices challenged by more traditional cultures. These issues make the dynamics of the global and local nexus more complex.

Photo 13.1   The Changing of the Guard is one of London's most famous spectacles, going back hundreds of years.
© Shuang Liu. Used with permission.

Scholarly discussions about global versus local, or about the homogenization and fragmentation of cultures, are gradually shifting away from a black-and-white view, as people recognize that 'cultural experience is both unified beyond localities and fragmented within them' (Skalli, 2006: 20). Despite the presence of global economy and mass cultural products, people still interpret what they see or have by drawing upon their local beliefs, values, and norms. Thus, at the same time that we recognize the far-reaching effects of technological, societal, and economic forces, we need to recognize that all messages that we experience are interpreted through the meaning systems of culture (Lustig and Koester, 2013). In focusing on the cultural dimensions of the integration–fragmentation dialectic, we cannot dissociate the economic and political aspects from the rest of the cultural realm. Rather, we view them through the lenses of culture and maintain their importance in the cultural prism.

Further online reading   The following article can be accessed for free on the book's companion website https://study.sagepub.com/liu2e: Winseck, Dwayne R. and Robert M. Pike (2008) 'Communication and empire: media markets, power and globalization, 1860–1910', *Global Media and Communication*, 4(1): 7–36.

THEORY CORNER

COORDINATED MANAGEMENT OF MEANING

Coordinated management of meaning (CMM) began as an interpretative theory focusing on interpersonal communication, but has now become a practical theory to improve patterns of communication. The term 'coordination' highlights the fact that whatever we do always intermeshes with the interpretations and actions of other people. CMM theorists (Pearce, 2005) believe that communication is, at the same time, idiosyncratic and social, and that it is necessary to describe the cultural context if we are going to understand communication within and/or across cultures. It is also necessary to understand individuals' interpretations of their communication.

CMM theorists have identified three goals of the theory: (1) to understand who we are, what it means to live a life, and how that is related to particular instances of communication; (2) to render cultures comparable while acknowledging their incommensurability; and (3) to generate an illuminating critique of cultural practices. Given that we have to engage in interactions with people who are not like us, the challenge is to find ways of acting together in order to create a social world where culture wars are minimized and people can find comfort and stability in their cultural traditions.

Reference

Pearce, Barnett W. (2005) 'The coordinated management of meaning (CMM)', in W. B. Gudykunst (ed.), *Theorizing about Intercultural Communication*. Thousand Oaks, CA: Sage. pp. 35–54.

Further reading on cultural hybridity and communication

Jacobson, Thomas (2000) 'Cultural hybridity and the public sphere', in K. G. Wilkins (ed.), *Redeveloping Communication for Social Change: Theory, Practice, and Power*. Lanham, MD: Rowman and Littlefield. pp. 55–69.

Theory in Practice

COORDINATED MANAGEMENT OF MEANING IN DISCRIMINATION DISCOURSE

According to CMM, individuals rely on an interpretative process that includes six levels of understanding to create meanings. The hierarchical model includes: (1) content (the words used to communicate); (2) speech acts (how we perform the content); (3) contracts (a system of formal and/or informal rules that guide two or more individuals' communication); (4) episodes (communication routines that consist of a describable sequence of speech acts); (5) life scripts (an individual's self-perceptions that shape, and are shaped by, communication); and (6) archetypes (understandings of speech acts, contracts, episodes, and life scripts that are shared by a particular social group) (Orbe and Camara, 2010).

Orbe and Camara (2010) examined how everyday discrimination is perceived by a diverse set of individuals. They collected 957 stories of discrimination as part of a larger study on uncertainty in oppressive forms of communication. Specifically, they focused on how a large, diverse group of individuals defined their experiences with discrimination – based on race, gender, age, sexual orientation, and abilities – in similar and different ways. Using the coordinated management of meaning theoretical framework, their analysis revealed that individuals make sense of everyday discrimination through a number of levels of meaning-making, such as content, speech acts, contracts, episodes, life scripts, and archetypes.

Questions to take you further

How are perceived acts of discrimination manifested within the cultural contexts of everyday interactions? What core elements define discrimination across a diverse set of experiences and contexts? Do you think discrimination is made up of a series of individual instances, or is it almost a way of life?

Reference

Orbe, Mark P. and Sakile K. Camara (2010) 'Defining discrimination across cultural groups: exploring the [un-]coordinated management of meaning', *International Journal of Intercultural Relations*, 34(1): 283–293.

Further reading on CMM in practice

Barnett, Pearce W. and Kimberley A. Pearce (2000) 'Extending the theory of coordinated management of meaning (CMM) through a community dialogue process', *Communication Theory*, 10(4): 405–423.

GLOBALIZATION AND LOCALIZATION

In the twentieth century, Jimmy Carter, the 39th President of the United States, commented: 'We become not a melting pot but a beautiful mosaic. Different people, different beliefs, different yearnings, different hopes, different dreams.' In the twenty-first century, however, the world can no longer be viewed as a mosaic with distinct parts (Cooper et al., 2007). With each contact between cultures, we leave some traces of our 'village' culture behind and add some new traits to it from other cultures. Albeit slowly, cultures are changing, and to some extent merging into one another. It is crucial to understand the dynamic interplay between localities and globalities around the world.

Critical thinking...

How can we understand the media's simultaneous involvement in both globalization and localization? Is it helpful to think about Western globalization as a process of tensions and contradictions, i.e., dialectically? How is globalization bringing other cultures to the West, and thus changing both?

Cultural diffusion and convergence

Through interaction between cultures, one culture may learn and adopt certain practices from another. *Cultural diffusion* happens when a culture learns or adopts a new idea or practice from another culture or cultures. Products can carry cultural values; many products represent a particular national identity and hence become cultural icons. An *icon* is a symbol that is idolized in a culture or is employed to represent it. For example, McDonald's represents the value placed on standardization, efficiency, and control in American culture; Japanese gardens reflect the value of harmony in Japanese culture; koalas and kangaroos represent Australia to many as a friendly, carefree, and relaxed country. It is believed that the receiving culture can unconsciously or uncritically absorb the values being transmitted via iconic products. For example, fast food has become an integral part of the life of people in China since it opened up to the world in the 1980s. The signs of McDonald's, KFC, and Pizza Hut can be seen in almost every city or town, as they can in the rest of the world. The concepts of efficiency, standardization, and quantification which are valued in Western cultures are infusing into the Chinese food culture, where harmony, balance, and perfection used to be valued in traditional Chinese cooking.

The increased sharing of information and agreement on mixing West with East leads to cultural convergence. *Convergence* is defined by Kincaid (2009: 189) as 'movement toward one point, toward another communicator, toward a common interest, and toward greater uniformity, never quite reaching that point'. Kincaid's convergence model was originally meant to address the shortcomings of the transmission model of communication, advancing the view that no two people can ever reach the same meaning for information; it is just a matter of a greater or lesser degree of similarity. Over the years, the term 'convergence' has been expanded to the economy, media, and culture. In cultural convergence, we can consider convergence to be more like the salad-bowl metaphor (a larger culture made up of different cultures, with each maintaining its own characteristics) as compared to the melting-pot metaphor (separate cultures all blended together into one larger culture). While the diffusion model focuses on what one culture does to another, the convergence model focuses on the relationship between individuals or groups of people who share information and converge over time towards a greater degree of mutual agreement (Jandt, 2007). In Russia, where more than 90 McDonald's outlets have been opened in the last ten years, McDonald's has to respond to local practices and cultivate local interests. Collective responsibility is very important in Russian culture, and McDonald's is situating itself as a responsible member of local communities by sponsoring sports events and making donations to children's programmes. Hence, globalization of products leads to cultural convergence.

Critical thinking...

Do you think globalization of the economy and products has resulted in the marginalization of regional cultures and traditional cultural products across the world? What evidence do you have for your viewpoint?

Cultural hegemony and colonialism

Some nations perceive the increasing popularity of culturally iconic products, particularly those from the West, as a form of *cultural hegemony*, or the structurally-enabled predominant influence of one culture over another. Cultural hegemony is faced not only by developing countries. For example, the French resistance to any linguistic influence of English is well documented in the literature, as are Japan's resistance to American movies and India's resistance to Coca-Cola. When products travel from one culture to another, they transmit cultural values to the receiving culture and change people's lives. Private ownership of cars was not popular in China in the 1980s. However, since the 1990s, a car has become more and more a 'necessity' for business people, government officials, and families – as a status symbol rather than a means of transportation. The ownership of foreign cars, in particular, shows the status of the owner: Toyota, Audi, Ford, and Hyundai are among the popular foreign models. In addition, imported televisions, cameras, mobile phones, refrigerators, washing machines, and cosmetic products, among others, all play a role in Westernizing the traditional Chinese ways of thinking and living. In this, the Chinese are doing what Western people have done for many years: showing their high status through their ownership of exotic goods and their knowledge of exotic cultural practices.

Contact between cultures may also lead to cultural colonialism. At the core of *cultural colonialism* is the concept of 'othering', predominantly used to refer to stereotypical images of non-white populations (Jandt, 2007). Cultural colonialism has a long history. When European seafarers discovered and colonized the Hawaiian Islands, they labelled the Hawaiians as 'the other' on the basis of their not being civilized by European standards. Similarly, in Australia, the Aboriginal people were labelled by Anglo-Saxon Australians as not evolved or civilized. Khan et al. (1999) argue that colonialism continues in many ways, including domination through the mass media. Mass media are not value-free, but carry important cultural values. They shape our perceptions of events and groups of people by providing a staple diet of news and entertainment to people in dispersed locations. The negative portrayal of the Muslim community in newspapers, for example, plays an important role in shaping our perception of that group, reinforcing stereotypes and sharpening the lines between 'us' and 'them'.

Cultural hybridization and branding

Local customs and traditions do not just fade away when global cultural products flow across borders. The transmission of cultural values and transformation of the lives of people via cultural products depend on how well the global products are received by the local cultures. *Cultural hybridization* refers to a new cultural form that combines elements of other cultures. For years, business people and corporations have devoted huge amounts of resources to adapt global products to local needs. For example, KFC is positioned as part of the fabric of life in China since its entry to Beijing in the 1980s as the first fast-food chain, and the chain has now spread to almost every city in China, with more than 100 KFC restaurants in both Beijing and Shanghai. One contributor to its huge success is that KFC has tailored its menu specifically to Chinese tastes. For example, the 'old Peking flavour' twister sandwich is styled after the way Peking duck is served, but with KFC's own brand of fried chicken and cucumber shreds. Instead of coleslaw, which is not part of traditional Chinese cuisine and does not appeal to Chinese tastes, customers can order seasonal vegetables, such as bamboo shoots in spring, lotus roots in summer, and rice porridge in the cold winter months. The localization of global products therefore plays an important role in their acceptance and sustainability in receiving cultures.

Further online reading The following article can be accessed for free on the book's companion website https://study.sagepub.com/liu2e: Hearn, Alison (2008) 'Meat, mask, burden: probing the contours of the branded self', *Journal of Consumer Culture*, 8(2): 197–217.

An important aspect of localizing the global is called 'branding', whereby business entities and nations position themselves and their products as globally recognizable. A brand is usually understood as the association of a product or service with a symbolic image that confers recognition, as well as additional value (or *added value*) to a product (Volčič, 2008). International brands competing in a global market-place, such as Nestlé, have to differentiate themselves from one another. Brand is something in the mind of consumers that motivates them to choose one product over another or to pay more for a product than they otherwise would. Brands are also capable of evoking beliefs and emotions, and prompting behav-iours. For example, in 1998, the British 'Cool Britannia' campaign attempted to move Great Britain from the traditional image of Queen, rain, aloofness, and snobbery to a 'cool' image. Other examples of cultural branding include attempts to globally brand a national (visual) image and transform it into commodities. Colombia is branded as *Café de Colombia*; Switzerland is powerfully represented by its delicious chocolates and cheese; Brazil is promoted by samba dancing, carnival, sex, magic, sports, adventure, and music; Singapore is known as a country *So Easy to Enjoy*; Poland as *The Natural Choice*; Turkey as *Welcome to Friends*. Such cultural branding encourages the employment of a marketable representation of difference, which emphasizes its local distinctiveness and even exoticism. When Baz Luhrmann released the film *Australia* in 2008, it was accompanied by the *Come Walkabout* print and a television advertising campaign commissioned by Tourism Australia. The advertisements used the ges-ture of national apology to the Stolen Generations (Indigenous people who had been forcibly removed from their families in order to assimilate them into white culture) to promote the nation.

Critical thinking...

A counter-culture is forming around the idea that the branding efforts of global consumer goods companies have spawned a socially destructive consumer culture. Nike, Coca-Cola, McDonald's, Microsoft, and Starbucks – the success stories lauded in marketing courses worldwide – are attacked by this new movement. How and why can branding cause trouble? What do you think is the best way to deal with the power of branding?

Along with the changes brought about by globalization is the need for us to redefine personal and cultural identities. At the same time people see themselves as 'global citizens', they identify themselves by a nation or a local community. The conceptualization of identity as multiple and fluid and changing according to situational characteristics, rather than a fixed product, gives people more freedom to define themselves along narrower categories. Similarly, while global cultural icons invoke Western cultural homogenization, these symbols at the same time may trigger a stronger desire for local cultures to form into distinctive communities and maintain their local traditions. The balance between global and local, when we view it through a cultural prism, occurs along a continuum rather than as an all-or-none phenomenon. Therefore, we cannot escape building up our cultural knowledge repertoire if we are to function effectively in both global and local contexts.

THEORY CORNER

CULTURAL SCHEMA THEORY

Cultural schema theory has been applied to study intercultural communication and cross-cultural adaptation (Nishida, 2005). Schemas are defined as generalized knowledge of past experiences organized into related categories and used to guide our behaviours in familiar situations. Cultural schemas are conceptual structures that enable an individual to store perceptual and conceptual information about his or her culture and interpret cultural experiences and expressions. When entering into communication with others, each of us brings a stock of knowledge about appropriate behaviours in our own culture. This pre-acquainted knowledge is referred to as cultural schemas. When a person interacts with members of the same culture over time, cultural schemas are generated in the mind. As the person encounters more of these similar situations, the cultural schemas become more organized, abstract, compact, and useable. Our communication becomes much easier through the application of cultural schemas. However, when sojourners enter into a new culture, they experience cognitive uncertainty and anxiety because of their lack of cultural schemas for the new situation. They usually go through two processes to adapt to the host culture: self-regulation and self-direction. In the self-regulation stage, sojourners try to resolve ambiguities and establish integration of information by drawing upon their home culture schemas. In the self-direction stage, they try to re-organize their home culture schemas or to generate host culture schemas to adapt to the new environment.

Reference

Nishida, Hiroko (2005) 'Cultural schema theory', in W. B. Gudykunst (ed.), *Theorizing about Intercultural Communication*. Thousand Oaks, CA: Sage. pp. 401–418.

Further reading on communication across cultures

Martin, Judith N., Mitchell R. Hammer and Lisa Braddord (1994) 'The influence of cultural and situational contexts on Hispanic and non-Hispanic communication competence behaviors', *Communication Quarterly*, 42(2): 160–179.

Theory in Practice

CULTURAL SCHEMAS IN ABORIGINAL ENGLISH

Cultural schemas have been used as a tool for describing culturally oriented mental models that give rise to action. They play a crucial role in cross-cultural sense making. As Palmer (1996: 63) states: 'It is likely that all native knowledge of language and culture belongs to cultural schemas and that the living of culture and the speaking of language consist of schemas in action.' In Aboriginal Australia, for example, kinship is the pillar of existence and the extended family is the essence of Aboriginal identity. For Aboriginal people, the company of extended family members is the source of security and solidarity as well as identity. Close family ties among Aboriginal Australians are clearly marked in the systems of kin terms in Aboriginal languages.

Malcolm and Sharifian (2010) examine how cultural schema theory has been employed in Aboriginal English oral discourse. The merit of this approach lies in the explanatory tools provided by cultural schema theory in accounting for those features of oral discourse in Aboriginal English. The term 'Aboriginal English' refers collectively to the range of distinctive varieties of English maintained by Aboriginal people and used primarily for communication within their own speech community. Malcolm and Sharifian (2010) noted that many features of Aboriginal languages instantiate Aboriginal cultural schemas and categories of Family. For example, the authors found that the word 'walk' stimulated ideas of extended family and kinship among speakers of Aboriginal English, which differed from speakers of Australian English, who may have viewed 'walk' as exercise or transport.

Questions to take you further

Do you agree that schematic cultural knowledge is inherent in the features of the environment? How much do you think culture and worldview provide a basis for the way languages of the world are patterned? How hard would it be for an Aboriginal Australian to understand and relate to contemporary media culture?

References

Malcolm, Ian G. and Farzad Sharifian (2010) 'Aspects of Aboriginal English oral discourse: an application of cultural schema theory', *Discourse Studies*, 4(2): 169–181.
Palmer, Gary (1996) *Toward a Theory of Cultural Linguistics*. Austin, TX: University of Texas Press.

Further reading on Aboriginal English dialects

Sharifian, Farzad (2006) 'A cultural-conceptual approach and world Englishes: the case of Aboriginal English', *World Englishes*, 25(1): 11–22.

DEVELOPING INTERCULTURAL COMPETENCE

The study of communication competence dates back to the time of Aristotle, as shown in his book *Rhetoric*, where the art of persuasion in public speaking is explored. The term 'communication competence' has been defined in various ways by scholars. This chapter adopts John M. Wiemann's (1977: 198) definition that conceptualizes *communicative competence* as 'the ability of an interactant to choose among available communicative behaviors in order that he [sic] may successfully accomplish his own interpersonal goals during an encounter while maintaining the face and line of his fellow interactants within the constraints of the situation'. This definition simultaneously highlights the importance of the ability of interactants in accomplishing their goals and showing concern to others in the interaction. As intercultural communication involves people who are culturally different, this definition applies well to the study of intercultural communication competence.

Further online reading The following article can be accessed for free on the book's companion website https://study.sagepub.com/liu2e: Krajewski, Sabine (2011) 'Developing intercultural competence in multilingual and multicultural student groups', *Journal of Research in International Education*, 10(2): 137–153.

Components of intercultural competence

Building on Brian Spitzberg and William Cupach's (1984) model, which emphasizes communication competence as context-specific behaviour, we describe four domains of intercultural communication competence: the knowledge component, the affective component, the psychomotor component, and the situational component.

The knowledge component

The knowledge component refers to the level of cultural knowledge a person has about another person or group with whom he or she is interacting. For example, touching the head of a child or showing the soles of one's shoes to other people are considered culturally inappropriate in Thailand, but these behaviours are considered as normal and acceptable in Australia. If an Australian and a Thai are in conversation, knowledge of each other's cultural taboos should prevent the occurrence of offence due to behaviour that is perceived as inap-

Photo 13.2   This artwork of dragons and phoenix at the international airport in Beijing symbolizes history and cultural tradition of ancient China. © Shuang Liu. Used with permission.

propriate. Knowledge may be both culture-specific, as in this example, and culture-general, which means knowledge about the dimensions of culture (see Chapter 5), aspects of culture (see Chapter 3), and the like. Although we often want specific knowledge about the practices of a culture we plan to visit, culture-general knowledge is sometimes more helpful in dealing with new cultures. Overall, the more knowledge people have about other cultures, the more likely they are to be perceived as interculturally competent.

The affective component

The affective component involves the emotional aspects of an individual in a communication situation, such as fear, like, dislike, anger, or stress. Emotions affect the motivation to interact with others from different cultures. For example, some people are more motivated to approach strangers and engage in an intercultural conversation, whereas others tend to be more apprehensive about communicating with 'foreigners'. Communicating with culturally different others suggests experiencing uncertainty and ambiguity when familiar cultural cues may not be adequate to interpret messages. Thus, an effective intercultural communicator needs to tolerate ambiguity and uncertainty.

The psychomotor component

The psychomotor component is the actual enactment of the knowledge and affective components. It involves the ability to use verbal and nonverbal codes to communicate messages in an interaction, and the degree to which one can communicate those messages in a culturally appropriate way. When we enter into communication with others, we assume certain roles. A role defines one's relative position in the communication event, together with an expected set of verbal and nonverbal behaviours. Roles vary significantly across cultures; the role expectations for a university student in North America differ from those in South Korea. Misunderstanding of role expectations may result in misunderstanding. Thus, both what we communicate and how we communicate determine communication outcomes.

The situational component

The situational component refers to the actual context in which intercultural communication occurs, including the environmental context, previous contact between the communicators, and status differential. For example, the degree of formality in word choice varies depending on status in a hierarchy and the relationship between the interactants. In a traditional Confucian family in China, children are taught to respect their elders and to obey their parents' decisions. They are not expected to 'talk back' to their parents. Similar principles apply to communication with teachers at school. It is not surprising to see first-generation Asian immigrants in the West finding it difficult to accept younger generations brought up in the new environment debating with their parents about decisions, for example about their careers.

The four components of intercultural communication competence are interrelated. Generally, as knowledge increases, one's attitudes to intercultural communication become more positive, and the motivation to engage in it increases. As motivation increases, one is more likely to translate it into behaviours; that is, to participate in intercultural communication. If the outcomes from intercultural encounters are successful, this positive experience functions as feedback and encourages the person to participate in future interactions. Greater opportunities for intercultural encounters enable the person to build a richer intercultural knowledge stock, which in turn facilitates subsequent communication.

Further online reading The following article can be accessed for free on the book's companion website https://study.sagepub.com/liu2e: Planken, Brigitte, Andreu van Hooft and Hubert Korzilius (2004) 'Promoting intercultural communicative competence through foreign language courses', *Business Communication Quarterly*, 67(3): 308–315.

Building empathy in intercultural communication

Intercultural awareness is one of the foundations of communication. It involves two qualities: one is the awareness of one's own culture; the other is the awareness of another culture. Intercultural awareness means the ability of standing back from one's own point of view and to become aware also of cultural values, beliefs, and perceptions of other cultures. However, the mere realization of cultural awareness is not enough. Many scholars claim that we also need to create a sense of empathy. As a word from the Greek *empatheia*, empathy means understanding others by entering their world or standing in somebody else's shoes. The concept of *empathy* has received much attention in intercultural communication and is described as the primary mechanism that makes understanding possible between two interdependent individuals. In recent years, several communication scholars have explored the nature and definition of empathy (Stock, 2012). Empathy is associated with many important aspects of communication behaviour, e.g., formulating communicative intentions and goals, devising strategies to accomplish communicative purposes, and constructing messages consistent with communicative strategies. These and other communication behaviours are usually seen as influenced by communicators' attempts to consider the perspective of the other person (Broome, 1991). As Broome (1991: 245) writes: 'An empathic encounter results in more than each individual developing a deeper understanding of the other – it leads to the creation of a unique whole that reflects a merging of each individual's construction of the other.'

Critical thinking...

Do you see empathy as a means to communicate across cultural gaps? What strategies can intercultural communicators employ to build empathy at an initial encounter? How is empathy related to knowledge, affect, and behaviour?

Strategies to develop intercultural communication competence

Increased intercultural contact provides opportunities for understanding between people as well as the potential for misunderstanding. How do we develop sufficient intercultural communication competence to ensure more success than failure when communicating with culturally different others?

Seek commonalities

In intercultural encounters, the first thing we tend to perceive is difference: differences in appearance, dress, language, diet, religion, customs, and even political orientations. If we adopt self-focused conversation strategies or use only our own cultural norms to guide us, intercultural communication is unlikely to be successful. To overcome the barrier of difference, we need to build mutual understanding with the other person. One way to achieve this is to focus on similarities rather than differences. As we gain more knowledge about each other, we may find that despite the visible differences, we share similarities in a number of ways. As Morris (1994: 6) describes: 'We may wear different hats but we all show the same smile; we may speak different languages but they are all rooted in the same basic grammar; we may have different marriage customs but we all fall in love.' Perceived similarities reduce uncertainty and hence facilitate intercultural communication.

Overcome stereotyping and prejudice

One of the most important barriers to intercultural competence is ethnocentrism, the degree to which other cultures are judged as inferior to one's own. Ethnocentrism is usually based on stereotyping and prejudice about outgroup members compared to the ingroup. Stereotyping and prejudice prevent us from seeing evidence that does not confirm our presumptions. In order for people to become more competent intercultural communicators, it is important to decrease ethnocentrism and avoid prejudiced attitudes.

One way to achieve this goal is to practise cultural relativism, which encourages us to understand the behaviour of others from their own cultural perspectives. However, we acknowledge that cultural relativism has its own limitations.

Develop flexibility and openness

Universally, communication is rule-governed behaviour, but rules vary from culture to culture. Cultural rules govern the distance that is perceived as appropriate between speakers, the loudness at which a person should speak during an interaction, the appropriate amount of gestures, and the appropriate information to be shared between speakers based on their relationship. When we enter an intercultural interaction, we may not know all the rules governing appropriate behaviours in the other culture. We must keep an open mind and be aware that what we practise in our culture may be neither the only correct way nor the best way of doing things, and we must be flexible in adapting our communication as the situation requires. Our knowledge of cultural dimensions and values will go a long way to help us adapt to new situations.

It is important to remember that communication across cultures takes place in context. For every encounter, there is an intergroup history, and that history can contain sources of tension, hostility, and prejudice, as well as (or instead of) more positive elements. There are circumstances where intercultural communication requires enormous skill, patience, and luck – communication competence is not enough. Fortunately, in many situations we can make use of the skills and strategies described here to help prevent misunderstandings and to achieve positive interactions.

SUMMARY

- The flow of many global cultural products, including movies, television programmes, music, cars, electric appliances, and food, has not only transmitted cultural values from one country to another, but also transformed people's way of living.

- Cultural homogenization and fragmentation work dialectically. Increasing economic and political interdependence and the spread of transport and communication technologies homogenize cultures. On the other hand, these same tendencies generate unique and culturally distinctive responses and opportunities for the expression and circulation of culturally specific products.

- Cultural colonialism, hegemony, diffusion, convergence, hybridization, and branding are all products and processes of contact between cultures. Globalization suggests multiple ways in which the global and the local cultural realms are articulated.

- Cultural differences can provide a rich resource for creative learning about the world, if culturally unlike individuals communicate effectively. Hence, becoming more intercultural is an important challenge for everyone.

- In order to develop intercultural communication competence, we need to specifically focus on seeking commonalities, overcoming stereotyping and prejudice, and developing flexibility and openness.

JOIN THE DEBATE

Will our attitudes become more 'provincial' in the global economy?

Global media, the internet, and travel have increased our exposure to cultural practices different from our own. One of the most prominent forms of response or resistance towards global dominance is when local brands present alternatives to global brands. An interesting example involves the many local and regional versions of the symbol of American global colonization and hegemony: Coca-Cola. In addition to the traditional colas that continue to be popular, such as the Italian drink chinotto, there are several examples of local colas that have been created either to imitate or resist the original one. For example, Mecca-Cola, targeting Muslim markets, was introduced as an ethical alternative to resist the American hegemony; Cola Turka, the Turkish equivalent of the popular soft drink, is another such example. The promotion of local and national colas illustrates how our attitudes and tastes can become more provincial. It may be that national and local touches will be employed in order to emphasize diversity in the global context. While some scholars argue that

Photo 13.3 Cola Turka – the Turkish version of Coca-Cola, standing in a public square in Istanbul.
© Zala Volčič. Used with permission.

diversity makes our thinking and being more global, others claim that diversity arouses new forms of ethnic and religious chauvinism – the more we inhabit a global world, the more we cling to our 'uniqueness', whether it is in language, music, food, or festivals. Could our attitudes and tastes become more provincial in the global economy?

CASE STUDY

Doctors without borders

Médecins Sans Frontières (MSF), or Doctors without Borders, is a global humanitarian and non-governmental organization best known for its projects in war-torn regions. The organization was created in 1971 by a small group of French doctors and medical journalists who were concerned with the plight of populations in emergency situations and who believed that everyone has the right to medical care, regardless of race, religion, creed, or political affiliation. Often, in crisis situations, people's lives shrink to the immediacy of survival. MSF believes that the needs of people supersede national borders, and it aims to avoid national bureaucracies and short-term goal-oriented international politics by providing rapid medical intervention in the face of crisis. Hence, Doctors without Borders started as a conscious, collective, and organized attempt to bring about large-scale change to needy regions by non-institutionalized means. Their mission statement, 'Doctors yes, borders no', reflects their motivation to go beyond national politics to provide real medical help to people.

MSF's borderless philosophy reflects one aspect of globalization – the recognition of increasing forms of interdependence as well as a commitment to human rights that transcends national or regional boundaries. MSF provides aid to those who are, in many cases, victims of international, economic, and political struggles associated with shifting balances of power, migration, and economic relations. Today, MSF is the world's leading independent international medical relief organization. Doctors from MSF work in over 60 countries affected by natural and social disasters, armed conflicts, and epidemics. The organization's funding comes mostly from private donors (approximately 80 per cent), while governmental and corporate donations make up the remaining 20 per cent, giving MSF an annual budget of approximately US$400 million. In addition to medical treatment, the organization also provides healthcare and medical training. MSF remains independent of any political, religious, or economic interests.

MSF received the 1999 Nobel Peace Prize in recognition of its members' continuing efforts to provide medical care in acute crises, as well as raising international awareness of potential humanitarian disasters. Dr James Orbinski, president of the organization at the time, accepted the prize on behalf of MSF with the words: 'Humanitarian action is more than simple generosity, simple charity. It aims to build spaces of normalcy in the midst of what is profoundly abnormal. More than offering material assistance, we aim to enable individuals to regain their rights and dignity as human beings.' In 2007, over 26,000 doctors, nurses, other medical professionals, logistical experts, water and sanitation engineers, and administrators provided medical aid all around the world. Over the past two decades, MSF has developed great technical capacity, lending credibility to its claim of being able to commence field operations almost anywhere in the world within 48 hours.

The organization mobilizes people around the idea that we need to deliver humanitarian and emergency care. MSF provides medical care to people who are caught in war zones and who may be injured by gunshot, knife, or machete wounds, bombings, or sexual violence. For example, MSF played a significant role in providing medical care in the wars of the 1990s in the former Yugoslavia – conflicts that resulted, at least in part, from the shifting balance of power in the post-Cold War era and tensions over the control of land and resources. The organization delivers surgical care in 25 countries, including the Democratic Republic of Congo, Haiti, Nigeria, Chechnya, and in northern Iraq, Iran, and Jordan for Iraqi civilians. MSF also provides medical care for refugees and internally displaced people who have fled to camps and other temporary shelters. Today, in places like Chad, Colombia, Somalia, and Sudan, MSF is running vaccination campaigns and water-and-sanitation projects, giving basic medical care through clinics and mobile clinics, building or rehabilitating hospitals, treating malnutrition and infectious diseases, and offering mental health support. In February 2014, MSF launched a vaccination campaign against measles in an attempt to control the epidemic that was declared by the government of Guinea on 14 January 2014. Working in cooperation with the Ministry of Health, MSF has deployed 32 teams throughout the Matam, Matoto, and Ratoma neighbourhoods of Conakry, the capital city of Guinea. They worked in areas such as community centres, private homes, and public spaces and were expected to have vaccinated over 390,000 children, aged from 6 months to 10 years.

MSF has a long history of responding to epidemic outbreaks of cholera, meningitis, measles, malaria, and other infectious diseases that spread rapidly and can be fatal if not treated. Over the past decade, MSF has been involved in the treatment of the pandemics of HIV/AIDS and tuberculosis. Through the Campaign for Access to Essential Medicines, MSF pushes for improved treatments for diseases that disproportionately affect the poor across the world. MSF has also called attention to the need for appropriate paediatric formulations for children with HIV/AIDS. In 1999, MSF co-founded the Drugs for Neglected Diseases initiative that brought together researchers, medical practitioners, and pharmaceutical companies to explore alternative ways of developing medicines. According to MSF International Activity Report 2012, MSF offered consultations to 8.3

million outpatients, treated 1.6 million patients for malaria, assisted 185,000 births, provided antiretroviral (ARV) treatment to 284,000 HIV patients, performed 78,000 surgical procedures, and treated 276,000 children for malnutrition.

MSF remains an inspiring source for global activists and humanitarian aid. Its medical teams often witness violence, atrocities, and neglect in the course of their work, largely in regions that receive scant international attention. At times, MSF speaks out publicly in an effort to bring a forgotten crisis to global attention, to alert the public to abuses occurring beyond the headlines, to criticize the inadequacies of the aid system, and to challenge the diversion of humanitarian aid for political interests. For example, in 1985, MSF spoke out against the Ethiopian government's forced displacement of hundreds of thousands of its population. The organization took the unprecedented step of calling for an international military response to the 1994 Rwandan genocide and condemned the Serbian massacre of civilians at Srebrenica in 1995. Since June 2012, MSF has been treating prisoners and ex-prisoners with drug-resistant tuberculosis (DR-TB) in the Donetsk region of Ukraine (the TB epidemic in Ukraine is among the most severe in the European region, with nearly 700,000 people infected). In thinking about cross-cultural connections, MSF is important because it adopts a borderless sense of space and an ethos of direct intervention and media involvement. Alongside Doctors without Borders, we now have reporters, pharmacists, engineers, sociologists, and even clowns 'sans frontières'. MSF has been recognized as an international organization embodying the insistence on a human right to health and the dignity of life that goes with it.

Reference

Medicins sans Frontieres [online]. Accessed 27 February 2014 at: www.msf.org.

Questions for discussion

1. What type of organization is Doctors without Borders and how did it come into existence?

2. What intercultural philosophy is the organization based on?

3. How do you think this organization helps to facilitate better intercultural understanding between peoples?

4. Why do you think it is important that MSF also speaks out about matters that call for public education?

5. What kinds of challenges or difficulties do you think MSF doctors encounter working in crisis or war regions?

FURTHER READINGS

All articles listed next to the mouse icon below can be accessed for free on the book's companion website: https://study.sagepub.com/liu2e

Globalization and localization

Hearn, Alison (2008) 'Meat, mask, burden: probing the contours of the branded self', *Journal of Consumer Culture*, 8(2): 197–217.

The article explores inflections of self-branding across several different mediated forms. Contemporary marketing literature identifies the construction of a branded persona as a central strategy in the negotiation of increasingly complex corporate environments. Recently, the practice and logic of personal branding has moved out of the board room and into the television studio. Television shows such as *The Apprentice* and *American Idol* invent a narrative of self-branding and simultaneously produce branded personae. Websites such as 2night.com extract value from partying young people: photographers take pictures at nightclubs and link them to advertisements online, blurring the distinction between product and consumer, private self and instrumental associative object. These forms of self-branding, which are found across several different kinds of media, illustrate the erosion of any meaningful distinction between notions of the self and the capitalist processes of production and consumption.

Imre, Aniko (2009) *Identity Games: Globalization and Transformations in the New Europe*. Cambridge, MA: MIT Press.

Eastern Europe's historically unprecedented and accelerated transition from late communism to late capitalism, coupled with media globalization, set in motion a scramble for cultural identity. In this book, Imre examined the corporate transformation of the post-communist media landscape in Eastern Europe. Avoiding both uncritical techno-euphoria and nostalgic projections of a simpler, better media world under communism, Imre argues that the demise of Soviet-style regimes and the transition of post-communist nation-states to transnational capitalism has crucial implications for understanding the relationships among nationalism, media globalization, and identity. Imre investigates the gaps and continuities between the last communist and first post-communist generations in education, tourism, and children's media culture, the racial and class politics of music entertainment (including *Roma Rap* and *Idol* television talent shows), and mediated reconfigurations of gender and sexuality.

Intercultural competence

Krajewski, Sabine (2011) 'Developing intercultural competence in multilingual and multicultural student groups', *Journal of Research in International Education*, 10(2): 137–153.

In times of accelerating globalization, intercultural competence emerges as one of the most desirable graduate capabilities for those who are likely to work in international environments. This article offers a case study with a focus on building intercultural competence through an assignment that invites experiential, self-directed learning. The assignment presented in the case study draws upon the expertise that individual students already have when they enter the classroom, and aims at further developing their intercultural skills. The article also includes an assessment of the assignment, based on a student survey conducted across several semesters. The results of the survey showed how students rate the usefulness of this particular assignment in comparison with other, more traditional, assessed tasks, such as essay writing.

Morley, Michael and Jean-Luc Cerdin (2010) 'Intercultural competence in the international business arena', *Journal of Managerial Psychology*, 25(8): 805–809.

Intercultural competence is presumed to be associated with global business success. Yet, the cumulative evidence from the international, comparative, and cross-cultural literatures remains mixed. This article identified four major threads in the international business literature dealing with cross-cultural competence, namely: a lack of agreement on what constitutes it; an almost total absence of studies of cross-cultural competence in international business, with few papers focusing on the knowledge, skills, and attributes that appear to be its antecedents; a tendency to ignore the larger environments in which expatriate managers operate; and a broad coverage of the topic in the workplace diversity and intercultural communications literatures.

Planken, Brigitte, Andreu van Hooft and Hubert Korzilius (2004) 'Promoting intercultural communicative competence through foreign language courses', *Business Communication Quarterly*, 67(3): 308–315.

The authors argue that foreign language courses can be contextualized to promote intercultural communication. In particular, foreign language courses should not only teach students the verbal language needed to communicate, but also promote the development of intercultural competence. This article examined a case study from an intercultural business communication (IBC) course at Nijmegen University in the Netherlands. This particular course promotes participation in the learning environment, as this is believed to better promote intercultural learning. Activities that help students develop intercultural awareness and foreign language competence can be divided into broadly two types: awareness-raising, requiring students to observe and analyse instances of business communication conducted in the foreign language; and production tasks, where students practise the skills they have learnt throughout the course.

GLOSSARY

Accommodating   One of Blake and Mouton's (1964) five conflict management styles; it refers to behaviours that conceal or play down differences by emphasizing common interests.

Acculturation   The adoption of the behaviour patterns of the surrounding culture; the modification of the culture of a group or individual as a result of contact with a different culture.

Activity orientation   One of Kluckhohn and Strodtbeck's (1961) value orientations; it refers to the use of time for self-expression and play, self-improvement, and work.

Affective conflict   Conflict arising from interpersonal tensions, which is largely emotional in nature.

Affective/instrumental communication style   One of Gudykunst and Ting-Toomey's (1988) four verbal communication styles; it is concerned with the extent to which communication is receiver-focused or sender-oriented, process-oriented, or outcome-oriented.

Agenda-setting   A theory that sees mass media as focusing our attention on certain aspects of life, and in doing so, setting the agenda for the public.

Anti-Semitism   A prejudiced perception of Jews, which may be expressed as hatred towards them.

Anxiety/uncertainty management theory   It posits that effective interpersonal and intercultural communication is a function of how individuals manage the anxiety and uncertainty they experience when communicating with others.

Attribution theory   The theory assumes that a person seeking to understand why another person acted in a certain way may attribute one or more causes to the behaviour in question.

Avoiding   One of Blake and Mouton's (1964) five conflict management styles; it refers to behaviours of physical withdrawal or refusal to discuss the conflict.

Belief   People's understanding of what is true in reality as viewed through their culture.

Bicultural identity integration   The degree to which a bicultural individual perceives the elements of his/her bicultural identity as compatible or conflictual.

Branding   The term stands for a distinct form of marketing practice intended to link products and services with resonant cultural meanings through the use of narratives and images.

Categorization   The process of ordering the environment by grouping persons, objects, and events based on their similarities.

Channel   The means by which a message moves from one person to another. The channel can be sound, words, letters, telephone, internet, fax, and so on.

Chronemics   The use of time, which influences our communication behaviour.

Closure   One of Goss' (1995) three common perceptual tendencies; it refers to humans' tendency to see things as complete wholes instead of incomplete configurations.

Cognitive conflict   Conflict arising from the perception of disagreements about the differences in viewpoints, ideas, and opinions.

Collaborating   One of Blake and Mouton's (1964) five conflict management styles; it refers to facing a conflict directly and examining possible solutions with the intention of achieving a win-win solution.

Collectivism   Cultures characterized by extended primary groups in which people see themselves as interdependent with others, and individual goals are secondary to those of the group.

Communication   The process by which people use shared verbal or nonverbal codes, systems, and media to exchange information in a particular cultural context.

Communication accommodation theory   The theory is based on three assumptions: (1) communication interactions are embedded in a socio-historical context including both intergroup and interpersonal histories; (2) communication is both about exchanges of referential meaning and negotiation of personal and social identities; and (3) interactants achieve the informational and relational functions of communication by accommodating their communicative behaviour through linguistic and non-linguistic moves, either treating others more as individuals or emphasizing intergroup relationships.

Communication style   How language is used to communicate meaning.

Communication technology   A range of technologies and systems used for gathering, storing, or transmitting information. It may include the internet, telephone, fax, mobiles, television, radio, or email.

Communicative ethical approach   This approach recognizes that humans are socialized into a particular set of cultural norms but believes that they are capable of critically reflecting upon and changing them.

Competing   One of Blake and Mouton's (1964) five conflict management styles; it refers to the use of power in satisfying one's position, even though it means ignoring the needs of the opponent.

Compromising   One of Blake and Mouton's (1964) five conflict management styles; it refers to behaviours that aim at finding a midpoint between the opposing viewpoints to achieve a mutually acceptable solution.

Conflict   The interaction of interdependent people who perceive opposition of goals, aims, and values, and who see the other party as potentially interfering with the realization of these goals.

Confucian work dynamism   Also known as long-term or short-term orientation, it is a cultural dimension which refers to the work practices and outcomes of dedicated, motivated, responsible, and educated individuals with a sense of commitment and organizational identity and loyalty.

Connotation   The cultural meanings that become attached to a word or an object.

Constructivist   Constructivists argue that language acquisition involves unveiling the patterns of language and requires interaction with a structured environment.

Context   The cultural, physical, relational, and perceptual environment in which communication occurs.

Contextual/personal communication style   One of Gudykunst and Ting-Toomey's (1988) four verbal communication styles; it is concerned with the extent to which the speaker emphasizes the self as opposed to his/her role.

Control   The ability to influence others, the environment and ourselves, along with the desire to be influenced by others (or not).

Creole   A new language developed from prolonged contact of two or more languages, which is a full, linguistically complex language in its own right with its own grammar, morphology, lexicon, phonetics, and phonology.

Cross-cultural adaptation   The process of increasing one's level of fitness in a new cultural environment.

Cultivation theory   Claims that exposure to vast amounts of violence on the screen conditions viewers to view the world as an unkind and frightening place.

Cultural activities   Manifestations of culture that can be expressed in technology, material objects, roles, rules, rituals, customs, communication patterns, and artistic expressions.

Cultural change   A dynamic process whereby the living cultures are changing and adapting to external or internal forces.

Cultural diffusion   A process that happens when one culture learns or adopts a new idea or practice from another culture or cultures.

Cultural hybridization   A process by which different cultures mix to form a new, third culture.

Cultural identity   Social identity based on cultural membership; it is one's identification with and perceived acceptance into a larger culture group.

Cultural relativism   The degree to which an individual judges another culture by its context.

Cultural schemas   Generalized knowledge of past experiences organized into related categories and used to guide peopole's behaviours in familiar situations.

Cultural value theory   Schwartz's taxonomy of seven cultural values: (i) conservatism; (ii) intellectual autonomy; (iii) affective autonomy; (iv) hierarchy; (v) mastery; (vi) egalitarian commitment; and (vii) harmony;

these were then summarized into three dimensions related to universal issues confronting all societies: (1) autonomy versus embeddedness; (2) hierarchy versus egalitarianism; and (3) mastery versus harmony.

Culture   The particular way of life of a group of people, comprising the deposit of knowledge, experience, beliefs, values, traditions, religion, notions of time, roles, spatial relations, worldviews, material objects, and geographic territory.

Culture shock   The feelings of disorientation and anxiety that a sojourner experiences when entering a new culture.

Cyber-bullying   Sending bullying messages to the victim by using communication technologies such as the internet and mobile phones.

Decoding   The process by which a receiver converts a message encoded in verbal or nonverbal codes back into meaning.

Denotation   The descriptive, literal meaning of a word or an object.

Digital media   Electronic communication where data is stored digitally.

Direct/indirect communication style   One of Gudykunst and Ting-Toomey's (1988) four verbal communication styles; it refers to how directly the speaker's intentions, wants, and desires are communicated in the interaction.

Discourse   Ways of thinking and producing meaning, either in written or spoken form.

Discrimination   Prejudicial treatment and disadvantaging of an individual based on their actual or perceived differences.

Diversity   The existence of different cultures within a larger society.

Elaborate/succinct communication style   One of Gudykunst and Ting-Toomey's (1988) four verbal communication styles; it refers to the quantity of talk a culture values.

Emic approach   The emic approach views each culture as a unique entity that can only be examined by constructs developed from inside the culture. See also *Etic approach*.

Empathy   Understanding others by entering their world or standing in somebody else's shoes.

Encoding   The internal process by which thoughts, feelings, and concepts are converted into a message by using shared verbal or nonverbal codes.

Ethical relativism   It denies the existence of a single universal set of values and norms and instead conceives them as relative to particular individuals or groups.

Ethical universalism   The proposed existence of a universal ethical principle that guides behaviour across all societies at any time – what is wrong in one place will be wrong elsewhere.

Ethics   Concerned with what is understood as right or wrong, good or bad; the standards and rules that guide the behaviour of members of a society.

Ethnic group   Identifiable groups of people who have a common heritage and cultural tradition.

Ethnic identity   A sense of belonging to or an identification with an ethnic group; ethnicity can be based on national origin, race, or religion.

Ethnocentrism   Seeing one's own culture as the point of reference and seeing other cultures as insignificant or even inferior.

Ethnography   A method used mainly by anthropologists to study culture in its natural setting.

Ethnolinguistic vitality   The degree of prestige, acceptability, and importance attached to a group's language.

Etic approach   The etic approach assumes that culture can be examined with predetermined categories that can be applied to all cultures in the search for cultural universals. See also *Emic approach*.

Expectancy violation theory   Assumes that humans anticipate certain behaviour from the people with whom they interact.

Expectations   One of Goss's (1995) three common perceptual tendencies; it refers to the idea that the more frequently we see something, the more inclined we are to form a 'fixed' image of that thing in our mind which informs our future expectations of it.

Face negotiation theory   Developed by Stella Ting-Toomey, it uses self-face concern and other-face concern to explain conflict management strategies.

Familiarity   One of Goss' (1995) three common perceptual tendencies; it suggests that people use their existing knowledge to identify what they see, and that we are more inclined to recognize the familiar than the unfamiliar aspects of things.

Feedback   Information generated by the receiver and made available to the source that allows the source to make qualitative judgements about the communication event.

Femininity   An aspect of Hofstede's masculinity–femininity cultural dimension; feminist culture permits more overlapping social roles for the sexes and places high value on feminine traits, such as quality of life, interpersonal relationships, and concern for the weak.

Folk culture   Consisting of the taken-for-granted and repetitive nature of the everyday culture of which individuals have mastery.

Fragmentation   Cultural fragmentation refers to the process through which different cultures maintain their own individual place, rather than merging with other cultures.

Gay, lesbian, bisexual, transgender and intersex identities (GLBTI)   Identities based on different sexual orientations.

Gender-neutral language   A verbal communication style that discourages the generic use of masculine pronouns in referring to persons of either sex.

Generative universal grammar   The idea that any language's rule structure allows speakers to generate sentences that have never before been spoken; from a finite set of sounds and rules, speakers of any language can create an infinite number of sentences, many of which have previously never been uttered.

Global village   Marshall McLuhan's description of a world in which communication technology brings news and information to the most remote parts of the world.

Globalist   Viewing globalization as an inevitable development which cannot be resisted or significantly influenced by human intervention through traditional political institutions, such as nation-states.

Globalization   The process of increasing interconnectedness between societies such that events in one place of the world are having more and deeper effects on people and societies far away.

Goal conflict   Conflict arising when people disagree about preferred goals and ends, such as an externally imposed goal being at odds with one's personal goals.

Halo effect   The tendency to presume that someone who has one good trait is likely to have other good traits.

Haptics   Refers to the use of touch.

High-context culture   One of Hall's cultural dimensions; members of high-context cultures typically gather information from the physical, social, and psychological context.

High-intensity conflict   Conflict which involves a series of intense, complex battles between conventional military forces; this may include sporadic violence such as ambushes or bombings.

Homogenization   Cultural homogenization refers to the transformation of different cultural practices into one blended, uniform cultural practice.

Human nature orientation   One of Kluckhohn and Strodtbeck's (1961) value orientations; it addresses the innate nature of humans – good versus evil.

Identity negotiation theory   It claims that there are particular influential identity domains that individuals acquire and that they further develop their identities through interaction with others.

Immigrants   People who leave their home country to live in another country on a permanent basis.

Implicit personality theory   Suggests that we organize our individual perceptions into clusters; individual personality traits are related to other traits, and when we identify an individual trait in someone, we assume they also possess other traits in the cluster.

Inclusion   A sense of belonging or of being involved with others, as well as of including others in our activities.

Individualism   An aspect of Hofstede's individualism–collectivism dimension; individualism emphasizes the individuals' goals over group goals.

Ingroup   A special class of membership group characterized by internal cohesiveness among its members, often with a shared culture, worldview, or interest, i.e., 'us'.

Integration   Immigrants' cross-cultural adaptation strategy; people who adopt an integration strategy maintain their heritage cultural traditions and practices while attempting to gain acceptance into the host culture.

Interactive model   Viewing communication as a process of creating and sharing meaning upon which context, experience, and perception exert influence.

Intercultural communication   Communication between individuals from different cultural or ethnic backgrounds or between people from subculture groups.

Intercultural competence   The ability to communicate effectively and appropriately with people of other cultures.

Intercultural conflict   Conflict arising due to perceived or actual incompatibility of goals, interests, resources, values, expectations, processes, or outcomes between two or more interdependent parties from different cultures.

Intergroup conflict   Conflict arising when two cultural or social groups perceive disagreements over resources, stereotypes, territory, policies, religion, or identities.

International conflict   Conflcit arising because of disputes and disagreements between nation-states.

Interorganizational conflict   Conflict arising because of disputes and disagreements between two or more organizations.

Interpellation   The process by which people ascribe identity to other people.

Interpersonal communication   The processing and sharing of meaning between two or more people when relatively mutual opportunities for speaking and listening occur.

Interpersonal conflict   Conflict arising when individuals are competing for scarce resources or having disagreements.

Interpretation   The process of verbally expressing what is said in another language; it can be either simultaneous or consecutive to the original speaker.

Intrapersonal communication   The processing and sharing of meaning within the self.

Islamophobia   Negative expressions against Islam or anything Muslim.

Kinesics   It refers to gestures, hand and arm movements, leg movements, facial expressions, eye contact, and posture.

Linear model   Representation of communication as a linear process whereby information 'packages' are transmitted from source to receiver, as if along a pipeline. It is also known as the *Transmission model*.

Localization   A process which reverses the trend of globalization by focusing on the local.

Long-term orientation   An aspect of Hofstede's long-term and short-term orientation cultural dimension; it encourages thrift, savings, perseverance towards results, and a willingness to subordinate oneself for a purpose.

Low-context culture   An aspect of Hall's cultural dimensions; members of low-context cultures gather information predominantly from the verbal codes.

Low-intensity conflict   Conflict which involves the limited and selective use of military armed forces at least by one party involved.

Man–nature orientation   One of Kluckhohn and Strodtbeck's (1961) value orientations; it refers to the relationship between humans and nature; humans can be subjugated to, in harmony with, or mastery over nature.

Marginalization   An acculturation strategy; it refers to individuals devaluing their cultural heritage and not having significant contact with the host society either.

Masculinity   An aspect of Hofstede's masculinity–femininity cultural dimension; masculine cultures strive for maximal distinction between male and female roles and attributes ascribed to them.

Mass communication   The process of understanding and sharing meaning through messages constructed specifically for and broadcast to a mass audience.

Message   The verbal and/or nonverbal form of ideas, thoughts, or feelings that one person wishes to communicate to another person or group within a specific context.

Migrancy   The movement of individuals from one location to another across national or cultural borders.

Monochronic time orientation   One of Hall's two categories of time orientations; people of monochronic time orientations view time as linear, progressive, and being able to be compartmentalized.

Morphology   The combination of basic units of meaning – morphemes – to create words.

Multiculturalism   At a descriptive level, multiculturalism can be used to characterize a society with diverse cultures; as an attitude, it can refer to a society's tolerance towards diversity and acceptance of equal societal participation.

Nativist   Nativists argue that language acquisition involves triggering pre-programmed models in the human mind (e.g., Chomsky).

Noise   Psychological, semantic, or physical elements that interfere with the travel of the message.

Nominalist   Nominalists argue that our perception of the external reality is not shaped by language but by material reality, and that any thought can be expressed in any language and can convey the same meaning.

Nonverbal codes   Any means, other than verbal codes, used to communicate meaning.

Olfactics   Refers to humans' perception and use of smell, scent, and odour.

Orientalism   Developed by Edward Said as a discourse for understanding the relationship between the East and the West; it is based on European cultural power and domination of political and economic interests.

Outgroup   A group whose attributes are dissimilar from those of the ingroup, i.e., 'them'.

Outgroup homogeneity effect   The tendency to see members of outgroups as 'all alike', without recognizing the individual differences.

Paralanguage   Vocal qualities that accompany speech; paralanguage can be divided into two broad categories: voice qualities and vocalizations.

Perception   An active process in which humans use sensory organs to identify selectively the existence of stimuli and then subject them to evaluation and interpretation.

Personal/contextual communication style   One of Gudykunst and Ting-Toomey's (1988) four verbal communication styles; it is concerned with the extent to which the speaker emphasizes the self as opposed to his/her role.

Phonology   The rules of a language that determine how sounds are combined to form words.

Pidgin   A makeshift language used when two people who do not share a common language come into contact.

Polychronic time orientation   One of Hall's two categories of time orientation; people of polychronic time orientation conceive time as cyclical and attempt to perform multiple tasks simultaneously.

Popular culture   Popular culture refers to artefacts and styles of human expression developed from ordinary people; it can include such cultural products as music, talk shows, soap operas, cooking, clothing, consumption, and the many facets of entertainment such as sports and literature.

Power distance   One of Hofstede's cultural dimensions; it refers to the extent to which a culture tolerates inequality in power distribution.

Pragmatics   The use of language in a social context.

Prejudice   A negative attitude towards individuals resulting from negative stereotypes.

Proxemics   Proxemics refers to the use of space, including territory, which stands for the space that an individual claims permanently or temporarily.

Racism   The belief that one racial group is superior and that other racial groups are necessarily inferior.

Receiver   The intended target of a message.

Referent   What a word or phrase denotes or stands for; however, there is no natural relationship between a word and its referent.

Relational orientation   One of Kluckhohn and Strodtbeck's (1961) value orientations; it addresses the modality of a person's relationship to other people.

Relativists   Relativists believe that our language determines our ideas, thought patterns, and our perceptions of reality.

Religious identity   Religious identity is the sense of belonging based on membership of a religious group.

Reverse culture shock   The culture shock experienced by people when they return to the home country after an extended period of stay in a foreign culture.

Rhetorical theory   This theory views communication as a practical art of discourse, and humans as rational beings who can be persuaded by compelling, carefully constructed arguments.

Sapir–Whorf hypothesis   This hypothesis proposes that language and thought are inextricably tied together, so that a person's language influences the categories of thought open to the person.

Selective perception   We selectively expose ourselves to certain kinds of information from our environment (selective exposure), pay attention to one element of it (selective attention), and retain the information that is likely to be used in the future (selective retention).

Self-fulfilling prophecy   A statement that causes itself to become true by directly or indirectly altering actions.

Semantics   The study of the meaning of words and the relationship between words and their referents.

Short-term orientation   An aspect of Hofstede's cultural dimension; it is consistent with spending to keep up with social pressure and a preference for immediacy.

Signified   In structural linguistics, the *signified* refers to the mental pictures, concepts, ideas, or objects which are attributed meaning by the signifier.

Signifier   In structural linguistics, the *signifier* refers to the spoken or written words in a language system.

Similarity attraction paradigm   It argues that if we perceive our attitudes as being similar to those of some people, we are attracted to them, because the similarity in attitudes validates our view of the world.

Social exchange theory   Exploring how individuals establish and continue social relations on the basis of their expectations that such relations will be mutually beneficial.

Social media   Networked interactive digital platforms that enable the formation of social groups connected by patterns of two-way communication either one-to-one or one-to-many.

Socialization   The process of learning a culture's rules, rituals, and procedures, including proper and improper behaviour and communication within the confines of these cultural rules.

Source   The sender, or origin, of the message being sent; a source is someone who has a need to communicate.

Stereotype   Preconceived beliefs about the characteristics of certain groups based on physical attributes or social status that may not be generalizable to all members of the group.

Structural linguistics   Structural linguistics views language as a coherent system whereby every item acquires meaning in relation to other items in the system.

Subculture   The smaller, coherent collective groups that exist within the larger dominant culture and which are often distinctive because of race, social class, gender, etc. (also referred to as co-culture or microculture).

Succinct/elaborate communication style   One of Gudykunst and Ting-Toomey's (1988) four verbal communication styles; it refers to the quantity of talk a culture values.

Symbol   An arbitrarily selected and learned stimulus that represents something else.

Syntax   The study of grammatical and structural rules of language which we use to combine words into sentences.

Time orientation   One of Kluckhohn and Strodtbeck's (1961) value orientations; it refers to the temporal focus of human life, i.e., past, present, or future.

Traditionalist   Traditionalists believe that most economic and social activity is regional, rather than global, and they see a significant role for nation-states.

Transformationalist   Transformationalists believe that globalization represents a significant shift, but they question the inevitability of its impacts; they argue that there is still significant scope for national, local, and other agencies.

Translation   The process of converting a source text, either spoken or written, into a different language.

Transmission model   See *Linear model*.

Transnationalism   The process by which migrants forge and sustain multi-stranded social relations that link together their societies of origin and settlement.

Uncertainty avoidance   One of Hofstede's cultural dimensions; it refers to a culture's tolerance of ambiguity and acceptance of risk and uncertainty.

Value orientation theory   The theory claims that cultures develop unique positions in five value orientations: man–nature orientation, activity orientation, time orientation, human nature orientation, and relational orientation.

Values   Concepts of ultimate significance and of long-term importance. Values inform the cultural group members of how to judge good or bad, right or wrong, true or false.

Verbal code   Spoken or written language; it comprises a set of rules governing the use of words in creating a message.

Worldview   The philosophical outlook a culture has about the nature of the universe, the nature of humankind, and the relationship between humanity and the universe.

REFERENCES

Adams, J. Michael and Angelo Carfagna (2006) *Coming of Age in a Globalized World: The Next Generation*. Bloomfield, CT: Kumarian Press Inc.

Adler, Peter S. (1975) 'The transitional experience: an alternative view of culture shock', *Journal of Humanistic Psychology*, 15: 13–23.

Adoni, Hanna and Sherrill Mane (1984) 'Media and the social construction of reality: toward an integration of theory and research', *Communication Research*, 11(3): 323–340.

Alba, Richard D. (1990) *Ethnic Identity: The Transformation of White America*. New Haven, CT: Yale University Press.

Allport, Gordon (1954) *The Nature of Prejudice*. New York: Macmillan.

Altman, Irwin and Dalmas Taylor (1973) *Social Penetration: The Development of Interpersonal Relationship*. New York: Holt, Rinehart and Winston.

Anderson, Benedict (1983) *Imagined Communities: Reflections on the Origin and Spread of Nationalism*. London: Verso.

Anderson, Jennifer (1987) 'Japanese tea ritual: religion in practice', *Man: Journal of the Royal Anthropological Society of Great Britain and Ireland*, 22(3): 475–498.

Ang, Ien (2000) 'Transforming Chinese identities in Australia: between assimilation, multiculturalism, and diaspora', in T. A. See (ed.), *Intercultural Relations, Cultural Transformation, and Identity*. Manila: Kaisa Para Sa Kaunlaran. pp. 248–258.

Ang, Ien (2001) *On Not Speaking Chinese: Living between Asia and the West*. London: Routledge.

Anti-Semitism Worldwide Report (2007) 'Report 2007' [online]. Accessed 18 September 2008 at: www.tau. ac.il/Anti-Semitism/asw2007/gen-analysis-07.pdf.

Ardizzoni, Michela (2007) *North/South, East/West: Mapping Italianness on Television*. Boulder, CO: Lexington Books.

Argent, Hedi (2003) *Models of Adoption Support: What Works and What Doesn't*. London: British Association of Adoption and Fostering.

Arweck, Elisabeth and Eleanor Nesbitt (2010) 'Young people's identity formation in mixed-faith families: continuity or discontinuity of religious traditions?', *Journal of Contemporary Religion*, 25(1): 67–87.

ASAPS – American Society for Aesthetic Plastic Surgery (2006) '11. 5 Million Cosmetic Procedures in 2005' [online]. Accessed 2 March 2009 at: www.surgery.org/public/news-release.

Asrul Hadi, Abdullah S. (2011) 'Foreign Worker Levy Hike in 2011', *The Malaysian Insider*. Accessed 2 January 2014 at: www.themalaysianinsider.com/malaysia/article/foreign-worker-levy-hike-in-2011/.

Augsburger, David (1992) *Conflict Mediation across Cultures*. Louisville, KY: Westminster/John Knox Press.

Australian Bureau of Statistics (ABS) (2005) 'Year Book Australia 2005' [online]. Accessed 2 October 2006 at: www.abs.gov.au/AUSSTATS/abs@nsf/Lookup/6A5AABD7621230ADCA256F7200832F77.

Australian Education International (AEI) (2013) 'International Student Data 2013' [online]. Accessed 30 October 2013 at: www.aei.gov.au.

Banks, Ingrid (2000) *Hair Matters: Beauty, Power and Black Women's Consciousness*. New York: New York University Press.

Barbour, Stephen (2002) 'Nationalism, language, Europe', in S. Barbour and C. Carmichael (eds), *Language and Nationalism in Europe*. Oxford: Oxford University Press. pp. 1–17.

Barker, Valerie, Howard Giles, Kimberly Noels, July Duck, Michael Hecht and Richarde Clement (2001) 'The English-only movement: a communication analysis of changing perceptions of language vitality', *Journal of Communication*, 51(1): 3–37.

Basch, Linda, Nina G. Schiller and Cristina S. Blanc (1994) *Nations Unbound: Transnational Projects, Postcolonial Predicaments, and Deterritorialized Nation-States*. Langhorne, PA: Gordon and Breach Publishers.

Baxter, Leslie (1988) 'A dialectical perspective on communication strategies in relationship development', in S. W. Duck (ed.), *Handbook of Personal Relationships: Theory, Research, and Interventions*. New York: Wiley. pp. 257–273.

Baylis, John and Steve Smith (2001) *The Globalization of World Politics: An Introduction to International Relations*. Oxford: Oxford University Press.

Beamer, Linda and Iris Varner (2008) *Intercultural Communication in the Global Workplace* (4th edn). Boston, MA: McGraw-Hill/Irwin.

Becker, An (2004) 'Television, disordered eating and young women in Fiji: negotiating body image and identity during rapid social change', *Culture, Medicine and Psychiatry,* 28: 533–559.

Bennett, Milton J. (1986) 'A developmental approach to training for intercultural sensitivity', *International Journal of Intercultural Relations*, 10(2): 179–95.

Bennett, Milton J. (1993) 'Towards ethnorelativism: a developmental model of intercultural sensitivity', in M. Paige (ed.), *Education for the Intercultural Experience*. Yarmouth, ME: Intercultural Press. pp. 343–354.

Berger, Charles R. and Richard J. Calabrese (1975) 'Some explorations in initial interaction and beyond: toward a developmental theory of interpersonal communication', *Human Communication Theory*, 1: 99–112.

Berlo, David (1960) *The Process of Communication*. New York: Holt, Rinehart and Winston.

Berry, John W. (1980) 'Acculturation as varieties of adaptation', in A. M. Padilla (ed.), *Acculturation: Theory, Models and Some New Findings*. Washington, DC: Westview Press. pp. 9–25.

Berry, John W. (1986) 'Multiculturalism and psychology in plural societies', in L. Ekstrand (ed.), *Ethnic Minorities and Immigrants in a Cross-Cultural Perspective*. Lisse, the Netherlands: Swets & Zeitlinger. pp. 35–51.

Berry, John W. (2001) 'A psychology of immigration', *Journal of Social Issues*, 57: 615–631.

Berry, John W. (2005) 'Acculturation: living successfully in two cultures', *International Journal of Intercultural Relations*, 29: 697–712.

Berry, John W. and Rudolf Kalin (1995) 'Multicultural and ethnic attitudes in Canada: overview of the 1991 survey', *Canadian Journal of Behavioral Science*, 27: 301–320.

Berry, John W., Rudolf Kalin and Donald M. Taylor (1977) *Multiculturalism and Ethnic Attitudes in Canada*. Ottawa: Ministry of Supply and Services.

Birdwhistell, Ray (1970) *Kinesics and Context: Essays on Body Motion Communication*. Philadelphia: University of Pennsylvania Press.

Bitzer, Lloyd F. (1968) 'The rhetorical situation', *Philosophy and Rhetoric*, 1: 1–14.

Blake, Robert R. and Jane S. Mouton (1964) *The Managerial Grid*. Houston, MA: Gulf.

Blank, Thomas, Peter Schmidt and Bettina Westle (2001) 'Patriotism – a contradiction, a possibility, or an empirical reality?', paper presented at the ECPR Workshop 26, National Identity in Europe, Grenoble, France.

Bogardus, Emory S. (1933) 'A social distance scale', *Sociology and Social Research*, 17: 265–271.

Bond, Michael H. (2009) 'Believing in beliefs: a scientific but personal quest', in K. Leung and M. H. Bond (eds), *Psychological Aspects of Social Axioms*. New York: Springer. pp. 319–342.

Bonvillain, Nancy (2014) *Language, Culture and Communication: The Meaning of Messages* (7th edn). Upper Saddle River, NJ: Pearson Prentice-Hall.

Boulding, Kenneth (1956) *The Image*. Ann Arbor, MI: University of Michigan Press.

Bourhis, Richard Y., Lena C. Moïse, Stephane Perreault and Sacha Senécal (1997) 'Towards an interactive acculturation model: a social psychological approach', *International Journal of Psychology*, 32(6): 369–386.

Bourhis, Richard Y., Shaha El-Geledi and Itesh Sachdev (2007) 'Language, ethnicity, and intergroup relations', in A. Weatherall, C. Gallois and B. M. Watson (eds), *Language, Discourse, and Social Psychology*. Basingstoke, England: Palgrave Macmillan. pp. 15–50.

Boussouar, Brice and Anne Mailliet (2008) *German Nudists versus Polish Puritans* [online]. Accessed 22 November 2013 at: www.france24.com/en/20080803-usedom-island-baltic-sea-border-germany-nudists-poland-puritans.

Brewer, Marilynn B. (1997) 'The social psychology of intergroup relations: can research inform practice?', *Journal of Social Issues*, 53: 197–211.

Brislin, Richard W. (1981) *Cross-Cultural Encounters*. Elmsford, NY: Pergamon.

Brislin, Richard W. (1988) 'Increasing awareness of class, ethnicity, culture and race by expanding on students' own experiences', in I. Cohen (ed.), *The G. Stanley Lecture Hall Series*, Vol. 8. Washington, DC: American Psychological Association. pp. 137–180.

Broome, Benjamin J. (1991) 'Building shared meaning: implications of a relational approach to empathy for teaching intercultural communication', *Communication Education*, 40(1): 235–249.

Brown, Wendy (2011) *Walled States, Waning Sovereignty*. New York: Zoned Books.

Brubaker, Roger (2001) 'The return of assimilation? Changing perspectives on immigration and its sequels in France, Germany, and the United States', *Ethnic and Racial Studies*, 24(4): 531–548.

Buruma, Ian (2007) *Murder in Amsterdam: Liberal Europe, Islam, and the Limits of Tolerance*. London: Powell Books.

Carbaugh, Donal, Michael Berry and Marjatta Nurmikari-Berry (2006) 'Coding personhood through cultural terms and practices: silence and quietude as a Finnish "natural way of being"', *Journal of Language and Social Psychology*, 25: 203–220.

Carey, James (1977) 'Mass communication research and cultural studies: an American view', in J. Curran, M. Gurevitch and J. Woolacott (eds), *Mass Communication and Society*. London: Sage. pp. 409–425.

Caspie, Avner and Paul Gorsky (2006) 'Online deception: prevalence, motivation, and emotion', *CyberPsychology & Behavior*, 9(1): 54–59.

Castells, Manuel (1997) *The Power of Identity*. Oxford: Blackwell.

Castles, Stephen (1992) 'The Australian model of immigration and multiculturalism: is it applicable to Europe?', *International Immigration Review*, 26(2): 549–567.

Castles, Stephen (2000) *Ethnicity and Globalisation*. London: Sage.

Chan, Yuet-Wah and Elisabeth Rudowicz (2002) 'The Chinese version of the Marital Comparison Level Index revisited', *Psychological Reports*, 91: 1143–1147.

Charon, Joel M. (2007) *Ten Questions: A Sociological Perspective* (6th edn). Belmont, CA: Wadsworth.

Chen, Guo-ming and William J. Starosta (2005) *Foundations of Intercultural Communication*. Lanham, MD: American University Press.

Chiang, Nora Lan-Hung (2011) 'Return migration: the case of the 1.5 generation of Taiwanese in Canada and New Zealand', *China Review*, 11(2): 91–123.

Chin, Christine B. N. (2003) 'Visible bodies, invisible work: state practices toward migrant women domestic workers in Malaysia', *Asian and Pacific Migration Journal*, 12(1/2): 49–74.

Chomsky, Noam (1968) *Language and Mind*. New York: Harcourt, Brace & World.

Chomsky, Noam (1975) *Reflections on Language*. New York: Pantheon.

Chomsky, Noam (1980) *Rules and Representations*. Oxford: Basil Blackwell.

Chouliaraki, Lilie (2006) *The Spectatorship of Suffering*. London: Sage.

Chouliaraki, Lilie (2012) 'The theatricality of humanitarianism', *Communication and Cultural Studies*, 9(1): 1–21.

Clark, Anna E. and Yoshihisa Kashima (2007) 'Stereotypes help people connect with others in the community: a situated functional analysis of stereotype consistency bias in communication', *Journal of Personality and Social Psychology*, 93(6): 1028–1039.

Clark, Virginia, Paul Eschholz and Alfred Rosa (1998) *Language: Readings in Language and Culture*. New York: St Martin's Press.

Clifford, James (1997) 'Diasporas', in M. Guibenau and J. Rex (eds), *The Ethnicity Reader: Nationalism, Multiculturalism and Migration*. Cambridge: Polity Press. pp. 283–290.

Cobley, Paul and Peter J. Schulz (2013) 'Introduction', in P. Cobbley and P. J. Schulz (eds), *Theories and Models of Communication*. Berlin/Boston, MA: Walter de Gruyter. pp. 1–15.

Coleman, Peter T. (2000) 'Power and conflict', in M. Deutsch and P. T. Coleman (eds), *The Handbook of Conflict Resolution*. New York: New York Press. pp. 115–123.

Colovic, Ivan (2002) *Politics of Identity in Serbia*. New York: New York University Press.

Condon, John C. (1977) *Interpersonal Communication*. New York: Macmillan.

Condon, John C. (1985) *Good Neighbors: Communicating with the Mexicans*. Yarmouth, ME: Intercultural Press.

Condon, John C. and Fathi S. Yousef (1975) *An Introduction to Intercultural Communication*. Indianapolis, IN: Bobbs-Merill.

Cooper, Andrew F. (2008) *Celebrity Diplomacy*. London: Paradigm Publishers.

Cooper, Pamela J., Carolyn Calloway-Thomas and Cheri J. Simonds (2007) *Intercultural Communication: A Text with Readings*. Boston, MA: Pearson.

Cooren, François (2012) 'Communication theory at the center: ventriloquism and the communicative constitution of reality', *Communication Theory*, 62(1): 1–20.

Couldry, Nick (2000) *The Place of Media Power*. London: Routledge.

Cox, Taylor H., Sharon A. Lobel and Poppy L. McLeod (1991) 'Effects of ethnic group cultural differences on cooperative and competitive behavior on a group task', *Academy of Management Journal*, 34(4): 827–847.

Craig, Robert T. (1999) 'Communication theory as a field', *Communication Theory*, 9(2): 119–161.

Dance, Frank E. X. (1970) 'The "concept" of communication', *Journal of Communication*, 20: 201–210.

Daniel, Jack (1976) 'The poor: aliens in an affluent society', in L. Samovar and R. Porter (eds), *Intercultural Communication: A Reader* (2nd edn). Belmont, CA: Wadsworth.

Davis, Kathy (1995) *Reshaping the Female Body: The Dilemma of Cosmetic Surgery*. New York: Routledge.

Dayan, Daniel and Elihu Katz (1992) *Media Events*. Cambridge, MA: Harvard University Press.

de Saussure, Ferdinand (1983) *Course in General Linguistics*, edited by C. Bally and A. Sechehaye, translated and annotated by Roy Harris. London: Duckworth.

Deetz, Stanley A. (1994) 'Future of the discipline: the challenges, the research and the social contribution', in S. A. Deetz (ed.), *Communication Yearbook 17*. Thousand Oaks, CA: Sage. pp. 565–600.

Denzin, Norman K. and Yvonna S. Lincoln (eds) (1998) *The Landscape of Qualitative Research*. London: Sage.

Department of Premier and Cabinet (2000) *Implementation of the Multicultural Queensland Policy, 1999–2000*. Brisbane: Multicultural Affairs Queensland.

DESA – Department of Economic and Social Affairs: Population Division (2013) *International Migration 2013*. Accessed 30 October 2013 at: www.un.org/en/development/desa/population/publications/pdf/migration/migration-wallchart2013.pdf.

Dines, Gail and Jean M. Humez (1995) *Gender, Race and Class in Media*. Thousand Oaks, CA: Sage.

Dion, Karen K. and Kenneth L. Dion (1993) 'Individualistic and collectivistic perspectives on gender and the cultural context of love and intimacy', *Journal of Social Issues*, 49: 53–69.

Dodd, Carley H. (1998) *Dynamics of Intercultural Communication* (5th edn). Boston, MA: McGraw-Hill.

Dupuy, Kat and Krijn Peters (2010) *War and Children: A Reference Handbook*. Santa Barbara, CA: Praeger Security International.

Dyer, Linda M. and Christopher A. Ross (2000) 'Ethnic enterprises and their clientele', *Journal of Small Business Management*, 38(2): 48–66.

Eadie, William F. and Robin Goret (2013) 'Theories and models of communication: foundations and heritage', in P. Cobley and P. J. Schulz (eds), *Theories and Models of Communication*. Berlin/Boston, MA: Walter de Gruyter. pp. 17–36.

Edwards, Richard and Robin Usher (2008) *Globalisation and Pedagogy: Space, Place and Identity* (2nd edn). Abingdon, Oxon, and New York: Routledge.

Ehrenreich, Barbara and Arlie Russell-Hochschild (eds) (2002) *Global Women: Nannies, Maids and Sex Workers in the New Economy*. New York: Henry Holt and Company.

Ekman, Paul and Wallace V. Friesen (1969) 'The repertoire of nonverbal behavior: categories, origins, usage, and coding', *Semiotica*, 1: 49–98.

Ekman, Paul and Wallace V. Friesen (1971) 'Constants across cultures in the face and emotion', *Journal of Personality and Social Psychology*, 17: 124–129.

Elliott, Deni (1997) 'The Great Hanshim earthquake and the ethics of intervention', in F. L. Casmir (ed.), *Ethics in Intercultural and International Communication*. Mahwah, NJ: Lawrence Erlbaum Associates. pp. 43–58.

Erjavec, Karmen and Zala Volčič (2007) 'The Kosovo battle: media's recontextualization of the Serbian nationalistic discourses', *Harvard Journal of Press and Politics*, 12(3): 67–86.

Evanoff, Richard (2004) 'Universalist, relativist, and constructivist approaches to intercultural ethics', *International Journal of Intercultural Relations*, 28: 439–458.

Everett, Daniel (2002) 'From threatened languages to threatened lives' [online]. Accessed 12 April 2009 at: http://yourdictionary.com/elr/everett.html.

Fair, Jo E. (2003) '*Francophonie* and the national airwaves: a history of television in Senegal', in L. Parks and S. Kumar (eds), *Planet TV: A Global Television Reader*. New York: New York University Press. pp.189–210.

Fairclough, Norman (2001) *Language and Power*. Harlow, UK: Longman.

Fairclough, Norman (2003) *Analysing Discourse: Textual Analysis for Social Research*. London: Routledge.

Fanon, Frantz (1990) *The Wretched of the Earth*. London: Penguin.

Fisher-Yoshida, Beth (2005) 'Reframing conflict: intercultural conflict as potential transformation', *Journal of Intercultural Communication*, 8: 1–16.

Fiske, John (1982) *Introduction to Communication Studies*. London: Methuen.

Frith, Katherine, Ping Shaw and Hong Cheng (2005) 'The construction of beauty: a cross-cultural analysis of women's magazine advertising', *Journal of Communication*, 55(1): 56–70.

Furnham, Adrian and Stephen Bochner (1982) 'Social difficulty in a foreign culture: an empirical analysis of culture shock', in S. Bochner (ed.), *Culture in Contact: Studies in Cross-Cultural Interaction*. New York: Pergamon. pp. 161–198.

Geertz, Clifford (1973) *The Interpretation of Cultures*. New York: Basic Books.

Gilbert, Dennis (2003) *The American Class Structure in an Age of Growing Inequality*. Belmont, CA: Wadsworth.

Giles, Howard, Richard Y. Bourhis and Donald M. Taylor (1977) 'Towards a theory of language in ethnic group relations', in H. Giles (ed.), *Language, Ethnicity and Intergroup Relations*. London: Academic Press. pp. 307–348.

Gitlin, Todd (1978) 'Media sociology: the dominant paradigm', *Theory and Society*, 6(2): 205–253.

Godin, Marie-Noelle (2006) 'Urban youth language in multicultural Sweden', *Scandinavian-Canadian Studies*, 16(1): 1–16.

Gordon, Milton, M. (1964) *Assimilation in American Life: The Role of Race, Religion and National Origins*. Oxford: Oxford University Press.

Goss, Blaine (1995) *The Psychology of Human Communication* (2nd edn). Prospect Heights, IL: Waveland Press Inc.

Gramsci, Antonio (2000) *The Antonio Gramsci Reader. Selected Writings: 1916–1935*. New York: New York University Press.

Greelis, Jim (2007) 'Pigeons in military history' [online]. Accessed 7 October 2013 at: www.theamerican pigeonmuseum.org/military.html.

Gudykunst, William B. (1983) 'Toward a typology of stranger–host relationships', *International Journal of Intercultural Relations*, 7: 401–415.

Gudykunst, William B. (2004) *Bridging Differences: Effective Intergroup Communication* (4th edn). Thousand Oaks, CA: Sage.

Gudykunst, William B. and Young Y. Kim (1984) *Communicating with Strangers: An Approach to Intercultural Communication*. New York: McGraw-Hill.

Gudykunst, William B. and Stella Ting-Toomey (1988) 'Verbal communication styles', in W. B. Gudykunst and S. Ting-Toomey (eds), *Culture and Interpersonal Communication*. Newbury Park, CA: Sage. pp. 99–115.

Gullahorn, John T. and Jeanne E. Gullahorn (1963) 'An extension of the U-curve hypothesis', *Journal of Social Issues*, 19: 33–47.

Gupta, Nilanjana (1998) *Switching Channels: Ideologies of Television in India*. New Delhi: Oxford University Press.

Hall, Bradford J. (2005) *Among Cultures: The Challenge of Communication* (2nd edn). Belmont, CA: Thomson Wadsworth.

Hall, Edward T. (1959) *The Silent Language*. Garden City, NY: Doubleday.

Hall, Edward, T. (1966) *The Hidden Dimension*. Garden City, NY: Doubleday.

Hall, Edward, T. (1977) *Beyond Culture*. Garden City, NY: Doubleday.

Hall, Edward T. and Mildred R. Hall (1990) *Understanding Cultural Differences: Germans, French, and Americans*. Yarmouth, ME: Intercultural Press.

Hall, Stuart (2001) 'Negotiating Caribbean identities', in B. Meeks and F. Lindahl (eds), *New Caribbean Thought: A Reader*. Jamaica, Barbados, Trinidad and Tobago: The University of the West Indies Press. pp. 122–145.

Hancock, Jeffrey and Catalina L. Toma (2009) 'Putting your best face forward: the accuracy of online dating photographs', *Journal of Communication*, 59(2): 367–386.

Hargreaves, Alec (1995) *Immigration, Race and Ethnicity in Contemporary France*. London: Routledge.

Harris, Philip R. and Robert T. Morgan (1987) *Managing Cultural Differences*. Houston, TX: Gulf.

Hartmann, Paul and Charles Husband (1972) 'The mass media and racial conflict', in D. McQuail (ed.), *Sociology of Mass Communications*. Harmondsworth: Penguin. pp. 435–455.

Harvey, David (2001) *Spaces of Capital: Towards a Critical Geography*. New York: Routledge.

Haviland, William A., Harald E. L. Prins, Bunny McBride and Dana Walrath (2011) *Cultural Anthropology: The Human Challenge* (13th edn). Belmont, CA: Wadsworth Cengage Learning.

Heidelberg Institute for International Conflict Research (2007) 'A 2007 Report' [online]. Accessed 18 October 2008 at: www.hiik.de/en/konfliktbarometer/pdf/ConflictBarometer_2007.pdf.

Hestroni, Amir (2000) 'Relationship between values and appeals in Israeli advertising: a smallest space analysis', *Journal of Advertising*, 29(3): 55–68.

Hirchman, Charles (2004) 'The role of religion in the origins and adaptations of immigrant groups in the United States', *International Migration Review*, 38(3): 1206–1233.

Hilton, James L. and William von Hippel (1996) 'Stereotypes', *Annual Review of Psychology*, 47: 237–271.

Hobsbawm, Eric (1983) *Nations and Nationalisms since 1780: Program, Myth, Reality*. Cambridge: Cambridge University Press.

Hoff, Erika (2001) *Language Development* (2nd edn). New York: Brooks/Cole.

Hofstede, Geert (1980) *Cultural Consequences: International Differences in Work-Related Values*. Beverly Hills, CA: Sage.

Hofstede, Geert (1991) *Cultures and Organizations: Software of the Mind*. New York: McGraw-Hill.

Hofstede, Geert (2001) *Culture's Consequences: Comparing Values, Behaviors, Institutions and Organizations across Nations* (2nd edn). Thousand Oaks, CA: Sage.

Hofstede, Geert and Michael H. Bond (1988) 'The Confucius connection: from cultural roots to economic growth', *Organizational Dynamics*, 16: 5–21.

Hogg, Michael A. and Dominic Abrams (1988) *Social Identifications: A Social Psychology of Intergroup Relations and Group Processes*. London: Routledge.

Hogg, Michael A. and Ben Mullin (1999) 'Joining groups to reduce uncertainty: subjective uncertainty reduction and group identification', in D. Abrams and M. A. Hogg (eds), *Social Identity and Social Cognition*. Oxford: Blackwell. pp. 34–45.

Hogg, Michael A. and Debborah J. Terry (2000) 'Social identity and self-categorization processes in organizational contexts', *Academy of Management Review*, 25(1): 121–140.

Houkamaua, Carla A. (2010) 'Identity construction and reconstruction: the role of socio-historical contexts in shaping Maori women's identity', *Social Identities*, 16(2): 179–196.

House, Robert J., Paul J. Hanges, Mansour J. Javidan, Peter W. Dorfman and Vipin Gupta (eds) (2004) *Culture, Leadership and Organizations: The GLOBE Study of 62 Societies*. Thousand Oaks, CA: Sage.

Hübinette, Tobias and Catrin Lundström (2011) 'Sweden after the recent election', *NORA: Nordic Journal of Feminist and Gender Research*, 19(1): 42–52.

Hui, C. Harry and Harry C. Triandis (1986) 'Individualism–collectivism: a study of cross-cultural researchers', *Journal of Cross-Cultural Psychology*, 17(2): 225–248.

Hutchinson, John (1987) *The Dynamics of Cultural Nationalism: The Gaelic Revival and the Creation of the Irish Nation State*. London: Allen and Unwin.

IDP Education (2008) 'Education replaces tourism as Australia's No. 1 services export' [online]. Accessed 26 June 2008 at: www.idp.com/about_idp/media/2008/February/tourism_no_services_export.

Institute of International Education (IIE) (2006) 'New enrolment of foreign students in the US climbs in 2005/06' [online]. Accessed 26 June 2008 at: http://opendoors.iienetwork.org/?p=89251.

International Education Advisory Council (IEAC) (2012) 'Discussion paper for the development of an international education strategy for Australia' [online]. Accessed 30 October 2013 at: https://aei.gov.au/IEAC2/Consultation(IEAC)/Documents/InternationalEducationAdvisoryCouncilDiscussionPaper.pdf.

International Organization for Migration (2006) 'World Migration' [online]. Accessed 24 July 2009 at: www.iom.int/iomwebsite/Publication/ServletSearchPublication?event=detail&id=4171.

Jandt, Fred E. (2007) *An Introduction to Intercultural Communication: Identities in a Global Community* (5th edn). Thousand Oaks, CA: Sage.

Jarvenpaa, Sirkka L. and Noam Tractinsky (1999) 'Consumer trust in an internet store: a cross-cultural validation', *Journal of Computer-Mediated Communication*, 5(1): 1–36.

Jaspars, Jos and Miles Hewstone (1982) 'Cross-cultural interaction, social attribution, and intergroup relations', in S. Bochner (ed.), *Cultures in Contact*. Elmsord, NY: Pergamon. pp. 127–156.

Jenkins, Richard (1996) *Social Identity*. London: Routledge.

Jitpiromsri, Srisompob (2006) 'Unpacking Thailand's southern conflict: the poverty of structural explanation', *Critical Asian Studies*, 38(1): 95–117.

Jitpiromsri, Srisompob (2008) '4.5 Years of the southern fire: the failure of policy in Red Zone', *DWS's Research Database* [online]. Accessed 18 September 2008 at: www.deepsouthwatch.org /index.php?l=content&id=265.

Jones, Gavin and Hsiu-hua Shen (2008) 'International marriage in East and Southeast Asia: trends and research emphasis', *Citizenship Studies*, 12: 9–25.

Katzenbach, Jon R. and Douglas K. Smith (2003) *The Wisdom of Teams: Creating the High-Performance Organization*. New York: Harper Business.

Kealey, Daniel J. (1989) 'A study of cross-cultural effectiveness: theoretical issues, practical applications', *International Journal of Intercultural Relations*, 13(3): 378–428.

Kearney, Michael (1995) 'The local and the global: the anthropology of globalization and transnationalism', *Annual Review of Anthropology*, 24(2): 547–565.

Khan, Fazal R., Abdus S. Abbasi, Mohammad N. Mahsud, Hashmat A. Zafar and Asmat U. Kaltikhel (1999) 'The press and Sindhi-Mohajir ethnic relations in Hyderland: do the newspapers cultivate ethnicity?', in A. Goonasekera and Y. Ito (eds), *Mass Media and Cultural Identity*. London: Pluto Press. pp. 129–191.

Kim, Young Y. (1988) *Cross-Cultural Adaptation: Current Approaches*. Newbury Park, CA: Sage.

Kimball, Charles (2002) *When Religion Becomes Evil*. New York: Harper Collins.

Kincaid, D. Lawrence (2009) 'Convergence theory', in S. W. Littlejohn and K. A. Foss (eds), *Encyclopedia of Communication Theory*. Thousand Oaks, CA: Sage. pp. 189–192.

Klopf, Donald W. (1995) *Intercultural Encounters: The Fundamentals of Intercultural Communication*. Englewood, CO: Morton.

Kluckhohn, Florence and Frederick Strodtbeck (1961) *Variations in Value Orientations*. Evanston, IL: Row, Peterson.

Knapp, Mark L. and Judith A. Hall (1997) *Nonverbal Communication in Human Interaction* (4th edn). Philadelphia, PA: Harcourt, Brace, Jovanovich.

Kolar-Panov, Dona (1997) *Video, War and the Diasporic Imagination*. New York: Routledge.

Kosic, Ankica, Lucia Mannetti and David L. Sam (2005) 'The role of majority attitudes towards out-group in the perception of the acculturation strategies of immigrants', *International Journal of Intercultural Relations*, 29: 273–288.

Kraidy, Marwan (2005) *Hybridity, or the Cultural Logic of Globalization*. Philadelphia, PA: Temple University Press.

Laclau, Ernesto (2006) 'Ideology and post-Marxism', *Journal of Political Ideologies*, 11(2): 103–114.

Lakoff, Robin (1975) *Language and Woman's Place*. New York: Harper & Row.

Lanigan, Richard, L. (2013) 'Information theories', in P. Cobley and P. J. Schulz (eds), *Theories and Models of Communication*. Berlin/Boston, MA: Walter de Gruyter. pp. 59–83.

Lasswell, Harold (1948) 'The structure and function of communication in society', in L. Boyson (ed.), *The Communication of Ideas*. New York: Harper. pp. 32–51.

Lee, Chol and Robert T. Green (1991) 'Cross-cultural examination of the Fishbein behavioral intentions model', *Journal of International Business Studies*, 21(2): 289–305.

Lee, Kang (2000) *Childhood Cognitive Development: The Essential Readings*. Oxford: Blackwell.

Lee, Tien-Tsung and Danis H. Wu (2004, May) 'Media use and attitudes toward Asian Americans', paper presented at 54th Convention of International Communication Association, New Orleans.

Lesko, Alexandra C. and Jennifer H. Corpus (2006) 'Discounting the difficult: how high-match-identified women respond to stereotype threat', *Sex Roles*, 54: 113–125.

Lévi-Strauss, Claude (1962) *The Savage Mind*. Chicago, IL: University of Chicago Press.

Levine, Timothy R. (2010) 'A few transparent liars: explaining 54% accuracy in deception detection experiments', in C. T. Salmon (ed.), *Communication Yearbook 34*. New York: Routledge. pp. 41–62.

Lewicki, Roy J., David M. Saunders, Bruce Barry and John Minton (2003) *Essentials of Negotiation* (3rd edn). Boston, MA: McGraw-Hill/Irwin.

Lewinsohn, Mark A. and Paul D. Werner (1997) 'Factors in Chinese marital process: relationship to marital adjustment', *Family Process*, 36: 43–61.

Liang, Ting-Peng and Jin-Shiang Huang (1998) 'An empirical study on consumer acceptance of products in electronic markets: a transaction cost model', *Decision Support Systems*, 24: 29–43.

Liebkind, Karmela and Inga Jasinskaja-Lahti (2000) 'The influence of experiences of discrimination on psychological stress: a comparison of seven immigrant groups', *Journal of Community & Applied Social Psychology*, 10(1): 1–16.

Light, Ivan H. and Steven J. Gold (2000) *Ethnic Economies*. San Diego, CA: Academic Press.

Lindemann, Stephanie and Nicolas Subtirelu (2013) 'Reliably biased: the role of listener expectation in the perception of second language speech', *Language Learning*, 63(3): 567–594.

Lippmann, Walter (1922) *Public Opinion*. New York: Macmillan.

Littlejohn, Stephen W. (1996a) 'Communication theory', in E. Enos (ed.), *Encyclopedia of Rhetoric and Composition: Communication from Ancient Times to the Information Age*. New York: Garland. pp. 117–121.

Littlejohn, Stephen W. (1996b) *Theories of Human Communication* (5th edn). Belmont, CA: Wadsworth.

Liu, Shuang (2006) 'An examination of the effects of print media exposure and contact on the subjective social reality and acculturation attitudes', *International Journal of Intercultural Relations*, 30: 365–382.

Liu, Shuang (2007) 'Living with others: mapping the routes to acculturation in a multicultural society', *International Journal of Intercultural Relations*, 31(6): 761–778.

Liu, Shuang (2011) 'Acting Australians and being Chinese: integration of ethnic Chinese business people', *International Journal of Intercultural Relations*, 35: 406–415.

Liu, Shuang and Guo-Ming Chen (1999) 'Assessing Chinese conflict management styles in joint ventures', *Intercultural Communication Studies*, IX(2): 71–88.

Liu, Shuang and Guo-Ming Chen (2002) 'Collaboration over avoidance: conflict management styles in state-owned enterprises in China', in G. Chen and R. Ma (eds), *Chinese Conflict Management and Resolution*. Westport, CT: Ablex Publishing. pp. 163–182.

Liu, Shuang and Eric Louw (2009) 'Cultural translation and identity performance of Chinese business people in Australia', *China Media Research*, 9(1): 1–9.

Looney, Rob (2004) 'Saudization and sound economic reforms: are the two compatible?', *Strategic Insights*, 3(2): 1–9.

Louw, Eric (2004a) 'Political power, national identity, and language: the case of Afrikaans', *International Language of Social Languages*, 170(1): 43–58.

Louw, Eric (2004b) *The Rise, Fall, and Legacy of Apartheid*. Westport, CT: Praeger.

Lowenstein, Ralph L. and John C. Merrill (1990) *Macromedia: Mission, Message, and Morality*. New York: Longman.

Luo, Shiow-Huey and Richard L. Wiseman (2000) 'Ethnic language maintenance among Chinese immigrant children in the United States', *International Journal of Intercultural Relations*, 24(3): 307–324.

Lustig, Myron W. and Jolene Koester (2013) *Intercultural Competence: Interpersonal Communication across Cultures* (7th edn). Boston, MA: Pearson.

Mader, Thomas F. and Diane C. Mader (1990) *Understanding One Another*. Dubuque, IA: Brown.

Marden, Peter and David Mercer (1998) 'Locating strangers: multiculturalism, citizenship and nationhood in Australia', *Political Geography*, 17(8): 939–958.

Markus, Hazel R. and Shinobu Kitayama (1991) 'Culture and the self: implications for cognition, emotion, and motivation', *Psychological Review*, 98: 224–253.

Martin, Judith E. and Thomas K. Nakayama (2001) *Experiencing Intercultural Communication: An Introduction*. Mountain View, CA: Mayfield Publishing Company.

Massey, Douglas and Edward J. Taylor (eds) (2004) *International Migration: Prospects and Policies*. Oxford: Oxford University Press.

Mastro, Dana E. and Bradley S. Greenberg (2000) 'The portrayal of racial minorities on prime time television', *Journal of Broadcasting and Electronic Media*, 44(4): 690–703.

Mayer, Vicki (2003) *Producing Dreams, Consuming Youth: Mexican Americans and Mass Media*. Piscataway, NJ: Rutgers University Press.

McCowan, Clint (2003) 'Imagining the Zapatistas: rebellion, representation and popular culture', *International Third World Studies Journal and Review*, XIV: 29–34.

McLuhan, Marshall (1964) *Understanding Media: The Extension of Man*. New York: McGraw-Hill.

McLuhan, Marshall and Quentin Fiore (1967) *The Medium is the Message*. New York: Random House.

McQuail, Denis (2005) *McQuail's Mass Communication Theory* (5th edn). London: Sage.

McSweeney, Brendan (2002) 'Hofstede's model of national cultural differences and their consequences: a triumph of faith – a failure of analysis', *Human Relations*, 55: 89–118.

Mehrabian, Albert (1982) *Silent Messages: Implicit Communication of Emotion and Attitudes* (2nd edn). Belmont, CA: Wadsworth.

Merry, Sally E. (1989) 'Mediation in cross-cultural perspective', in K. Kressell and D. Pruitt (eds), *The Mediation of Disputes: Empirical Studies in the Resolution of Social Conflict*. San Francisco, CA: Jossey-Bass. pp. 75–103.

Miller, Daniel (2011) *Tales from Facebook*. Cambridge: Polity Press.

Minkov, Michael and Geert Hofstede (2012) 'Hofstede's fifth dimenions: new evidence from the World Values Survey', *Journal of Cross-Cultural Psychology*, 43(1): 3–14.

Mohanty, Chandra Talpade (2003) *Feminism without Borders: Decolonizing Theory, Practicing Solidarity*. Durham, NC: Duke University Press.

Morley, David (2000) *Home Territories: Media, Mobility and Identity*. London and New York: Routledge.

Morley, David and Kevin Robins (1995) *Spaces of Identity: Global Media, Electronic Landscapes and Cultural Boundaries*. London: Routledge.

Morris, Desmond (1994) *The Human Animal: A Personal View of the Human Species*. New York: Crown Publishers.

Mortensen, C. David (1972) *Communication: The Study of Human Interaction*. New York: McGraw-Hill.

Mulder, Niels (1996) *Inside Thai Society: Interpretations of Everyday Life*. Amsterdam: Pepin Press.

Mullen, Brian and Li-Tze Hu (1989) 'Perceptions of ingroup and outgroup variability: a meta-analytic integration', *Basic and Applied Social Psychology*, 10: 233–252.

Nacos, Brigitte (2007) *Mass-Mediated Terrorism: The Centrality of the Media in Terrorism and Counterterrorism*. Lanham, MD: Rowman & Littlefield.

Naficy, Hamid (1993) *The Making of Exile Cultures: Iranian Television in Los Angeles*. Minneapolis, MN: University of Minnesota Press.

Neuliep, James (2012) *Intercultural Communication: A Contextual Approach* (5th edn). Thousand Oaks, CA: Sage.

Newbold, Chris (1995) 'The media effects tradition', in O. Boyd-Barrett and C. Newbold (eds), *Approaches to Media: A Reader*. London: Hodder Arnold. pp. 118–123.

Niehoff, Arthur (1964) 'Theravada Buddhism: a vehicle for technical change', *Human Organization*, 23: 108–112.

Nielsen Wire (2012) *State of the Media: Social Media is Coming of Age* [online]. Accessed 28 November 2013 at: www.nielsen.com/us/en/reports/2012/state-of-the-media-the-social-media-report-2012.html.

Nisbett, Richard E. and Yuri Miyamoto (2005) 'The influence of culture: holistic versus analytic perception', *Trends in Cognitive Sciences*, 9(10): 467–473.

Nua Internet Survey (2007) 'How many online' [online]. Accessed 18 April 2008 at: www.nua.ie.surveys/how_many_online/index.html.

Oetzel, John G. (2002) 'The effects of culture and cultural diversity on communication in work groups: synthesizing vertical and cultural differences with a face-negotiation perspective', in L. R. Frey (ed.), *New Directions in Group Communication*. Thousand Oaks, CA: Sage. pp. 121–137.

Office for Democratic Institutions and Human Rights (ODIHR) (2008) *Anti-Semitism Worldwide Report* [online]. Accessed 18 April 2008 at: www1.yadvashem.org/about_holocaust/holocaust_antisemitism/media_holocaust.html#FAQS.

Ogden, Denise T., James R. Ogden and Hope J. Schau (2004) 'Exploring the impact of culture and acculturation on consumer purchase decisions: toward a microcultural perspective', *Academy of Marketing Science Review*, 3 [online]. Available at: www.amsreview.org/articles/ogden03_2004.pdf.

Okabe, Roichi (1983) 'Cultural assumptions of East and West', in W. B Gudykunst (ed.), *Intercultural Communication Theory*. Beverly Hills, CA: Sage. pp. 21–44.

Østergaard-Nielsen, Eva (ed.) (2003) *International Migration and Sending Countries: Perceptions, Policies and Transnational Relations*: New York: Palgrave Macmillan.

Pacanowsky, Mochael E. and Nick O'Donnell-Trujillo (1983) 'Organizational communication as cultural performance', *Communication Monographs*, 50: 126–147.

Park, Robert, E. (1924) 'The concept of social distance', *Journal of Applied Sociology*, 33(6): 881–893.

Park, Hyun-Sun and Allen Rubin (2012) 'The mediating role of acculturative stress in the relationship between acculturation level and depression among Korean immigrants in the US', *International Journal of Intercultural Relations*, 36(5): 611–623.

Pearce, Barnett W. (2005) 'The coordinated management of meaning (CMM)', in W. B. Gudykunst (ed.), *Theorizing about Intercultural Communication*. Thousand Oaks, CA: Sage. pp. 35–54.

Pearson, Judy C. and Paul E. Nelson (1997) *An Introduction to Human Communication: Understanding & Sharing* (2nd edn). Boston, MA: McGraw-Hill.

Pedersen, Paul B. and Fred E. Jandt (1996) 'Culturally contextual models for creative conflict management', in F. E. Jandt and P. B. Pedersen (eds), *Constructive Conflict Management: Asia Pacific Cases*. Thousand Oaks, CA: Sage. pp. 3–26.

Pettigrew, Thomas F. (1997) 'Generalized intergroup contact effects on prejudice', *Personality and Social Psychology Bulletin*, 23: 173–185.

Pew Internet (2010) *Internet, Broadband, and Cell Phone Statistics*. Accessed 29 November 2013 at: www.pewinternet.org/~/media//Files/Reports/2010/PIP_December09_update.pdf.

Pew Research Report (2008) *Reports: Religious Landscape Survey* [online]. Accessed 31 October 2013 at: http://religions.pewforum.org/reports.

Piaget, Jean (1977) *The Development of Thought: Equilibration and Cognitive Structures*. New York: The Viking Press.

Pondy, Louis R. (1967) 'Organizational conflict: concepts and models', *Administrative Science Quarterly*, 12: 296–320.

Potter, Jonathan and Stephen Reicher (1987) 'Discourses of community and conflict: the organization of social categories in accounts of a "riot"', *British Journal of Social Psychology*, 26(1): 25–40.

Putnam, Linda L. and Marshall S. Poole (1987) 'Conflict and negotiation', in F. Jablin, L. Putnam, K. Roberts and L. Porter (eds), *Handbook of Organizational Communication*. Newbury Park, CA: Sage. pp. 549–599.

Ramsey, Sheila J. (1979) 'Nonverbal behavior: an intercultural perspective', in M. Asante, E. Newmark and C. Blake (eds), *Handbook of Intercultural Communication*. Beverly Hills, CA: Sage. pp. 105–143.

Ritzer, George (2004) *The Globalization of Nothing*. Thousand Oaks, CA: Pine Forge Press.

Robins, Kevin (1996) 'Interrupting identities: Turkey/Europe', in S. Hall and P. Du Gay (eds), *Questions of Cultural Identity*. London: Sage. pp. 61–86.

Robinson, Peter W. (1996) *Deceit, Delusion, and Detection*. Thousand Oaks, CA: Sage.

Robinson, Piers (1999) 'The CNN effect: can the news media drive foreign policy?', *Review of International Studies*, 25: 301–309.

Rogers, Everett M. (1995) *Diffusion of Innovations* (4th edn). New York: The Free Press.

Rogers, Everett M. (1999) 'Georg Simmel's concept of the stranger and intercultural communication research', *Communication Theory*, 9(1): 1–25.

Rogers, Everett M. and Steinfatt, Thomas M. (1999) *Intercultural Communication*. Prospect Heights, IL: Waveland Press.

Rohmann, Anette, Arnd Florack and Ursula Piontkowski (2006) 'The role of discordant acculturation attitudes in perceived threat: an analysis of host and immigrant attitudes in Germany', *International Journal of Intercultural Relations*, 30: 683–702.

Rubin, Alan M. (1986) 'Uses, gratifications, and media effects research', in J. Bryant and D. Zillmann (eds), *Perspectives on Media Effects*. Hillsdale, NJ: Lawrence Erlbaum Associates. pp. 281–301.

Sachdev, Itesh and Tej Bhatia (2013) 'Language attitudes in South Asia', in H. Giles and B. M. Watson (eds), *The Social Meanings of Languages, Dialects, and Accents: International Perspectives on Speech Styles*. New York: Peter Lang. pp. 141–156.

Said, Edward (1994) *Culture and Imperialism*. New York: Vintage Books.

Salih, Ruba (2003) *Gender in Transnationalism: Home, Longing and Belonging among Moroccan Migrant Women*. London: Routledge.

Samovar, Larry A., Richard E. Porter, Edwin R. McDaniel and Carolyn S. Roy (2013) *Communication between Cultures* (8th edn). Boston, MA: Wadsworth.

Sayegh, Liliane and Jean-Claude Lasry (1993) 'Immigrants' adaptation in Canada: assimilation, acculturation, and orthogonal cultural identification', *Canadian Psychology*, 34(1): 98–109.

Schramm, Wilbur (1971) 'The nature of communication between humans', in W. Schramm and D. F. Roberts (eds), *The Process and Effects of Mass Communication: Revised Version*. Urbana, IL: University of Illinios Press. pp. 3–53.

Schutz, William (1966) *The Interpersonal Underworld*. Palo Alto, CA: Science and Behavior Books.

Schwartz, Sholom (1994) 'Beyond individualism/collectivism: new cultural dimensions of values', in U. Kim, H. C. Triandis, C. Kagitcibasi, S. C. Choi and G. Yoon (eds), *Individualism and Collectivism: Theory, Method, and Applications*. Thousand Oaks, CA: Sage. pp. 85–119.

Schwartz, Sholom (1999) 'A theory of cultural values and some implications for work', *Applied Psychology: An International Review*, 48(1): 23–47.

Scollon, Ron, Suzanne W. Scollon and Rodney H. Jones (2012) *Intercultural Communication: A Discourse Approach* (3rd edn). London: Wiley-Blackwell.

Segall, Marshall H. (1979) *Cross-Cultural Psychology: Human Behavior in Global Perspective*. Monterey, CA: Brooks/Cole.

Seib, Philip (1997) *Headline Diplomacy: How News Coverage Affects Foreign Policy*. London: Praeger.

Seton-Watson, Harry (1977) *Nations and States: An Enquiry into the Origins of Nations and the Politics of Nationalism*. Boulder, CO: Westview Press.

Shannon, Claude and Warren Weaver (1949) *The Mathematical Theory of Communication*. Urbana, IL: University of Illinois Press.

Shepherd, Gregory J. (1993) 'Building a discipline of communication', *Journal of Communication*, 43(3): 83–91.

Sidanius, Jim and Felicia Pratto (1999) *Social Dominance: An Intergroup Theory of Social Hierarchy and Oppression*. Cambridge: Cambridge University Press.

Simic, Olivera (2010) 'Breathing sense into women's lives shattered by war: DAH Theatre Belgrade', *Law Text Culture*, 2(1): 117–133.

Simmel, Georg (1950) *The Sociology of Georg Simmel*, translated by Kurt H. Wolff. New York: The Free Press.

Singer, Marshall (1987) *Intercultural Communication: A Perceptual Approach*. Englewood Cliffs, NJ: Prentice-Hall.

Sitaram, K. S. and Lawrence W. Haapanen (1979) 'The role of values in intercultural communication', in M. K. Asante and C. A. Blake (eds), *The Handbook of Intercultural Communication*. Beverly Hills, CA: Sage. pp. 147–160.

Skalli, Loubna H. (2006) *Through a Local Prism*. Lanham, MD: Lexington Books.

Slobin, Dan I. (2000) 'Verbalized events: a dynamic approach to linguistic relativity and determinism', in S. Niemeier and R. Dirven (eds), *Evidence for Linguistic Relativity*. Amsterdam/Philadelphia, PA: John Benjamins. pp. 107–138.

Smith, Anthony D. (1995) *Nations and Nationalism in a Global Era*. Cambridge: Polity Press.

Smith, Anthony D. (2007) 'Nations in decline? The erosion and persistence of modern national identities', in M. Young, E. Zuelow and A. Sturm (eds), *Nationalism in a Global Era*. London: Routledge. pp. 16–30.

Snikars, Peller and Patrick Vonderau (eds) (2009) *The YouTube Reader*. Stockholm: National Library of Sweden.

Soysal, Yasemin N. (1994) *Limits of Citizenship: Migrants and Postnational Membership in Europe*. Chicago, IL: University of Chicago Press.

Spitzberg, Brian H. and William R. Cupach (1984) *Interpersonal Communication Competence*. Beverly Hills, CA: Sage.

Steele, Claude M. and Joshua Aronson (1995) 'Stereotype threat and the intellectual test performance of African Americans', *Attitudes and Social Cognition*, 69: 797–811.

Steele, Claude M., Steven Spencer and Joshua Aronson (2002) 'Contending with group image: the psychology of stereotype and social identity threat', *Advances in Experimental Social Psychology*, 34: 379–440.

Stephan, Walter G., Oscar Ybarra and Guy Bachman (1999) 'Prejudice toward immigrants', *Journal of Applied Social Psychology*, 29(11): 2221–2237.

Stewart, Edward and Milton J. Bennett (1991) *American Cultural Patterns: A Cross-Cultural Perspective.* Yarmouth, ME: Intercultural Press.

Stock, Cheryl (2012) 'Adaptation and empathy: intercultural communication in a choreographic project', *Journal of Intercultural Studies*, 33(4): 445–462.

Sveningsson, Elm (2007) 'Young people's presentations of relationships in a Swedish internet community', *Young*, 15(2): 145–156.

Synnott, Anthony (1996) 'Sociology of smell', *Canadian Review of Sociology and Anthropology*, 28(4): 437–460.

Tadmor, Carmit T. and Philip E. Tetlock (2006) 'Biculturalism: a model of the effects of second-culture exposure on acculturation and integrative complexity', *Journal of Cross-Cultural Psychology*, 37(2): 173–290.

Tajfel, Henri (1978) 'Social categorisation, social identity and social comparison', in H. Tajfel (ed.), *Differentiation between Social Groups: Studies in the Social Psychology of Intergroup Relations*. London: Academic Press. pp. 61–76.

Tajfel, Henri (1982) *Social Identity and Intergroup Relations*. Cambridge: Cambridge University Press.

Tajfel, Henri and Joseph P. Forgas (1981) 'Social categorisation: cognitions, values and groups', in J. P. Forgas (ed.), *Social Cognition: Perspectives on Everyday Understanding*. London: Academic Press. pp. 113–140.

Tannen, Deborah (1990) *You Just Don't Understand: Women and Men in Conversation*. New York: William Morrow/Ballantine.

Tannen, Deborah (1994) *Talking from 9 to 5: How Women's and Men's Conversational Styles Affect Who Gets Heard, Who Gets Credit, and What Gets Done at Work*. New York: Oxford University Press.

Ting-Toomey, Stella (1994) 'Managing intercultural conflicts effectively', in L. Samovar and R. Porter (eds), *Intercultural Communication: A Reader* (7th edn). Belmont, CA: Wadsworth. pp. 360–372.

Ting-Toomey, Stella (2005a) 'Identity negotiation theory: crossing cultural boundaries', in W. B. Gudykunst (ed.), *Theorizing about Intercultural Communication*. Thousand Oaks, CA: Sage. pp. 211–233.

Ting-Toomey, Stella (2005b) 'The matrix of face: updated face-negotiation theory', in W. B. Gudykunst (ed.), *Theorizing about Intercultural Communication*. Thousand Oaks, CA: Sage. pp. 71–92.

Ting-Toomey, Stella and Leeva C. Chung (2005) *Understanding Intercultural Communication*. Los Angeles, CA: Roxbury.

Tomlinson, John (1999) *Globalization and Culture*. Oxford: Polity Press.

Training and Development (1999, November) 'Training & development annual trend reports', *Training and Development*, 53(1): 22–43.

Trammell, Key, Alek Tarkowski, Justyna Hofmokl and Amanda Sapp (2006) 'Examining Polish bloggers through content analysis', *Journal of Computer-Mediated Communication*, 11: 702–722.

Triandis, Harry C. (1977) *Interpersonal Behavior*. Monterey, CA: Brooks/Cole.

Triandis, Harry C. (1984) 'A theoretical framework for the more efficient construction of culture assimilators', *International Journal of Intercultural Relations*, 8: 301–330.

Triandis, Harry C. (1989) 'The self and social behavior in differing cultural contexts', *Psychological Review*, 60: 649–655.

Triandis, Harry C. (1995) *Individualism and Collectivism*. Boulder, CO: Westview Press.

Triandis, Harry C., Christopher McCusker and C. Harry Hui (1990) 'Multi-method probes of individualism and collectivism', *Journal of Personality and Social Psychology*, 59(5): 1006–1020.

Tuchman, Gaye (1978) *Making News: A Study in the Construction of Reality*. New York: The Free Press.

Turner, Graeme (1994) *Understanding Celebrity*. London: Sage.

Vivian, Bradford (1999) 'The veil and the visible', *Western Journal of Communication*, 63(2): 115–140.

Volčič, Zala (2005) 'The notion of "The West" in the Serbian national imaginary', *European Journal of Cultural Studies*, 8(2): 155–175.

Volčič, Zala (2008) 'Former Yugoslavia on the World Wide Web: commercialization and branding of nation-states', *International Communication Gazette*, 70(5): 395–413.

Vukeljic, Marijana (2008) *Vpliv medijev na oblikovanje identitete druge generacije Srbov v Sloveniji* [*The Effects of Media on Forming Identities of the Serbian Second Generation in Slovenia*]. Maribor: Univerza Maribor Press.

Ward, Colleen and Miles Hewstone (1985) 'Ethnicity, language and intergroup relations in Malaysia and Singapore: a social psychological analysis', *Journal of Multilingual and Multicultural Development*, 6: 271–296.

Ward, Colleen and Anthony Kennedy (2001) 'Coping with cross-cultural transition', *Journal of Cross-Cultural Psychology*, 32(5): 636–642.

Ward, Colleen, Yutaka Okura, Antony Kennedy and Takahiro Kojima (1998) 'The U-curve on trial: a longitudinal study of psychological and sociocultural adjustment during cross-cultural transition', *International Journal of Intercultural Relations*, 22(3): 277–291.

Wasko, Janet (2001) *Understanding Disney: The Manufacture of Fantasy*. Cambridge: Polity Press.

Waters, Malcolm (1995) *Globalization*. New York and London: Routledge.

Weber, Elke U. and Christopher Hsee (1998) 'Cross-cultural differences in risk perception, but cross-cultural similarities in attitudes towards perceived risk', *Management Sciences*, 44: 1205–1217.

Whitty, Monica T., Andrea J. Baker and James A. Inman (2007) *Online Matchmaking*. New York: Palgrave Macmillan.

Whorf, Benjamin L. (1956) *Language, Thought and Reality: Selected Writings*, edited by J. B. Carroll. Cambridge, MA: Technology Press of MIT.

Wiemann, John M. (1977) 'Explication and test of a model of communicative competence', *Human Communication Research*, 3(3): 195–213.

Williams, Raymond (1989) *Resources of Hope: Culture, Democracy, Socialism*. London: Verso.

Wittgenstein, Ludwig (1922/2001) *Tractatus Logico-Philosophicus*. London: Routledge.

Woodrow, Lindy (2006) 'Anxiety and speaking English as a second language', *RELC Journal*, 37: 308–327.

Xi, Changsheng (1994) 'Individualism and collectivism in American and Chinese societies', in A. Gonzalez, M. Houston and V. Chen (eds), *Our Voices: Essays in Culture, Ethnicity, and Communication*. Los Angeles, CA: Roxbury. pp. 125–167.

Yamaguchi, Susumu (1998) 'Biased risk perceptions among Japanese: illustration of interdependence among risk companions', *Asian Journal of Social Psychology*, 1: 117–131.

Ye, Xiang (2010) 'Cultural invasion and cultural protection: should Chinese celebrate Christmas?', *Asian Social Science*, 6(1): 157–160.

Yum, June O. (1988) 'The impact of Confucianism on interpersonal relationships and communication patterns in East Asia', *Communication Monographs*, 55: 374–388.

Zagefka, Hanna and Rupert Brown (2002) 'The relationship between acculturation strategies, relative fit and intergroup relations: immigrant–majority relations in Germany', *European Journal of Social Psychology*, 32(2): 171–188.

Zhang, Shuangyue and Susan L. Kline (2009) 'Can I make my own decision? A cross-cultural study of perceived social network influence in mate selection', *Journal of Cross-Cultural Psychology*, 40: 3–23.

Zhou, Lianxi and Michael K. Hui (2003) 'Symbolic value of foreign products in the People's Republic of China', *Journal of International Marketing*, 11: 36–43.

Zubrzycki, Jerzy (1997) 'Australian multiculturalism for a new century: towards inclusiveness', *Immigration Policies and Australia's Population*. Canberra: Australian Ethnic Affairs Council.

INDEX

Page numbers in **bold** indicate tables and in *italic* indicate figures.